Plus

OF 7

Modern Christianity and Cultural Aspirations

Lincoln Studies in Religion & Society, 5

Modern
Christianity
and
Cultural
Aspirations

edited by
David Bebbington and Timothy Larsen

SHEFFIELD ACADEMIC PRESS
A Continuum imprint
LONDON • NEW YORK

Published by Sheffield Academic Press Ltd
The Tower Building, 11 York Road, London SE1 7NX
15 East 26th Street, Suite 1703, New York, NY 10010.

www.continuumbooks.com

British Library Cataloguing-in-Publication Data

A catalogue record for this book is available from the British Library

Typeset by Sheffield Academic Press
Printed on acid-free paper in Great Britain by Bookcraft Ltd, Midsomer Norton, Bath

ISBN   0-8264-6262-6

In Honour of Professor Clyde Binfield, OBE

A Portrait by Trevor Stubley, RP
Photography courtesy of Clyde Binfield, OBE

CONTENTS

Contents

Foreword

The Lincoln Studies in Religion and Society series was originally designed to explore and examine the changing shape of the churches in contemporary society. Boldly conceived, this series of books sets out to challenge many of the common assumptions about the place of religion that tend to prevail within the public domain and much of the academy. Each book assesses, from a different perspective, the extent to which contemporary society might be said to be 'truly' secular, or continues to be infused with sacred motifs and spiritual values. Equally, the volumes take seriously the adaptability and living organic residue of religions as they mutate within contemporary culture, as surely as the religions themselves continue to shape and develop the contexts within which they are immersed. Previous studies have looked at the culture of management and organization (LSRS 1), sacred and secular time (LSRS 2), religion and society (LSRS 3) and the nature of religious resilience (LSRS 4).

The Lincoln Studies in Religion and Society—while undeniably focused on studying Christianity and the churches—are also radically committed to interdisciplinarity. Each of the volumes 'reads' contemporary culture and cultural studies thoughtfully, regarding this as a key area of interface for the complex panoply of theological disciplines, as well as for other discrete arenas of academic endeavour such as the sociology or anthropology of religion. It is through the themes and methodological approach in each book that readers can begin to make more nuanced and discerning judgments about the shape, place and capacity of religion within contemporary society.

Eschewing the normative chasmic antinomy between the sacred and the secular worlds that shape most analytical paradigms, the Lincoln Studies are characterized by their perception of religion in relation to contemporary culture as being more equivocal. Religion continues to cultivate and fashion society; society continues to make and mould religion. Rather than trying to understand religion and culture as things apart, the volumes in this series treat them as inextricably intertwined, making for a richer, engaging and penetrating type of study. The original meaning of the word 'religion' is, after all, derived from a Latin term meaning 'to persistently bind together'—something each volume in the Lincoln Studies series seeks to honour in its analytical tenacity and theological acuity.

A final word about Lincoln. The Lincoln Theological Institute was set up in 1997 to further the (postgraduate and postdoctoral) study of religion and society. Originally established at the University of Sheffield, the Institute is now an adjunct centre within the Department of Religions and Theology at the University of Manchester. The Institute owes its origin to the former Lincoln Theological College (in the city of Lincoln) that once trained men and women for the ordained ministry in the Church of England and, latterly, the Methodist Church. The Institute, like its parent theological college, is committed to understanding the relationship between society and religion, and reflecting upon this theologically. Some might say that the closure of the theological college confirms, in a modest way, the gradual secularization of society. Perhaps, if nothing further had happened, this might be true. However, the forming of the Institute in 1997, and its contribution towards the academy since then, provides further evidence for the rationale of this series. Religious institutions seldom die. They change, resurrect and live on in new guises, perhaps less distinct and 'private' than they once were, and yet no less definite in their capacity to participate in the public domain and the academy as they emerge, freshly created, to salt the earth and leaven the lump once more.

In this fifth volume of the series, David Bebbington and Timothy Larsen bring together a formidable array of authors to explore modern Christianity and cultural aspirations. Sections explore popular culture, architecture, education, politics and ecclesiology. The volume is dedicated to Professor Clyde Binfield OBE, one of the leading scholars of Nonconformity. I cannot think of a more deserving person for such a book. The publication of *Modern Christianity and Cultural Aspirations* pays handsome tribute to Professor Binfield—a most estimable colleague who has enriched the public arena and the academy with his careful and illuminating scholarship, coupled with his warmth, friendship and integrity.

Canon Professor Martyn Percy
Director, Lincoln Theological Institute

PREFACE

The essays collected in this volume were originally delivered as papers during a conference held at Westminster College, Cambridge, in July 2001 to mark the retirement from the University of Sheffield of Professor Clyde Binfield, OBE. The editors want to express their warm thanks to the principal and staff of the college for their hospitality, to the United Reformed Church History Society for supporting the occasion and especially to its treasurer, Margaret Thompson, who coordinated the business affairs of the whole event, repeatedly going the extra mile in order to ensure its success. They are also grateful to the contributors to this volume for their generous and wholehearted cooperation. The other conference attenders deserve our gratitude as well. The conference was booked to capacity with others regrettably turned away; and the good-natured and insightful participation of numerous people made for an exceptionally congenial occasion. A special word of thanks should be given to those who agreed to chair sessions: Alan Argent, William Jacob, Peter Nockles, Doreen Rosman, Mark Smith and Martin Wellings. The editors are also grateful to Sheffield Academic Press for agreeing to publish the volume in their Lincoln Studies in Religion and Society series.

David Bebbington and Timothy Larsen

David Bebbington is Professor of History, University of Stirling

Clyde Binfield is Professor Associate in History, University of Sheffield, and President of the United Reformed Church History Society

John Briggs is Senior Research Fellow in Church History, Regent's Park College, Oxford

Richard Carwardine is Rhodes Professor of American History, University of Oxford, and Fellow of St Catherine's College, Oxford

David Cornick is General Secretary of the United Reformed Church

Sheridan Gilley is Emeritus Reader in Theology, University of Durham

John Handby Thompson is a former President of the Chapels Society

John A. Hargreaves is Honorary Secretary, Halifax Antiquarian Society

Elaine Kaye is Past President of the United Reformed Church History Society

Frances Knight is Senior Lecturer and Chair of the Department of Theology and Religious Studies, University of Wales Lampeter

Timothy Larsen is Associate Professor of Theology, Wheaton College, IL, USA

Hugh McLeod is Professor of Church History, University of Birmingham

Alan Sell was formerly Professor of Christian Doctrine and Philosophy of

Religion, United Theological College, Aberystwyth, within the Aberystwyth and Lampeter School of Theology of the University of Wales

David Thompson is Fellow of Fitzwilliam College, Cambridge, and Director of the Centre for Advanced Religious and Theological Studies, University of Cambridge

Reg Ward is Emeritus Professor of Modern History, University of Durham

John Wigley is Head of Economics at Haberdashers' Aske's Boys' School, Elstree, Hertfordshire

INTRODUCTION

On 10 February 1852 Thomas Binney, minister of the King's Weigh House Congregational Church in London, spoke in the Exeter Hall under the auspices of the London Young Men's Christian Association. His audience of junior clerks and shopkeepers' assistants lapped up his words as he discussed the question, 'Is it possible to make the best of both worlds?' He assured them that they could achieve resounding success in this world as well as everlasting life in the next. 'The pious, excellent, philanthropic men' who were the backbone of the religious societies that met regularly on the same premises, he contended, proved his case. Once young men themselves, they had risen to prosperity, comfort and eminence. Each one of them had no cause to be ashamed of the lifestyle he had achieved. 'His house, appointments, habitual expenses, are all to be such as are suitable to his property and rank, according to what is customary with his class, and furnished by the improvements of the particular age in which he lives.' The enjoyment of wealth, Binney went on, was entirely legitimate. The 'sudden outburst of Pentecostal communism' that had marked the early Church, as recorded in the book of Acts, was rightly transient. The rich were not commanded in Scripture to cease to be rich or to be known as rich. In Victorian England (Binney was speaking less than four months after the closure of the Great Exhibition of 1851) there was no reason why they should not enjoy the good things of life. 'Because', he argued, 'once there were no carpets, nor curtains, nor rosewood chairs, nor beautiful engravings, to be seen in the houses of certain classes…that is no reason why it should be thought wrong to have them now.' There was no harm in their wives possessing two or three gowns or taking pleasure in the imitative arts. There was no necessity for Christians to avoid such opportunities of modern days. 'They might as well…decline using the railways.'[1] Christianity was a world-affirming faith that his youthful hearers could take with them to the pinnacles of their future careers.

1.   T. Binney, *Is it Possible to make the Best of Both Worlds? A Book for Young Men* (London: James Nisbet & Co., 9th edn, 1855), pp. 118-21.

This welcome message was wide in its application. The aspiring audience learned from its speaker that Christianity enabled a man to make the best of everything: it promoted health, cheerfulness, financial welfare, reputation and 'a green old age'. Most of all, according to Binney, the Christian faith encouraged 'the culture of the intellect', which he coupled with its nourishment of consolation under the trials of life.

> Knowledge with its substantial realities, in all the diversified departments of truth; Beauty with its variety of attractive forms, as exhibited in the works of God, in the utterances or the achievements of genius, in words or things, in poetry or eloquence, in writing or discourse, in painting, music, statuary, and song:—these are high sources of personal enjoyment.

Under a capable teaching ministry these tastes would be fostered from the pulpit. A regular sitter in the pews (Binney no doubt had his own congregation in mind) would hear 'discussions on controverted topics, and has to balance evidence and form an opinion'.

> The religious man becomes of necessity a thinker and reader. He is a logician and philosopher in his way; for he becomes a theologian, and learns to follow trains of reasoning as well as to indulge the impulses of piety. He gets to know something of ancient history, sacred and profane; of the developments of truth through successive dispensations; of the grounds of national prosperity; the laws of the Divine government; the principles of moral science.

His mind would be elevated, his knowledge would be augmented and he would gain the means to collect a personal library. He would acquire a taste for the elegant and beautiful that would find expression in 'the pictures on his walls and the arrangements in his garden'.[2] A London Nonconformist could become a thoroughly cultured man.

It was an ideal appropriate to the age, as the huge sales of the published version of Binney's lecture showed. It was to reach a ninth edition within three years, a fifteenth eventually. Self-improvement was in the air, a possibility for larger numbers than in the past because of the growing prosperity of the country. Before the decade was out Samuel Smiles, the prophet of self-help, was urging the maxim that 'Any man can do what any other man has done'.[3] That spirit permeated the world of the YMCA of which Binney was the ideologue. He was also its exemplar, for he

---

2. Binney, *Is it Possible?*, pp. 38, 41-42, 80, 81.
3. S. Smiles, *Self-Help with Illustrations of Conduct & Perseverance* (ed. A. Briggs; London: John Murray, 1958 [1859]), p. 120.

himself had once been a humble shop assistant (to a bookseller) but had risen to the leading pulpit of metropolitan Dissent. The young men who bought his book eagerly aspired to get on, to make a tidy competence and move to the burgeoning suburbs of Clapham or Highgate. But the YMCA was predominantly an Evangelical agency, a body designed to mobilize those same young men to win souls for the world to come. It was a profoundly Evangelical decade, one of the junctures in English history most immersed in the values of popular Protestantism. Since 1848 the Church of England had possessed, for the first time, an Evangelical Archbishop of Canterbury; while Evangelical Nonconformity, as the census of 1851 revealed, represented not far short of half the churchgoing population. At least in its respectable reaches, it was a remarkably religious nation. That was Binney's premise. A portion of society, as he put it, was 'pervaded by the Christian element'. If a person were brought up in that setting and remained under its 'holy influences' during the vulnerable years of early manhood, he was likely both to prosper and to acquire good taste. True religion would envelope him, virtue would be rewarded and refinement would follow. That would be the outworking of divine laws, for it was the purpose of the Creator that vital Christianity should be associated with success and the perfection of the human spirit. In the particular sphere of the English religious classes would be witnessed the 'benign and favourable working in human affairs of *that constitution of things*, which in a perfectly righteous and religious age, would work benignly and favourably for the whole body'.[4] The conditions of the millennium, Binney was supposing, were already approaching in the circles he knew best. That is why he could anticipate so confidently that the members of the YMCA would go on to become men of great riches and elegant attainments. It was no less than the will of God.

Binney was providing an anticipatory rebuttal of Matthew Arnold. In 1869 Arnold's *Culture and Anarchy* launched an elaborate attack on English Evangelical Nonconformity, claiming that it was vulgar, mediocre and, in a new usage that was to become standard in the language, 'Philistine'. This species of Christianity, according to Arnold, was incompatible with culture. Arnold, the son of the celebrated headmaster of Rugby School, was a poet, a literary critic and an exponent of the benefits of a classical education. In theology he was the broadest of Anglican Broad Churchmen (though High Church in his religious practice), and one of his

4.   Binney, *Is it Possible?*, pp. 105, 106.

greatest complaints was that Evangelical Nonconformity was narrow. It so concentrated on the Hebrew values associated with intense religiosity that it neglected the Hellenic principles of 'sweetness and light'. Arnold did not level the charge against Binney, and even playfully suggested that in other circumstances Binney might have held a position of influence in the established Church.[5] Perhaps the minister of the King's Weigh House was too urbane to be a target of his ridicule. In any case it might have been Binney's whole purpose in life to roll away Arnold's reproach. He held ambiguous views about the training in the ancient languages of the nation's elite. Nothing, he held, could supply the lack of the classical culture instilled by a university education; yet he was sure that a person without Latin or Greek could master the art of writing so thoroughly as to be able to surpass a scholar steeped in antiquity. He reprinted a stern critique of the stylistic deficiencies of George Grote, the historian of ancient Greece, who regularly resorted to 'an uncouth Greek compound when he might easily express the same idea in two or three English words'.[6] Culture was essentially independent of an elite training. A man could attain 'virtue', a classical term he deliberately prefers to any biblical description of righteousness in *Is it Possible?*, through the outworking of his faith without any recourse to the Stoics or the *Nicomachean Ethics*. Binney did not, to use Arnold's word, go in for Hebraizing, employing the argot of the chapels, but on the contrary translated scriptural notions into everyday language.

Samuel Morley, one of Binney's members at the King's Weigh House, the embodiment of his minister's ideal layman and another person mentioned by Arnold as a representative Nonconformist,[7] claimed that he learned the lesson of breadth from the teaching he heard. Morley, originally a Nottingham hosier, prospered to become a millionaire, entered parliament as a prominent Dissenter and was the agent of countless acts of philanthropy. Binney, he used to say, 'had marvellously helped him to aim at independence of character, to take large views of life…to attempt great and generous things in life'. As a result, according to a minister who knew them both well, Morley had 'a certain largeness of feeling and aim which

---

5.   M. Arnold, *Culture and Anarchy* (ed. J. Dover Wilson; Cambridge: Cambridge University Press, 1935 edn), p. 25.

6.   T. Binney, *Authorship* (Lecture before the YMCA, 24 January 1854, London, n.d.), pp. 12-13, 27.

7.   Arnold, *Culture and Anarchy*, p. 209.

saved him from all that was narrow and contracted'.[8] Morley, despite Arnold's allusion to him, was no Hebraizer. In the lives of men such as Morley Binney's reconciliation of gospel and culture seemed to be triumphantly vindicated.

The best modern appreciation of Thomas Binney is to be found in the work of the historian Clyde Binfield, to whom this book is dedicated.[9] Perhaps the most prominent thread running through his historical writing is the way in which Christianity in the modern era has interacted with culture, not least the desire for self-improvement so near the heart of the YMCA. It is no accident that he received the OBE for his services to the international YMCA in the twentieth century. His *oeuvre*, furthermore, demonstrates more clearly than any other body of writing that Nonconformity was capable of generating a cultured sector.[10] It is, in a sense, an extended commentary on the realization of Binney's contentions in 1852. When a conference was planned to mark Clyde's retirement as Professor of History at the University of Sheffield, the theme of modern Christianity and cultural aspirations appeared the most appropriate subject for the gathering. The papers contained in this volume were all given during the conference at Westminster College, Cambridge, in July 2001. The historical papers that form the bulk of the book are preceded by two essays about Clyde. One is an exercise in autobiographical reflection; the other is a critical appreciation of his published writings by a fellow historian, Reg Ward. The scope of the subsequent papers reflects some of Clyde's main interests. Binfield, like Binney, comes from the Nonconformist tradition—in its Congregational branch—and so there is a concentration on that strand in modern Christianity. Eleven of the papers, in fact, deal with various aspects of English Nonconformity in the nineteenth and twentieth centuries, with special emphasis on the Victorian period about which Clyde has written extensively. One (by David Cornick), for example, considers how Presbyterians, once essentially a Scottish denomination, turned themselves into a branch of English Nonconformity in the 1840s. Another

8. E. Hodder, *Life of Samuel Morley* (London: Hodder & Stoughton, 1888), p. 273.

9. J.C.G. Binfield, *George Williams and the Y.M.C.A.: A Study in Victorian Social Attitudes* (London: Heinemann, 1973), pp. 24-34.

10. E.g., J.C.G. Binfield, 'Hebrews Hellenized? English Evangelical Nonconformity and Culture, 1840–1940', in S. Gilley and W.J. Sheils (eds.), *A History of Religion in Britain: Practice and Belief from Pre-Roman Times to the Present* (Oxford: Basil Blackwell, 1994), pp. 322-45.

(by Alan Sell) deals with the much later adaptation, in the 1960s, of the church order of the Congregational body. Other contributions range more widely. The paper on Abraham Lincoln (by Richard Carwardine) is a reminder that many of Binney's values were shared across the Atlantic; the discussion of the Welsh clergy (by Frances Knight) shows that criticisms such as those mounted by Matthew Arnold against Nonconformity could also be turned against members of the established Church; and the account of the design of the Oratory (by Sheridan Gilley) illustrates that architecture was at least as controverted a subject within the Roman Catholic communion as it was (as Clyde has shown on several occasions) in Nonconformity.

The word 'culture', as Raymond Williams demonstrated, has undergone many metamorphoses, and it has passed through more since he wrote on the subject in 1958.[11] It came to signify, in Arnold's writings, the literary and artistic attainments of the human race. High culture, the meaning that Arnold attached to the term, is usually taken to encompass architecture, the subject of two of the papers here. Apart from the consideration of the Oratory, there is an analysis of a process of chapel building in nineteenth-century Nonconformity (by John Handby Thompson). There are also three papers concerning the attainment of culture in this superior form by means of higher education. One (by Timothy Larsen) is about the chief of its outward trappings, the honorary degree, which suggests that there was no reliable correlation between the badge and what it was supposed to represent; a second (by Elaine Kaye) is about the first cohort of students at a Nonconformist theological college in Oxford; and a third (by David Thompson) is about the Nonconformists who went to the other ancient English university, Cambridge. Culture also has a popular dimension, and that, too, is covered by papers in this volume. One (by John Briggs) discusses the material culture of the pottery industry in its various intersections with Nonconformity; another (by Hugh McLeod) takes for its subject the attitude of the Free Churches to sport, in many ways the essence of popular culture at the turn of the twentieth century. A further contribution (by John A. Hargreaves) discusses the laying of the foundations of Christian understanding in Methodist institutions for the young that at one time were closely interwoven with the popular culture of their area. The broadest sense of the word 'culture', its common meaning in anthropology, embraces every aspect of human thought and activity. It

---

11. R. Williams, *Culture and Society, 1780–1850* (London: Chatto & Windus, 1958).

certainly includes politics, which is discussed in three essays. Apart from the one on Lincoln, there is a study of the opening of the Dissenting disestablishment campaign in the 1830s (by David Bebbington) and another on the 1906 Education Bill (by John Wigley), the frustrating anti-climax of the most intense agitation ever mounted by the Nonconformists. So the interaction of Christianity with culture, interpreted widely and variously approached, is the common theme of the various contributions contained in this book.

It would be vain to expect some overall conclusion from a body of essays written independently by a range of scholars working in different fields. Nevertheless there are recurring themes. One is the compatibility of high social ambitions with strongly held religious belief, something that Binney would not have found strange. Another is the permeation of society at large by the views of the Christian groups under discussion and the converse penetration of the religious bodies by contemporary social attitudes. A third (prominent in Chapters 4, 5, 9 and 10) is the importance of family connections reinforcing religious allegiance, a theme central in much of Clyde Binfield's work. These, it may be suggested, are significant findings: modern Christianity was interwoven with social aspirations; the gospel interacted with its host society; and Christian belief was sustained by the family. If these points are unsurprising, they merit emphasis for a historiographical reason. The role of religion in wider affairs has been too much neglected in writing about the modern period in Britain. If these essays help to restore to the centre of discussion the relationship between, on the one hand, Christianity and, on the other, ambitions, attitudes and families, they will have served their purpose.

David Bebbington and Timothy Larsen

A Dissenting Historian's Formation

Clyde Binfield

What formed me as a historian? That must begin with my grandmother, my mother's mother. She was a woman of radical intelligence and views, with looks to match though never the income to exploit those looks. She had a compelling capacity for communicating (which involves so much more than mere telling) a story, to which she allied an infectious interest in unlikely family links, a Victorian's respect for useful lists and a firmly held Whig-Dissenting view of history. Thus she knew the counties of England in alphabetical order and their county towns. She knew the states of the United States and their seats of government and she could reel off the Lord Wardens of the Cinque Ports. It goes without saying that Protestant martyrs were best (and she claimed descent from one) and so were Roundheads, Cromwellian Independents, Huguenots, Waldensians, F.B. Meyer, who baptized her as a believer, and Charles Silvester Horne, under whom she sat as a young woman rather than go either to R.F. Horton's Lyndhurst Road with the two ladies to whom she acted as companion in grand Fitzjohn's Avenue or to Lyndhurst Road's Kentish Town Mission whither they directed their servants. Brought up as a Liberal, she turned to Labour well before the First World War.

And all this she clothed, understandably if not wholly logically, in the novels of Charlotte Yonge, Elizabeth Rundle Charles and Edna Lyall, together with Harrison Ainsworth, *The Cloister and the Hearth* and, more frivolously, Stanley Weyman and Rafael Sabatini. I am not at all sure that her literary tastes—at least as far as they ran to Ainsworth, Reade, Weyman and Sabatini—are not still mine and I am quite sure that her view of history remains mine. I have from time to time been accused of having a Whig view of history. That has never been meant as a compliment, although I have always taken it as such. Perhaps I have been, after all, keeping the faith. Certainly what my grandmother taught me was a feeling for the past and confidence that I might know it as it was.

There were, of course, crisper disciplines in store. The first was having the same history master from Upper One to the Upper Sixth. That was at Dover Grammar School and it worked. E.W. Lister was rigorous, the sort whose quality is best savoured in retrospect, although none of us was ever in doubt as to his command of his subject. He was a tribute to the quality of the Leeds History School and especially to his mentor, Professor Turberville. He believed in the grounding—indeed the grinding—of facts, the shaping of essays, and the reading of books from cover to cover. I am still perversely fascinated by Napoleon III, whose Second Empire was our A Level Special Subject. Above all he had a determined eye for who should go to Cambridge, Oxford too, London as well, and he got them there. In my case he prevailed against the better judgment of headmaster (who was also a historian) and form master, Methodists both (the latter more by marriage). He crammed relentlessly with extra tuition but it was, as I now realize, an expertly judged cramming and it was a cramming which lasted. It was foundational.

So was Cambridge or, to be more precise, Emmanuel College. That was chosen chiefly because I liked the look of its buildings. Their quality was patent, without any of the biscuit-tin allure of The Backs. There was, of course, its traditionary Puritanism, though there really had been little enough of that after 1660. And my school had had a notable recent scholarship success there. Anyway, History at Emmanuel proved dangerously formative for me.

This is not the place for celebrating the humane and civilized liberation which was Cambridge in the late 1950s. My present purpose is quirkier. Emmanuel was then a thoroughly quirky college. It was no place in which to plot fame or fortune. Certainly it had founder's kin, men whose thoroughbred birth was patent because they looked like horses, but in fact more of its members were grammar school men from the deeper sticks than otherwise. It also had an unusually large number of intending ordinands, Low Church, High Church and Broad Church in roughly equal numbers. And it had The Master.

Emmanuel men (they all then, of course, were men) of Edward Welbourne's time are bound on meeting to reminisce of Welbourne, who for us is 'The Master' as the great Duke of Wellington was always 'The Duke', in ways that all others must find quite incomprehensible. The Master was famously opinionated, wickedly prejudiced, and his notoriously idiosyncratic admissions policy could not even be excused by success because it really did not work very well (I, incidentally, was admitted in the year when he was off ill, or so I understand). Yet for us he was The Master. He knew us without ever letting on that he did and he set his mark on each of us. I owe much to his fierce yet thoughtful kindness—the sort of thing that took him each year to the Cheshunt College Commemoration because Cheshunt's president at that time was Eric Pyle, an Emmanuel man, and because years back Welbourne's greatest friend had been Bernard Lord Manning, that famous bursar for Jesus who held a similar watching brief for Cheshunt.

And for History? The Master made lateral thinkers of us all, the more outrageously so the better. Why were there so few Catholics in East Anglia? Because there are no railway tunnels. Could anything be more obvious? More prosaically there was his description of the horse, a perfectly straightforward animal, with a leg at each corner.

More to the immediate point I had a weekly formation, essay by essay, one to one, at the hands of a characterful assortment of supervisors.

In my first year there was that rogue Methodist (why are Methodist historians often such naughty rogues?) John Kent. He was perfect for a priggish 17-year-old straight from a smallish grammar school. His method was wafer biscuits and coffee. The coffee was on the tepid side but the courtesy was much appreciated. Then he would take my essay, read the first sentence, launch for an hour into nothing to do with the subject in hand, return with meticulous timing to the last sentence, and that would be that. The only time he ever complimented me on an essay was when I had written on Politics in the Reign of Anne under the influence of 'flu. John Kent had, of course—it was hard not to be—been bitten by Welbourne. That must explain his remark that the newly enthroned Archbishop Michael Ramsey was so Anglican because he wasn't really an Anglican at all.

My second and third years presented me with a study in contrasts. Goulding Brown was in his eighties and looked 50 years older. He was a Ronald Searle cartoon figure to the life. He had been taught by Maitland, or so we were told, and if he had not heard Acton lecture then he should have done. He firmly disapproved of reading much beyond the primary sources. Alas, like most undergraduates I wanted my Machiavelli mediated racily and accessibly second-hand and that was not how I got it. Yet Goulding Brown was no slouch. The college was convinced that he was in financial straits; in fact he left a tidy sum. And he was disconcertingly up-to-date in his reading, however much he tried to hide the fact and even if, when he died, it was with a volume of Sydney Smith's open on his lap.

John Derry was quite different. He too was tinged with Welbournism and as with many Liberals he was right and has moved further right. He was engaged, bracing, cutting edge and he convinced me of the importance and the attractiveness of the eighteenth century and, too, of the impossibility that I would ever get a sentence right about it, let alone join it up with any other sentence. He was a Butterfield man but in introducing me to Namier (though my history master had in fact begun that introduction) he aroused my distaste at the apparent determination of 1760s man to divest history of both principle and progress. It was only some years later, when faced with giving first-year lectures the following morning, that I returned to Namier and fell for his genius for at once encapsulating and releasing a whole world of possibility in one brisk, crisp sentence of summation. I have been captivated ever since.

Another contrast followed with David Newsome. His championship of the elect tradition of schoolmaster-turned-don-turned-headmaster probably explains my sense that if only there were time what riches might be shared...

It was in my third year that I was slowly reconciled to the medium of the lecture. So far lectures had been the cause of headaches, since they always seemed to be too critical of the work of other historians, and it was such a waste of time getting to the lecture room (then usually still in Mill Lane) and back again.

But there were exceptions. News got round that David Newsome's lecture on the Marian martyrs was wither-wringingly unmissable. I know now that I lost as much as I gained by not going to lectures. For instance, I went just once to hear Geoffrey Best. Recently I came across my notes of that lecture and I now realize how good it was. Forty years on it could be given fresh as new. Yet that was not how it felt at the time—not Elton, not Ullmann, not Postan, not Brogan, not even young John Elliott, not Geoffrey Best. What waste of opportunity; and what suggestive exceptions—Denis Mack Smith on Italian Art of the Renaissance and Owen Chadwick on the Oxford Movement (or, to be more precise, and such precision proved important when the examination came, the Oxford Movement, Parliament and the Churches). Chadwick's audience, that first time round, had gone to uncover the secret of Catholicism and be converted too. They were disappointed. I had no such expectations but I was fully converted to his lectures. They were an unfailing pleasure. I still regard that doubtless mannered charm as lecturing perfection.

So to research. That meant Kitson Clark, with a benign surveillance from David Newsome when Kitson was out in Australia. Had I been older and sooner, or had he been younger and later, it would have meant Frank Salter. Both of them were rich in Dissenting genealogy, but what a gold mine was Frank Salter's! Kitson Clark held an apparently loose rein. It amounted to one supervision a term. I now know that had he disapproved he would have been down on me like a ton of bricks. I also know that what he made me do in my first year of research has served me well ever since, and at no subsequent time could I possibly have found time to do it. I read, year by year, each *Congregational Year Book* and *Baptist Handbook*, and as many *General Baptist Year Books* and *Minutes* of assorted Methodist Conferences as I could. In the case of the first I cut the pages with a paper knife, knowing that no other Cambridge library eye had even glanced at them. That fact greatly amused Kitson, since he had been put on to the trail by Frank Salter, for whom the thought had clearly yet to father the deed. And once I slipped into the mode, how good those apparently predictable chairman's and president's addresses were. These were my sort. Better yet were the obituaries, what early *Year Books* called the 'Necrological Information'. Those gleamed with connection. Like the architectural descriptions they were often most revealing where most conventional. Lady Bracknell and young Mr Worthing were not more fascinated by the *Army Lists* of the 1890s than I was by the *Congregational Year Books* of the 1850s, 1860s, 1870s and 1880s.

What is to be gleaned from this obviously imperfect formation? It encouraged independence, but it also bred a loner. It liberated an almost improperly romanticized passion for connection and continuity, above all where least expected or likeliest to be discontinuous. It developed an eye for the unlikely, a determination to see all the world in a single atom, the Church catholic in the narrowest back lane. It nurtured a predisposition for the brilliant densities of a historian like John Vincent and what was to become known as the Peterhouse School, and generally for all rigorously naughty historians. It fostered a self-contained temper which became marvellously companionable because it gave every journey or stop or chance encounter a potential significance and a certain interest.

But liberating though all this has been, it has also proved terribly inhibiting. For such a temper shies away from the broad sweep or large confident view. It is such a temper as drove Ruskin mad. And it explains the sort of tension that the papers in this volume so honestly explore. My formation as historian brings in its train the faith that I might know it all, in tension with the knowledge that I can know no such thing and that, even if I could, such knowledge so objectively sought must nonetheless be refracted through my limited personality. What a self-indulgent thing is History. How literally self-ish it is, this story that is meaningless, indeed existenceless, unless it is communicated to others, unless it is projected beyond self—as, indeed, my Victorian grandmother first taught me.

PROFESSOR CLYDE BINFIELD: A CRITICAL APPRECIATION

Reg Ward

To introduce a celebration of Clyde's friendship and scholarship is both a thankful and a thankless task, necessarily ambiguous in a colleague at whom Clyde permitted himself a characteristically sly dig in my own Festschrift as 'that most iconoclastic of evangelical historians'.[1] Others can speak more knowledgeably than I of his services to his department and to his denomination; but it is impossible not to know of the burden of departmental chores and hospitality which he has borne, the Saturday morning seminars,[2] the chaplaincy work, the relentless round of editing the denominational historical journal, his advocacy of the work of the YMCA, indeed his apparently ageless personification of the smoother, City-going, non-table-tennis-playing kind of YM. Only the second president of the Ecclesiastical History Society to be elected before his elevation to the professoriate, he was not overshadowed by his predecessor in this distinction, Geoffrey Nuttall. Less eminent societies, not all with a Dissenting bias, have reason to be grateful for his active support. Yet with all his selfless public service, Clyde has stuck to his last. A tardy university has at length acknowledged his services; a United Reformed Church adrift on the ecumenical tide could do (and will do) much worse than make him a bishop; and we as his professional colleagues wish to mark his quite extraordinary contribution to historical studies. Clyde's bibliography runs to well over a hundred items, exclusive of the journals he has edited, and the book reviews that are part of every scholar's routine output.

Clyde's scholarship, however, is more than fertile, it is distinctive. Con-

1.   J.C.G. Binfield, ' "We Claim our Part in the Great Inheritance": The Message of Four Congregational Buildings', in K. Robbins (ed.), *Protestant Evangelicalism: Britain, Ireland, Germany and America, c.1750–c.1950* (Oxford: Basil Blackwell, 1990), pp. 201-223 (223).

2.   J.C.G. Binfield (ed.), *Sainthood Revisioned: Studies in Hagiography and Biography* (Sheffield: Sheffield Academic Press, 1995), p. 7.

centrated at first on the period between the middle of the nineteenth century and the First World War, which happened to be the golden age of Congregationalism, and almost encompassing the 90 years which he has established as the life of a suburban church[3] (Congregational clogs to clogs in three generations, so-to-speak), he has steadily moved forward in time and constantly sought to orientate the *petites histoires* of which he is a master by the broader perspectives of the teaching that has provided his bread and butter and served Sheffield so well. These broader perspectives will be crucial to the major works which have been deferred to his retirement, and especially the *Life* of Gladstone and the nineteenth-century British volume of the *Oxford History of the Christian Church*. Already he has done his bit for secular Sheffield as initiator, editor and contributor to the *History of the City of Sheffield, 1843–1993*. This work was the more excellent for being, like some of Clyde's celebrations of Congregationalism, a slightly sad work of piety. For if a Congregationalism which had claimed all sorts of catholic virtues for Independency now quietly threw in its lot with a Presbyterianism having a quite different image of self-esteem, Sheffield, a noble enterprise indeed, had suffered the ultimate humiliation of being pipped as the capital of the new South Yorkshire by, of all places, Barnsley.

Clyde cut his scholarly teeth on the history of Nonconformity in East Anglia, and emerged sharing the conviction of George Eliot that Dissent was like asthma, it ran in families. Families were indeed his stock in trade, and no one has ever known so much about the Dissenting cousinhoods, nor the vexatious way they would run off into alien territory in Wesleyanism or the Church of England (his favourite bishop of Sheffield was the son of the Congregational manse). There was nothing specially remarkable in the emergence of a Nonconformist Namierite—I had been one myself; but in *George Williams and the Y.M.C.A.* and in *So Down to Prayers*, Clyde made his family studies the key to a wide-ranging theory about the history of Nonconformity and of British social history generally in the second half of the nineteenth century. Williams had come into a vast Dissenting cousinhood by chapel membership, a kind of Nonconformist aristocracy not only like the intellectual aristocracy charted for the Church of England by Noel Annan, but in touch with it, and eventually marrying and moving into it. In his view the success of the YMCA was based on the

---

3.   J.C.G. Binfield, 'True to Stereotype? Vivian and Dorothy Pomeroy and the Rebels in Lumb Lane', in Stuart Mews (ed.), *Modern Religious Rebels: Presented to John Kent* (London: Epworth Press, 1993), pp. 185-205 (187-88).

forces that were bringing the two aristocracies together; the Association's apparent decline from desperate dormitory evangelism to that evidence of a misspent youth, the billiard table, was the secular counterpart of the mind-opening that was taking place as the Congregationalists moved from the fringes of society into official culture, from backstreet Bethels into whopping Gothic masterpieces, from a narrow fundamentalism into who-knew-what, from being the whipping-boys of Matthew Arnold to the heirs of civilization. As if this cosmic perspective were not enough, it was so adorned with learned general *aperçus* from Clyde's nineteenth-century teaching that I commended it in a review as worthy 'to become the bedside companion of the cannier kind of undergraduate for it is stuffed with author's asides which are likely to reappear as quotations for discussion in examination papers for years to come'. I knew that disclosing this tit-bit was no breach of professional confidence since the review appeared in the *Durham University Journal*,[4] a periodical so seldom read as almost to qualify for the *genre* of curious literature, and one whose very existence was veiled from undergraduates.

Nevertheless I had the feeling that Clyde and I were two Namierites confronted eyeball to eyeball, he affirming and I wondering whether this genealogical evidence was indeed the open window upon the vista.[5] Everyone knew that Namier had invented his method to illuminate a period in which in domestic politics not much was happening, when ideas, though not absent, and very clearly present in the cleft between Church and Dissent, were at a lower ebb than at any other time in the century; if politics had become to so great a degree a struggle after hogwash, then blood was certainly thicker than water, and family and county networks were the rage. Where ideas and conflicts abounded, family ties were likely to replicate rather than occasion ideological congruity;[6] where things were changing fast, the cousinhood would be hard pressed to keep up.

At one point Clyde frankly admitted to a difficulty by comparing his Dissenting elite with the birthright membership of the Quakers, that public

---

4.   *Durham University Journal* 66 (1974), p. 327.

5.   These hesitations were most clearly expressed in a review of *So Down to Prayers* in the same recondite journal, *Durham University Journal* 72 (1979), pp. 103-105.

6.   Clyde himself came to state this view cogently in 'Jews in Evangelical Dissent: The British Society, the Herschell Connection and the Pre-Millenarian Thread', in M. Wilks (ed.), *Prophecy and Eschatology* (Studies in Church History, Subsidia 10; Oxford: Basil Blackwell, 1994), pp. 225-70 (250).

sign that an origin in aggressive evangelism had been foresworn and forgotten. Of course the Congregationalists were still growing vigorously; but something was coming over them. Not long before the personal networks had been of a spiritual nature; B, C and D had been recalled as the converts of A and the seals of his ministry, as X, Y and Z were in turn the fruit of theirs. The enormous impetus given to Independency by people converted under George Whitefield owed little to the flesh but much to the Spirit. It would appear that minds being opened in one direction were being closed in others. The nearest so nice a man as Clyde comes to being nasty is a comment that on a certain cast of mind evangelicalism has a very damaging effect, and if he wishes to be severe upon his own denomination it is that Matthew Arnold was right about them; they failed either to measure up to official culture or to offer an alternative. Yet Clyde's 'mind-opening' theme was essential to three of the main vistas that he wished to open, the reconciliation and interpenetration of the intellectual aristocracies, the Dissenting championship of an 'improved' Gothic, and the ultimate commitment of Congregationalism to the ecumenical movement.

Yet none of these parts quite fit. The last ploy was the most desperate of all for it involved Clyde in the messianism of the ecumenical spin-doctors. He wrote at one time as though the ecumenical movement was on the threshold of cosmic triumph, then growled most uncharacteristically that delay was all due to the immobility of the Church of England. But if, after all, the mind-opening that was the key to Congregational progress had led to absorption in an official culture ecclesiastically represented by the Church of England, and so complete that Congregationalists had now nothing to dissent from but their own past, they might just as well pack up with or without an ecumenical cachet. And at the very least it was patent that neither the ecumenical viewpoint nor the genealogy to which Clyde had contributed so generously[7] made sense of the denominational *Geistesgeschichte*.

Congregationalism was not a linear history stretching unbroken from blinkered hypers to smooth liberal men of the world; even if it had been, it would have started from men who believed that they were clarifying an important international current of thought, a current they knew was powerfully represented in the Church of England. I think it is true that

---

7.   What the genealogy could do was to reveal the formation of a market for an enterprise; applying this to an intermediate stage of women's education brought Clyde to one of his most delightful and informative studies, *Belmont's Portias: Victorian Nonconformists and Middle-Class Education for Girls* (Friends of Dr Williams's Library 35th Lecture; London: Dr Williams's Trust, 1981).

Congregationalists in company with other Nonconformists have often made the mistake of thinking that if they were doing better than the Church establishment they were doing well enough, oblivious of the fact that the English establishment was a Church of very low achievement. But as the English establishment began to turn in on itself in the eighteenth century and turn away from such religion as the English people had, the Independents did a profitable business in importing theologies from abroad. English-language theology can hardly get more highbrow than Jonathan Edwards, but, as everyone knows, the first edition of the *Surprising Work of God* was published in England with a commendation by Isaac Watts and John Guyse to the effect that it offered the common plain Protestant doctrine of the Reformation, that it was the Baxterian middle way. And in the 1840s, half a century before Clyde's bourgeois arrivistes were broadening their minds by expensive continental holidays, the *British Quarterly Review* was full of notices of German theological literature.

It is this in-and-out character of Congregational intellectual history which makes it comprehensible that a highbrow Protestant like P.T. Forsyth should emerge in the midst of a liberal flood, and that Nathaniel Micklem, laudably attempting to state a gospel which was more positive than that of mere Dissent, should try all our patience by rhetoric about the catholicity of Protestantism.[8] We are all losers from the fact that the editors of recent symposia about Forsyth have not entrusted Clyde with any of the contributions in intellectual history.[9] We did not need Clyde to remind us of the curious propensity of the distinguished Reformed to fetch up as college principals[10] from long before Jonathan Edwards to long after Charles

---

8. It is nice to be able to record Micklem's generous understanding of this doctrine in the help he gave by personal assistance and the use of his vast private library to the German prisoners-of-war in Norton Camp near Mansfield (1945–48). This camp (with a Catholic commandant) proved to be an astonishingly successful venture in Protestant theological education. Its most distinguished graduate was Jürgen Moltmann. K. Loscher, *Studium und Alltag hinter Stacheldraht* (Neukirchen–Vluyn: Neukirchener Verlag, 1997), pp. 9, 37.

9. E.g., J.C.G. Binfield, 'P.T. Forsyth as Congregational Minister', in T. Hart (ed.), *Justice the True and Only Mercy: Essays on the Life and Theology of Peter Taylor Forsyth* (Edinburgh: T. & T. Clark, 1995), pp. 168-96.

10. Still, according to Clyde, exercising an indirect pastoral role. J.C.G. Binfield, ' "Bridled Emotion": English Free Churchmen, Culture and Catholic Values, c. 1870 to c. 1945', in A.C. Duke and C.A. Tamse (eds.), *Britain and the Netherlands. VII. Church and State since the Reformation* (The Hague: Nijhoff, 1981), pp. 176-206 (186).

Finney. But for what he thinks of Forsyth's place in the intellectual pedigree we shall have to wait until the large works he has on the stocks are before us.

If family history is unlikely to offer the key to either a movement coping with differences in ideas or one in which things are happening quickly, I am convinced by Clyde's arguments that the history of Congregationalism in his preferred period was quite largely made in this way to a degree which has never been matched in Methodism. Certainly my Primitive forebears who scoured the country on foot looking for souls as they went also on foot looking for work were not able to function in this way. It was also clear that the forces which transformed Lancashire Independency from a village religion of working men to one of an urban elite who formed their own cousinhoods were not of this kind. Again, why was the affinity between the Dissenting cousinhoods and the Gladstones so glorious when the propensity of their epigone to heed the siren songs of Lloyd George was so dreadful?[11] Moreover as Clyde's mind developed and particularly as he turned to the boom years of Sheffield,[12] the cousinhoods disappear.

They are, however, central to another of Clyde's distinctive enterprises, the history of Nonconformist architecture, a general study of which is promised. Here there is no alternative to proceeding building by building and congregation by congregation, and the *petites histoires* which have occupied much of Clyde's writing life become the building blocks of the Gothic proto-cathedral to which he aspires. This work is the more important because its evidences are fragile. Whether or not 90 years is the life of a congregation, a century is roughly the life of the buildings they erected in their grandiose days, buildings which are now threatened by both the contempt of ministers and congregations which want to centre their existence on social service rather than worship, and by the ecumenical philis-

11. J.C.G. Binfield, 'Networking through Sound Establishments: How Gladstone Could Make Dissenting Sense', in D. Bebbington and R. Swift (eds.), *Gladstone Centenary Essays* (Liverpool: Liverpool University Press, 2000), pp. 133-62. (My best thanks are due to Professor Bebbington for letting me have a copy of this work hot from the press.) The full horror of the Lloyd George period Clyde leaves to John le Carré: J.C.G. Binfield, 'Sir Makepeace Watermaster and the March of Christian People: An Interaction of Fiction, Fact and Politics', in J.P. Parry and S. Taylor (eds.), *Parliament and the Church, 1529–1960* (Edinburgh: Edinburgh University Press, 2000), pp. 165-84.

12. J.C.G. Binfield, 'Religion in Sheffield', in J.C.G. Binfield *et al.* (eds.), *A History of the City of Sheffield* (3 vols.; Sheffield: Sheffield Academic Press, 1993), II, pp. 364-428.

tinism of the BBC which, in England at least, thinks that pictures fit even for *Songs of Praise* can only be generated from parish churches. Yet the myopia of the BBC is not different from that of our forebears who thought that if it was a church that was wanted they must demonstrate that Nonconformists could build churchwardens' Gothic better than churchwardens, or, if they were Wesleyans, at least show that they were not as the heathen Primitives down the road.

Clyde believes that the improved Gothic educated congregations towards that vaguely conceived higher life to which so many of them aspired, and, shrewdly anticipating what I might say on an occasion such as this, has assured the world that my 'own Methodism...in Durham as now in Petersfield...has sat down in spired Gothic'.[13] Vain assurance, for that part of the sitting down has not been from pleasure! I have failed so far to find in Clyde an explanation why an inherited style which had been such an incubus on Protestant worship in the Church of England since the Reformation, and which had been joyfully abandoned by even Central European Catholics in a rush into the baroque, was now thought obligatory, even mind-opening, for aspiring Protestant Dissenters. He is right of course in commending an improved Gothic, and he has my total support in perceiving the improvement (as he repeatedly assures us) in 'ample lavatory and cloakroom accommodation',[14] not to mention Jennings Patent Washbasin and Urinal for the minister,[15] or even, in what seems to be Clyde's favourite architectural fantasy, Coats Memorial Baptist Church, Paisley, where already the tiled lavatories were like reception halls, a provision against the church's going over from immersion to sprinkling, drinking fountains like fonts![16] Congregationalists had not yet come to the point of installing Gothic projection rooms, though anyone who has used the Gothic electric-light switches in the John Rylands Library must regard this as a possibility, while Tottenham Court Road Congregational Church

13. Binfield, ' "We Claim our Part" ', p. 223.

14. J.C.G. Binfield, ' "A Crucible of Modest though Concentrated Experiment": Religion in Sheffield', in H. McLeod (ed.), *European Religion in the Age of Great Cities* (London: Routledge, 1995), pp. 196-215 (196).

15. J.C.G. Binfield, 'A Chapel and its Architect: James Cubitt and Union Chapel, Islington, 1874–1889', in D. Wood (ed.), *The Church and the Arts* (Studies in Church History, 28; Oxford: Basil Blackwell, 1992), pp. 417-48 (440).

16. J.C.G. Binfield, 'A Working Memorial? The Encasing of Paisley's Baptists', in W.M. Jacob and N. Yates (eds.), *Crown and Mitre: Religion and Society in Northern Europe since the Reformation* (Woodbridge: Boydell, 1993), pp. 185-202 (193).

in a splendid spirit of enterprise resolved to out-palace if not to out-gin all the local gin-palaces. 'The electric light [we read] is unsparingly used, and before the great arc-lights outside the illuminations of gin-palaces hard by pale into yellow insignificance.'[17]

It is quite plain from what Clyde tells us that there were plenty of people about who understood that what Nonconformists needed was a building which could be preached in, which encouraged congregational singing, and, as Henry Allon prudently observed, which enabled the minister to lead the congregation in extemporary prayer without having to shout at God.[18] What could doubtless be taken for granted in the prestige buildings to which Clyde has devoted most of his attention, was that unless an additional suite of buildings could be provided for Sunday school, smaller meetings and social activities, the main worship room must be adaptable for these purposes too. On every score the Gothic buildings were worse than the classical buildings which preceded them. To cap all they were less durable. The Methodist Chapel Committee has known for 50 years that the Gothic chapels are coming down much faster than the older classical buildings. Spires which were a poor engineering concept, roofs the poor ventilation of which encouraged dry rot, and the complicated construction of which disguised the entry of water and the onset of wet rot, were not a recipe for longevity. Where Clyde sees broadening of mind the historian of Methodist architecture sees the obscuring of architectural vision;[19] having sat under two lots of the 'spired Gothic' for the last 40 years and watched them gradually disintegrate in the same sequence, baffled trustees constantly perceiving unaccountable acts of God, my own judgment on the question is somewhat biased. And perhaps Clyde's mind has moved a little in the same direction. For after appearing to endorse R.W. Dale's claim that Mansfield College embodied the whole spiritual and intellectual heritage of the west, and that such missing worthies as found no place in its importunate iconography owed their misfortune to lack of reliable portraiture, he admits that such claims are over the top, 'God's variant of the Whig view of history',[20] and perhaps not even God's.

17. J.C.G. Binfield, *So Down to Prayers: Studies in English Nonconformity, 1780–1920* (London: J.M. Dent, 1977), p. 204.

18. Binfield, 'A Chapel and its Architect', p. 430.

19. G.W. Dolbey, *The Architectural Expression of Methodism* (London: Epworth Press, 1964).

20. Binfield, ' "We Claim our Part" ', pp. 204-209; the title of 'Hebrews Hellenized?', in S. Gilley and W.J. Sheils (eds.), *A History of Religion in Britain: Practice and Belief*

Even those who do not share Clyde's architectural enthusiasms are bound to be grateful for the energy and skill with which he has gone about his cataloguing, and for two very notable qualities he has brought to the task. Any minuscule temptation I might ever have had to attempt anything of the kind fell victim a few years ago when I had an hour to kill at Zurich Hauptbahnhof, and popped into a local gallery to see an exhibition about a municipal housing scheme. There were the original plans and the bold ideas; there were the political processes and the changes made to accommodate this pressure group or that financial squeeze; and there was the final outcome which bore no perceptible resemblance to the first concept. Clearly the attempt to infer ideas from an architectural creation was in the last degree hazardous, and the attempt to document the transition from one to the other was beyond the energy I could spare from other things. It has not been beyond Clyde's; and whether it was the substantial change of use which would have been occasioned at the City Temple had the Congregational Union camped out within its portals, or whether it was the idiocies of the town planners in Bournemouth, Clyde has devoted some of his most learned and hilarious passages to the architecture that never was, the virtual building which expensively preceded the building that ultimately happened.[21] We all know that ecclesiastical history, and not merely chairs in it, has a fight to survive, threatened as it is by the mutually supporting contempt of secularists and theologians; it had better be entertaining, and Clyde is never less. On architecture he is at his most entertaining.

A final branch of Clyde's achievement is closely associated with the buildings: the congregations which erected and used them. Clyde's history of the Baptist Church at Queen's Road, Coventry,[22] seems to me to be as good a chapel history as one can ever expect, and it is not surprising that it has exposed him to demands for more of the same. The book left me feeling envious that so few Methodist churches have cared sufficiently for their records ever to receive a memorial of this kind. If it has a weakness, it is that in the early section where the documentation is thinnest Clyde

from Pre-Roman Times to the Present (Oxford: Basil Blackwell, 1994), pp. 322-45, also contains a grandiose cultural assumption against which my old colleague Professor Jo Skemp used to deploy his great Hellenistic learning.

21. J.C.G. Binfield, 'Victims of Success: Twentieth-Century Free Church Architecture', in J. Shaw and A. Kreider (eds.), *Culture and the Nonconformist Tradition* (Cardiff: University of Wales Press, 1999), pp. 142-81.

22. J.C.G. Binfield, *Pastors and People: The Biography of a Baptist Church: Queen's Road, Coventry* (Coventry: Queen's Road Baptist Church, 1984).

most indulges his fondness for fine writing. This may seem an odd subject of complaint and indeed impertinent from one who finds the plain style appropriate to the earthen vessel which is our common theme hard to achieve, but it is characteristic of all Clyde's work. One of Clyde's favourite words is the word 'traditionary', a word I have come across nowhere else than in the *Shorter Oxford English Dictionary*. My edition is admittedly immediately pre-Clyde, but it produces only two examples of the word, the most recent dating from 1749. Being these days (in the vulgar phrase) *into* visions I thought that *Sainthood Revisioned* might contain some new ones, but Clyde's contribution did not, and I am not sure what the title meant. That I was not the only one perplexed by the fine style was made clear by MS evidence in the copy I obtained from a West of England university library by inter-library loan. There in the neatest of pencil a laborious Japanese had applied to an English dictionary for explanations of some of Clyde's abstract nouns and metaphors, achieving a steady beta minus level, before translating the result into Japanese. All went tolerably until Clyde pronounced that 'when Professor Kumpera delivered his paper Comenius studies were rapidly emerging from their Communist carapace'. For 'carapace' the dictionary had yielded 'on the back of a tortoise' and the effort to find acceptable Japanese for the emergence of Comenius studies on the back of a Communist tortoise was altogether too much for our earnest reader, who gave up the enterprise and deprived posterity of the advantage of his exegesis. None of us wish Clyde's volume in the *Oxford History of the Christian Church* to suffer in the Japanese market because of high style.

One of the reasons for the high style is of course that Clyde is often unashamedly evocative.[23] The attempt to conjure up ethos is, of course, entirely legitimate and is particularly valuable when the ignorant are likely to produce postmodernist reasons for pretending otherwise. But it does not really help to make a metaphor out of a staple trade. Thus Leeds is 'woven' into the fabric of Yorkshire society while Sheffield is a 'crucible' (though a modest one) of religious experiment. My beloved Manchester comes badly out of this process, producing only Cottontots, who sound

---

23. And never more impressively than in 'Freedom through Discipline: The Concept of the Little Church', in W.J. Sheils (ed.), *Monks, Hermits and the Ascetic Tradition* (Studies in Church History, 22; Oxford: Basil Blackwell, 1985), pp. 405-50, in which the Congregational approach to children c. 1880 to c. 1939, the theme of which is the disappearance of original sin and the emphasis on beauty, is recaptured with all the presumed innocence of the children to whom it was addressed.

like elder siblings of the Teletubbies.[24] But Clyde's style, like his outlook, has matured; he introduces the history of Sheffield by turning a cliché into a memorable epigram; Sheffield was 'a town of tools and cutting edges'.[25] And what is lacking in his evocations is lacking in the work of almost all of us which we must put right while we still can, and that is what the working substance of the religion of his Congregationalists was. He is well able to do it. His paper on 'Jews in Evangelical Dissent' is an important study in eschatology; but in his general work, apart from advice on Bible reading, there is very little. The Congregational pulpit was there to provide drama, but until the last generation it always attracted upwardly mobile Methodists who wanted to escape their own sort of drama. What prayers appealed? What reading was recommended, and what actually undertaken? What was it about the old Independent defence of orthodoxy which led so many Congregational churches rapidly to emulate the *Shipley Times*'s definition of the YMCA in 1905 'as a kind of institutional church without the church as such being included'?[26] These are all questions which Clyde will doubtless elucidate with his usual charm in the big works still to come.

24. Binfield, *So Down to Prayers*, p. 57; Binfield, 'A Crucible of Modest though Concentrated Experiment', pp. 191-215. Clyde tells us that one member of the Taylor family of Ongar 'was overpolished, as thoughtful Nonconformists were apt to be, another wrote "Twinkle, Twinkle, Little Star" ': *So Down to Prayers*, p. ix.

25. Binfield, *History of Sheffield*, II, p. 1.

26. J.C.G. Binfield, *George Williams and the Y.M.C.A.: A Study in Victorian Social Attitudes* (London: Heinemann, 1973), p. 315.

Part I

POPULAR CULTURE

'THEWS AND SINEWS': NONCONFORMITY AND SPORT

Hugh McLeod

In June 1893 the Baptists of College Street, Northampton, were looking for a successor to their veteran pastor, the Revd J.T. Brown. The search had dragged on for over a year, since any candidate who won the admiration of one part of the church was regarded with suspicion by another part.[1] In that month the *Northamptonshire Nonconformist*, a journal produced by members of the chapel's Young Men's Society, published an article entitled 'How to Choose a Minister'. It consisted of a series of letters prompted by the ministerial vacancy at the 'Statusquo Chapel, Letherville'. The first letter came from Miss Dora Featherweight, who favoured one of the candidates because he had a nice moustache and she had played tennis with him. A more pious note was struck by Mr Simon Saintly, who began his letter 'The dear Lord has still left us as sheep having no shepherd', and went on to insist that they should continue to remain in this state, rather than select a candidate who smoked cigars. The next contributor was a shoe manufacturer, Mr Jeremiah Gripper, who apparently combined a rigid form of Calvinism with unethical business practices. Finally, there was Mr Ernest Stiremup, who wanted to convert the chapel into a swimming bath and gymnasium.[2]

One may surmise that Mr Stiremup would have found some sympathy among the publishers of the journal. The Young Men's Society had been involved in a long-running dispute with the trustees over their request that one of the schoolrooms be used as a gym. In spite of pleas that the Society and presumably by implication the church itself were losing members to

1. Northamptonshire Record Office [hereafter NRO], CSBC/65: College Street Baptist Church, Northampton [hereafter CSBCN], Church Minute Book 1888–94, 27 April 1892, 30 November 1892, 28 December 1892, 3 May 1893, 16 August 1893, 11 November 1893, 14 February 1894 (when the church voted by 247 to 66, with 10 absentions, to invite the Revd Philip Smith—in spite of objections that he was not a pledged abstainer).

2. *Northamptonshire Nonconformist*, June 1893 (Northamptonshire Central Library, Northamptonshire Studies Room [henceforth NCL, NSR]).

other Baptist or Congregational churches in the town which did have their own gym, the trustees refused to budge.[3] While refraining from direct attacks on named individuals or bodies, the young men, and some young women, who produced the *Northamptonshire Nonconformist* regularly used the columns of their paper to further the cause of sport generally and chapel-based sport in particular. The second issue in February 1889 introduced a sports column headed 'Thews and Sinews' and signed 'Biceps':

> From month to month I purpose saying a few words on what young Non-conformists are doing in the athletic world, as I believe with all my heart in the trite but true maxim, *Mens sana in corpore sano*. There's nothing to beat a sound mind in a sound body. Without the latter, in many cases the former is impossible.
>
> Any healthy physical recreation shall receive my hearty support. Give me good sound sport, free from cruelty and torture of dumb animals—that is barbarity not sport—and I am happy. Were the Studds any worse missionaries because they were the foremost cricketers of the day? Is a man a poorer Christian because he can pull stroke in an eight, do a spin across country, play a sound game at football, or distinguish himself on the cricket field? Nay, I trow not.

The writer went on to praise the College Street hockey team for some notable victories and the cricketers for sportsmanship and determination in the face of defeat. At Doddridge, the leading Congregational chapel in the town, the schoolroom was transformed once a week into 'a capital gym-nasium': 'the Powers-that-be are inclined to view with favourable eyes the efforts of the coming generation to expand their chests and strengthen their biceps'. And, in an allusion which his readers would be unlikely to miss, he added, 'It is a wise policy, contrasting well with some places where whispers tell me opposition is put in the way rather than encouragement given'. The young ladies of Doddridge also had the opportunity for weekly calisthenic exercises under the direction of Miss Jeannie Mayger, 'to the manifest improvement of their physique'.[4]

'Biceps' brought to his journalistic endeavours a degree of missionary ardour. In 1889 there were still some Nonconformists who regarded sport as being at best a waste of time and as often an occasion for sin. There were probably some who thought sport unladylike. And there were many more

3.   NRO, CSBC/167: CSBCN, Minutes of Young Men's Society [hereafter MYMS] 1887–94, 19 May 1888, 23 July 1890, 19 December 1890, 22 August 1891, 30 September 1892; Annual Report 1890.

4.   *Northamptonshire Nonconformist*, February 1889.

who accepted that both men and women had some need for recreation, but who thought it wrong that anything so worldly should take place on chapel premises or under the auspices of the church. Thus in March 1889 'Biceps' was lambasting a 'doubtless well-meaning, though sadly mistaken' gentle-man, who had 'contributed a bitter tirade to the columns of the *Baptist* on the ungodliness of football', and he was expounding the benefits to women's health of bicycling and tricycling.[5] A conference in Northampton later that year on 'The Church and Amusements' gave both sides an opportunity to state their case. The *Northamptonshire Nonconformist* presented the debate mainly in generational terms. Older speakers warned of 'the danger of mak-ing amusements the *only* work of the church', and suggested that where this was done the amusements were not sufficient to retain younger people. Younger speakers at the conference tended to take a more positive view, 'arguing that the Church should aim at elevating humanity and touching life at *all* points, and that the young *lodgers* of our town need evening homes, as also do many of our poorer brethren'.[6]

At the beginning of the 1890s there was a fairly even balance within the chapels between those who eagerly embraced the growing national passion for sport and those who were more cautious, or even hostile. But as the debate in Northampton had indicated, time was on the side of the sportsmen. In the 1870s and early 1880s the idea that there could or should be any overt connection between Nonconformity and sport would have seemed incon-gruous to many people, and those who advocated such a connection knew that they would have to prepare their ground carefully.[7] By the early 1900s the battle had been won. Not only did most chapels provide sporting facili-ties, or at least sponsor a range of teams, but the minister frequently took a close interest in this aspect of the church's work, and sometimes participated himself. And by the 1920s and 1930s sport was as much taken for granted as tea meetings had been 60 years earlier. They were an integral part of Non-conformist life, and in many parts of England chapel-based clubs made a major contribution to the growth of amateur sport in this period. Research by Jack Williams suggests that in the 1920s over half of those who played competitive cricket regularly in some of the Lancashire cotton towns were playing for teams based on a place of worship, and that the majority of these

5.   *Northamptonshire Nonconformist*, March 1889.
6.   *Northamptonshire Nonconformist*, December 1889. See also CSBCN, MYMS 1887–94, Annual Report 1889.
7.   For examples of the persistence of more negative views, see R. Currie, *Methodism Divided* (London: Faber & Faber, 1968), p. 132.

teams were associated with a Nonconformist chapel. In Lancashire, church and chapel teams also played a major role in the male sports of soccer and billiards, the female sport of rounders, and the mixed sports of tennis, table tennis and hockey, though there were other sports where places of worship were less significant, including rugby, golf, bowls and darts.[8] There were also sports in which Anglicans and Catholics participated more readily than Nonconformists—but I shall return to that below. Though Williams suggests that the link between churches and sport in the inter-war years was stronger in the north than the south, it was also strong in the midland town of Northampton. For instance in 1922 out of the 17 strongest cricket teams in the borough, 5 were based in an Anglican church and 5 in a Nonconformist chapel (2 Baptist, and one each from the Congregationalists, Unitarians and Primitive Methodists).[9] Indeed at a somewhat earlier date, in 1900, Jeff Cox has noted that as many as 26 out of 43 teams in the Lambeth cricket league were linked with a chapel.[10]

In this paper I intend to trace the successive stages in the growing affinity between Nonconformists and certain branches of sport. The first stage was the spontaneous formation of cricket, football or athletic clubs for the purposes of fellowship and fun by the members of Bible classes, Mutual Improvement Societies, and similar groups of young men already attached to a chapel. The second was the formation of clubs or the provision of facilities for the purpose of retaining teenage boys who had been attending Sunday school or other chapel institutions, but were thought to be in danger of falling away. The third was the provision of facilities for sport and for other kinds of leisure as a way of attracting outsiders, and as an alternative to less wholesome forms of amusement. The fourth was the advocacy by ministers and other chapel leaders of sport as something necessary to the good life, and thus as essential to every chapel programme and to the personal development of each individual. The final stage was when chapel-based sport and participation therein was so taken for granted that it no longer needed any justification.

8.   J. Williams, 'Recreational Cricket in the Bolton Area between the Wars', in R. Holt (ed.), *Sport and the Working Class in Modern Britain* (Manchester: Manchester University Press, 1990), pp. 101-120; *idem*, 'Churches, Sport and Identities in the North, 1900–1939', in J. Hill and J. Williams (eds.), *Sport and Identity in the North of England* (Keele: Keele University Press, 1996), pp. 113-36 (114-17).

9.   G. Sibley, *Northampton Club Cricket: A Centenary History* (Northampton: Town Cricket League, 1986), p. 55.

10.   J. Cox, *English Churches in a Secular Society: Lambeth 1870–1930* (Oxford: Oxford University Press, 1982), p. 85.

The Origins of Chapel Sport

The popularity of cricket, athletics, gymnastics and both codes of football grew rapidly from the later 1860s. Clubs founded at that time mostly charged high subscriptions and attracted young men of the upper middle class. Then, in the 1870s, organized sport began to attract large numbers of men from the lower middle and working classes as well. A crucial factor here was the increasing practice of closing factories and offices around the middle of the day on Saturday and of closing shops on a Wednesday or Thursday afternoon. It was in the 1870s that Saturday afternoon became the principal time for sporting events; Wednesday or Thursday afternoon were soon established as the major alternatives.[11] Young men connected with Nonconformist chapels were among the beneficiaries of these new leisure opportunities, and many of them fully shared the contemporary passion for sport and physical fitness. Some, no doubt, joined clubs based on their locality or place of work; but if their closest friends were fellow chapel-goers, it was natural that they should band together to form chapel-based clubs. At College Street, Northampton, the Young Men's Society, the sporting enthusiasm of whose members was mentioned at the beginning of this paper, had its origins in a Bible class picnic in 1884, during which the idea of such a society was mooted.[12] In the 1870s clubs of this kind were multiplying, though at this stage there seem to have been considerably more sports teams attached to Anglican parishes. It has been estimated that in the later 1870s there were 96 football or cricket clubs linked to Anglican parishes in Birmingham, but only 46 attached to Nonconformist chapels, and that in Leicester in 1893 11 out of 16 church-based football clubs were Anglican[13]—though it should be

---

11. J. Lowerson, *Sport and the English Middle Classes, 1870–1914* (Manchester: Manchester University Press, 1993), pp. 96-98 and *passim*; D. Molyneux, 'The Development of Physical Recreation in the Birmingham District from 1871 to 1892' (MA thesis, University of Birmingham, 1957), pp. 2, 25-26, and *passim*; T. Mason, *Association Football and English Society, 1863–1915* (Brighton: Harvester, 1980), pp. 2-3. For the significance of Thursday, see NRO, PSBC/21/1: *Princes Street Baptist Church Magazine*, September 1898, April 1901, showing that in Northampton Thursday afternoon was a favourite time for cycle runs as well as for other chapel social events.

12. CSBCN, MYMS 1887–94, Annual Report 1890.

13. D.A. Reid, 'Labour, Leisure and Politics in Birmingham, c. 1800–1875' (PhD thesis, University of Birmingham, 1985), pp. 136-39; J. Crump, 'Amusements of the People: The Provision of Recreation in Leicester, 1850–1914' (PhD thesis, University of Warwick, 1985), p. 378.

noted that Anglican clubs, with names like St Silas or Holy Sepulchre, are often more easily identified than their Dissenting counterparts.

The earliest chapel-based sports clubs tended to leave few traces behind them. How much would we know about the football club formed in 1874 by members of the Young Men's Bible Class at Villa Cross Wesleyan Chapel if it had not subsequently become Aston Villa? And in spite of that team's subsequent fame, very little seems to be known about its early years.[14] One of the fullest accounts of teams of this kind comes in the autobiography of William Kent, born in a lower-middle-class Wesleyan family in south London in 1884, and in his youth and young manhood an adherent first of a Congregational mission and then of a Congregational church. At the mission, Kent took a very active part in the Bible class and Mutual Improvement Society, wrote articles for the magazine and played for the cricket team, having earlier played for a Rechabite XI. Rather than being alternatives, as was often alleged by critics of 'amusements', these various activities flowed naturally into and out of one another. Close friendships were formed at the church which naturally spilled over into leisure hours. Young men whose prayers, reading of the Bible and absention from intoxicating liquor made them vulnerable to charges of 'cant', 'pharisaism', 'goody-goodiness', and much more, were all too ready to prove that they could enjoy themselves as well as the next man—though they preferred to do it in company where swearing during the match and drinking afterwards were not mandatory.[15]

While the idea of a chapel cricket or football club was new in the 1870s, a variety of favourable influences were making this idea possible. In the first place, even the most austere religious communities found a place in their programme for purely social events. Tea meetings were a well-established part of Nonconformist life, and generally agreed to be both enjoyable in themselves and a valuable means of building up fellowship. This was even more so in the case of the Sunday schools, which competed with one another to provide the most attractive outing and the most sumptuous feast. Outings often included cricket, rounders or races, and teachers participated as eagerly as children. When a cricket or football team was formed for or by the older children, this was merely taking long-established practice one stage further. While outings were generally recognized as a necessary and even desirable aspect of the Sunday school, some congregations were by the later 1850s introducing outings and treats for their

14. There is a brief account of Aston Villa's early history in Molyneux, 'Development of Physical Recreation', pp. 66, 88.

15. W. Kent, *Testament of a Victorian Youth* (London: Heath Cranton, 1938).

adult members. A pioneer was the undenominational Church of the Saviour in Birmingham, which in the 1850s and 1860s held a 'Christmas Gathering', with 'quiet games', music and dancing, and a summer outing, with cricket, football and athletics. Their pastor, George Dawson, was one of the first Nonconformist preachers to attack puritanism and to argue the need for healthy recreation. For some time to come the strongest advocates of recreation would be, like Dawson, theological liberals, convinced that the church had a duty to work for social amelioration. Dawson's less outspoken, but more widely influential Birmingham colleague, R.W. Dale, was prepared in 1867 to make a more modest defence of recreation as a necessary precondition for efficent work. He noted as a fact that there was a relaxation 'everywhere of the stricter habits of our forefathers'.[16]

Most of the pioneers of religiously sanctioned recreation were Anglicans, and Anglican inspirations and examples played a part in the changing currents of Nonconformist thought and practice. From the 1850s Anglican clergy were beginning to provide sporting facilities for their parishioners, and it was also in the 1850s that sport began to be an important part of the curriculum in the Anglican public schools.[17] The Nonconformist Mill Hill was not far behind: the first mention of the School XI and the School XV comes in 1860, and according to Roddy Braithwaite, the school's historian, the inter-house rugby competition soon became 'the high point of School life'.[18] Meanwhile, Nonconformist employers were beginning to provide sporting facilities for their workforce. For instance, the Cadbury brothers already had a works cricket team when their cocoa business was still based in central Birmingham in the 1860s and 1870s; after the move to Bournville on the outskirts of the city, in 1879, sporting facilities on a very large scale were provided for workers of both sexes. In Leicester, too, Nonconformist employers were beginning to set up works cricket teams in the 1860s.[19]

If the early clubs were often founded by sports enthusiasts, who wished to

16. Reid, 'Labour, Leisure and Politics', pp. 115-18, 127-29; Church of the Saviour, Birmingham, *Monthly Record*, January 1865 (Birmingham Reference Library [henceforth BRL]).

17. Reid, 'Labour, Leisure and Politics', pp. 102-107, 113-14; M. Tozer, *Physical Education at Thring's Uppingham* (Uppingham: Uppingham School, 1976), pp. 22-30, 53, 57. For the ideal of 'Christian manliness' and its roots in liberal Anglicanism, see N. Vance, *The Sinews of the Spirit* (Cambridge: Cambridge University Press, 1985).

18. I am very grateful to Roddy Braithwaite for allowing me to read sections of his forthcoming history of Mill Hill.

19. J. Bromhead, 'George Cadbury's Contribution to Sport', *Sports Historian* 20 (2000), pp. 97-117; Crump, 'Amusements of the People', pp. 333-35.

play in congenial company, they were soon being set up by those for whom they were 'a means to an end, rather than an end in itself', as the Unitarian Home Missionary, David Heap, put it in 1881. Heap ran a mission and Sunday schools in connection with the Church of the Messiah, a wealthy and influential congregation in central Birmingham, which included Joseph Chamberlain among its members. In 1879, Heap had set up cricket and athletic clubs, as well as facilities for indoor games, in connection with his schools. The vestry committee in their annual report felt the need to justify these innovations.

> The object in introducing these new features has been to give your insti-tutions greater cohesiveness and strength by keeping among us the older scholars of your Sunday Schools, and to act as a counterforce to the many insidious and demoralising influences which in large towns especially are ever militating against the welfare of the rising generation. Your Committee believe that amusement in some form or other must necessarily form an important element in every young and healthy life, and that hence by pro-viding innocent recreation they are doing good work and one that is calculated to produce the most beneficial results.

Young men were recognized as a problem group by most churches. They had in mind especially young men of the working class. But young men of other classes too were regarded as irregular churchgoers, and as a prey to all kinds of vices. Sport was at the very least a means of keeping them within the orbit of the church, and it was hoped that the experience of healthy pleasures would reduce the appetite for unhealthy pleasures. In 1908, at a conference of Sunday school teachers in Leicester, one of the speakers claimed that sport was the means of making the Sunday school 'the vestibule of true manhood rather than the vestibule of the public house'. Sport, it was claimed, taught self-mastery and it was also a means of getting on the wave-length of the pupils: 'You may be interested in David, or Jonah, or Daniel; but it is more than probable that they are interested in the doings of Ran-jitsinghi or C.B. Fry.'[20]

One stage further down this road was the formation of an 'institute' or guild. The prototypes were provided by the YMCAs which from the mid-1870s, inspired by American models, offered an increasingly ambitious recreational programme. In 1874 the *Young Men's Monthly* published an article by a member of the Manchester branch criticizing the existing facilities and calling for the construction of a central building including 'two

20. Church of the Messiah, Birmingham, *Annual Reports*, 1879, 1881 (BRL); Crump, 'Amusements', p. 176.

lecture halls…comfortable refreshment rooms, reading room and library, committee rooms, gymnasium, swimming and other baths, &c'. The new building opened in 1876 included most of these features, and at about the same time a new central YMCA on similar lines was opened in Birmingham. By the turn of the century, the YMCA in most large towns had a palatial headquarters, with a wide-ranging programme of religious, educational and sporting activities. The rationale was explained by the Anglican Canon Denton Thompson in a meeting in Birmingham in 1907 where he declared that Christianity 'sanctified the whole of life. That idea was well represented in the YMCA building by its reading rooms, study rooms, play rooms, and smoke rooms, all under the same roof as the rooms where they held religious meetings.'[21]

The YMCAs often attracted a large membership of whom the majority were not church members. In 1907 the central Birmingham branch had 249 'Members' (who had to be committed evangelical Christians), but 1529 'Associates'. Few churches could offer the range, or indeed the quality, of facilities provided by the YMCA, whose Birmingham branch claimed in 1904 to have 'THE MOST UP-TO-DATE GYMNASIUM IN THE MIDLANDS'.[22] But the 'institutional' principle was beginning to be adopted in the 1880s, especially in working-class areas with conspicuous social needs and large numbers of non-churchgoers. One of the earliest examples was Melbourne Hall, a Baptist mission founded by F.B. Meyer in Leicester in 1880, with coffee being served in the evenings, and 83 attached organizations.[23]

By the 1890s, when Charles Booth was collecting material on 'Religious Influences' for his monumental series of volumes on the *Life and Labour of the People in London*, there were institutes everywhere. Any large Anglican parish or Dissenting chapel was likely to have special premises for social and athletic activities next to or close to the church, and mission churches were quite often known as an 'institute', which usually indicated a multipurpose building, in which some rooms were designated for worship and others for gymnastics, concerts or public meetings. As Booth commented in respect of Lyndhurst Hall Mission in Kentish Town, an offshoot of R.F. Horton's famous Lyndhurst Road Church in Hampstead, 'both Dr Horton

21. YMCA Archive (Birmingham University Library), A27: Annual Reports of the Manchester Association 1875, 1877; A45: *The Young Men's Magazine* (1873), p. 781, Annual Report of Birmingham Association 1880; A47: Annual Report of Birmingham Association 1907.

22. YMCA Archive, A46: *Birmingham YMCA Record*, October 1904.

23. Crump, 'Amusements', pp. 152-55.

and those who work under his inspiration look upon religious and social work as inextricably mixed and the accepted lines of action are very broad'.[24] In his general observations on middle-class Nonconformity in north London, Booth wrote:

> There is no trace of sourness and severity in their theories of life. Pleasure is not tabooed. The young are trusted and encouraged, happiness is directly aimed at, but is associated with the performance of duty: duty to themselves and to each other, and in various ways to the world around. Their pastors preach this ideal and boldly act up to it. They use their churches without hesitation for any purpose which is not actually irreligious. Concerts, popular lectures, debates on social and political questions; all find a place. Even on Sunday in special services, they do not hesitate to combine the mundane with the spiritual. All may be done to the glory of God; but the immediate effect is the brightening and deepening and widening of human lives.[25]

Similar points were made in the annual report for 1890 of the Young Men's Society at College Street Baptist Church.

> In these days of broader conceptions of religion, not only is stress laid on man's spiritual nature, but the church is waking up to the fact that man has a body to be cared for and a mind to be cultivated. We hold that there is nothing antithetic between the 'Service of Man' & the 'Service of God' & that to promote the well-being of the life that now is is to promote the well-being of that which is to come. To the former of these such societies as ours can supply any want.[26]

The underlying principle was the rejection of any division between the spiritual and the secular. But almost equally important was the rejection of this 'sourness and severity', which was still too often a part of the Nonconformist stereotype. Biographies of Nonconformist ministers of this period were often at great pains to emphasize that their hero combined boundless energy with an irrepressible sense of humour. So the biographer of the Primitive Methodist preacher A.T. Guttery claimed:

> The home life itself was ideal in its atmosphere and freedom. When 'A.T.G.' was there his humour and wit kept things lively, and the other members of the family shared his frolics and fun... There were jokes and pranks and everything which could contribute to the true home feeling.

24. C. Booth, *Life and Labour of the People in London* (Three Series; London: Macmillan, 1902–1903), 3rd series, 'Religious Influences', I, pp. 177-79.

25. Booth, *Life and Labour*, 3rd series, I, p. 121.

26. NRO, CSBC/167.

Silvester Horne's daughter recalled that the Congregational preacher and Liberal MP 'gave himself to holiday-making with tremendous joy and zest. In all our excursions, picnics and games he was the life and soul of the party, and just as full of excitement as any of us.'[27] But even those Nonconformists who were incapable of relaxation could agree that Christians must further the cause of social progress. In particular, it was argued, churches had in the past failed the working class. They had a duty to do all they could to improve the living and working conditions of the people and to provide them with healthy recreation and amusement. So, for instance, at the Christian Institute in Hoxton Market, one of the poorest districts of London, and also reputedly one of the most criminal, there were not only Bible classes and temperance organizations, but also a gymnasium, a cricket club, a chess club and a library. According to Booth, each of these was seen as one of the steps 'by which the rough Hoxton boy will, it is hoped, be raised into an upright self-respecting citizen'.[28]

The Triumph of Chapel Sport

Dorothea Hughes in her biography of her father, Hugh Price Hughes, mentioned his enthusiasm for cricket almost in passing, and suggested that many of his admirers would be surprised to learn of it.[29] Yet, by the early twentieth century, Nonconformists often knew as much about their pastor's sporting activities as about his views on the Bible. A striking example was the Revd J.A. Roxburgh, who came to Princes Street Baptist Church, Northampton, in 1906 after a pastorate in Dudley. A newspaper report on his arrival at Princes Street declared:

> He has all along pleaded for the entire development of manhood and woman-hood—body, mind and spirit. He is athletic and a lover of all legitimate sport, an all-round cricketer, having captained several clubs, a swimmer and a seasoned cyclist, although in sport he modestly describes himself as 'Jack of all trades and master of none'... Perhaps the most outstanding features of his character are his manliness and brotherliness. His piety is of the robust

---

27. J.C. Bowran, *The Life of Arthur Thomas Guttery* (London: Holborn, 1922), p. 290; W.B. Selbie, *The Life of Charles Silvester Horne, M.A., M.P.* (London: Hodder & Stoughton, 1920), pp. 270-71. For Horne, see also J.C.G. Binfield, *So Down to Prayers: Studies in English Nonconformity, 1780–1920* (London: J.M. Dent, 1977), pp. 189-213.

28. Booth, *Life and Labour*, 3rd series, II, pp. 120-22.

29. [D. Hughes], *The Life of Hugh Price Hughes*, by his daughter (London: Hodder & Stoughton, 1907), p. 152.

order, and will appeal to young men in particular, in whose interests a large part of his active life has been spent.[30]

Not only was Roxburgh himself a keen player, he was also an evangelist in the cause of sport. The already extensive sporting programme at his church was further extended, he filled the church magazine with references to sporting events and appeals for yet more sport, and even when writing on other topics drew readily on sporting metaphors. Meanwhile in the more austere atmosphere of the nearby Abbey Road Baptist Church, where the magazine devoted most of its space to reports of evangelistic work and attacks on the Boer War, the congregation showed their appreciation of their pastor in 1900 by presenting him with 'an up to date safety bicycle'. In a speech of thanks he referred to it as 'a beautiful machine'.[31]

Cricket and cycling were the pre-eminent Nonconformist sports of these years. Cricket was primarily the sport of young men, requiring strength and speed, but also science; fiercely competitive, yet also synonymous with principles of 'sportsmanship' and 'fair play'; a team game, yet one which offered unrivalled scope for individual achievement. It was also associated in memory, if not always in reality, with long warm summer afternoons. Cycling offered its devotees a unique sense of freedom. It offered 'escape' from the town and the world of work. Like cricket it was a summer sport, associated with country lanes overhung with elm and beech branches in full leaf. It had connotations of adventure. Cyclists discovered remote villages, and sometimes had strange encounters with their inhabitants. Church magazines provided blow-by-blow accounts of big cycle runs—sometimes literally so. Returning from Bidford on Avon by dark, in 1904, two cyclists from the Birmingham YMCA were stopped by highwaymen:

> but our two heroes were too smart for them, for in addition to riding them down, one of our two heroes planted his big left fist in the face of the 'gentleman of the road' in passing, just by way of leaving an impression.

On one of their Ladies' Days they arrived home after midnight, and 'before parting we asked the lady, who had now ridden 80 miles, if she felt tired. She replied "No" but a little bird whispers to me that she missed morning church on Sunday.'[32] So cyclists could enjoy their own strength and fitness, they could commune with nature, take advantage of the fact that normal

30. File of press cuttings on Baptists (NCL, NSR, 198-695).

31. NRO, PSBC/24/6, NARBC/24: *Princes Street Magazine*, May, June, July, August 1907; *Abbey Road Baptist Church Magazine*, March 1900.

32. YMCA Archive, A46: *Birmingham YMCA Record*, October 1904.

restraints and disciplines were temporarily relaxed, and savour the possibilities of romance. Cycling also came to acquire a variety of special meanings in the years around 1900. For many young people at this time a Sunday
spent cycling in the country was the perfect alternative to a Sunday shut up
in church.[33] On the other hand, a writer in the *Northamptonshire Nonconformist* suggested that the invention of the bicycle was providential, coming
as it did 'in the very darkest hour of the need of the villages'. Teams of
Christian cyclists could now pedal out from the towns to preach on village
greens or participate in chapel anniversary services and teas in tiny rural
chapels.[34] Clyde Binfield himself once referred to an article of 1894 in the
Ipswich Nonconformist, which declared the bicycle to be 'a thoroughly
Christian machine', and went on to assert that 'a minister can preach better
on Sunday if he rides a bicycle on Saturday'.[35]

If 'King Willow', together with the 'trusty wheeler', reigned supreme in
the hearts of sporting Nonconformists, other sports, including both codes of
football, swimming and gymnastics, all had a considerable following, and by
the early 1900s tennis was fast growing in popularity, at least in the more
affluent chapels. But as the Revd J.A. Roxburgh had indicated, Nonconformist approval was limited to 'legitimate' sports. This excluded at the least
all those which involved cruelty to animals or in which gambling was an
intrinsic part. In practice this meant that horse racing was unacceptable—
though in 1893, when the *Northamptonshire Nonconformist* was campaigning for a ban on the town races, the Unitarian minister claimed that if the
betting were stopped, 'I do not think the most puritanical amongst us would
object to the races being held. It is not the sport which we desire to put a stop
to, but the evils which have come in its train.'[36] Boxing was a more disputed

---

33. D. Rubinstein, 'Cycling in the 1890s', *Victorian Studies* 21 (1977–78), pp. 7-28;
H. McLeod, *Religion and Society in England 1850–1914* (Basingstoke: Macmillan 1996),
p. 199.

34. *Northamptonshire Nonconformist*, August 1897. See also N. Hardyment, *West
Street Story: A History of Maidenhead United Reformed Church* (Maidenhead, n.d.),
pp. 76-77, which describes a long day out in 1898 when 3 Maidenhead Congregationalists
cycled to Stokenchurch for the chapel anniversary, arriving late, and getting back at 11
p.m. as a result of bad weather and mud.

35. J.C.G. Binfield, 'Congregationalism's Baptist Grandmothers and Methodist Great
Aunts: The Place of Family in a "Felt" Religion', *Journal of the United Reformed Church
History Society* 2.1 (1978), pp. 2-9 (8).

36. *Northamptonshire Nonconformist*, May 1893. At about the same time the pastor
of Steelhouse Lane Congregational Church, Birmingham, was fiercely opposing the proposed establishment of a racecourse in Birmingham, *Ebenezer Magazine*, May 1894

case. In the form of prize-fighting it had been clearly unacceptable to Non-conformists, but in its new reformed version, there were at least some who were prepared to give it the accolade of being 'manly'. However, it was probably a minority who did this. At Wheatsheaf Hall, a Congregationalist mission in south London, the proprietor, W.S. Caine MP, initially allowed boxing in the Young Men's Institute, but in 1904 he agreed to a ban after a deputation, apparently supported by the majority of those attached to the mission, protested that this sport was 'contrary to the spirit of the Sermon on the Mount'.[37] Certainly boxing never acquired the vogue among Noncon-formists that it had in some Anglican circles in the later nineteenth and early twentieth centuries. There were Test cricketers like Herbert Sutcliffe and later Len Hutton who began their careers by playing for chapel teams,[38] but there were no Nonconformist counterparts to the Anglican boys' clubs in the East End of London which turned out future professional fighters.[39] And while some Anglican clergy kept up the tradition of the 'hunting parson' right through the nineteenth century, I have found no evidence that any of their Nonconformist counterparts joined them.[40]

The scale of Nonconformist sporting activity probably reached its highest point in the 1920s and 1930s. By this time sport was no longer in any way controversial. Gambling before and during or drinking afterwards, or sport

(BRL). For Nonconformist opposition to horse-racing, see also M. Huggins, *Flat Racing and British Society* (London: Frank Cass, 2000), pp. 205, 215-16, 220 (though most of his examples come from the first half of the nineteenth century).

37. Kent, *Testament*, pp. 110-12. Attitudes to boxing related to one of the most frequently disputed issues in Nonconformist chapels at this time, namely the question of whether they should support youth organizations of a militaristic character, and if not, whether the Boys' Brigade or the Scouts fell into that category. See S. Yeo, *Religion and Voluntary Organisations in Crisis* (London: Routledge, 1976), pp 165-67, 369.

38. R. Holt, 'Cricket and Englishness: The Batsman as Hero', *International Journal of Sports History* 13 (1996), pp. 48-71 (62); L. Hutton, *Cricket is my Life* (London: Hutchinson, 1949), pp. 26-30. (While Hutton stresses his Moravian roots, he very quickly moved on to a stronger [Anglican] cricket team.)

39. For the role of Anglican parishes and settlements in promoting boxing in work-ing-class areas of London, see S. Shipley, 'The Boxer as Hero: A Study of Social Class, Community and the Professionalisation of the Sport in London, 1890–1905' (PhD thesis, University of London, 1986), pp. 290-96, 315, 353.

40. While participation in hunts by Anglican clergy may have peaked in the later eighteenth and early nineteenth centuries, it continued at a reduced level throughout the nineteenth century and into the 1920s. As one example, see G. Paget, *The History of the Althorp and Pytchley Hunt, 1634–1920* (London: Collins, 1937), pp. 10, 65, 210-11, 236.

of any kind on Sundays, were all still taboo.[41] But the need for healthy recreation was accepted even in the most evangelical churches, and with their keen eye for evangelistic opportunities, the latter were aware of the propaganda value of the 'Christian athlete'.[42] Eric Liddell, 'the Flying Scot', had plenty of admirers south of the border, and C.T. Studd remained a name to conjure with long after he exchanged the cricket field for the mission field. Jack Williams's work on Lancashire suggests that the number of cricket and football teams based on a place of worship peaked between about 1922 and 1930.[43] The final blow to any lingering resistance to chapel-based sport was dealt by the returning serviceman, whose demands for better recreational facilities could not be refused. Thus Doddridge Memorial Congregational Church, Northampton, finally set up an Institute, with recreational facilities for both sexes, at the end of the First World War, though even then there was some opposition.[44]

The two rising sports were now golf and tennis. Tennis was open to accusations of 'unmanliness',[45] but, of course, owed a large part of its appeal to the fact that it was one of the few sports that men and women played together. Tennis clubs were regarded as marriage markets[46]—and this reputation gains support from the fact that the Ferme Park Baptist Tennis Club in north London had to reply in 1901 to allegations of 'improper behaviour' by members in the field adjoining the courts. Tennis clubs could also be places for celebrating the joys of companionate marriage. The membership at Ferme Park in the early twentieth century included several married couples, though most of the women members seem to have been unmarried.[47] The growing number of Nonconformist tennis clubs was evidence of the increasing social respectability and middle-classness even of those branches of Dissent whose plebeian credentials had once been strongest. The same

41. J. Williams, *Cricket and England: A Cultural and Social History of the Inter-War Years* (London: Frank Cass, 1999), pp. 150-54.

42. P. Scott, 'Cricket and the Religious World in the Victorian Period', *Church Quarterly* 3 (1970), pp. 137-40; Vance, *Sinews of the Spirit*, pp. 168-72.

43. Williams, 'Recreational Cricket', p. 115.

44. E.F. Poole, *The History of Doddridge Memorial Congregational Church, Northampton* (London: Independent Press, 1947), p. 46.

45. Crump, 'Amusements of the People', pp. 373-74, citing a speaker at a cricket club meeting in 1913.

46. Lowerson, *Sport and the English Middle Classes*, pp. 96-98.

47. London Metropolitan Archives [henceforth LMA], Acc 2732/17: Ferme Park Baptist Church Institute, Crouch End, Minutes of Tennis Section 1901–1908, 11 July 1901, 23 April and 8 May 1900, 21 April 1902, 20 April 1903.

was even more emphatically true of golf. J.D. Jones 'of Bournemouth', one
of the most respected Nonconformist leaders of the 1920s and 1930s always
tried to fit in 18 holes on Monday morning, and his sporting tastes were of a
piece with his enthusiasm for Stanley Baldwin, which was also characteristic
of the ministerial elite of that generation.[48]

The Meaning of Chapel Sport

G.S. Barrett in his chairman's address to the autumn assembly of the Congregational Union in 1894 chose as his theme 'The Secularization of the
Church'. He complained that the church's spiritual mission had been sub-
ordinated to social and philanthropic work, and he criticized the 'worldliness
of spirit and of tone among the members of the Church'. In the past the
church had suffered from 'an unhealthy and unwise retreat from the world',
but now the danger was in the opposite direction: 'the old-fashioned distinction between the Church and the world has become partly obliterated, and in
some cases it is difficult to see where the world ends and the Church begins'.
He went on to note that the 'Puritan family' was in decay, and that novels,
theatres, ballrooms, billiards, cards and concerts were now accepted by
'Christian parents'.[49]

Some historians have interpreted the changes in English Dissent during
the later Victorian period in similar terms. Robert Currie sees this as a period
of relentless secularization, in which Methodists gradually relinquished
everything that made them distinctive, and thereby prepared the way for
decline and eventual extinction. Mark Johnson has argued a similar case in
respect of Congregationalism.[50]

While Currie's critique of late Victorian Methodism is frequently
entertaining, it seems to me mistaken both in its underlying assumptions and

48. A. Porritt, *J. D. Jones of Bournemouth* (London: Independent Press, 1942),
pp. 154-55; P. Williamson, 'The Doctrinal Politics of Stanley Baldwin', in Michael
Bentley (ed.), *Public and Private Doctrine* (Cambridge: Cambridge University Press,
1993), pp. 181-208 (205-208).

49. G.S. Barrett, 'The Secularization of the Church', *Congregational Year Book*
(1895), pp. 45-47.

50. Currie, *Methodism Divided*, pp. 112-40; M.D. Johnson, *The Dissolution of
Dissent, 1850–1918* (New York: Garland Press, 1987). The ultimately damaging effects
of changes in church and chapel around the turn of the century are also noted—though in
much more nuanced and less polemical fashion—by Yeo, *Religion and Voluntary Organisations*, and S.J.D. Green, *Religion in the Age of Decline: Organisation and Experience
in Industrial Yorkshire, 1870–1920* (Cambridge: Cambridge University Press, 1996).

in its reading of the specific situation. The assumption that old methods should be adhered to and old taboos observed, without any regard for the ways in which the world had changed, may be possible for a church that aspires to be a faithful remnant, but is impossible for one possessed, as Victorian Nonconformists were, by a strong missionary drive and a keen sense of social responsibility. Any such church is neither unambiguously 'in' 'the world' or 'out' of it. It is engaged in a process of selective separation and adaptation, in which the areas of life where its members conform to contemporary norms and those in which they remain most distinct are both continually changing. Moreover, Currie's depiction of a 'cheerful, happy, unambitious' Methodism[51] completely misses the note of militancy, and often aggression, which underlay much of the Nonconformity of this era.

Returning to the Northampton Baptists mentioned at the start of this paper: Currie's version makes sense of Dora Featherweight, but not of Ernest Stiremup. Rather than being a surrender to the hedonism of the day, Nonconformist enthusiasm for sport was pursued with a zeal which any true hedonist would have found embarrassing. It was also part of a wider vision of life, in which condemnation of personal or social sin and of a variety of pseudo-pleasures was combined with the insistence that true pleasure was not sinful, but a gift of God to be enjoyed by all. Again the pages of the *Northamptonshire Nonconformist* illustrate the fact that the gospel of sport often came as part of a package. Articles on cycling, cricket or swimming ran alongside those condemning drink, gambling, cruel sports and Anglican privilege, supporting trade unions, and advocating pacifism, the social gospel and respect for true Christians of whatever denomination. An unexpected example of the latter was a long poem entitled 'Columbus', which condemned the Spanish conquest of the Americas, but rather than drawing the predictable anti-Catholic moral, highlighted the championing of the indigenous people by the Catholic Las Casas.[52] Thus in the 1880s and 1890s Nonconformist promotion of sport was a part of a more generally 'progressive' stance. It had a variety of symbolic meanings, which by the 1920s would have completely vanished.

It is significant that Barrett did not include any sport other than billiards in his critique. Similarly, preaching on 'Amusements' at his north London chapel in 1885, the Congregationalist J. Ossian Davies laid down criteria for

51. Currie, *Methodism Divided*, p. 140.
52. *Northamptonshire Nonconformist*, October 1889, March 1891, February 1893, March 1893, August 1893, May 1893, July 1897.

acceptability which excluded most contemporary forms of leisure, but was still able to conclude:

> A young Christian should attend the gymnasium as well as the prayer meeting. We should patronize all healthful amusements in the open air that are not productive of evil. No man is too pious to play. We have a physical as well as a spiritual nature.[53]

One of the great attractions of cricket or football, cycling or gymnastics, was that they enabled Nonconformists to connect with a central dimension of contemporary culture, without any sacrifice of principle. Sporting passion was a way in which Dissenters could refute the accusations of 'puritanism' or of being 'killjoys', which they frequently faced.

On the other hand the wholesale adoption of 'legitimate' sport was, as I have shown, in no way indiscriminate. On the contrary, Nonconformists continued to reject horse-racing, one of the most popular of contemporary sports, and their condemnation of the gambling that was an integral part both of horse-racing and of many other recreations, made them targets for continuing anti-puritan attacks. Support for the temperance movement also remained at a high, and even increasing, level during this period. In Leicester, according to Crump, from the 1870s onwards, the involvement of the churches in the provision of 'healthy' amusements went hand in hand with increasingly severe attacks upon drinking and gambling.[54] Indeed it was characteristic of the Nonconformity of the later nineteenth and early twentieth century that enthusiasm for sport and for temperance tended to go together. Sport was advocated as an alternative to the pub. But at a deeper level, both passions reflected a preoccupation with fitness, and an insistence that physical, intellectual and spiritual strength are interconnected. As Jowett of Carr's Lane told the Birmingham YMCA in 1907, 'Goody-goody men could not do the work of the strong son of God. He wanted young men of strong will, clear head, and fervent faith to get hold of other young fellows.'[55] The fullest embodiment of this synthesis of faith with physical fitness was the missionary—the supreme role model for Nonconformists of this era, and a figure inevitably missing from those accounts which present chapels as places for having a good time. Clyde Binfield has provided a vivid example in the Congregationalist missionary martyr, Oliver Tomkins, who arrived in New Guinea in 1899, and two years later was clubbed to death and subsequently

53. LMA, N/C/69/109: *New Court Chapel Magazine*, March 1885.
54. Crump, 'Amusements of the People', p. 187.
55. YMCA Archive, A47: Annual Report of Birmingham YMCA 1907.

eaten. His letters home combined accounts of reconnaissance trips to remote districts with a description of his attempts to teach New Guineans to play football. He reported that they had 'rolled in delight' at their first sight of the game.[56]

These 'muscular Christians' were aiming for a balance between the physical, the intellectual and the spiritual, each of which was necessary to the development of full humanity. The cricket match or cycle run on Saturday afternoon took its place alongside the Literary and Debating Society on Friday evening and chapel and Bible class on Sunday. Even at the time some people doubted if the balance could be maintained. In 1897 the President of the Young Men's Bible Class at College Street was complaining that 'In these days it seems as though the strain of recreation on Saturday afternoon is so great that it needs some effort to attend a Sunday morning Bible Class'.[57] In the long run these fears were to be fully justified. Saturday afternoon spread forward into Sunday and backwards into the weekday evenings, and the ideal of balance was dismissed as part of the legacy of Victorian 'puritanism' and 'cant'. Like many other aspects of later Victorian and Edwardian Christianity it has often been treated merely as a part of the story of religious 'decline'. The ideal was nonetheless a noble one, and the attempt to achieve it deserves to be seen as an important and creative phase in our religious history.

56. Binfield, *So Down to Prayers*, pp. 224-31.

57. NRO, CSBC/600: *Manual* of College Street Baptist Church, Northampton, 1897, Report by President of Young Men's Sunday Morning Bible Class.

NONCONFORMITY AND THE POTTERY INDUSTRY

John Briggs

So concerned was John Calvin about the prohibition against making images that he split the first commandment into two, in order that there should be a separate and specific ban on the creation of graven images.[1] Notwithstanding this, the impact of this proscription upon the folk life of the Dissenting tradition seems to have been a matter of ambivalent response. Such artistic representations were in Calvin's language 'examples of the most abandoned lust and obscenity'.[2] Accordingly, the image of a saint or the figure of the Virgin Mary in a Roman Catholic or Tractarian church all too often provoked Protestant mutterings about idols and idolatry, not least because Protestants, in a Reformed and evangelical tradition, proudly announced themselves as people of the book, as those living under the all-authoritative Word.[3] Thus while there is a clear iconoclastic emphasis within the Reformed tradition—indeed, Patrick Collinson speaks of the tradition suffering from 'visual anorexia'—that is not its sole judgment. Alongside concern for the misuse of images has to be set more positive teaching as to the educative function of the visual, if not in the sanctuary,

1.   Exod. 20.3-4. To accommodate this variation, Calvin amalgamates the last two commandments. See J. Dempsey Douglas, 'Foreword', in P.C. Finney (ed.), *Seeing Beyond the Word: Visual Arts and the Calvinist Tradition* (Grand Rapids, MI: Cambridge, MA: Eerdmans, 1999), p. xi.

2.   John Calvin, *Institutes of the Christian Religion*, 1.11.106, cited by D.W. Hardy, 'Calvinism and the Visual Arts: A Theological Introduction', in Finney (ed.), *Seeing Beyond the Word*, pp. 12-13.

3.   Rich testimony to this position will be found in the life and writings of John Elias (1774–1841) who is one of those whose image was subsequently to be moulded in ceramic, and after whom the library at Westminster College, where this paper was originally given, is named. See J. Harvey, *Image of the Invisible* (Cardiff: University of Wales Press, 1999), p 1. Unfortunately Professor Harvey does not bring the pottery figures discussed in this paper within his purview, his only ceramic illustration being of a 'Thou God Seest Me' plaque (p. 71).

then in the home, though with the qualification, as set out in the *Institutes*, 'Only those things are to be sculpted or painted which the eyes are capable of seeing'.[4]

John Harvey is right, in his particular situation, to talk about the different ways in which Welsh Nonconformity reinforced its own particular culture by 'imaging the Word': 'Within this tradition invisible religious concepts such as doctrine, biblical narrative, and spiritual experience, are given tangible expression in visual, literary and conceptual imagery.'[5] Word and common experience here found incarnation in various concrete manifestations—embellishments of the sanctuary, illustrations in the Family Bible, and the potted figures here considered—which became so conspicuous a part of the Nonconformist way of living. Such images were no respecters of intellectual achievement, being accessible and immediate to people of all levels of intelligence: this was the appeal to the perhaps underexercised Dissenting eye.

Philip Benedict makes the point that rather than doctrinal prescription, the explanation of an absence of visual representation within the Reformed tradition may in part be ascribed to a lack of technical skills among Calvinist communities.[6] If this is so, then the capacities of the Staffordshire potters would offer explanation as to why there should be a regional reversal of this tradition in just that period when Staffordshire began to undertake the specialist production of pottery for the whole nation. Indeed, it is worth pointing out that you will search the earlier potters' product in vain for the kind of subject matter with which I am concerned: you will not find them in Chelsea or Vauxhall or Lowestoft, though in Staffordshire post-1780 they are forthcoming in abundance.

The religious figures here discussed can be seen, therefore, as a function of the interface between the industrial revolution and the religious revival of the late eighteenth century and following. It is with such figures and images, cast in ceramic rather than graven in stone, together with those who made them, that this paper is concerned—not, on this occasion, with those who made and badged chapel tea ware or who supplied entrepreneurial chapels with bazaar china, though several pottery firms ran special bazaar departments, so closely attuned were they to chapel culture.

4. Calvin, *Institutes*, 1.11.1.2, cited in Finney (ed.), *Seeing Beyond the Word*, p. 32. In this respect Professor Harvey's title for his study of Welsh Nonconformist culture—*Image of the Invisible*—is nicely challenging!

5. Harvey, *Image of the Invisible*, p. 1.

6. P. Benedict, 'Calvinism as a Culture', in Finney (ed.), *Seeing Beyond the Word*, pp. 19-48 (34).

The notion that these folk figures were never meant to be more than a cheerful ornament in a farmhouse or a labourer's cottage has been challenged, but that does not take them out of the range of popular culture. The full catalogue P.D.G. Pugh argues

> is reminiscent of a nineteenth-century *Dictionary of National Biography*. Staffordshire portrait figures provided the 'news of the day' in much the same way as the pictorial dailies of the twentieth century and for this reason had just as broad an appeal throughout the land.[7]

But such a *DNB* would be a very selective one, posing questions as to the whys and wherefores of the principles of selection, and even more revealingly, of omission.

This selection of themes and subjects could be a question about choices made by producers or it could be a question about market demand, but most likely is a combination of both. The Staffordshire potters nicely distribute themselves between Church and Dissent. It fairly quickly becomes clear that there is not a one-to-one relationship between products of interest to the Nonconformist conscience or tradition and the confession of those producing them. However, it can be argued that there were sufficient Nonconformists among the master potters for their interests not to be overlooked.

Their influence was, of course, there right at the centre of the industry because of Wedgwood and Bentley's association with Unitarianism, or, as far as the latter is concerned, with heterodox religion.[8] Thus the connection of the Wedgwood family with the Old Meeting in Newcastle is of considerable interest. Josiah's sister Katherine married William Willetts, minister of the Old Meeting from 1727 to 1776, which was perhaps the most flourishing half century of its history. Willetts was a close friend of Joseph Priestley, sometime his near neighbour at Nantwich. The great Josiah appears in the chapel history as 'its leading member' with traditions as to his provision of both communion table and communion cup.[9] Wedgwood, of course, was the manufacturer of one of the most telling ceramic persuaders in the whole history of the industry. This was the cameo designed by himself and modelled by William Hackwood, which shows a

---

7. P.D. Gordon Pugh, *Staffordshire Portrait Figures of the Victorian Era* (Woodbridge: Antique Collectors' Club, 1987), p. 95.

8. A. Burton, *Josiah Wedgwood: A Biography* (London: Andre Deutsch, 1976), pp. 36-37.

9. G. Pegler, *A History of the Old Meeting House, Newcastle-under-Lyme* (Hanley, n.d. [but post 1922]), p. 15.

shackled and kneeling slave, crouched beneath the legend: 'Am I not a man and a brother?' These cameos, Wedgwood, passionate in the cause, both made available free to the leaders of the Society for the Suppression of the Slave Trade, such as Thomas Clarkson, and also sent to friends of influence, such as Benjamin Franklin, asking them to ensure their wise distribution. Anti-slavery meetings were widely held in the pottery towns with associated petitions being signed to secure the suppression of the trade.[10]

Josiah Wedgwood's commitment to Unitarian beliefs may be seen in the fact that Thomas, his youngest son and pioneer in photography, had a Unitarian tutor, while Francis, the third son of the second Josiah, was a trustee and occasional preacher at the Old Meeting. Josiah II himself is described as taking great interest. Later generations, up to Colonel Jos Wedgwood, are recorded as subscribers but not as more directly involved.

A Miss Byerly[11] kept the family well informed of what was happening at the meeting house. In 1819 she writes of a plot 'to get the chapel and funds into the hands of the Calvinist minister at Newcastle' under the pretence of nominating to the ministerial vacancy a student from Doddridge's academy, with the proposal that he would take only a single service each Sunday at Newcastle. The trustees were upset: Samuel Parkes, the chemist and also a trustee, became involved and Josiah II was invoked. The threat lay in the ambiguity of the product from Doddridge's academy; rather than a rationalist minister to their taste and edification they could all too easily, as the correspondence makes clear, find a hellfire enthusiastic Methodist occupying their pulpit, unless they acted with great prudence. The trustees were alerted to the threat, and certainly, unlike in some other Staffordshire towns, the meeting house in Newcastle remained in Unitarian hands.

A greater threat came, however, from within the congregation, for the Revd Edward Lomas, Latin tutor to Wedgwood's sons, and minister from 1797 to 1804, managed to empty the chapel with great efficiency so that it was closed for some fourteen years during the first two decades of the century. Miss Byerley, energetic in attempts to reopen the chapel, was in correspondence with Josiah II about this, but for much of the century the cause had only minimal success. It was too weak to exercise much influence on the industry or to provide the spiritual home for its leaders, a

10. Burton, *Josiah Wedgwood*, p. 176, facing, pp. 199-203.
11. Tom Byerly was Wedgwood's nephew and sometime partner but he had 7 daughters, and it is not clear which one is the correspondent here referred to.

very different situation from the 300-strong congregation that Willetts had presided over.[12]

The activities of the great Methodist manufacturers are well known, especially those of the New Connexion,[13] but other denominations, more obviously in the Reformed tradition, also played their part in the industry. The Baptist presence in the potteries was relatively small and faltering,[14] but they nevertheless made their impact upon the pottery industry. For example, Jacob Phillips, who belonged to a family that ran a London china dealership in Oxford Street, and who was a deacon of the Little Wild Street Church, had by 1818 moved to the potteries, where, in partnership with a John Bagster, he purchased the Church Works in Hanley. These works had previously been run by James Neale, Robert Wilson and Elijah Mayer. All three were trustees of Hanley Tabernacle, alongside such worthies as Jonathan Scott, Rowland Hill and John Whitridge.[15]

In 1819, Phillips invited L.J. Abington, a fellow deacon at Little Wild Street, and, according to Llewellyn Jewitt, a 'clever modeller' and 'a fair chemist', to join him. Deploying his artistic skills, Abington, in his London years, had assisted Benjamin Wyatt with the decoration of Drury Lane Theatre and was entrusted by Sir John Soane with much of the ornamental detail on the Bank of England. Reluctance to undertake Sunday work and health reasons are given as part of the explanation of his willingness to move to North Staffordshire. Abington fairly soon entered into partnership with the Congregationalist Joseph Mayer, son and successor to Elijah Mayer and cousin to the Methodist Ridgways, and by this means subsequently became partner to William Ridgway and, after 1845, his son, E.J. Ridgway. The firm traded as Ridgway and Abington from 1848 to 1860, when Abington was able to retire, being the recipient of a

12. Pegler, *Old Meeting House*, pp. 6-8, 14-15.

13. See, e.g., my article, ' "The Radical Saints of Shelton": The Ridgway Family, Methodist Pottery Manufacturers', in D.J. Jeremy (ed.), *Business and Religion in Britain* (Aldershot: Gower, 1988), pp. 47-71.

14. Newcastle-under-Lyme's seventeenth-century Baptists were taken over by the Quakers. Preaching recommenced at the end of the eighteenth century with places for worship registered in 1814, 1832 and 1839, but the church became extinct in 1854, only to restart in 1867. Hanley started falteringly in 1789 and was re-established in 1820. Burslem began around 1806, Stoke in 1841 and Longton in 1853, the latter two being General Baptist New Connexion churches.

15. All are named in a Trust Deed dated 4 January 1789, cited in a pamphlet entitled, *Congregational New Tabernacle Church Buildings at Hanley* [reprinted from the *Staffordshire Sentinel*, 17 October 1881], p. 7.

substantial legacy from Joseph Mayer. Labelled a Radical by the *Victoria County History*, he for a short time edited the *Pottery Mercury*, and was a leading spirit within the Pottery Philosophical Society.

In 1845 Abington's partner, William Ridgway, began to simplify his industrial network; the Church Works, in which Abington had an interest, went to his son, E.J. Ridgway, who married Mary Akroyd of the Halifax Methodist New Connexion family that became Anglican, as did E.J. Ridgway himself. The Broad Street Works, which had been purchased in 1835 and operated under the style of Ridgway, Morley, Wear and Co., was transferred to his son-in-law, Francis Morley, of the Nottingham Congregationalist hosiery family, as sole owner. In 1851 on the bankruptcy of C.J. Mason, the patentee of Mason's ironstone, Morley purchased his patents, moulds, copper plates, indeed his entire business.[16] In these marriages the significance of the Dissenting network is once more to be seen.

Another Baptist pottery interest focuses around a remarkable female entrepreneur named Eleanor Coade, who emerges as 'a most benevolent, useful member' of James Upton's Chapel in Blackfriars, in south London. The family came from the west country, where she developed an association with the Baptist chapel in Lyme Regis, which suggests she may have had interests in the supply of west country clays. Around 1769 she established 'Coade's Lithodipyra, Terracotta, or Artificial Stone Manufactory', to exploit the patent of the artificial stone that bears her name, a ceramic imitation of natural stone. This impressive creation is to be found in use at Buckingham Palace, St George's Windsor and the Royal Naval College. In fact Eleanor Coade, who is sometimes allocated to the wrong gender, seems to have been a member of a group of Dissenting or evangelical craftsmen that worked in association with John Bacon, sculptor and clay modeller, who oscillated between Dissent and Evangelical Anglicanism.[17]

16. L. Jewitt, *Ceramic Art of Great Britain* (Poole, Dorset, New Orchards Reproduction, 1985 [repr. from 2nd edn, 1883]), pp. 491-92; G. Godden, *Jewitt's Ceramic Art of Great Britain, 1800–1900* (London: Barrie & Jenkins, c. 1972), pp. 62-63; J.G. Jenkins (ed.), *Victoria County History: Staffordshire* VIII (28 vols.; London: Oxford University Press, 1963), p. 165. There is confusion as to the chronology here, but the chronology given above is in my judgment more reliable than the variations to be found in the two versions of Jewitt.

17. Jewitt, *Ceramic Art*, pp. 93-94; D. Rosman, *Evangelicals and Culture* (London: Croom Helm, 1984), pp. 158-62, and the entries on Bacon and Coade in D.M. Lewis (ed.), *The Blackwell Dictionary of Evangelical Biography, 1730–1860*, I (Oxford: Basil Blackwell, 1995), pp. 44-45. See also *Baptist Magazine*, February 1822, p. 65,

It must be by total accident that the next entry in Jewitt concerns the London Pottery of James Stiff and Sons, in High Street, Lambeth, and subsequently of the Albert Embankment. In the ownership of the Stiff family from 1840, it was described in 1883 as 'among the largest in London' employing about 200 people, occupying a 2-acre site with its 14 kilns. A very extensive export trade was well served by the company's own private dock, developed on the Albert Embankment site: in 1913 it was taken over by the neighbouring Doulton enterprise. Some of its terracotta can still be found, with signature, on London Baptist churches.[18] One of the 'Sons' was William Stiff (1837–99) who became a member of the same Upton Chapel in 1864, serving 26 years as deacon and 21 as treasurer. His wife, who was associated with Upton from birth for nigh on 80 years, contributes a moving testimony to chapel life in its history.[19] While Matthew Arnold might have been inclined to scoff at the vulgarity of Staffordshire figures which are the main concern of this article, there is evidence also of high-quality craftsmanship which is far from being philistine, and was of sufficient quality to attract the patronage of many aristocratic and metropolitan clients.

The two worlds, moreover, are not entirely separate because both Bacon and Coade were involved in the early ceramic representations of the personage of John Wesley. An article in the *Wesleyan Methodist Magazine* for 1896 refers to Coade making a cast of Wesley around 1769, from which undoubtedly copies were produced by this innovator in artificial stone. When, in 1830, Conference wished to commission a life-size replica of the founder, it was to Samuel Manning, a pupil of John Bacon, Junior, that they went. Initial sculpting did not, however, go well and the outcome was deemed unworthy of the founder. Adam Clarke became involved, and on his advice, the famous Enoch Wood bust, of which Clarke possessed a copy, was used for Wesley's head on the full-size figure, much to the advantage of the overall presentation. I am here interested in two interrelated phenomena, first the existence of a network of highly skilled

and A. Kelly, *Mrs Coade's Stone* (Upton Upon Severn: Self-Publishing Association, 1990).

18. Jewitt, *Ceramic Art*, pp. 94-96, and presentation to the Listed Buildings Advisory Committee of the Baptist Union of Great Britain, Case Number 70 (Kenyon Chapel, Solon Road, Brixton), September 2000. The autographed building is dated 1884.

19. S.J. Price, *Upton: The Story of One Hundred and Fifty Years* (London: Carey Press, 1935), pp. 138-39, 167-68, 197-99.

craftsmen and artists associated with Dissent, and through this network the existence of a linkage which connected the world of high art and the more popular productions of the potteries.[20]

Dissenters were also involved in linking together the clay extraction end of pottery production with its manufacture in Staffordshire. And here I claim a personal connection since for 30 years I lived in the house (21 The Villas, Stoke on Trent) once occupied by the person to whom I wish now to refer. His name was W.H. Grose and he was born near St Austell in 1815. As agent for the West of England China Stone and Clay Company, he came to live in Stoke-on-Trent some time after 1845. Prospering in business, he became the principal in two firms, W.H. Grose and Sons, Clay Merchants, and Grose and Stocker, who specialized in selling plaster for plaster moulds. He also dabbled in pottery manufacture under the incorporation of Grose and Sons at the Bridge Works in Stoke. Initially one of Abington's deacons in Hanley, in the late 1860s Grose transferred his membership to the Stoke Church, nearer to his home in the newly constructed 'Stokeville', Stoke's attempt to create an immediate bourgeois neighbourhood in 24 houses of Italianate design.

Nearly every aspect of Baptist life found him a willing sponsor, and he frequently provided the finance to bail ailing churches out of debt, his total generosity adding up to a very considerable benefaction. His special delight was his 60-strong Bible class. Improvement Commissioner and Poor Law Guardian, he was vice chairman to the Revd Lovelace Stamer of the Stoke-on-Trent School Board. Indeed Stamer, by then elevated to be the first Bishop of Shrewsbury, pronounced the benediction at Grose's funeral in 1890, and I wonder whether this may have been the first time that an Anglican bishop participated in a Free Churchman's funeral.[21]

The Stoke Stocker was Grose's son-in-law, but the relationship between the two families was clearly of longer duration, for the West of England China Clay Company was largely the creation of Thomas Stocker and had a very considerable reputation for the fair treatment of its workers. A philanthropic Baptist, he largely financed the building of the St Austell Baptist Church. The next generation produced Thomas Medland Stocker, who trained at the Camborne School of Mines and who was responsible for much technical improvement—the introduction of new filter presses

20. A.D. Cummings, *A Portrait in Pottery* (London: Epworth Press, 1962), pp. 21-23, pp. 44-45.

21. J.H.Y. Briggs, 'Civic Engagement and Ecumenical Relations', *Baptist Quarterly* 36 (1995), pp. 105-107.

and the application of electricity—in an otherwise conservative industry. Medland Stocker also invented the compacting of clay into granular form, a process that offered considerable economies in things like tile manufacture because the clay did not have to have water added to it for processing, only to have it taken out again in firing. These granules were still known in the trade (at least as late as 1985) as 'Stockalite'. Medland Stocker also perceived the need for company amalgamation and so the industrial conglomerate, English China Clays, was his creation, and it has been said that its incarnation was possible only because of his personal high standing in the industry. It was he, too, who secured the democratic style of management for which English China Clays became renowned. He followed his father in the life of the St Austell church where he served as organist and choirmaster, its organ being his personal gift.[22]

A further example of how the Dissenting network operated concerns another migrant who came to the potteries from the wholesale china trade in London. This was Henry Wileman, a member of John Clifford's Praed Street congregation. He came to the potteries in 1853 as a man of sufficient substance to lease Longton Hall from the banker, Charles Harvey. In the same year he went into partnership with Joseph Knight at the Foley Potteries in Fenton. Alongside new business enterprises, in July 1853 he also took the initiative, supported by the General Baptist Association, in establishing services in the Town Hall, which were immediately successful with a congregation of 200 the first evening. An early setback occurred when the first minister, the Revd T. Freckleton, seceded to the Unitarians, becoming minister of the Old Meeting in Newcastle, where, though attracting large congregations, he was paid only a modest salary of £78, which 'he eked out by sketching and photography in the services of Wedgwoods'.[23]

Wileman became sole partner on Knight's retirement in 1856 and so remained until his death in 1864. In 1860, he built the new Foley Works for the production of china while the old factory continued to produce earthenware, creating a remarkably successful enterprise with tea and dinner ware as well potted as any within the industry at that time. His sons joined the firm and continued it after Henry Wileman's death in 1864; in

22. K. Hudson, 'Thomas Medland Stocker', in D.J. Jeremy (ed.), *Dictionary of Business Biography*, 5 (London: Butterworths, 1986), pp. 343-44.

23. Pegler, *Old Meeting House*, pp. 9-10. An earlier Baptist cause in Longton in the 1820s is referred to by A.G. Matthews, *The Congregational Churches of Staffordshire* (London: Congregational Union, 1924), p. 176.

1872 J.B. Shelley became a partner, and eventually the Wileman enterprise was subsumed under his name.[24] While Henry was much involved with the Longton church, his sons seemed to have conformed to the Church of England. This is, of course, a process worthy of a separate study, but it can certainly be traced in families as significant as the Ridgways and the Doultons.

What is happening here? Certainly, as members of the new entrepreneurial classes moved around the country, they used their chapel networks to put down roots in new locations. This process is illustrated by the usefulness of their chapel connections to Abington, Coade and Grose, who link together the west country, the metropolis and Staffordshire. In the case of Henry Wileman, it looks as if his business move from Paddington to the potteries in part caused the establishment of the new General Baptist Church in Longton, both occurring in 1853. In the case of the Hanley church, the arrival of London-trained businessmen and craftsmen helped to revive a faltering cause.

Having sketched in something of the Dissenting network and its impact on the pottery industry, I want to move from producers to product. The genre of Staffordshire figures reflects on larger questions of popular culture, for across all subjects there is a left-of-centre bias in favour of that which was Liberal, or radical, or anti-establishment, notwithstanding ongoing concern to celebrate the monarchy and national military success. Pugh notes that while there are only two figures of Disraeli, and they are both pairs to corresponding figures of Gladstone, the Liberal leader appears in many versions both in statuary and in flatware.[25] To Gladstonian Liberalism must be added a number of other reformist causes. Duncombe, presenter of the 1848 petition, represents Chartism.[26] O'Connell, Parnell, Sexton and O'Brien together with historical celebrations of Wolfe Tone, McCracken and Lord Edward Fitzgerald represent Irish nationalism,[27] while Peel, Cobden and Bright represent the anti-corn law movement.[28] The success of the American Revolution, a conflict of particular but changing interest to the Dissenting conscience, is reflected in images of

24. D. Stuart (ed.), *People of the Potteries: A Dictionary of Local Biography*, I (Keele, Staffordshire: University of Keele, Dept of Adult Education, 1985), p. 230.

25. Pugh, *Staffordshire Portrait Figures*, p. 16.

26. Pugh, *Staffordshire Portrait Figures*, pp. 179, 182-83.

27. Pugh, *Staffordshire Portrait Figures*, pp. 179-81, 183-86, 188, 196-98.

28. Pugh, *Staffordshire Portrait Figures*, pp. 179-83, 185, 191-95.

Washington, Jefferson and Benjamin Franklin,[29] while the perpetuation of black slavery in the USA produced a glut of figures of John Brown, Uncle Tom and Eva, Aunt Chloe, Topsy, George and Eliza Harris, with Abraham Lincoln depicted as the liberator,[30] fairly mirroring Dissenting interest in the emancipationist cause.

True there are myriad images of Wellington, who is often the partner to Napoleon. Napoleon competes with Wesley to be the most reproduced image of all, ambivalently representing both revolutionary change and conservative authority. Some of these figures of Napoleon, but by no means all, were specially manufactured for the French market.

One of the early collectors of Staffordshire figures, Dr Glaisher, confessed that his attraction to this genre was a concern to understand what he called 'speaking pottery' because of the witness it bore to ceramic and more general history. If we can talk of 'speaking pottery' then it is also appropriate, with due acknowledgment to Conan Doyle, to listen to the voice of the 'dog that does not bark', that is the voice we might legitimately expect to find and which simply is not there.[31] It is in this context that we have to measure the absence of Anglican clerical representation, especially since we have at least one, admittedly rare, representation of a rabbi at the door of his synagogue.[32]

This Anglican clerical absence is the more peculiar since no such inhibition existed with regard to Roman Catholic figures, where Pionono, Cardinal Manning, Mother O'Hallahan, Père Moulaert, Father Mathew and St Sebastian all exist as Staffordshire figures. This may not constitute the most representative group of nineteenth-century Catholics, but therein lies an aid to understanding. Margaret Hallahan, who was of poor Irish descent, founded a Dominican community in Coventry in 1844, extending her activities to the potteries seven years later. Here, with her chaplain, the Belgian Dominican Père Molaert, she opened schools for the poor,

29. Pugh, *Staffordshire Portrait Figures*, pp. 179-81, 188, 199-203.

30. Pugh, *Staffordshire Portrait Figures*, pp. 179-81, 204-209; some are also to be found in parian: C. Shinn and D. Shinn, *Victorian Parian China* (London: Barrie & Jenkins, 1971), p. 81. Lincoln appears once on horseback in the Staffordshire series and three times in parian. Pugh, *Staffordshire Portrait Figures*, pp. 202-205; P. Atterbury (ed.), *The Parian Phenomenon* (Shepton Beauchamp, Somerset: Richard Dennis, 1989), pp. 206, 233, 266.

31. Dr Glaisher, as cited by T. Balston, *Staffordshire Portrait Figures of the Victorian Age* (London: Faber & Faber, 1958), p. 14.

32. Pugh, *Staffordshire Portrait Figures*, p. 524.

including night schools for pottery workers: Pugh wisely comments, 'The figures of Moulaert and Hallahan were potted by those whose children they taught and whose sick they nursed, and the condition of whose lives they sought to ameliorate.'[33]

Less wisely Pugh discounts the significance of local factors in the potters' choice of subjects: on the contrary a local event or experience often triggered production.[34] Kossuth, for example, was not only the champion of Hungarian nationalism, but had brought himself to local attention by giving a public lecture in the new Market Hall in Hanley.[35] Moreover, it cannot be an accident that the potters produced a monumental figure of Arthur Orton, claimant to the Tichborne fortune, but in fact the twelfth child of a Wapping butcher. The connection is there in terms of his defending counsel, Dr E.V. Kenealey, the Irish barrister, who not only defended Orton but had earlier defended William Palmer, the Rugeley murderer, who also appears as a pottery figure. In 1875, by one of the strangest whims of democratic decision making, after 'numerous solicitations' to contest the parliamentary seat of Stoke-on-Trent, Kenealey was elected MP with a handsome 2,000-plus majority in a poll of some 10,000 votes. Kenealey made of the Orton case one of the longest trials in history, taking it to some 188 days, following 104 days spent on a first trial. Specializing in gratuitous attacks on Roman Catholic institutions, for the Tichbornes were an old Catholic family, Kenealey seems to have won popular sympathy for his client among the half-educated who were invited to suspect sinister Jesuit plots against Orton. For his troubles, especially his abuse of the bench, Kenealey was depatented by the Lord Chancellor and expelled from Gray's Inn. Such was his reputation that no fellow MP would present him to the House of Commons, so that on the motion of Disraeli the ceremony was dispensed with.[36]

33. Pugh, *Staffordshire Portrait Figures*, p. 322, where Pugh makes reference to an article by M. Littledale in *The Antique Dealer and Collector's Guide* for January 1954. See also J.G. Jenkins (ed.), *Victorian County History of Staffordshire*, VIII, p. 273. Pionono also appears in the parian sequence (Atterbury [ed.], *Parian Phenomenon*, p. 229), as do Cardinal Newman, Cardinal Manning and Leo XIII (Atterbury [ed.], *Parian Phenomenon*, p. 234).

34. Pugh, *Staffordshire Portrait Figures*, p. 95, where he discounts the local factor.

35. Pugh, *Staffordshire Portrait Figures*, pp. 14, 16. 21, 48, 180, 198-99. He also appears in the parian sequence: see Atterbury (ed.), *Parian Phenomenon*, p. 185.

36. Pugh, *Staffordshire Portrait Figures*, pp. 15, 25, 95, 466, 477-78; *DNB*: E.V. Kenealey and Arthur Orton. Kenealey appears in parian: see Atterbury (ed.), *Parian*

But there was more than local enthusiasm to the selection of whose like-nesses to set in ceramic. The local may have triggered the potter's mind, but he needed to be certain that there was a large market of would-be buyers with a purchasing desire to be satisfied. This is where the selective nature of the product suggests a large and distinctive popular appetite among nineteenth-century Dissenters. All three adjectives are important, for the scale of the enterprise was important, and the initial cost was modest enough—pence rather than shillings for a small Wesley, for example—for the product to attract a mass market. Beyond this, the more the phenomenon is studied the more distinct the taste becomes.

Such distinctiveness of taste is reinforced when, alongside Staffordshire figures, consideration is given to figures produced in 'statuary porcelain' or parian, an impervious, lustrous, sometimes transparent, white, marble-like, ceramic body especially used for the reproduction of busts and figures. Prior to 1845, the year in which parian was invented, it seems simultaneously by both the Minton and the Copeland and Garrett factories, such figures were made in unglazed fine biscuit, but in that process the firing had to be perfect because there was no glaze to conceal staining in firing or small firing cracks that could normally be obliterated in the glazing process. Moreover the surface of biscuit ware remained porous and so the figures were vulnerable to discolouration.[37] As with the Staffordshire series, so in parian ware, classical, folk and other allegorical imagery and biblical and religious figures all rub shoulders with one another.

The cultural feel, however, of the parian figures is quite different from that of Staffordshire ware, where the potter has tried to translate a flat image from an engraving into a more or less three-dimensional figure. By contrast the parian figures are accurate reproductions of existing marble or bronze figures by the foremost artists of the day, very often using Chever-ton's reducing machine, which in effect offered the possibilities of three-dimensional tracing and reduction of statuary in a single process.[38] So whereas the Staffordshire figure makers only needed an engraving, painting or even a self-executed sketch of their subject, the parian designer was dependent, for the most part, on access to a previously existing statue, thus very clearly limiting options. Later on some modellers produced work specially commissioned for parian production. Whatever the source, how-

Phenomenon, pp. 238, 245. It is sometime said that John Bright, out of respect for the electoral process, however flawed the outcome, introduced Kenealey to the Commons.

37. Atterbury (ed.), *Parian Phenomenon*, pp 9-10.
38. Atterbury (ed.), *Parian Phenomenon*, p. 8.

ever, the same bias in subject matter is to be found. Produced in great quantity, parian figures vary greatly in quality, with inferior ware produced by some manufacturers because of their greediness in attempting to take too many casts off the one mould. By contrast good-quality ware— and the best is superbly crisp in depth and detail—was not cheap to produce and would be 'found only in the homes of relatively prosperous families'.[39]

While the parian range is wider than the Staffordshire series, the same biases in the selection of material emerge, even if not in quite so absolute a fashion. Given that the treatment of political themes is more even-handed, the selectivity in the handling of religious subjects remains significant, with a preference for Nonconformist figures, some representation of Roman Catholic interests, but only rare Anglican depiction.

Analysis needs to be contextualized by the way in which, first the grand contours of Scripture, and then the story of the Church, is depicted in pottery. From the late eighteenth century come figures from the Old and New Testaments, both pious and robust, mirroring the images in the Family Bible, but again this was a rather selective Bible in terms of the individuals and events celebrated, with a preference for vivid action narrative. In Staffordshire ware there are lurid depictions of Abraham about to slay Isaac, but with the patriarch apprehensive of divine intervention. The one which most appeals to me bears the simple legend, 'Abraham Stop'.[40] Samuel is found anointing David, who later appears complete with harp looking remarkably similar to a figure of Apollo.[41] Elijah, with the defining raven, is often found paired by a figure of the widow of Zarephath.[42] Later prophets are represented by Jeremiah, 'preserved by Scripture', concerning which the spectator is invited to consult Jeremiah 34.[43]

From the Old Testament, in parian ware there are figures of Adam and Eve,[44] Cain and Abel,[45] Abraham and Isaac.[46] Hagar and Ishmael represent

39. Shinn and Shinn, *Victorian Parian China*, p. 12.

40. P. Halfpenny, *English Earthenware Figures, 1740–1840* (Woodbridge: Antique Collectors' Club, 1991), pp. 228, 256, 271.

41. Halfpenny, *English Earthenware Figures*, p. 275 and cf. pp. 56 and 62.

42. Halfpenny, *English Earthenware Figures*, pp. 140, 219, 224, 240.

43. Halfpenny, *English Earthenware Figures*, pp. 254-55.

44. Atterbury (ed.), *Parian Phenomenon*, pp. 109, 140, 255; Shinn and Shinn, *Victorian Parian China*, p. 94.

45. Atterbury (ed.), *Parian Phenomenon*, p. 76.

46. Atterbury (ed.), *Parian Phenomenon*, p. 190.

a different aspect of the Abraham story. Rebekah[47]is well moulded and completes the patriarchal series. An interesting group, entitled 'Interpretation: Moses before Pharoah', also shows the presence of a rather intent Potiphar.[48] The series continues with representations of Moses in the bulrushes,[49] Naomi and her daughters-in-law,[50] Ruth, on her own,[51] 'The Infant Samuel',[52] 'David's Triumph and Reward' or simply David and Goliath[53] and 'Daniel Saved'.[54] A pair of mother and child figures are identified as Hannah (and Samuel) and Pharaoh's Daughter (with the infant Moses).[55] Another pair focus on two royal scenes: 'The Queen of Sheba's visit to Solomon' and Esther and her royal husband.[56]

In Staffordshire ware from the gospels come clearly designated evangelists, anticipated representations of Virgin and Child in domestic genre, with a range of representations of the flight into Egypt. The only parables represented are those of the lost coin and lost sheep.[57] John 3, with its familiar text concerning the need for new birth, seems to have been of particular interest to the potters, with their various representations of Christ teaching Nicodemus, in the 1820 period.[58] How many sermons on this chapter, heard by the potters in their several Bethesdas and Zions, are reflected in the production of such an image, one can only speculate. Christ's agony in the garden of Gethsemane[59] is another focus of their attention. In parian a range of gospel themes is handled. In addition to numerous angels and Madonnas, representations of Christ himself and moving presentations

47. Atterbury (ed.), *Parian Phenomenon*, p. 151. Rebekah is also found with Isaac: (Atterbury [ed.], *Parian Phenomenon*, pp. 192, 255); see also Shinn and Shinn, *Victorian Parian China*, p. 71, Plate 46.

48. Atterbury (ed.), *Parian Phenomenon*, p. 194; Shinn and Shinn, *Victorian Parian China*, Plate 99, shows a Wedgwood version.

49. Atterbury (ed.), *Parian Phenomenon*, pp. 96, 190, 255.

50. Atterbury (ed.), *Parian Phenomenon*, p. 67; see also Shinn and Shinn, *Victorian Parian China*, p. 91, Plate 63B.

51. Atterbury (ed.), *Parian Phenomenon*, pp. 151, 255; see also Shinn and Shinn, *Victorian Parian China*, Plate 36.

52. Shinn and Shinn, *Victorian Parian Phenomenon*, Plate 63E and p. 88.

53. Atterbury (ed.), *Parian Phenomenon*, pp. 78, 119; Shinn and Shinn, *Victorian Parian China*, p. 94.

54. Atterbury (ed.), *Parian Phenomenon*, p. 88.

55. Atterbury (ed.), *Parian Phenomenon*, p. 252.

56. Atterbury (ed.), *Parian Phenomenon*, p. 255.

57. Halfpenny, *English Earthenware Figures*, pp. 64, 141, 164, 182, 189, 253.

58. Halfpenny, *English Earthenware Figures*, pp. 217, 255.

59. Halfpenny, *English Earthenware Figures*, pp. 249, 271.

of the crucifixion,[60] there are depictions of the 'Flight into Egypt',[61] St Joseph,[62] a youthful study of John the Baptist and Jesus.[63] From Christ's mature ministry there are portrayals of 'The Prodigal's Return', one of which is inscribed 'Father I have sinned',[64] again almost certainly reflecting the preacher's emphasis in handling this parable. The blessing of the children,[65] Christ with Mary the sister of Martha,[66] 'The Magdalene',[67] 'Christ on the Mount', [68] 'Christ healing the Blind Man',[69] all graphically capture particular incidents. The three Marys as found at the foot of the cross [70] are to be found alongside 'Christ and his Disciples'.[71]

From the Acts and the epistles, Staffordshire ware has representations of Peter, Paul and Philip,[72] including in particular Peter raising the lame man of Acts 3,[73] together with rather bizarre portrayals of Faith, Hope and Charity.[74] Faith, Hope and Charity are also frequently presented in parian,[75]

60. Atterbury (ed.), *Parian Phenomenon*, pp. 103-104; Shinn and Shinn, *Victorian Parian China*, p. 91.

61. Atterbury (ed.), *Parian Phenomenon*, p. 69; Shinn and Shinn, *Victorian Parian China*, p. 91.

62. Shinn and Shinn, *Victorian Parian China*, p. 91.

63. Atterbury (ed.), *Parian Phenomenon*, p. 255.

64. Atterbury (ed.), *Parian Phenomenon*, pp. 13, 111, 169; see also Shinn and Shinn, *Victorian Parian China*, p. 71.

65. Atterbury (ed.), *Parian Phenomenon*, p. 108; Shinn and Shinn, *Victorian Parian China*, p. 93.

66. Atterbury (ed.), *Parian Phenomenon*, pp. 156, 212, 218.

67. Shinn and Shinn, *Victorian Parian China*, pp. 89-90.

68. Atterbury (ed.), *Parian Phenomenon*, p. 190.

69. Atterbury (ed.), *Parian Phenomenon*, p. 194.

70. Atterbury (ed.), *Parian Phenomenon*, p. 69; Shinn and Shinn, *Victorian Parian China*, p. 93.

71. Atterbury (ed.), *Parian Phenomenon*, p. 109; Shinn and Shinn, *Victorian Parian China*, p. 94.

72. Halfpenny, *English Earthenware Figures*, pp. 135, 141, 217.

73. Halfpenny, *English Earthenware Figures*, p. 275.

74. Halfpenny, *English Earthenware Figures*, pp. 65, 83, 155, 169, 218, 232, along with such other virtues as Innocence, Prudence, Fortitude and Tenderness. There are also two sets of Faith, Hope and Charity listed in a sales ledger of 1785 as being sold to John Edwards by John Wood for five shillings, though another set of three were charged at only four shillings and sixpence. King David commanded one shilling and nine pence, while a Vicar and Moses was sold to a Mr Mundy in June 1786 for two shillings and sixpence, but one with gilt decoration later commanded three shillings. Halfpenny, *English Earthenware Figures*, pp. 315, 319, 321. A dozen men carrying lost sheep cost nine shillings from Ralph Wood in 1783, though lost sheep and lost

while from the book of Revelation come Michael and Satan.[76]

The history of the Church is reflected in the depiction of St Sebastian, figures of whose martyrdom seem to have been in constant production from the 1820s right through to the early twentieth century. Though clearly not images, along with the *pietà*, St Barbara, and some of the more Catholic Virgin and Childs, of appeal to the Nonconformist market,[77] such figures do indicate a parallel Roman Catholic attraction. Church history in parian likewise witnesses an array of saints, nuns and friars, including a figure of the mysterious St Filomena (Philomena),[78] who became something of a cult figure among French ultramontanes around 1850. From contemporary piety come images like 'Maternal Devotion' or 'The Prayer'[79], as do representations of 'The Fount of Mercy' paired by 'The Rock of Ages', both underlining the total sufficiency of the cross,[80] and witnessing to patterns of contemporary piety.

In the late eighteenth century, pottery became a vehicle for ecclesiastical satire. In their commentary upon the contemporary Church scene, the potters ironically expose the sins of the establishment. Figures of 'The Vicar and Moses', appearing from the 1780s onwards,[81] celebrate the laity's lack of respect for the expository skills of the Anglican pulpit. The vicar in his elevated pulpit has fallen asleep while the clerk below continues to read the service, portraying the very opposite of what Nonconformists were to celebrate among their own number with their Gothic pulpits offering the

coin together, coloured, fetched two shillings: Halfpenny, *English Earthenware Figures*, pp. 322-23.

75. Atterbury (ed.), *Parian Phenomenon*, pp. 154, 191, 202, 206.

76. Atterbury (ed.), *Parian Phenomenon*, pp. 33, 73; Shinn and Shinn, *Victorian Parian China*, p. 92.

77. Halfpenny, *English Earthenware Figures*, pp. 190, 199-202, 286, 287, 288.

78. Atterbury (ed.), *Parian Phenomenon*, pp. 109, 154. This selection compares interestingly with Philip Benedict's analysis of the ownership of paintings in Metz in the seventeenth century where he notes that Calvinist owners largely eschewed displaying canvasses of the Virgin, the saints, the crucifixion and the Magdalene, focusing instead on Old Testament histories, New Testament stories and depictions of the nativity, a pattern confirmed by J.M. Montias's research on Amsterdam. See P. Benedict in Finney (ed.), *Seeing Beyond the Word*, p. 40.

79. Atterbury (ed.), *Parian Phenomenon*, p. 68; see Shinn and Shinn, *Victorian Parian China*, pp. 91 and 107, for reference to matching figures of 'Prayer' and 'Belief'.

80. Atterbury (ed.), *Parian Phenomenon*, p. 226.

81. Halfpenny, *English Earthenware Figures*, pp. 73, 84, 288.

greatest of their orators permanent elevation six foot above contradiction. The contrast is between a seriously neglected pulpit and a pulpit as the focus for eager anticipation of the Church's exposition of divine revelation.

Even worse, perhaps, than 'The Vicar and Moses' is the figure of the 'Parson and Clerk', which also appears under the title 'Inebriation'.[82] The parson now appears in need of the clerk to guide his intoxicated person back to his vicarage ere even greater harm befall him. Such a popular image brought together not only an incipient concern for the temperate life, but also an attack on the time-serving nature of the clergy who far from expounding the gospel could not even model the moral life. Gentle mocking of the ecclesiastical establishment in such images, though not exclusive in appeal to Nonconformists, echoed their judgment upon the effectiveness of the ministry of many a parish church. Rougher treatment of the failings of the establishment was to appear in literary form in *The Black Book*, from 1820 onwards, and *The Extraordinary Black Book*, 1831. The image was of a Church which cost vast sums to maintain but which served the nation so ill, a Church which could command vast wealth but so signally failed to provide adequate pastoral service.

The other figures of import here are the various depictions of the impact of tithe upon the inhabitants of rural England, which were produced by Derby from the 1760s onwards and from the 1780s in Staffordshire.[83] The farmer and his wife stand alongside the rector (strictly so-called) who claims one-tenth of all their produce, cattle, sheep, eggs and grain. The farmer's wife tellingly nurses the baby, whose well-being is threatened by such taxation and hence the tenth child is also being offered to the Church. That there is a cause here, which cannot be limited to either Dissenting grievance or to those who suffered from the burdens laid upon those who derived their living from the land, is indicated by the fact that the figure is found not only in earthenware but in high-quality porcelain. Owen Chadwick argues that 'tithe, however irritant, was not an authentic grievance of dissenters as dissenters' but that what was really a 'war of conservative and radical became partly identified with a war of churchmen versus dissenters'.[84] While it was hoped that the contentious issue of tithes could be put to rest by the Commutation Act of 1836, the impact of tithe and the memory of tithe lingered on, partly because certain crops like hops and

82. Halfpenny, *English Earthenware Figures*, p. 288.

83. Halfpenny, *English Earthenware Figures*, pp. 204, 221, 257.

84. O. Chadwick, *The Victorian Church* (2 vols; London: A. & C. Black, 1966–70), I, p. 61.

market gardening were not included in the 1836 act. This led to further disputes, while in the 1870s and 1880s, tithe again became contentious because the agricultural depression lowered a number of clerical incomes to a position of acute poverty. At the same time, the commuted charges still remained an intolerable burden on depressed agriculture. Final resolution only came a hundred years after the 1836 act when the 1936 Tithe Act secured the income for tithe owners, both lay and clerical, by way of 3 per cent treasury stock, which was to be funded by the farming community purchasing annuities over a 60-year period. This in part at least explains why tithe groups were still being potted by Staffordshire potters anxious to exploit the sinister side of the Church right up to the end of the nineteenth century, and indeed by those who reproduce antique figures beyond that.[85]

Figures representing the Nonconformist tradition as such must start with a late eighteenth-century representation of Oliver Cromwell clearly based on an engraving in Frederick Raymond's *New Universal History of England* published in 1787, whose production unnecessarily worries Pat Halfpenny.[86] John Milton appears much more frequently, but is less easily identified with the Dissenting tradition.[87] He is also much found in parian, paired either with John Bunyan or with a fierce-looking Cromwell. With the Methodist Revival come the characteristic figures, not only of the brothers Wesley, but also of George Whitefield together with Hugh Bourne and William Clowes and other leaders.

So Reformed anathemas of the creation of graven images did not inhibit an array of Wesleys (John 1703–91; Charles 1707–88) and Spurgeons (1834–92), Moodys (1837–99) and Sankeys (1840–1908) being displayed upon pious mantle shelves; visual images outside church came now to receive an approbation not given to such imagery within sacred space, unless encased within the stained glass of leaded windows.

Amid other Dissenting images are those of a remarkable set of Welshmen. One was John Bryan (1770–1856), a Wesleyan preacher who translated many of Wesley's hymns into Welsh and championed his

85. G.F.A. Best, *Temporal Pillars: Queen Anne's Bounty, the Ecclesiastical Commissioners, and the Church of England* (London: Cambridge University Press, 1964), pp. 187–89, 465–79.

86. Halfpenny, *English Earthenware Figures*, p. 137. Atterbury (ed.), *Parian Phenomeon*, p. 235.

87. Halfpenny, *English Earthenware Figures*, pp. 332-35.

Figure 1. *Staffordshire figure of John Wesley* (Photography courtesy of The Potteries Museum and Art Gallery, Stoke-on-Trent).

Arminianism within a Welsh context: though he retired from the full-time ministry in 1824, he continued to preach as a layman, first in Leeds and then in Caernarfon. Others were John Elias (1774–1841), high Calvinist and political conservative from north Wales who was nevertheless an enthusiast for both the Bible and the (London) Missionary Societies; Christmas Evans (1766–1838), autocratic Baptist minister who spent most of his life as 'bishop' of the Baptist churches on the island of Anglesey, sometimes termed the 'Bunyan of Wales'; Robert Evans (1824–1901), Welsh Congregationalist who undertook much temperance advocacy; and Evan Roberts (1878–1951) of 1904–1905 revival fame. These Welsh figures, some of which have been attributed to Sampson Smith's factory in Longton, clearly demonstrate the Staffordshire potters' sensitivity to a potential market. And they clearly judged well, for it was some of the earlier of these figures that the migrating Welsh took with them, as a tangible memory of home and the old life in Wales, into Patagonia, where they perpetuated their piety in a new land. One figure found in a homestead in Southern Argentina is clearly inscribed 'Made by Sampson Smith, Loughton [sic], 1851'.[88]

Other traditions and themes are represented by General Booth (1829–1912) of the Salvation Army; Henry Cooke (1788–1868), Irish Presbyterian opponent of the proposed disestablishment of the Irish Church; and Fletcher of Madeley (1729–85), whose saintliness has been widely celebrated. Wesley's own testimony was: 'In four score years I have known many excellent men, holy in heart and life, but one equal to him I have not known, one so uniformly devoted to God.'[89] One of the two Congregational Joseph Fletchers, the elder (1784–1843) of Blackburn and Stepney, and the younger (1816–76) of Hanley, is listed. I am strongly of the judgment that the right identification is the younger Fletcher, not least because the vestry at Trinity, Hanley, before its closure had within it a figure of Hanley Tabernacle's first minister, Fletcher's eighteenth-century predecessor, James Boden (1757–1841), who had been involved both in home mission and in the founding of the London Missionary Society. This figure is not recorded elsewhere. Fletcher the younger is known as one who, though initially sceptical as to the advisability of Dissenting ministerial support for the Anti-Corn Law League, subsequently became most enthusiastic in the cause. He was a Congregational historian and thus properly finds his place in this paper.[90]

88. A.F. Tschiffely, *The Way Southward* (1940), cited in Pugh, *Staffordshire Portrait Figures*, p. 94.

89. As cited in Pugh, *Staffordshire Portrait Figures*, p. 322.

90. All of these feature in Pugh, *Staffordshire Portrait Figures*, Section D, pp. 322-44. Other figures I would expect to appear in local situations, as, for example, the parian figure of Alexander Kilham brought to the attention of the Cambridge conference in honour of Professor Clyde Binfield in July 2001.

Figure 2. *Staffordshire flatback of C.H. Spurgeon* (Photography courtesy of
The Potteries Museum and Art Gallery, Stoke-on-Trent).

Others broadly in the Independent tradition include Rowland Hill
(1744–1833), who sustained a 30-year ministry at the Surrey Chapel, and
William Huntington, SS (1745–1813), whom Kenneth Dix has shown us
was more influential than the limitations of his creed might suggest.[91]

91. K. Dix, 'English Strict and Particular Baptists in the Nineteenth Century'

Finally, Thomas Raffles (1788–1863), long-serving minister of Great George Street Chapel, Liverpool, and an early chairman of the Congregational Union, is represented using the same mould that was deployed for the Staffordshire Fletcher. When titled that represents no problem, but the figure also exists untitled and then antique collectors despair: I have seen the same figure labelled Fletcher and Raffles in successive fairs, or on different stalls at the same fair.

In parian, to the Wesleys (John appearing more frequently than Charles, though the hymn-writer is also present), must be added Rowland Hill, Adam Clarke and John Fletcher, all of whom appear in the Staffordshire series.[92] From a later period come Robinson and Leadbeater busts of the Revd Dr F.E. Clark, the founder of the Christian Endeavour movement, the Revd Charles Garrett of the Methodist Forward Movement and Dr Joseph Parker of the City Temple, as well as C.H. Spurgeon, the great Baptist preacher.[93] All of these figures represent important aspects of Nonconformist consciousness: for example, the Christian Endeavour movement in providing a method for training the laity in active church-manship had a wide following not dissimilar to that afforded by the Alpha movement for evangelism and discipleship training in today's church. The Forward Movement, too, had a significance that, around the 1890s, spread out from Methodism to the other churches, indicating a new willingness to tackle the problems of the city, while Parker and Spurgeon represent two of the giants of the metropolitan pulpit. General Booth, whose Salvation Army embraced both evangelism and a commitment to social relief, was modelled by several firms, notably by both Goss and Robinson and Leadbetter.[94]

Here is the heart of the puzzle that I have tried to present in this paper: that notwithstanding Calvin's concern for the second commandment, that is on his own peculiar counting, the evidence suggests a markedly Dissent-

(unpublished PhD thesis, University of Keele, 1999), especially ch. 1.

92. Atterbury (ed.), *Parian Phenomenon*, pp. 94 and 101-102, 198, 102, 94, 234, 245, 247. One rather rare figure is a c. 1870 figure of John Wesley at his mother's tomb. See also Shinn and Shinn, *Victorian Parian China*, pp. 80, 84, 88-90.

93. Atterbury (ed.), *Parian Phenomenon*, p. 235. The Leadbetter part of the partnership was closely associated with Trinity Presbyterian Chuch, both James and E.J. Leadbetter being long-serving elders, the latter serving as secretary and president of the Hanley Ragged Schools for over 40 years. W.H. Shaw, *Centenary Souvenir and Historical Review, 1824–1924* (Hanley, 1924), p. 17.

94. Shinn and Shinn, *Victorian Parian China*, p. 78.

ing preference for image-making. For as Pugh notes in his authoritative study of *Staffordshire Portrait Figures of the Victorian Era*, while some 20 or so Nonconformist preachers can be identified, only one Anglican attribution has been made, and even that one is extremely rare and clouded in uncertainty. This is an authoritative cleric in a well-cushioned pulpit labelled Coulburn. After searches in the *Dictionary of National Biography* and the printed catalogue of the British Library, this proves to be an unidentifiable name, and accordingly it has been suggested that the references should be to the Revd Edward Goulburn, sometime headmaster at Rugby (1849–57) and subsequently Dean of Norwich (1866–97).[95] This is only a suggestion and I am not even sure that the figure is clerical at all, for the dress is not convincingly Anglican; in that respect the figure could as well be Henry Goulburn, the Chancellor of the Exchequer who was much concerned with the setting up of the Ecclesiastical Commissioners. Suffice it to underline that the only possible Anglican prelate in the Staffordshire series has extremely dubious provenance.

Even within the Nonconformist figures presented a hierarchy of number emerges. While most of the figures were produced in fairly small editions, some subjects stand out as being immensely more popular than others. For example, there are some 18 different figures of the Wesleys, mainly John but also Charles, deriving from the Victorian period (that is in addition to the busts that originate in pre-Victorian years) and most have been designated as either average or common in their availability. Two editions of Moody and Sankey and two of the three editions of Spurgeon also fall into the commonly available category. Moreover I know of no good reason why some figures might have survived in greater proportions than others within the general category of Nonconformist preachers. Thus while other figures are rare, the subjects identified above were high-volume products. Does this suggest that Nonconformists were more prone to attachment to the individual, more given to the personality cult, than those in churches where synodical and episcopal government obtained?

Alongside preachers some lay persons are also represented, often for secular rather than religious reasons. Thus, for example, Sir Henry Have-

---

95. Pugh, *Staffordshire Portrait Figures and Allied Subjects of the Victorian Era* (London: Barrie & Jenkins, 1970), p. 16. Balston, *Staffordshire Portrait Figures*, p. 69, suggests that only one copy of the Goulburn is known, but Pugh thinks there may be up to ten surviving. L. Hallinan, *British Commemoratives* (Woodbridge: Antique Collectors' Club, n.d.), p. 195, out of sheer desperation even seeks to make Spurgeon into an Anglican!

lock was often modelled,[96] but since the figure nearly always pairs a figure of Sir Colin Campbell the interest would seem to be military, even though Havelock did achieve fame as a cult figure in the mould of the Bible-reading, praying commander of men, popularly called, because of the notice-able difference of their behaviour, 'Havelock's saints'. He was associated by marriage with the Serampore missionaries, his wife being a Marshman. The other widely regarded Christian soldier was 'Chinese' Gordon who again appears in both Staffordshire ware and parian.[97]

The immediate occasion for the provision of some of these figures is pretty obvious: the Moody and Sankey figures may with some confidence be assigned to the crusade years of 1873–75 and 1883, and they have in fact been assigned initially to the first visit. Among the most enterprising of Staffordshire Baptist ministers was one of Spurgeon's own students, the Revd George Dunnett, who came to minister to the struggling cause in Newcastle-under-Lyme in 1876. To aid its building fund he commissioned Robinson and Leadbeater to produce small busts of Spurgeon to sell at a guinea each, or so say the church minutes in 1878, which also reproduce a letter from Spurgeon, commending Dunnett and the infant Newcastle cause. But when I further investigated I found it was not just one figure but a range, for the great man comes in three sizes, on two different kinds of pedestal and on a stand of Bible and hymn book. The figures themselves tell their own story: on the back you will discover reference to Mr Dunnett, as publisher, to Robinson and Leadbeater as manufacturer, and to John Adams Acton as sculptor—he added Acton to his name in 1869. The parian figures of Spurgeon represent the mature preacher as over against the more youthful expositor in the Staffordshire figures which have been dated about 1856, that is to say depicting a Spurgeon who is only 22 years old.

Subsequent to my earliest researches, I discovered that the Revd Clarence Chambers, first minister of the Fenton Church (and incidentally father of the devotional writer, the Revd Oswald Chambers), adopted a similar strategy in 1881–82 in liaison with the Spode factory, but these Spode fig-ures are much less often seen. The provenance of a terracotta figure in my collection, also derived from the Acton sculpture, I have yet to discover.

---

96. Hallinan, *British Commemoratives*, pp. 14, 87, 214, 261-62, 268, 270, 289-92. He also features frequently in parian as well: see Atterbury (ed.), *Parian Phenomenon*, pp. 187, 196, 203, 240, for a bust by Ridgway, Bates and Co. And also Shinn and Shinn, *Victorian Parian China*, pp. 72, 75, 94.

97. Pugh, *Staffordshire Portrait Figures*, pp. 15-16, 27, 30, 34, 56, 68, 89, 96, 99, 213, 308-13. Atterbury (ed.), *Parian Phenomenon*, pp. 236, 245-46.

With Spurgeon as the leader of something rather like a connectional group-ing within the Baptist denomination, and with an increasing throughput of students through the college he had founded, there should have been a good demand factor. How much immediate success the selling of figures brought I do not know. Certainly both ministers concerned had moved to new charges within a year, so the profits may lie with the antique trade rather than the church building funds. Maybe Robinson and Leadbeater did better out of the enterprise than the churches, because there exist figures without the provenance statement on the back, and these I would imagine to be later continuations.

At last in the parian sequence a representative of the bench of bishops appears with the likeness of C.J. Ellicott of Gloucester and Bristol, who was widely read as a conservative commentator on Scripture, much in-volved with the production of the Revised Version, active in the Lambeth Conferences and a conservative temperance reformer.[98] There is also a late Robinson and Leadbetter parian figure of the Rt Revd Sir Lovelace Stamer, long serving rector of Stoke and the first suffragan bishop of Shrewsbury. Clearly here the local factor can be seen to be playing very strongly, for Stamer was highly influential in the area. The Disruption north of the border prompts an image of Thomas Chalmers, whereas for all the high-land soldiers and lassies there is no representation of the kirk in the Staffordshire series.[99]

Reflecting missionary experience, Minton produced both David Living-stone and H.M. Stanley, and the less well-known Hope Waddell, an Irish-man who pioneered Scottish missions in Jamaica and was later involved in developing mission work in the Calabar Delta in Nigeria, where Mary Slessor became his much more famous associate.[100] Granted the enthusiasm for overseas missions, this also represents a surprising neglect: no William Carey, pioneer of modern missions in India, no William Knibb, sworn enemy of slavery, no Congregational martyrs such as John Williams or James Chalmers. Only Livingstone and Waddell appear, and they only in parian.

Preachers and evangelists are those who most engage the attention of

98. Atterbury (ed.), *Parian Phenomenon*, p. 203; *DNB*; and B. Harrison, *Drink and the Victorians* (Keele, Staffordshire: Keele University Press, 2nd edn, 1994), p. 249.

99. Atterbury (ed.), *Parian Phenomenon*, p. 103; see also Shinn and Shinn, *Victorian Parian China*, p. 91.

100. Atterbury (ed.), *Parian Phenomenon*, pp. 86, 123; Shinn and Shinn, *Victorian Parian China*, pp. 96-97.

the Staffordshire potters but three themes dear to the heart of most Victorian Nonconformists also play their part: Protestantism, philanthropy and temperance.

The theme of Protestantism seems to have flourished around the time of the so-called 'No Popery'/'Papal Aggression' crisis of 1851, which may explain this particular flurry of figures, all made, it is suggested, by Thomas Parr of Burslem. This may or may not be of significance in so far as Burslem had a succession of fiercely Protestant Irish incumbents and became what seems to have been the centre of anti-Catholicism in the potteries, though the leadership was in Low Anglican rather than Nonconformist hands. It is represented by celebratory figures of Ridley and Latimer separated by a stake and set upon lively faggots and flames, with the familiar quotation, 'Be of good comfort master Ridley, and play the man: we shall this day light such a candle, by God's grace, in England, as I trust shall never be put out'. In very similar vein, a separate figure of Cranmer appears with the date of his Oxford burning given as 21 March 1556.[101]

A rather more contentious figure on this theme has been identified by Surgeon Commander Pugh as deriving from a *Punch* cartoon of March 1851, which is entitled 'The Kidnapper—A Case for the Police'. The monk, who is holding forth the sought-after veil, and the innocent young girl, who seeks the life of the cloister, appear similarly placed in both representations, but in the figure she carries a bag of cash labelled '£10,000' which has become the popular title of the figure, whereas in the cartoon it is simply labelled '£.s.d.' The image most exactly reflects the nature of that popular Protestantism that Geoffrey Best has so effectively expounded. The fact that the reflected source is of the 1850s is important in confirming this group of figures as belonging to the No Popery Crisis of the 1850s rather than the Catholic Emancipation campaign of the 1820s.[102]

Figures of 'Popery' and 'Protestantism' are similarly polemical. In these cases the process of imaging the Word is put into reverse for these figures embrace fairly lengthy textual messages. A didactic Protestantism is here reversing the earlier tradition with its failure to resist the temptation of

101. Pugh, *Staffordshire Figure Portraits*, pp. 57, 323-26; also Balston, *Staffordshire Figure Portraits*, pp. 43, 67, plate 38. Again it may be significant that it is the English Reformation that is celebrated. No British representations of continental reformers have been found.

102. G.F.A. Best, 'Popular Protestantism in Victorian England', in R. Robson (ed.), *Ideas and Institutions of Victorian Britain* (London: G. Bell & Sons, 1967), pp. 115-42.

texting the image. Significantly, while Popery is represented by a young priest, who carries a copy of the Scriptures quite clearly chained and closed, the young woman representing Protestantism carries an open book clearly inscribed Holy Bible. The priest also reveals a document, reinforcing the symbolism. It reads, 'Either we must root out the Bible or the Bible will root out us. The translators of the English Bible are to be abhorred to the depths of Hell. It would be better to be without God's law than without the Pope', a quotation assigned to 'Dr Troy, Archbishop of Dublin, 1816'. On the reverse is further text: 'He that committeth his conscience to the keeping of another is no longer a free man. Freedom of conscience and freedom of thought are essential to the freedom of a nation. Therefore a nation of Catholics is a nation of slaves.' The text on the scroll in the Protestant figure refers the reader to a series of biblical texts: 'Search the Scriptures', John 5.39; 'Prove all things', 1 Thess. 5.21; 'Let the word of Christ dwell in you richly', Col. 3.16; 'To the Law and to the Testimony: if they speak not according to this word, it is because there is no light in them', Isa. 8.26. On the reverse of the scroll is the reinforcing message: 'The Bible, the open Bible, is the Religion of Protestants. It is like everything else from God, free as the air we breathe. It spurns alike indulgences and penance.'[103]

In celebration of philanthropy, a few Anglican lay persons appear in the Staffordshire sequence but only when they are seen to be evangelical and Reformist: several untitled figures of men of substance befriending boys have been suggested as either Wilberforce where the costume is late eighteenth-century, or Shaftesbury where the costume is later.[104] Here the identification is aided by comparison with Sir Francis Grant's portrait of Shaftesbury in the House of Commons collection. A female figure of a similar kind, this time holding a book, which it has been suggested might be a Bible, is thought to be of Elizabeth Fry. Her fellow Quaker and kinsman, J.J. Gurney, also appears in Staffordshire ware, while the memory of William Penn (1644–1718) is also celebrated by an unmarked but fairly obvious figure. To these must be added further Evangelical Anglican leaders and philanthropists who appear in parian: Minton's figures of Hannah More and Wilberforce reflect subjects already available in the Staffordshire series, but Charles Simeon, Dean Close and Hugh McNeile are new and obviously Evangelical Anglican figures.[105]

103. Pugh, *Staffordshire Figure Portraits*, pp. 324-26.
104. Pugh, *Staffordshire Figure Portraits*, pp. 179, 182-83, 514, 530.
105. See Minton's figures of Hannah More and Wilberforce, Atterbury (ed.), *Parian*

One High Church figure who does appear in the more comprehensive parian sequence is Sister Dora, but this may be explained by her cross-denominational appeal and like her Catholic counterpart, Sister Margaret Hallahan, her ministry had been local to Staffordshire, in her case Walsall.[106] One of the most interesting of all figures is the representation of a group of George Müller's orphans. This is one of a trio of figures focusing on Bristol charities, the others showing a girl from the Red Maid's School and a boy from Colston's Hospital, all three produced in the Parr Kent style of pottery and dating to the 1880s.[107]

The temperance theme on the Protestant side is represented by organizations rather than by individuals, though on the Catholic side there are three very rare figures of Father Mathew who achieved remarkable things for the temperance cause in Catholic Ireland—the cutting of the consumption of spirits by a half, though still leaving annual consumption at over five million gallons. In 1843, the year to which the figures are dated, he came to England and campaigned for people to sign the pledge, was accepted by temperance reformers of all denominations, secured a pension from the queen, but did not repeat the spectacular success he had achieved in Ireland.

The two organizations frequently found are, first, the Band of Hope, and, secondly, the Independent Order of Good Templars. Four different Band of Hope figures exist which are fairly frequently found. They are dated to 1847 when the organization, a temperance society for children, was founded in Leeds. Some of the figures may be later. The less well coloured ones, either of behatted children holding out a scroll labelled Band of Hope, or a watch holder held by three children beneath flags declaring the Band of Hope, are likely to be the earliest.[108] The rather more colourful figures may be later. In these Hope in female form, stands bare-headed carrying a shield with a cross on an orange ground. Beside her is a child carrying a tall flag which varies according to the version of the figure being studied. On the other side of Hope a serpent insidiously twines itself around a dead tree trunk.[109]

Phenomenon, p. 94; Charles Simeon, p. 98; Dean Close, p. 95; and Hugh McNeile, p. 102. See also Shinn and Shinn, *Victorian Parian China*, Plates 5 and 6, p. 89.

106. Atterbury (ed.), *Parian Phenomenon*, p. 245.

107. Pugh, *Staffordshire Portrait Figures*, pp. 512, 525.

108. The suggestion that the presence of a watch in the family indicated a non-drinking household (because the first thing pawned was always the watch) is I think far-fetched since watch holders are such a common pottery artefact.

109. Pugh, *Staffordshire Portrait Figures*, pp. 323-24, 342-44.

The independent Order of Good Templars comes in four forms, all dated to 1868 when the order was introduced to the United Kingdom. Many of these figures are almost totally without colour in a porridgy kind of earthenware, but some are coloured. Pugh notes three variants, together with a wholly different figure associating the order with the virtues of 'Faith, Hope and Charity', which is inscribed on the figure, and depicted by three women, the last of whom holds a waif, perhaps the child at risk in a drunken family. The other clue you need for understanding temperance figures is that any figure with a fountain in it is likely to represent this interest. One of these is dated 1861, at a time when the temperance societies were worried about the reduction of duties on the sale of certain types of alcohol. Given the insanitary nature of water supplies earlier in the century it is not surprising that it was the late 1850s before the 'water reformers' became active through organizations such as the Metropolitan Free Drinking Fountain Association which by 1872 had 300 fountains to its credit. Lord Shaftesbury's enthusiasm probably got the better of him when he suggested that if drinking fountains were established in the East End 'water would carry the day over gin, beer, or anything else of an intoxicating character'.[110] Illustrative of Shaftesbury's hopes is another Parr figure whose meaning is quite clear: it is the Janus-like double-facing figure, which in one direction reveals all the miseries of the gin drinker, but turn the figure round and the happiness of the water drinker is fully revealed.[111] Representing temperance is also Sir Wilfred Lawson, nephew of Sir James Graham, a man whose career cuts across all one's expectations in nineteenth-century history. A landowner from a Dissenting family, he had a Congregational tutor. A keen sportsman, he became the parliamentary spokesman of the United Kingdom Alliance. Keenly in favour of Irish disestablishment, he opposed all ecclesiastical establishments. He was against the South African War and in favour of votes for women, and his image was reproduced in parian.[112]

110. Harrison, *Drink and The Victorians*, p. 292.

111. The figure appears in Halfpenny, *English Earthenware Figures*, p. 288, as a novelty figure in a William Kent catalogue of 1955 as an example of Walton and Enoch Wood figures that were still being produced. Temperance as a virtue appears in the parian sequence but the mood is very different. Atterbury (ed.), *Parian Phenomenon*, p. 115; and Shinn and Shinn, *Victorian Parian China*, p. 91.

112. Atterbury (ed.), *Parian Phenomenon*, pp. 232, 266. The religious outlook of this, the younger Wilfred Lawson (1829–1906), is not quite clear. David Bebbington labels him 'an Anglican of undenominational Evangelical background', while Clyde

Staffordshire pottery offers its own positive, yet selective, unguarded and for the most part unselfconscious representation of the life of Dissent. This is to be seen not only in the figures that were produced, but also through the negative evidence of the invisible testimony of that which failed to appear. In both these ways the artefacts of the pottery industry suggest their own profile of the scope of Nonconformist cultural interests and aspirations. Like other artefacts—pictures, architecture, Sunday school prizes and so many other material things—they survive for us to touch and handle knowing that they communicate with us something beyond the written document of how these people felt and what they thought important. The picture presented is very broad-brush, but its emphases are indicative of attitude and choice at both popular and bourgeois levels, where Nonconformity had a firmly established constituency.

Binfield notes him as a 'fox-hunting squire' with 'a Congregational upbringing and kinsmen', noting of his father that he 'fostered congregational causes from his Cumbrian estates'. D.W. Bebbington, *The Nonconformist Conscience* (London: Allen & Unwin, 1982), p. 47; J.C.G. Binfield, *So Down to Prayers: Studies in English Nonconformity, 1780–1920* (London: J.M. Dent, 1977), pp. 4, 83. See also Harrison, *Drink and the Victorians*, pp. 23-34.

Part II

ARCHITECTURE

'AN IMPORTANT WORK': BUILDING A VICTORIAN CHAPEL

John Handby Thompson

In 1996, a paper appeared in the *Bulletin of the Hornsey Historical Society* under the title, 'Behind the Bath Stone Façade, Josiah Viney, T. Roger Smith and Pond Square Chapel'. The meticulously composed title, the sense of mystery behind the stone façade and the hint of complex relationships to be resolved, all unmistakably pointed to Clyde Binfield as the author. When researching his subject, he was assured, I understand, that the records of this chapel in Highgate at the time of its construction in 1859 had gone up in smoke a century on. Certainly, the hall Viney later built behind the chapel was burned down in 1978 while being used as a temporary home by a congregation of Jews, and the chapel vestry above it and most of the Congregational records were lost in the blaze. But when, more recently, I came to write the history of Dissent in Highgate[1] I was fortunate to find an old tin trunk in the gallery of the chapel which had somehow survived and had been forgotten. The contents revealed just how Viney, a renowned benefactor and supporter of chapel building, had built this one.[2]

This paper, which in part is based on the contents of the trunk, is not however intended as an addendum to Professor Binfield's. My purpose is to offer a self-standing case study of Victorian chapel building and relate it in a final section to the wider chapel building activity of Congregationalists in the nineteenth century. In the steps of the master, however, I shall not hesitate to unravel familial and churchly relationships, where possible, just for the fun of it.

---

1. J.H. Thompson, *Highgate Dissenters: Their History since 1660* (n.p., 2001).
2. The contents of the trunk were: (1) some at least of the replies to the appeal for funds to build Viney's Pond Square Chapel and other related correspondence from 1857–59; (2) a notebook recording the building of the earlier Congregational chapel in Highgate between 1817 and 1822; (3) the minute book kept by successive Highgate ministers between 1816 and 1883.

Figure 1. *Josiah Viney—Congregational Minister 1857–84* (Portrait courtesy of Highgate United Reformed Church).

Josiah Viney accepted a call to the Congregational church in Highgate
in 1857. His recurrent ill-health and sense of strain after 13 years as minister in Bethnal Green seem to have influenced his decision against Hackney and in favour of Highgate, which was still then a village on a hill, well
above and beyond the smoke and noise of London, surrounded by woods,
hayfields and birdsong but, with piped water replacing the ponds in Pond
Square, set to grow. Viney recorded in the ministers' minute book that he
had consented to come 'for the present at least, to minister the word of
God' and only later, when he was stronger, to take 'oversight' of the congregation. What better tonic than to build a new chapel?

The existing one, opened only in 1822, he found 'small, inconvenient
and unattractive'. It was, even so, the second Independent chapel to have

been built in Highgate since an evangelical secession at Michaelmas 1782 from the century-old Presbyterian meeting, by then become a place of Unitarian preaching. I look first at the struggle to fund the building of these two earlier chapels, before denominational boundaries had hardened and church extension had become a popular movement, in order to show how much more effectively the Victorians did it.

Three London ministers sponsored the seceders' petition for funds in 1782.[3] One was Samuel Brewer, Independent minister in Stepney. The second was Thomas Wills, minister of the Countess of Huntingdon's church at Spa Fields. (The third was Wills's assistant.)[4] Brewer had studied at Deptford under Abraham Taylor, a firmly orthodox Calvinist. He would have been very close in belief (one imagines), if not in 'enthusiasm', to the seceders, and it was he who was invited to preach at the opening. Wills, a former Anglican minister, had by now been obliged to leave the Church of England, in company with the countess. He had married her favourite niece, was among her closest advisers, and saw himself as her successor. His formal duties included responsibility for her chapels. Highgate was never one of those but, if (as one must suppose even for those days) the sum of precisely £133 raised from 120 donors and carefully recorded on the reverse of the petition was insufficient for the very modest building which resulted, Wills would be well placed to find the difference. That he did so is suggested by his nomination of the minister who would lead the new congregation. He was Thomas Williams, one of the countess's students.

In the result, another of the countess's former students, Edward Porter, became the secessionists' minister, and he was called by the church in Independent fashion, not appointed. He ministered from 1786 until his death in 1812. As late as 1809, when the Baptist historian Dr Ivimey visited Highgate and acquired the old meeting house for a Baptist congregation, Porter's congregation, he was told, were 'Calvinistic Methodists'.[5]

3. The original petition hangs in the vestry of Highgate United Reformed Church (Pond Square Chapel), as does the original of the Highgate Case of 1817 (see below).

4. For Brewer, see D. Bogue and J. Bennett, *The History of Dissenters* (2 vols.; London: F. Westley & A.H. Davies, 2nd edn, 1833), II, pp. 632-35; for Wills, see B.S. Schlenther, *Queen of the Methodists* (Durham: Durham Academic Press, 1997), *passim*, and for his later career as an Independent minister, P. Temple, *Islington Chapels* (London: Survey of London, Royal Commission on the Historical Monuments of England, 1992), pp. 24 and 73.

5. Thomas Williams is recorded in G.F. Nuttall, 'The Students of Trevecca 1768–1791', *Transactions of the Hon. Society of Cymmrodorion* (1967), part 2, p. 277; three letters from Porter to the countess survive from his itinerancy in Lincolnshire, two in

Whatever the village might label the chapel, it did not become part of the Countess of Huntingdon's Connexion. Porter named it 'Salem' and referred to himself as an Independent pastor. One of his daughters married a Congregational minister, Thomas Toke Lynch, himself a later Highgate pastor, and Porter appears in the index of deceased Congregational ministers in the 1900 *Congregational Year Book*. His two sons attended the Congregational School at Lewisham, and both became Congregational ministers. The elder emigrated to Canada and later, on leaving the ministry, became an educationalist. The younger served churches in Lancashire and Glasgow, retiring to north London, where in his eighties he wrote a note recording his friendship as a young man in Highgate with the elderly poet, Samuel Taylor Coleridge. Indeed, it was the young Porter, fresh from school and apprenticed to the village apothecary, who (unknown to Coleridge's doctor) regularly refilled Coleridge's laudanum bottle. The note he wrote was prompted by the 'monstrously incredible' account of Coleridge's consumption of opium in Highgate, in the newly published *Dictionary of National Biography*. He was able to correct it with unquestionable authority.[6]

Edward Porter's chapel did not long survive him. By 1816, when his successor, John Thomas, was called, it was falling to pieces. Thomas set up a sinking-fund for a new chapel and issued an appeal, called 'the Highgate Case', in 1817. Several factors had changed since the petition of 1782, not least prices as a result of inflation during and after the Napoleonic wars: the new chapel (admittedly bigger, with stone portals and an organ) would cost £1,700. To whom could Thomas look to support an appeal for an amount of this kind? Who would be his Wills?

'The Highgate Case' refers to the 'liberality of the congregation, with that of other kind friends'. The notebook Thomas kept shows that the congregation's gifts amounted to £69, apart from his own donation of £20. Everything plainly depended on the 'kind friends' who appear to have provided some £1,300 in total before the appeal or in response to it.

Thomas had two outside constituencies. The first was the Village Itinerancy Society, for whom he had preached and from whom he had later received his ministerial training at Hackney. The larger individual dona-

his own hand, in the Cheshunt Archive, Westminster College, Cambridge, FI 490, FI 518 and FI 616; Ivimey's visit to Highgate is recorded in a manuscript note by a later Highgate Baptist minister, Dr J.H. Barnard, kindly made available by Mrs S.J. Mills, librarian and archivist of the Angus Library, Regent's Park College, Oxford.

6.   See E.L. Griggs, 'Samuel Taylor Coleridge and Opium', *Huntingdon Library Quarterly* 17 (1954), pp. 357-78 (357).

tions—none is bigger than £30 but they dwarf the others—appear to be from those associated with that formally non-denominational society, and the language of the 'Case' is noticeably catholic. The connection between the society and the chapel was maintained. Thomas felt it incumbent to report periodically to the society on the progress of his ministry in Highgate; and some years later, when the chapel fell on hard times, it was given into the hands of the society, who sent a supply preacher, Henry Townley, late of Calcutta and Bishopsgate Chapel, until the congregation was again strong enough to call a minister of its own.

Thomas's other source of outside support was from the Independent chapels in London. The appeal was supported by 19 ministers, headed by Rowland Hill of Surrey Chapel, Blackfriars' Road, Alexander Waugh of the Scots' Church in Wells Street and William Bengo Collyer of Hanover Chapel, Peckham. Their varied religious backgrounds—Countess of Huntingdon itinerancy, Scottish Presbyterian and Congregational respectively—gave force to the religious breadth of the appeal. Through the 19 ministers, subscriptions were sought of their congregations. The response was good, at an average donation of a pound from many scores of contributors. But there were no big givers and Porter and his village congregation were left to raise £300.

Impressive as this is as an example of mutual support in the days of Independency, it took five years from the start of the sinking-fund to the opening of the chapel, and it took seven years to clear the debt, each small additional contribution from his village congregation duly recorded by Thomas in the notebook. There was no denominational fund to help him; no Wilson or Morley in the wings. Thomas himself had no ministerial stipend, just £120 a year from seat-rents, and the chapel anniversary collections. He had to run a small boarding school for boys to make ends meet. When he died in 1830, aged just 50, his congregation erected a tablet in his memory. His principal achievement, it said, was his chapel, built by 'means of his persevering exertions'.

It is not easy, therefore, to forgive Viney, 27 years and 5 ministers later, for his slighting comments on Thomas's chapel. Viney's exertions, as we shall see, were more easily rewarded, because of a number of changes since Thomas's day, both local and denominational, which greatly assisted chapel building.

The local changes were organizational and societal. The Highgate congregation became formally Congregationalist under John Thomas in 1827. The first church meeting was held in March 1831 under his successor,

Robert Blessley. By 1848, under Thomas Toke Lynch, Highgate was in the West Middlesex Association of Congregational Ministers and Churches. Under Viney's immediate predecessor, Ebenezer Cornwall, who had trained for the ministry in Edinburgh and seems to have had a nose for good order, 'an improved plan for the more effective working of the church' was adopted in April 1856. This allotted duties to 'brethren' appointed by the minister. The very first duty provided that 'one of the brethren shall be treasurer of all monies belonging to the church' and further that

> an evening shall be appointed once or twice a year when the pecuniary accounts of the church shall be open for the inspection of any members who may wish to be acquainted with them. The treasurer is…to wait in the vestry for that purpose.

I take this to be a clear indication that, village chapel though it was, there were now some in the Highgate congregation whose giving was large enough for them to want to know how it had been spent, who could understand accounts and who would generally expect to share the responsibilities of running the church with the minister. When Viney arrived 18 months later, in poor health but resolved to build a new chapel, he found a congregation used to taking responsibility and a treasurer in post well able to run an appeal and account acceptably for its progress.

The changes outside Highgate were even more significant. I shall look at them in greater detail later, but note here the three most salient: first, the establishment by London Congregationalists in 1848 of a Chapel Building Society; secondly, Joshua Wilson's recommendation to the Congregational Union of England and Wales that the second centenary of the Great Ejectment should be commemorated by opening 50 new chapels by St Bartholomew's Day, and laying the foundation stones of 50 more by then; and thirdly, the successful development of church extension into a popular movement among Congregationalists, in which evangelism and the satisfaction of social aspiration were both factors.

Highgate fits easily into this picture. The membership of 45 when Viney arrived was no bigger than in Thomas's day. As with the earlier chapels, outside help would be needed, and there was now a denominational fund to be called on. In due course the London Congregational Building Society granted Highgate's new chapel appeal £500. The Highgate cause had had three ejected ministers among its first leaders, so that a new chapel would be an apposite celebration of its beginnings, as well as fitting within Wilson's suggested time-frame of national commemoration of the Ejectment.

Viney's address at the stone laying took his hearers back to 1662.[7] The third factor, the satisfaction of social aspiration and progress in evangelism, requires longer exposition.

Figure 2. *Pond Square Chapel, Highgate in the year of the opening, 1859*
(Photograph courtesy of the Highgate Literary and Scientific Institution).

As I have already hinted, the social composition of the Highgate congregation had begun to change, like the village itself, as the middle classes moved there in the 1850s. They came at first mainly from the City, Hackney and Islington, all fading strongholds of Old Dissent. Part of Viney's resolve to build was his realization that a fine new building in the centre of the village would draw these new arrivals in a way that Thomas' gloomy out-of-the-way chapel would not; more than this, that they would be willing to help build it.

The first appeal letter, from which, incidentally, the title of this paper is taken, shows that already when the public appeal was launched on 15 April

7.   Published in 1858 as *Foundation Truths: or, Why we are Dissenters*. There is a reference to the publication in H. Johnson, *Josiah Viney: A Record of his Life and Work* (London: E. Stock, 1899), p. 100.

1858 the congregation had raised £1,700, as much as Thomas' appeal had raised in 12 years of struggle. The first five names gave £1,450 between them, but only one of these, and it was the smallest donation, was from a long-standing member of the congregation.

The first, marked 'from a Friend', was all too obviously from Viney himself. Viney had a number of unusual characteristics for a Congregational minister of the time, at any rate in combination. He had attended university, was without formal theological training, had had a short career in business, and was a man of independent means. His wealth came from his own family and his wife's, and they had no children. His later social benefactions in Highgate—model dwellings for the poor, a working men's institute and library, and a plain mission chapel at the poorer end of the village— were substantial; the £500 for his new chapel in keeping with them.[8]

It was equalled by the church treasurer's donation. He was William Patrick, a retired sugar refiner. Patrick had transferred his membership from the Congregational church in Poplar in April 1853, and on Viney's arrival had sold his house to him to use as the manse. This house, Fernwood, was set in three acres and backed by woodland, offering a style of living which suggests a further distinction between Viney and the general run of Congregational ministers of the day. But it was a signal to the great and good of Highgate that Dissent knew how to live in style.

The third donation, of £200, came from William Warton, a City solicitor. He was church secretary and had been received into membership 'by testimonial from the church under the care of the Rev'd Mr Galloway in Bishopsgate Street' in February 1853. Warton also lived in a fine Highgate house, Southwood Lawn—its garden so large it is now several roads of houses—and like Patrick he had brought his servants into membership as well. He provided an interest-free bridging loan of £600, and probably arranged another of £500, to allow building to proceed while the results of the appeal were collected.

The fourth donation—we are down to single £100s now—came from William Sargant, who had transferred his membership to Highgate from

8.   Viney studied for the ministry under the Revd T.S. Guyer of Ryde, Isle of Wight. He then attended University College, London. His mother, Elizabeth Elliot, was a member of the family that owned Frith Sands, an East India shipping firm. His father had a substantial business as a trunk-maker near St Paul's. The father of Viney's wife, Anna, was Thomas Piper, a successful London builder, and senior deacon at the King's Weigh House, where her sister was wife of the minister, Thomas Binney. Mrs Binney when widowed became a Highgate member.

Finsbury Chapel in 1854. The fifth came from the father-in-law of the architect—the T. Roger Smith of Professor Binfield's title—and was therefore perhaps a special case.[9] The sixth, as already noted, was the one sizeable donation (£50) from a long-standing Highgate resident and church member, Joseph Clarke.

Apart from the level of their donations to the building fund, the wealth and respectability of Viney's leading supporters—all except the architect's father-in-law became deacons and chapel trustees—sent a message to the village, and its newer residents. Dissenters in a place like Highgate were still not quite socially acceptable, but attendance at a chapel supported by the respectable certainly provided a social lift. It is unsurprising to read in Viney's diary soon after the chapel was opened, 'congregation trebled, many interesting families added'.

And to Viney, as well as his deacons, numbers were a measure of successful evangelism. The new chapel, its commanding position in the village and its carved Bath stone façade strikingly white and gracious, quickly justified itself as an agency of evangelism. Although Highgate after its mid-century growth remained relatively small until the big houses were pulled down (long after Viney's day), he received 750 members during his 26-year ministry and christened 250 babies. Membership rose and began to average 280, with a Sunday school of 300. Extensions and elaborations in 1861, 1871 and 1876, included a gallery, a new organ, stained glass and a new Sunday school building. They do not seem to have required further appeals. Viney was a saintly man, but he liked success and his chapel in Highgate gave him that. He did not use notes in the pulpit and when on two occasions words embarrassingly failed him he knew it was time to retire from the ministry. That was 1883. He was careful to record in the minister's minute book, however, that retirement 'was not from failure of health, or character, or success', but because he was encountering the weaknesses of old age.

What of the responses of those outside Highgate to the appeal? In 1782 and 1817, the practice had been to set out a case in one document, rather like (to use a modern term) a mission statement, and refer to it, or produce

---

9.   Smith was a son of the manse. Pond Square Chapel was his first serious commission and he was appointed without a competition, a trust he repaid in part by remitting some of his fees. He was later known for his public buildings in India. He was twice elected president of the Architectural Association and became Professor of Architecture at University College, London. See *Dictionary of National Biography, Second Supplement*.

it, when soliciting funds. In 1858 there was of course a reliable postal service and printing was cheap. Viney's appeal appeared on that strong but tissue-like paper associated with devotional prayer books and was despatched by Patrick throughout the kingdom. Many replies are reminders of the extent of contemporary chapel building.

> Mr…presents his compliments and regrets that he has already given as much aid for chapel building as he can afford this year.

> It would afford me much pleasure to be a liberal donor to the good work you are about to undertake…were it not that at this time I am engaged to the full extent of my ability in two, nay three, operations in this locality.

> What with the dullness of the wine trade this year and having had to meet a similar call from a friend last week, I regret exceedingly that I am unable to contribute.

Another concern of some recipients was the evident failure of the Victorian virtue of self-help in Highgate.

> I should have thought such a sum ought to be made up by two or three persons such as yourself.

> I am sorry you are obliged to go from home for aid.

Despite these extracts, outright refusal was rare. Such comments were more often a reason for a conventional five or ten pound note, or a promise to send a donation when the roof was on, or the chapel was opened. The relative absence of refusals may have been due in part to Viney's good name as himself a generous donor to many causes, but much more probably it represents a strong sense of obligation to support church extension born of the times. The responses are usually unfulsome, even business-like, but a few letters use the contorted language of evangelical pietism. ('I find it impossible to remember unceasingly and to act out the conviction that we are but stewards…and that time, property and life all belong to Him, who in his goodness honours us to hold them in trust for Him and his service.') Such letters come usually from an older generation, and the one quoted was accompanied by £50.

Patrick cast the net wide. He secured £5 from the Baptist railway magnate, Sir Morton Peto. It was grandly conveyed by a secretary after the opening and just before Peto's insolvency. Some local Anglicans contributed to the appeal, usually conveyed anonymously through a chapel neighbour, but not Highgate's most illustrious resident, Miss Angela Burdett-Coutts. Patrick sent her a specially drafted letter during her sojourn in Torquay, but does not seem to have had a reply.

Connections, as always, were fully used. Patrick dunned his old partners, the McFies, in Sugar House, Liverpool, for four guineas (cannily split between the two of them) and received an invitation to tea. For a small church treasurer, however, he had a much more valuable and surprising connection. A letter to him from John Morley in response to the appeal, beginning 'My dear Brother', was the clue. At first, I took this to be an early intimation of John Morley's gradual shift from Congregationalism to the Plymouth Brethren, but the language was altogether too intimate. A hint from Professor Binfield, and a visit to the Morley tomb in Abney Park cemetery, revealed that the two were brothers-in-law: William Patrick's sister, Lydia, was John Morley's wife. Patrick, I then discovered, was from an old Upper Clapton (Hackney) family, suggesting that this union might have been a chapel romance. The cheque accompanying the brotherly letter was for £100 and a further £50 followed the chapel opening. More than this, John's brother, Samuel Morley, agreed to lay the foundation stone and gave £50 to the appeal for the honour. A specially composed letter to the Morleys' cousin, John Remington Mills, supposedly the richest commoner in England, seems to have been unrewarded.[10]

Viney collected £10 each from the Spicer brothers, and the Crossley brothers of Dean Clough Mills, Halifax, sent £5 each. Joshua Wilson gave £50. Viney's father-in-law, Thomas Piper, another eminent Congregational layman, contributed £100 just before he died. William Piper, who took over the family building firm, and later built Portsmouth Docks, gave £100 and promised more if it was needed. He was to be superintendent of the Pond Square Sunday school in retirement, though he was never successful in the deacons' elections. Viney's brother, John, who took over his father's business, became master of the Leathersellers, and retired at 42, gave £35 and £5 for each of his daughters.

I have written enough to show in outline how the job was done: loyalties—local, familial and religious—were fully exploited and faithfully rewarded, business connections and good offices were exhaustively pursued, all undergirded by a denominational church extension movement the nature and extent of which now remain to be explored. First, however, for the record, the building contract for Pond Square Chapel was let for £3,880 in September 1858, the foundation stone was laid the following month and, blessed by a dry winter, the church was opened six months

---

10. In fairness to Remington and Miss Coutts, I should make clear that the correspondence I am drawing on may not be complete. Nor, unless donations were passed on by letter, are there references to money handed over in person.

later, virtually free of debt, on 30 April 1859. The final cost was £4,684. The extras included a turret and a short spire which carried steps to the projected gallery. This practical purpose was the reason for the spirelet, but I like to think that it was also Viney's rejoinder to Dr Blomfield, Bishop of London, who was known to resent the full-blown steeple and spire on the Gothic church Viney had built earlier in Bethnal Green. The bishop's fear was that such ornamented schismatic buildings might lead Anglicans to stray into them under the impression that they were entering 'mother church'.

The church extension movement in Congregationalism had two main justifications. The first, which pervades, for example, Joshua Wilson's *Memoir* of his father, Thomas,[11] the denomination's earliest and probably most influential supporter of chapel building, was the disparity between the general population and church provision as a whole. This was due to large overall population growth, but intensified in towns and cities by the movement of the population there from the country. Neither national nor local growth had been matched to any significant extent by new church building. The simple assumption that a growing population required a large number of new churches allowed scope for all denominations to take part, to the extent that they could afford it. It would be naive to say that this was undertaken in an uncompetitive spirit, but the prime duty was to evangelize, and one simple calculation appeared to be sufficient: the number of existing sittings for all denominations, compared with the size of the population in the locality. It was of course very unusual to find the sittings sufficient.

Thomas Wilson's importance to Congregational church extension was arguably as much the example he set to a later generation as the sums he disbursed in his own. He started rescuing, repairing and re-establishing dilapidated chapels from his own purse as early as 1799. After inheriting a further fortune from his uncle, John Remington, in 1813, he began to advance money for the construction of large new chapels in centres of population. Craven Chapel, Paddington Chapel and Claremont Chapel, all in London, cost him in total some £25,000, a nearly unimaginable figure in today's money. In each case he advanced the money at no interest. Though he looked for repayment of capital over a period, he wrote off in the end about a fifth of this sum. In addition, he continued to assist chapel causes all over the country, with big sums or small, by gift or loan, free or con-

11. J. Wilson, *A Memoir of the Life and Character of Thomas Wilson Esq, Treasurer of Highbury College* (London: John Snow, 1846).

ditional, according to circumstance, for 40 years. The *Memoir* records each with filial duty. His benevolence, and the business-like discrimination by which it was exerted, designed both to encourage self-help and regenerate resources, became later the model for others of means throughout the chapel building period. His final contribution to a denomination still pronouncedly Independent was to show the benefits of pooled resources. In 1837 he formed, and became first chairman of, the Metropolis Chapel Fund Association, the earliest of the chapel building societies. Its aim was to collect large donations from wealthy individuals and disburse them in support of new chapels in the destitute areas of London, which as always were bearing the brunt of population growth. The fund's main achievement was the construction of Westminster Chapel, in the festering environs of parliament and the palace, to which Wilson himself gave £1,000, having already paid as much again towards the cost of acquiring the freehold.

The other justification of Congregational church extension was a good deal less openly dispassionate: Anglican 'aggression'. Dissent, still with its disabilities unrelieved, resented the establishment in 1818 of the Church Building Commission and the allotment of public funds to build new Anglican churches. Lord Liverpool had, after all, been frank. The purpose was 'to remove Dissent'. Later, the chapel builders' cry was to be 'Tractarian aggression'. John Angell James's speech to the Congregational Union of 1839 is perhaps the most spirited expression of this chauvinist justification of chapel building.

> It seems to be the present policy of the Church of England to build us *down* and to build us *out*. Its members suppose that our congregations continue with us only because there are no Episcopalian places to receive them; and acting upon this mistake they are multiplying their churches and chapels, many of which are erected in the immediate vicinity of ours, for the purpose of drawing into them the people we have gathered. To prevent this, we must keep pace with them in this blessed spirit of building. Enlargements, re-erections and erections must go on among us, according to our ability, and with an energy in some measure resembling the Church of England... We must catch the building spirit of the age. We must *build, build, build.*

And later:

> For this, money, much money, far *more* money, will be wanted. We must give it. The time is come when Nonconformists must prove their love for their principles by the sacrifice of poverty.

You will not find this speech, or any reference to the subject, in R.W. Dale's reverential *Life* of James. It is altogether too down-to-earth and partial for the statesmanlike portrait Dale wishes to draw. We owe the preservation of James's speech to Albert Peel, who predictably adds the comment, 'with a policy of this kind it is easy to see how chapel debts arose'.[12]

James's speech is worth marking in two other respects. The first is the ease with which he brushes aside the objection that a policy of church extension is likely to be inimical to one of the defining principles of Congregationalism, 'the gathered church': 'We cannot multiply our persons until we multiply our places. We must not wait for congregations to be gathered before we build. We must build to gather.' 'Church planting' was of course widely practised by other denominations. Presbyterians typically put in an interim session, borrowed from a neighbouring church, until the planted church had taken root. James recommended sending off 'as a nucleus for the new congregations, colonies from such as are already large and overflowing'. The dividing line, between gathering and building could, of course, be thin. When Thomas Wilson built his London chapels, he acted in concert with a small group like himself already committed elsewhere, who either severed their connections with their former churches or (like Wilson himself) remained spiritually engaged for a time with the new chapels when they opened, usually until a minister was called.

The second difficulty which James raises is overseas missions and the risk that large sums devoted to chapel building would draw off support from them. This, such as it is, is his answer:

> Nor must we allow our denomination to be lost in the splendour and magnitude of foreign missions. I would not have a single shilling withdrawn from these to support Dissent and multiply Dissenting places of worship, but I would have Dissenting places and congregations multiplied to the support of foreign missions... We must bestir ourselves and build more places; this I repeat, and urge again and again...

He sums up thus: 'We must seek to *increase*, we have the means; there is room for us; and I believe God will bless the attempt.'

I have dwelt at length on John Angell James's speech in order to let it show the temper of the times, so different from our own. I have drawn attention to its rhetoric and its partisan nature, in order to emphasize the emotions he sought to arouse. By such speeches, in national and county forums, and echoed in hundreds of pulpits, support for chapel building was

---

12. A. Peel, *These Hundred Years, 1831–1931* (London: Congregational Union of England and Wales, 1931), p. 149.

encouraged and a responsive movement created. It was never as wide-spread as missionary giving because (as at Highgate) it was primarily directed at the prosperous among Dissent, able in smaller ways to emulate Thomas Wilson. (It still of course enthused local church members to give as they were able.) In Congregationalism, it was aided by their stronger sense of denominational identity after the formation of the Congregational Union of England and Wales in 1831, and by the Union's furtherance of a new home missions policy and organization. A particular stimulus, as noted, was the commemoration of the second centenary of the Great Ejectment in 1862—365 new chapels were reported by 1867.[13] The growth of a varied denominational press was also a factor in encouraging new building and the sacrifices this entailed. There is no space to develop these themes here, but reference must be made to the biggest factor of all, the chapel building societies.

Thomas Wilson here, as in the widespread but judicious disbursement of his private resources to individual appeals, provided a lead and an example. The Metropolis Chapels Fund Association, set up in 1837 and chaired by him, was the first attempt to gather in substantial contributions and disburse them to chosen chapel building causes. It provided the givers with an assurance that their donations would be responsibly spent and thus encouraged them to give more than they would to an individual non-local appeal. It was also hoped thereby to end the sad procession of ministers from debt-ridden chapels calling, cap in hand, on likely donors. The association was followed by the London Chapel Building Society (1848), of which Joshua Wilson was treasurer. A similar body was set up in Manchester in 1852, called the Lancashire and Cheshire Congregational Chapel and School Building Society.

The leading figure in the Congregational chapel building society movement was J.C. Gallaway. An architect *manqué*,[14] from 1848 he was minister of Bishopsgate Chapel.[15] He also acted as secretary of the London Chapel

13. R.T. Jones, *Congregationalism in England 1662–1962* (London: Independent Press, 1962), p. 296. For a recent account of the more polemical aspect of the 1862 commemorations, see T. Larsen, 'Victorian Nonconformity and the Memory of the Ejected Ministers: The Bicentennial Commemorations of 1862', in R.N. Swanson (ed.), *The Church Retrospective* (Studies in Church History, 33; Woodbridge: Boydell, 1997), pp. 459-73.

14. He actually designed and himself built a brick chapel during a visit to Nova Scotia in 1843.

15. As such he was minister to W.H. Warton, the later church secretary of High-

Building Society. The paper he read to the Congregational Union's autumnal meeting in Northampton in 1851 became the foundation of the Union's policy on chapel building. The paper is easily accessible[16] and I need only refer in outline to its main arguments. The first is the timeliness of an extension of chapel building now because it is 'a financially propitious moment' and because the 'antics of the Puseyites and the aggressiveness of the Papists' have opened the public mind to the dangers of 'priestism'. Among the modern aspects of society, which he claims are 'breaking up the last strong-holds of bigotry', he lists the free trade movement, the electric telegraph, the railway, the press, the schoolmaster and 'the general elevation of the masses'. A chapel building movement would advance and advertise 'pure religion', and would be entirely consistent with the voluntaryist, educational and missionary nature of Congregationalism, yet any map would show 'that a very large portion of the population are at present untouched by our ministry'.

The rest of the paper is heavily practical, yet of interest in that it advocates making buildings both prominent in position and attractive in appearance to be faithful 'to the openings of Divine Providence'. Those for whom they were to build 'have taste but not religion', yet 'through the gratification of the one' they may be led 'ultimately to the full enjoyment of the other'. Even those already attracted to religious services are not unsusceptible to tasteful surroundings.[17] Gallaway was to be a great advocate of the Gothic church, partly because of the economy of its design and construction, but also because of a desire to separate the image of Dissent from the barn-like meeting house.

If James had been cavalier in his dismissal of the 'gathered church' as an impediment to chapel building, Gallaway addresses the problem at length, suggesting that in some minds it remained a stumbling block. He acknowledges that the best way to evangelize a new district is to form a spiritual nucleus out of which a building ultimately arises. This can be done by a portion of the members of an established church 'swarming off',

gate. It is therefore perhaps unsurprising to find among the Highgate correspondence a letter from Warton to Patrick, the treasurer, beginning: 'It appears to be thought both in Highgate and London that we are rather sleepy about our new chapel' and going on to suggest in some detail how and when the building should be undertaken.

16. *Congregational Year Book, 1851*, pp. 84-94.

17. Samuel Morley was unpersuaded. Considering too much was spent on ornament, he offered £500 for any chapel built for under £5,000 if the rest could be raised, giving in this way over £14,000 between 1864 and 1870.

or by starting a Sunday school or preaching station in a destitute area from which a church eventually emerges. But he also points to the need for a building to aid evangelism, the inconveniences of the hired hall, and the value, therefore, of a new chapel from the start.

The Congregational Union decided in the light of Gallaway's paper that an English Congregational Building Society should be formed, to operate everywhere except London, Lancashire and Cheshire, where the existing societies would continue.[18] It began in 1853. Initially it reported annually to meetings of the Union, but essentially it ran itself. Gallaway was appointed secretary, John Crossley guaranteeing his stipend for three years. The society was guaranteed an annual income of £2,000 for ten years.

Like the London and Lancashire societies, the English society received donations and disbursed grants or loans, but unlike them only assisted projects on which it had been able to offer advice at a preliminary stage. This was an attempt, difficult in an independent-minded denomination, to influence expenditure and location. The aim, according to a commentator in the *Evangelical Magazine*, was to produce 'satisfactory undertakings', that is, satisfactory in origin and need, size, character and cost, in local support, in the concurrence of neighbouring churches, in the provisions of the trust deed and in the prospect of the early extinction of debt.[19] The society asked well-known architects to prepare model plans, which were made available to chapel building committees, and they compiled *Practical Hints on Chapel Building* (1858). Loans were widely used to encourage self-help. Sums lent carried no interest, and repayment allowed resources to be used again. A church receiving a grant was expected to contribute to the society regularly and voluntarily.

In 1878, at the end of 25 years' service, the society had assisted the building of 521 churches and chapels (nearly twice as many as planned), containing 240,000 sittings, at a total cost of £1,050,000, towards which the society had paid or promised £140,000.[20] The figures show the effectiveness of the society in stimulating support for church extension, but they also demonstrate, as at Highgate, how much the promoters of new chapels were still dependent on the willingness of church members and the respondents to an appeal to give. This was even more true by the end of

18.   The English society also covered Wales and the Channel Islands. A Liverpool Congregational Chapel Building Society was formed in 1872.

19.   *Evangelical Magazine* (1879), pp. 475-80.

20.   *Evangelical Magazine* (1879), pp. 475-80.

the Victorian era when the Congregational building societies as a whole had helped to build just short of 1,000 chapels and manses. Chapel building societies were an expression of the church extension movement, even a product of it, but never more than part of it.

To those of us of the rationalizing, adapting, closing generation, the chapel building era is not so much a puzzle, as an embarrassment. We admire their zeal, but wish they had got their sums right. At heart, however, it was their response to the challenge of the great unwashed; it was evangelism on a big scale, using the technology they knew, based on preaching and a place to preach. Our embarrassment may be in part that we have found no answer to the same call, and attempted none.

The chapel building movement was a voluble declaration of Nonconformist confidence and relative prosperity in mid- nineteenth-century England. It gloried in self-help, receiving not a penny from the state. Expansion was firmly along denominational lines and therefore in unashamed competition with other churches. In a society which was very much Church and chapel, building maintained, even enhanced, the place of the chapel, and with it that of socially aspiring chapel-goers. Chapel building was even justified as a rejoinder to those who, for the first time for over a century, appeared to threaten Reformation principles. Almost every one of these characteristics of the chapel building movement is at variance with our experience of Nonconformity today, and our attitudes to the wider Church. In our uneasiness we forget the confidence of Victorian religion, which could not have found expression without the builders. Like Albert Peel, we prefer to mutter about the debt they left behind. But those of us who can still use a chapel they built, such as Pond Square, Highgate, Gothic and ornamented as Gallaway would have wished, still honour the memory of the builders and their movement.

NEWMAN, PUGIN AND THE ARCHITECTURE OF THE ENGLISH ORATORY[1]

Sheridan Gilley

I first met Clyde Binfield in 1971, when he gave a paper on the Nonconformist antecedents of Mr Asquith.[2] He was three hours late, but he was
worth waiting for, and I became an instant convert Binfieldian. Gothic pinnacles, the families of mercantile manufacturers and fine writing—these
elements in his work singled out by Professor Ward—I loved 'em all. I
thought, therefore, that the only thing that would suit this volume in his
honour would be an offering on architecture, a subject which Clyde has
made his own; and the only topic that would do would be slightly over the
top, an excursion into English Roman Catholic Gothic and Baroque. Clyde,
for all his Nonconformity, has something of the Gothic if not the Baroque
about him. He has certainly shown a most Catholic delight in the form, spirit
and substance of Protestant church buildings. Moreover, as representing the
Catholic side of Clyde, and the Roman Catholic branch of English Nonconformity, I feel called to make a popish contribution on the subject of Roman
Catholic ecclesiology (the study of church buildings, not of the doctrine of
the Church), in an area more or less adjacent to the realm of the Victorian
Nonconformist buildings about which Clyde has written and lectured to
delight us all.

This is, moreover, an archaeological area, where the angel of destruction
has been busily assailing both lowly chapel and great cathedral. Margaret

1.   There is one essay on my theme, J. Patrick, 'Newman, Pugin, and Gothic',
Victorian Studies 24 (1981), pp. 185-207, but this makes a somewhat different selection and use of themes and material.

I am grateful to Gerard Tracey of the Birmingham Oratory, and to Richard Pickett
for reading this essay in draft. He has just completed his thesis, 'The Churchmanship
of A.W.N. Pugin' (MA thesis, University of Durham, 2001).

2.   Published in part as 'Asquith: the Formation of a Prime Minister', *Journal of
the United Reformed Church History Society* 2 (1981), pp. 204-42.

Visser, in her wonderful work, *The Geometry of Love: Space, Time, Mystery and Meaning in an Ordinary Church*,[3] has described what a Roman Catholic church ought to be. Let me describe what it is not. Recently on a walk in the backwoods of northern Yorkshire, where it borders on County Durham, I came across a small, late Victorian, stone Gothic church with a connected house for its minister. The present owner offered to show me the building, which he had bought from the Roman Catholic diocese of Middlesbrough. Its last restoration took place perhaps a decade ago. A flat low internal roof had been introduced, of public-house varnished pine. The sanctuary had been stripped of almost everything except a wooden table, though a lamp still flickered by the tiny tabernacle on the old east wall. Stalls, possibly from some abandoned convent, had been placed length-wise along the south side of the nave, facing another raised modern altar of two massive rough and irregular blocks of stone, suggesting a place of infant sacrifice. Any one could see what is wrong. The church is high and narrow, and was designed as a longitudinal building leading the eye to a vertical sanctuary. The violent wrenching round of the seating to face the nave wall had produced an effect both comic and tragic, a sort of architectural rape, in which the underlying idea, the creation of community, had failed to respect the building as it was. Nothing in the Second Vatican Council's decree on liturgy requires such desecration.[4] The present lay custodian is contemplating a more sensitive re-restoration, but it is difficult to imagine the spiritual and aesthetic grossness of the priestly mind which had perpetrated the present horror, and of the architect or builder who had carried it out. Here, then, is a template of what not to do to a church. The internal sack of so many English Roman Catholic shrines is significant of an essential lack in the character of most of the Roman clergy, not merely of aesthetic training, but of an elementary sense of the unity of spiritual things, an unBinfieldian blindness to the needs of the spirit in what it sees.

Our present visual condition of the spirit is being rendered worse by the disappearance of religion from the public landscape, in the closure and demolition of church buildings. The Victorian boom in both population and churchgoing made the fortunes of a myriad of architects and builders, including Roman Catholic ones, who have for decades been the subject of serious scholarly enquiry. The importance of this enquiry is one theme of this paper, but even now it has not triumphed in public opinion, which is still

3.   (London: Viking, 2001).

4.   See 'Constitution on the Sacred Liturgy: Sacrosanctum Concilium', *The Documents of Vatican II* (London: Geoffrey Chapman, 1967), pp. 137-78.

too often as described by P.G. Wodehouse in 1937, that 'whatever may be said in favour the Victorians, it is pretty generally admitted that few of them were to be trusted within reach of a trowel and a pile of bricks'.[5] In the year of Victoria's accession, 1837, the Institute of British Architects received its royal charter of incorporation, a milestone in their emergence as a profession, to be dignified by the great Anglican ecclesiastical architects, Scott and Street, Butterfield and Pearson, who built thousands of new churches and restored nearly every existing one. Any Victorian cleric worth his salt built or restored at least one church, and though this was hardly his primary interest, even the greatest of Victorian converts to Rome, John Henry Newman, the subject of this essay, had a major part in building four. Almost any Victorian cleric could be depicted like a founder saint, with a model of his building in his hands. As Dr John Thompson has reminded us, this nineteenth-century heritage of religious buildings was stimulated by social ambition, by an enormous denominational self-confidence and by fierce interdenominational rivalry, to put the boldest and most beautiful face towards the world, in faith graven in stone.

But the losses of Victorian buildings have been enormous. There were over 14,000 Methodist chapels in England and Wales at the Methodist union of 1932. By 1980, this number had halved to about 7,000. Many, no doubt, were unprepossessing; many, however, were the only attractive buildings which communities possessed. This loss is most apparent in the poorest areas which can afford it least.

This scale of church closures, among other denominations, has yet to be felt among Roman Catholics, though the loss of convents and monasteries must be considerable, and certain abandoned buildings have become notorious, like the Franciscan Church of St Francis in Gorton, Manchester, one of the most remarkable shrines in England, and the historic Church of the Oblates of Mary Immaculate in Leeds, whose lay custodian converted the church's marbles into decoration for his swimming pool. Roman Catholic churches are especially vulnerable. In spite of the existence since 1994 of diocesan committees on architecture, Roman Catholic churches are not protected by a proper internal planning system like the Anglican structure of consistory courts; and while it is now very difficult to demolish a mediaeval building, Roman Catholic churches are overwhelmingly in the vulnerable categories of nineteenth-century buildings, because the vast increase in the Roman Catholic population took place through the nineteenth-century Irish immi-

5.   *Summer Moonshine* (Harmondsworth: Penguin Books, 1966 [1937]), p. 17.

gration, and it was in the nineteenth century that both rich and poor Catholics poured a fortune into the construction of chapels and churches.

These churches, however, now need protection from the Church itself. We have seen in our own lifetime the second round of what Dr Eamon Duffy has called the stripping of the altars at the Reformation:[6] the sledgehammer destruction of sacred interiors and objects by modern liturgical iconoclasts. I shudder when I think of the lovely little church designed by the greatest of Victorian Roman Catholic church architects, Augustus Welby Northmore Pugin, at Crook in County Durham, where bits and pieces of the old sanctuary have been exploded round the building like trophies of a barbarian war;[7] or the once lovely Cathedral of St Barnabas, Nottingham, also designed by Pugin, whose custodians had the brass effrontery to advertise their work of destruction to the recent Pugin exhibition in the Victoria and Albert Museum. There is vast scope for more such vandalism. Augustus Pugin designed a number of Roman Catholic cathedrals and scores of churches, and his energies were ferocious; he married thrice, the last time to Jane Knill, whom he called 'a first-rate Gothic woman',[8] and fathered eight children, before dying exhausted after a bout of insanity in 1852, at the age of forty. I owe to my research student Christabel Powell in her doctoral dissertation the insight that Pugin's imagination was essentially liturgical, and his argument for Gothic was that, simply and supremely, it was the finest and most functional setting for Catholic worship.[9] While he had no love of the Italian Oratory which Newman introduced into England, as we shall see, the English Oratories, in a period of drought, have yet maintained Pugin's principle, the spiritual unity of worship with its form and setting, which has been nothing less than keeping faith with their sixteenth-century and Victorian founders. Where other Catholic clergy and other orders have seen their role as the radical recasting of their tradition, with the worst philistine results in the ordering of their churches and the character of their liturgy, the

6.   *The Stripping of the Altars: Traditional Religion in England c. 1400–c.1580* (New Haven: Yale University Press, 1992).

7.   On Our Lady Immaculate and St Cuthbert, Crook, see N. Pevsner and E. Williamson, *The Buildings of England: County Durham* (Harmondsworth: Penguin Books, 1983), pp. 134-35.

8.   Cited C. Wainwright, ' "Not a Style but a Principle": Pugin and his Influence', in P. Atterbury and C. Wainwright, *Pugin: A Gothic Passion* (New Haven: Yale University Press; London: Victoria and Albert Museum, 1994), pp. 1-21 (5).

9.   C. Powell, 'The Liturgical Vision of Augustus Welby Northmore Pugin' (PhD thesis, University of Durham, 2002).

English Oratories have, almost alone, been true to the ideals which once formed them.

Some of the most hideous reorderings, however, have arisen from the difficulty of reconciling the demands of modern liturgy with buildings constructed on the model of Pugin's Victorian Gothic, with long naves and sanctuaries, intended in Romantic manner to restore the elements of awe, mystery and wonder to religion, in a sort of inspissated gloom, and to inspire, not a cosy communal spirit of togetherness but the trembling adoration of the most high God. There was in this the paradox that Pugin's ideas reflected the pre-Puginian Romantic Gothic conception of the picturesque, the 'cloisters by moonlight' that Pugin most despised: the inspiration of Keats's misconception, in 'The Dream of St Agnes', that the moonlight could cast the coloured light of stained glass on Madeleine's fair breast, known to the unpoetic young as Madeleine's white chest. As Rosemary Hill, Pugin's latest biographer, has reminded us, quoting Payne Knight, the effectiveness of Pugin's type of Victorian neo-Gothic lay in the 'dim and discoloured light diffused through unequal varieties of space, divided but not separated'. Pugin thought that the spectator

> should see new views at each stage in his passage through a church. The progress from one space to the next was directed towards the central drama of the sanctuary, its power enforced on the mind of the laity by being partly hidden from their sight.[10]

Pugin was one of the few great English makers of a cultural revolution, one of half a dozen English converts to Roman Catholicism who have made a serious difference to English culture, with Newman and Gerard Manley Hopkins, and there is no underestimating his transforming influence upon the English imagination, which adopted Gothic as the style not only for churches and schools but for banks, sewage works and railway stations. Pugin's model for worship was that of the high middle ages; so that anything later, from St Peter's in Rome to the smallest Baroque candlestick, was the product of the corruption of the Church by Renaissance paganism. Although Dr Duffy has taught us all to see how the mediaeval laity did participate in the liturgy in a range of ways, indeed that at Low Mass in a side chapel or chantry chapel, they were all but next to the altar, Pugin's leading idea was the separation of a long or deep sanctuary from the nave by a pierced or open rood screen, through which the faithful looked through a golden gauze

---

10. R. Hill, '"To Stones a Moral Life": How Pugin Transformed the Gothic Revival', *Times Literary Supplement*, 18 September 1998, pp. 21-22.

of Gothic crocketing to a sacral area confined to priests and servers, and certainly to men. Pugin denounced the enemies of rood screens as screen vandals or 'ambonoclasts', and divided them into four categories, the Calvinist, the Pagan, the Revolutionary and the Modern, the last describing Newman's Oratorians.[11] Pugin's own genius for design, which furnished the new Houses of Parliament with Gothic desks, thrones, umbrella stands and inkwells, and still more famously, the Lord Chancellor's Gothic wallpaper, supplied the whole paraphernalia of the mediaeval sanctuary down to pyxes, paxes and orphreyed baudekins.

Pugin's argument was a compelling one. There is the most intimate connection between a religion and culture and its outward expression, and the Gothic was the only architectural and artistic style which Christendom had created for itself.

> The Catholic Church, she never knew—
>   Till Mr. Pugin taught her,
> That orthodoxy had to do
>   At all with bricks and mortar.[12]

Oddly enough, the Puginian mediaevalist vision of the Church had, through the Anglican Camden or Ecclesiological Society, founded in 1839 by John Mason Neale, its greatest influence on the Church of England, so much so as almost to conflate the terms Gothic and Anglican.[13] This was in spite of the fact that the Anglicans possessed a fine inheritance of classical and Baroque church buildings, like Wren's metropolitan churches and Thomas Archer's splendid church, later a cathedral, of St Philip in Birmingham. Yet the great majority of Victorian Anglican church buildings came to embody, however distantly, the Puginian vision. While Gothic in England did not quite become the national style, as it did in nineteenth-century Catholic Belgium,[14] it was Pugin who taught subsequent generations of ordinary Englishmen indelibly to associate religion with pointed arches,

---

11. See his *A Treatise on Chancel Screens and Rood Lofts* (London: Charles Dolman, 1851), pp. 76-99.

12. B. Ferrey, *Recollections of A. N. Welby Pugin and his Father, Augustus Pugin* (London: Edward Stanford, 1861), p. 115.

13. J.F. White, *The Cambridge Movement: The Ecclesiologists and the Gothic Revival* (Cambridge: Cambridge University Press, 1979).

14. See J. De Maeyer, 'The Neo-Gothic in Belgium: Architecture of a Catholic Society', in J. De Maeyer and L. Verpoest (eds), *Gothic Revival: Religion, Architecture and Style in Western Europe, 1815–1914* (Leuven: Universitaire Pers Leuven/ KADOK, 2000), pp. 19-34.

crocketed choir stalls and screens, brass eagle lecterns and candle sticks, encaustic tiles and neo-mediaeval stained glass.

A return to mediaeval Gothic was not, of course, quite the Roman way— there is only one important and unambiguously Catholic Gothic church in Rome itself, Santa Maria-sopra-Minerva. Nor was Pugin's conception of the sanctuary Roman. Pugin was explaining in St Barnabas's in Nottingham that no layman was permitted to set foot in the Holy of Holies behind the rood screen, when the future Cardinal Wiseman swept by with a lady on either hand.[15] Even in the nineteenth century, Rome had no feeling for Pugin's conception of a church, and though it did not prescribe or proscribe any single architectural or artistic style, canon law and the Congregation of Rites required

> that the congregation must take an active part in the Mass; that formidable barriers should be avoided; that chancels should be spacious and wide rather than deep, the intended implication being that the model for planning, furnishing and worship should be the unaltered practice of the genuine basilican churches in Rome.

This

> encouraged a set pattern for the disposition of the various parts of the church: a west end porch or narthex supporting a gallery for the choir and the organ [rather than the Anglican Camdenian ideal of a surpliced chancel choir]; a baptistery or mortuary chapel at the west end of the aisles; relatively wide aisles with widely spaced arcades to the nave; an east end arrangement of a shallow chancel, often containing a massive reredos; side altars dedicated to Our Lady and to the Sacred Heart or St Joseph; altars at the east end of the aisles; and spacious sacristies for priests and for altar boys. There would be communion rails, occasionally with a hanging rood but never with a screen.[16]

This produced the so-called '"Jesuit" planning' of 'Counter-Reformation structures in Gothic dress'.[17] The nineteenth-century Church had something already of the more modern obsession with visual participation in liturgy, and Rome's instinctive preference was for an architecture of equal light, so

15. W. Ward, *The Life and Times of Cardinal Wiseman* (2 vols.; London: Longmans, Green & Co., 1897), I, p. 359.

16. J. Sanders, 'Pugin & Pugin and the Diocese of Glasgow', in *Architectural Heritage: The Journal of the Architectural Heritage Society of Scotland*. VIII. *Caledonia Gothica: Pugin and the Gothic Revival in Scotland* (Edinburgh: Edinburgh University Press, 1997), pp. 95-96.

17. B. Little, *Catholic Churches since 1623* (London: Robert Hale 1966), p. 130.

that Roman rubrics pointed less to Gothic than to classical or Baroque.

It says much for Pugin's influence that in spite of this, the great majority of Victorian Catholic churches were Gothic ones. This was in part because the Roman arrangement, of a nave hall church in which almost everyone could fully see the Mass, with a west gallery choir and organ, and an open view of the High Altar and no screen, could be translated into a Gothic without gloom, as the two younger Pugin sons, Edward Welby and Peter Paul, demonstrated in the churches they designed. This can also be seen in the third English Oratory church, in Oxford, dedicated to St Aloysius, originally contracted by the Jesuits on a site provided by the convert third Marquess of Bute, said to be the richest man in Britain and one of the greatest benefactors of the Church in these islands.[18] Bute translated the 3,000 pages of the Roman Breviary into English and maintained the whole Roman ritual in a tin cathedral in Oban. St Aloysius, Oxford, designed by Joseph Aloysius Hansom (who was the architect of the Duke of Norfolk's great church, later a cathedral, originally dedicated to St Philip Neri at Arundel), has a west gallery for choir and organ with an unscreened and untrammelled view of a shallow chancel, 'giving a Gothic building a wholly un-Gothic spatial character',[19] the serried ranks of saints on the sanctuary wall forming an imposing reredos behind the altar. The saints must have been more imposing still before they were all painted in battleship grey.[20]

As a Roman Catholic, Newman, however, looked not to the middle ages but to the sixteenth-century Oratory, a confessedly modern institute of priests, not a mediaeval one, the proud possessor of numerous Baroque churches, not least the great Chiesa Nuova in Rome, S. Maria in Vallicella, rebuilt by the Oratorian founder, the 'Apostle of Rome', St Philip Neri,[21] from 1575, with its decorations by Pietro da Cortona, and its noble adjoining house, the work of one of the greatest of Baroque architects, Francesco Borromini.[22] As an Anglican, however, Newman had thought in Gothic, and

18. See R. Hannah, ' "Alive to Kindness": The Early Life and Achievement of John Patrick Crichton-Stuart, Third Marquess of Bute, 1847–1881' (PhD thesis, University of Durham, 2000).

19. J. Sherwood and N. Pevsner, *The Buildings of England: Oxfordshire* (Harmondsworth: Penguin Books, 1974), p. 63.

20. J. Bertram, *St Aloysius' Parish Oxford The Third English Oratory: A Brief History and Guide, 1793–1993* (Oxford: Oxford University Press, 1993).

21. M. Trevor, *Apostle of Rome: A Life of Philip Neri 1515–1595* (London: Macmillan, 1956).

22. R. Toman (ed.), *Baroque: Architecture. Sculpture. Painting* (Cologne: Könemann, 1998), p. 27.

indeed it had been 'near the center of his programme for the reformation of Anglicanism during the years before 1839'.[23] He raised the money for the new Oxford Church of St Clement's in the 1820s, and in the 1830s he built a simple Gothic church, dedicated to SS. Mary and Nicholas, for his poor parishioners at Littlemore, a church designed by Henry Underwood and conceived as a typical English village church. Indeed Pugin may have had a hand in the decoration. Its most moving feature is its white marble memorial to Newman's mother. Newman never joined the Camden Society, but he was, in 1839, with his ecclesiologically minded curate John Rouse Bloxam, a founding member of the Oxford Society for Promoting the Study of Gothic Architecture.[24]

Even as an Anglican, however, Newman's first architectural love was for his college chapel of Trinity, where he received his first communion, amid its splendid wooden classical furnishings. Even in the presence of Milan Cathedral, he declared that 'however my reason may go with Gothic, my heart has ever gone with Grecian. I loved Trinity Chapel at Oxford more than any other building.'[25] He was at first stunned by Pugin's show-church of St Giles at Cheadle, financed by the munificent Earl of Shrewsbury: 'the most splendid building I ever saw… The Chapel of the Blessed Sacrament is, on entering, a blaze of light—and I could not help saying to myself "Porta Coeli".'[26] Yet the moment passed. Newman was no mediaevalist, and knew nothing of mediaeval theology. His doctrinal arguments as a High Anglican constituted an appeal, not to the Church of the middle ages but to the early Church of the Fathers, and his Oxford Tractarians, who published a Library of the Fathers and of the Anglo-Catholic divines, published no equivalent series on mediaeval theology. The chief Anglican support of the Gothic Revival, the Ecclesiological or Camden Society, was founded at Cambridge, not Oxford, and the leading enthusiasts for the mediaeval period, like the Leicestershire squire Ambrose Phillipps, later Phillipps de Lisle, the Romantic writer Kenelm Digby and Pugin himself, were converted to Roman Catholicism and confirmed in it, at least in part by their vision of the splendour of mediaeval civilization, without benefit of the Oxford Movement or its theology. The architectural interest led into an interest in

23. Patrick, 'Newman, Pugin, and Gothic', pp. 206-207.
24. Patrick, 'Newman, Pugin, and Gothic', p. 190.
25. Newman to Henry Wilberforce, 24 September 1846, in C.S. Dessain (ed.), *The Letters and Diaries of John Henry Newman* (henceforth cited *L&D*) (London: Nelson 1961), XI, p. 252.
26. Newman to Elizabeth Bowden, 21 July 1846, *L&D*, XI, p. 210.

mediaeval ritual, but Newman himself had no great interest in ritual except musically, in his editions and translations of the Latin breviary hymns. There was, of course, a mediaeval interest among the Tractarians, as shown in the Tractarian *Lives of the Saints*, in Richard Hurrell Froude's work on Thomas à Becket, published in his *Remains*, and John William Bowden's *The Life and Pontificate of Gregory the Seventh*.[27] But for all 'the last enchantments of the middle age' in Gothic Oxford, Newman was of all the Oxford converts one of the least influenced by mediaeval Romanticism, and this his church building was to show.

This tension became apparent even by 1848, when Pugin had a row with Mrs Elizabeth Bowden, who was the widow of Newman's closest friend in his undergraduate days, John William Bowden, and who was the mother and aunt of three future Oratorians. The cause was Mrs Bowden's refusal to allow a rood screen in the Gothic Church of St Thomas of Canterbury which Pugin designed for her in Fulham. It was of this building that Newman remarked of Pugin:

> his altars are so small that you can't have a Pontifical High Mass at them, his tabernacles so low that you can scarce have exposition, his East windows so large that every thing else is hidden in the glare, and his skreens so heavy that you might as well have the function in [the] Sacristy, for the seeing it by the Congregation.[28]

Equally unenthusiastic was Newman's disciple Fr Frederick (in religion Wilfrid) Faber, the first superior of the Brompton Oratory, who had a grand confrontation with Pugin and Ambrose Phillipps in 1848 over the Oratorians' lack of a rood screen. According to Faber, Pugin said to him 'I never saw such a man as you are; it's beastly, it's positively beastly'. '*Pugin*', noted Faber, then '*receives a crack on his back from Father Wilfrid.*' Phillipps declared that 'we have no right to see the Blessed Sacrament', at which Faber asked him, 'what do monstrance and Exposition mean?' Phillipps thought that the Oratorians were 'copying a wretched people (Italians) who are now throwing off the faith, and persecuting the Church'. Faber, challenged on what he would do with rood screens, roundly replied that he'd 'Burn 'em all'. More pacifically, he continued, 'Live and let live: I will let you alone behind your screen: you let us alone without one'. 'The laity must be separated from the Sanctuary', declared Phillipps, to which Faber retorted that 'tailors in copes and black whiskers occupy the stalls at St Chad's' [in

27. (2 vols.; London: J.G.F. and J. Rivington, 1840).
28. Newman to Maria Rosina Giberne, 6 June 1848, *L&D*, XII, p. 215.

Birmingham]. The conversation climaxed with Phillipps's proclamation to Faber that God would 'curse and destroy your order', and Pugin remarked that he had 'always thought I [himself] was the only moderate man in the world'. The combatants then made it up, Phillipps, who had become a Catholic on discovering that Mahomet and not the pope was Antichrist, launched into a three-quarters of an hour lecture on millennial prophecy, and they all went off together to dine in high Victorian style on veal and suet pudding.[29]

This and the subsequent row in the periodical *The Rambler* over the desirability of Gothic[30] may seem trivial, but it was of some significance. The Oratorians constituted the primary obstacle to the total re-creation of the English Catholic Church in Pugin's Gothic style. Even the high Roman ultramontane Henry Edward Manning built a Gothic church for his Oblates of St Charles Borromeo, St Mary of the Angels, and was to contemplate the creation of a Gothic cathedral for London, and for long Manning made do with a Gothic pro-cathedral, George Goldie's Our Lady of Victories in Kensington.[31] 'Despite Manning's advocacy of the Roman styles mid-Victorian Catholic churches in the classical tradition are extremely rare',[32] which shows how little even the most fervent ultramontanes tried to counter the incoming Gothic tide. Elsewhere, ultramontanism might be not Baroque but eccentrically eclectic, a mingling of all the styles, as the monstrous basilica of Notre Dame de Fourvière in Lyon shows.[33]

Newman's own architectural principles were stylistically eclectic or pluralist and were summed up in a letter to Ambrose Phillipps:

> Mr Pugin is a man of genius… His zeal, his minute diligence, his resources, his invention, his imagination, his sagacity in research, are all of the highest order… But he has the great fault of a man of genius, as well as the merit. He is intolerant, and, if I might use a stronger word, a bigot… The Canons of Gothic architecture are to him points of faith, and everyone is a heretic who would venture to question them.

29. R. Chapman, *Father Faber* (London: Burns & Oates, 1961), pp. 183-85.

30. See J.L. Altholz, *The Liberal Catholic Movement in England: The 'Rambler' and its Contributors, 1848–1864* (London: Burns & Oates, 1960), pp. 14-18.

31. See, on Goldie, A. Felstead, J. Franklin and L. Pinfield, *Directory of British Architects, 1834–1900* (London: Mansell, 1993), p. 357.

32. Little, *Catholic Churches*, p. 140.

33. See N. Davenport, 'Fortress Catholicism: The Art of Ultramontanism at Notre Dame de Fourvière', in L. Woodhead (ed.), *Reinventing Christianity: Nineteenth-Century Contexts* (Aldershot: Ashgate, 2001), pp. 37-66.

Yet the classical and Baroque were the architecture of half the Catholic world, including Rome, even if one excludes 'the Greek and Oriental bodies'. Moreover, there had been no '*uninterrupted tradition* of Gothic architecture from the time it was introduced till the present day... Mr Pugin is notoriously engaged in a revival...' Pugin's conception of revival contradicted Newman's own idea of doctrinal development, in which there had to be both a continuity and permanence in what was essential, while the Church, wrote Newman, was

> ever modifying, adapting, varying her discipline and ritual, according to the times. In these respects the Middle age was not what the First Centuries were, nor is the Age Present the Middle age. In order that any style of Architecture should exactly suit the living ritual of the 19th century, it should be the living architecture of the 19th century—it should never have died—else, while the ritual has changed, the architecture has not kept pace with it... Gothic is now like an old dress, which fitted a man well twenty years back but must be altered to fit him now. It was once the perfect expression of the Church's ritual...it is not the perfect expression now. *It must be altered in detail* to become that expression. That is, it must be treated with a freedom which Mr Pugin will not allow...for Oratorians, the birth of the 16th century, to assume the architecture simply and unconditionally of the 13th, would be as absurd as their putting on them the cowl of the Dominicans or adopting the tonsure of the Carthusians. We do not want a cloister or a chapter room but an Oratory. I, for one, believe that Gothic can be adapted, developed into the requisitions of an Oratory. Mr Pugin does not; he implied, in conversation with me at Rome, that he would as soon build a mechanic's [sic] institute as an Oratory. I begged him to see the Oratory of the Chiesa Nuova, he gave me no hope he would do so. Now is it wonderful that I prefer St Philip to Mr Pugin?

Newman went on to point out that he had never subscribed to the Camden Society or what he called the 'Rubric movement' in the Church of England or even to 'Pusey's movement for the London Churches': 'there seemed to me', he concluded, 'something excessive and unreal in it'.[34]

Newman wanted to create a sort of Mechanics' Institute in Birmingham, for working-class young men, an institution which Pugin considered simply Voltaireian, and there is a wonderful comic air about Newman's failing to persuade Pugin to visit the Chiesa Nuova—what one would give to have been a fly on the wall—but Newman's own principles are not perfectly clear. On the one hand, there is the implication of his letter to Ambrose Phillipps that the Oratory should be true to a sixteenth-century style; on

---

34. Newman to A. Lisle Phillipps, 15 June 1848, *L&D*, XII, pp. 220-22.

another, that it can employ any style, including Gothic, by adapting it to modern worship. It might seem that Newman is offering the most radical liberty to our modern architects and liturgical modernizers. I think, here, however, that his justification of change was a cautiously developmental one. It was in exactly this sense that he was opposed to Pugin, who like any revolutionary, was demanding that the Church must conform to the style and worship of a single past age: as the liturgical modernizers insist on rejecting the whole tradition of Catholic worship in favour of the real or imagined liturgies of the third or fourth centuries. Indeed Pugin was a revolutionary modern in his underlying principles, being among the first to proclaim what have become some of the central arguments of the modern movement in architecture, that every part of the building should be functional, and be morally honest and in accordance with '*convenience, construction, or propriety*',[35] so that decoration, if any, should be honestly subordinate to structure and illustrate it.[36] This doubtful principle may have been 'no more than the Vitruvian conventions of the drawing school'[37], but it led straight on to the Bauhaus and Le Corbusier, who took one step further in rejecting decoration altogether. In the same way, Pugin in his demand for the destruction of anything classical or Baroque, as departing from his 'true principles', was very like the modern architect or liturgist who in the name of one principle demands that everything old be swept away.

Not so the Oratorians. Pugin therefore wrote that 'The Oxford men with some few exceptions have turned out the most disappointing people in the world. They were three times as Catholic in their ideas before they were reconciled to the Church.'[38] Newman's very choice of an Oratory was both unmonastic and unmediaeval. In his last years, Pugin wrote to urge a reconciliation between Rome and the Church of England, now being rebuilt by properly Gothic High Anglicans. Newman himself feared that Pugin's ideas concealed a sort of nationalist heresy, and said so in a Latin letter of 10

---

35. A.W.N. Pugin, *The True Principles of Pointed or Christian Architecture* (London: John Weale, 1841), p. 1. See M. Bright, 'A Reconsideration of A.W.N. Pugin's Architectural Theories', *Victorian Studies* 22 (1979), pp. 151-72.

36. D. Watkin, *Morality and Architecture: The Development of a Theme in Architectural History and Theory from the Gothic Revival to the Modern Movement* (Oxford: Clarendon Press, 1977).

37. R. Hill, 'Reformation to Millennium: Pugin's *Contrasts* in the History of English Thought', *Journal: Society of Architectual Historians* 58 (1999), p. 40.

38. Cited M. Trappes-Lomax, *Pugin: A Mediaeval Victorian* (London: Sheed & Ward, 1932), p. 224.

November 1848 to the papal secretary Monsignor Palma, who was assassinated by a Garibaldian before he received it to pass on to the pope.[39] Newman now seemed to fear Gothic for what Pugin extolled as one of its characteristics, its Englishness. In *The Idea of a University*, Newman considered that Gothic

> is endowed with a profound and a commanding beauty, such as no other style possesses…and which probably the Church will not see surpassed till it attain to the Celestial City. No other architecture, now used for sacred purposes, seems to be the growth of an idea, whereas the Gothic style is as harmonious and as intellectual as it is graceful…but to English Catholics at least it would be a serious evil, if it came as the emblem and advocate of a past ceremonial or an extinct nationalism [for] an obsolete discipline may be a present heresy.[40]

Indeed the Oratory initially dared to dispense not just with Gothic, but with permanent church buildings. The original Oratories in Birmingham and London were, respectively, in a former gin distillery in Alcester Street, which was still lined with spirit vats when Newman saw it first, and the former Lowther Rooms near the Strand, an assembly room and then a whisky store. The latter inspired the infinite disgust of Pugin, who described it to his patron the Earl of Shrewsbury as

> a place for the vilest debauchery, masquerades, &c.—one night a MASQUED BALL, next BENEDICTUS. This appears to me perfectly monstrous, and I give the whole order up for ever. What a degradation for religion! Why, it is worse than the Socialists… I always said they wanted rooms, not churches, and now they have got them.[41]

Newman himself thought it better first to build a house for his priests and only then a church, partly because a church, unlike a house, would attract subscriptions. Both Newman and Faber commissioned temporary church buildings, the present London Oratory having been built after Fr Faber's death, as Faber's memorial, as the Birmingham Oratory was to be Newman's.

One hope for our inheritance lies in the scholarly appreciation of its achievement, and the Oratorian buildings constitute a rich subject for study of both the Catholic architectural profession and of the patrons who financed them, among the friends and converts of the Oratory who belonged to the

39. Newman to Monsignor G.B. Palma, 10 November 1848, *L&D*, XII, pp. 324-28.
40. J.H. Newman, *The Idea of a University Defined and Illustrated* (London: Longmans, Green, & Co., 1891), p. 82.
41. Ferrey, *Recollections*, pp. 127-28.

aristocracy and richer laity. The original Oratory at Brompton, which stood until 1880, externally resembled a brick warehouse; one historian of the order says, 'It was badly lit and worse ventilated…something put up on the cheap to comply with the laws of the Metropolitan Building Act'.[42] This can have hardly prepared the visitor for the interior, a riot of rich polychrome, with its sanctuary floor and choir stalls made of precious inlaid woods, the gift of the convert Duchess of Argyll. The duchess was not a snappy dresser, and is said to have been originally sent away by the verger with the words, 'Father Faber is engaged: go off to Dr Manning, he is good enough for the likes of you'.[43]

The first Brompton Oratory was designed by Joseph John Scoles,[44] whose churches again were mostly Gothic, including St George's in Edgbaston, though they included a classical Catholic chapel at St Winifride's in Wales. Scoles had been apprenticed to his kinsman Joseph Ireland, Bishop John Milner's architect, Milner himself being an early pioneer of the proto-Gothic revival in his new church in Winchester.[45] In his youth, Scoles toured the continent and Near East in the company of another popular young Catholic architect, Joseph Bonomi, drew the plan of the Norman Church of the Holy Sepulchre in Jerusalem, published a survey map of Nubia, and returned to London to design the interior of Gloucester Terrace, Regent's Park, for John Nash. He also designed a suspension bridge at Great Yarmouth which 'in 1845 gave way with fatal results'.[46] This eclectic formation was much commoner among architects than pure Puginianism, most of whom showed this perfect adaptability, the willingness to design in any style, which Pugin loathed, but it is significant that so many of Scoles's works were Gothic, showing again how deeply the Pugin bug had bitten Catholics. Scoles's best-known churches are the Immaculate Conception in Farm Street and St Francis Xavier's in Liverpool, both Gothic. St John's, Islington, is Norman, was funded by two pious ladies, the Misses Gallini, and satisfied everyone but Pugin, who attacked the building in the *Dublin Review*, as 'built on the

42. *The London Oratory* (London, 1963), p. 15.

43. *The London Oratory*, p. 19.

44. See Felstead, Franklin and Pinfield, *Directory*, p. 808.

45. See P.P. Bogan, 'Beloved Chapel: The Story of the "Old Chapel" of St. Peter's, Winchester' (Winchester: Culverlands Press, n.d.), which corrects the impression in K. Clark, *The Gothic Revival: An Essay in the History of Taste* (Harmondsworth: Penguin Books, 1962), pp. 87-89.

46. See *DNB*.

Figure 1. *The First Oratory at Brompton* (Published with the permission of the Fathers of the London Oratory).

all front principle of Dissenters'.[47] On the other hand, Scoles's surviving residence for the London Oratorians is a light and perfectly plain and pleasant building described by Pevsner as in 'stock brick and very restrained'.[48] It has nothing external that is ecclesiastical about it, and is, like the house of the Birmingham Oratory, crowned with a magnificent library. Of his truly Victorian family of four sons and eight daughters, two of Scoles's sons, Ignatius and Alexander, were trained as architects. One became a secular priest, the other a Jesuit, and are said thereafter to have 'practised [architecture] only in a clerical capacity':[49] by which I suppose is meant that Alexander at least financed the churches which he designed.[50]

When, in the 1870s, the Brompton Oratorians decided to replace Scoles's church, they arranged for a competition and brought in as an advisory assessor the greatest of late Victorian architects, Alfred Waterhouse,[51] who was not a Catholic but designed the vast Romanesque cathedral to science a few paces down the road from the Oratory, the Natural History Museum. It was notoriously Waterhouse/who thought a house/should be

> partly chateau,
> and partly gateau,
> but chiefly municipal slaughterhouse.[52]

At one point in the competition to build the London Oratory, 'there were almost as many plans as there were Fathers'.[53] Of the thirty competitors, disguised by Latin and Italian pseudonyms like *Ut puto*, *Laetatus sum* and *Con amore*, nine or ten were Catholics, the runner-up being Henry Clutton, the architect of Newman's house in Birmingham. The winner, Herbert Augustine Keate Gribble, was an assistant to another prolific

47. A.W.N. Pugin, *The Present State of Ecclesiastical Architecture in England... Republished from the Dublin Review* (London: Charles Dolman, 1843), p. 116.

48. N. Pevsner, *The Buildings of England: London Except the Cities of London and Westminster* (Harmondsworth: Penguin Books, 1974), p. 245.

49. H.M. Colvin, *A Biographical Dictionary of British Architects, 1600–1840* (New Haven: Yale University Press, 1995), pp. 854-55.

50. See Little, *Catholic Churches*, pp. 149-50; Felstead, Franklin and Pinfield, *Directory*, p. 808.

51. M. Girouard, *Alfred Waterhouse and the Natural History Museum* (London: Natural History Museum, 1999), p. 64.

52. C. Cunningham and P. Waterhouse, *Alfred Waterhouse, 1830–1905: Biography of a Practice* (Oxford: Clarendon Press, 1992), p. 199.

53. R. O'Donnell, 'The Architecture of the London Oratory Churches', in M. Napier and A. Laing (eds), *The London Oratory Centenary, 1884–1984* (London: Trefoil, 1984), p. 32.

Figure 2. *Herbert Gribble's decorative design for the interior of the Bromp-ton Oratory* (Published with the permission of the Fathers of the London Oratory).

Roman Catholic architect, Joseph Aloysius Hansom. Gribble himself was a convert received into the Church at the Oratory, and seems to have been the choice of Fr Stephen Keogh, who also brought to England the magnificent seventeenth-century Lady Altar with its wonderful front of coloured stone pietre dure, adorned with Dominican saints, St Pius V and St Rose of Lima, all rescued from an abandoned Dominican church in Brescia. Equally happy was the Oratory's acquisition of the great seventeenth-century Baroque statues of the Twelve Apostles, with St Paul replacing St Matthias, designed by Giuseppe Mazzuoli and discarded by Siena Cathedral in a nineteenth-century fit of Puginian Gothic purification. The ground plan of the new London building follows the standard fifteenth-century model of Leone Battista Alberti's S. Andrea in Mantua, which is most famously repeated in St Peter's, with a cross groundplan of sanctuary, nave and transepts, the nave leading to a central crossing dome raised upon a drum. Gribble made a significant concession to the northern lack of light by roofing the nave and sanctuary, not with a tunnel vault but with small iron-framed and glazed cupolas, thereby making use of a new material. Gribble also designed the iron church which stood in front of the house and was used while the new church was being built. It was later said 'to be doing duty as a Sailors' Institute at Alexandria'.[54]

Newman's former pupil the Duke of Norfolk gave £20,000 for the building. St Wilfrid's chapel, in memory of Faber, was the gift of Mrs Bowden, while the outer dome was funded by Mrs Daglish-Bellasis; the Bellasis brothers were also Oratorians. The Duke of Norfolk gave St Philip's Altar, and the Duchess of Argyll the organ. It has been said 'that a walk round the Oratory consoles the man who wishes to go to Italy but cannot afford it'.[55] Dr O'Donnell describes the completed work in all its glory, with 46 chandeliers and over a thousand candles, for the tercentenary of St Philip Neri's death in 1895. It was, until the opening of Westminster Cathedral, the most stunning Roman Catholic church in the metropolis, indeed the largest in England, and one which now in its modern liturgy maintains above every other, the splendour of Roman worship, so largely lost.

The Oratory's house in Birmingham, designed by Clutton, is again wholly unmonastic in its external appearance, apart from the suggestion of Romanesque in the cloister. Newman's own final liking seems to have been less even for Baroque than for the early basilicas he saw in Rome.

---

54. E. Kilburn, *A Walk Round the Church of the London Oratory* (London: Sands, 1980), p. 11.

55. *The London Oratory*, p. 24.

His first plan for a church was not Gothic but eclectic, an exercise in the 'compromise classicism' mingling elements of the 'Lombard style' or 'style Latin' which were Christian styles supposed to have followed the classical period but to have preceded Romanesque. The building, designed by the French architect Louis-Joseph Duc, was to be in masssive brick, with round arched windows and round arched arcades, with an open raftered roof like an early Christian basilica, and with a huge dome; it would have stretched along the Hagley Road instead of being, like the later church, at right angles to it, and punctuated the Edgbaston skyline.[56] The building was the victim of Newman's trial for libelling the notorious Protestant rapist and seducer Giacinto Achilli: having raised such huge sums for his legal expenses, Newman did not feel that he could go to the public again. Instead he settled for a big provisional rectangular barn-like building, of four plain brick walls with the ready-made and second-hand roof from a disused factory,[57] which was dedicated to the Immaculate Conception in 1853. The building was subsequently extended by John Hungerford Pollen, an Oxford convert who was from a gentry family, with a baronet brother who was also a convert. Pollen had been a curate of Dr Pusey's great church of St Saviour's, Leeds, and married the daughter of Manning's curate La Primaudaye. Pollen was to befriend Benjamin Woodward, the architect of the Oxford Union, and with Dante Gabriel Rossetti and other Pre-Raphaelites, painted the now all but obliterated frescoes in the Union's Old Library. Like Pugin, he designed stained glass, tapestry, carpets and furniture. Pollen also published some famous art catalogues as editor of the Department of Art and Industry at the Victoria and Albert, and with Walter Crane, founded the Arts and Crafts Exhibition Society. Of his ten children, two became Jesuits and one an Oratorian.

Newman launched Pollen upon his career in 1854, by making him Professor of Fine Art in the Catholic University in Dublin, wanting him to 'give the subject a Christian character and separate it from the sensuality which is often considered part of it, without running into the extravagancies of the Ultra-Puginians'.[58] Pollen also designed the enchanting little basilica chapel for the Catholic University in Dublin, partly funded with the surplus from the money raised to pay Newman's expenses for the Achilli trial. It is quite

56. R. O'Donnell, ' "Louis-Joseph Duc in Birmingham": A "Style Latin" Church for Cardinal Newman, 1851', *Gazette des Beaux Arts* (Paris) 97.6 (1981), pp. 37-44.

57. H. Tristram, *Cardinal Newman and the Church of the Birmingham Oratory* (Gloucester: British Publishing, 1980), p. 21.

58. Newman to C.J. La Primaudaye, 17 November 1854, *L&D*, XVI, p. 301.

the best church that Newman contracted, and is chiefly what earns him a place, in a very inaccurate essay by Hugh Maguire, in Jane Turner's magnificent *Dictionary of Art*.[59] The narrow entrance by way of a passage from St Stephen's Green is no adequate preparation for the richly decorated rectangular interior, lined with Irish marbles and painted canvas panels copied from Raphael's tapestries for the Sistine Chapel, these being divided by the figures of the Apostles copied from the Tre Fontane Church in Rome. A letter from Newman in Rome to Pollen sets out the dimensions of the design and gives the cost:

The expense, each Apostle 15 scudi—Each quadro, 60 scudi:

$$12 \times 15 \quad 180 \text{ scudi}$$
$$10 \times 60 \quad \underline{600 \text{ scudi}}$$
$$780 \text{ scudi}$$

? at 46 scudi to £10 Somewhat under £180[60]

Newman had difficulty getting Archbishop Cullen to bless the church, he despaired of matching its expenses with collections, and he ran up a massive debt in building it. It was to have cost £3,500. It cost £6,000, at a time when interest rates were high, and Newman feared that it might be seized for debt. In the end, the university trustees bought it from him. But the building gave him great satisfaction. 'Pollen has made the Church gorgeous', he wrote to Henry Wilberforce before its opening in 1856.[61] Newman was closely involved in its further decoration. There is a raised choir gallery adjoining the sanctuary in the semi-circular apse, painted by Pollen with the Virgin as Sedes Sapientiae and elements copied from the apse mosaic in the Roman church of San Clemente. Dublin has some magnificent neo-classsical Roman Catholic churches, but as the reproduction of an early Christian basilica, the University Church is a unique gift to Ireland.[62]

Newman's correspondence with Pollen shows the care he took with architectural detail. On his giving up the rectorship of the Catholic University in Dublin, he turned to the improvement of his church in Birmingham. Pollen designed an added aisle on the epistle side in 1858 and then a transept and an apsidal sanctuary in 1860, and the complete building was reopened in

59. J. Turner (ed.), *The Dictionary of Art* (34 vols.; London: Macmillan, 1996), XXIII, p. 30.

60. Newman to Pollen, 1 February 1856, *L&D*, XVII, p. 142.

61. Newman to Henry Wilberforce, 29 April 1856, *L&D*, XVII, p. 229.

62. See E. Kane, *John Henry Newman's Catholic University Church in Dublin* (Dublin: Irish Messenger Publications, n.d.).

1861. The wooden High Altar was raised on seven steps, and the plain design allowed for numerous altars, including a Sacred Heart altar, the Lady Altar, with its fine copy of the statue of Our Lady of Victories in Paris, and the altar of St Valentine with the relics of the saint brought by Newman from Rome, for a feast kept on Newman's birthday of 21 February. There was a raised platform for the boys from the Oratory school. To mark the half century of the Oratory in Birmingham to 1899, the congregation gave a new High Altar in green Connemara marble designed by Dunstan Powell on the model of that of the Charterhouse at Pavia with a tabernacle copied from one at St Peter's. The altar was re-erected in the modern church, with the baldacchino or canopy which is a memorial to the Pollens. Various other relics of the old church were to pass into the new one, including the Altar of the Sacred Heart. Father Tristram described the old building as 'dingy, shabby and dowdy, although quaint and attractive in many ways, and entirely devotional'.[63] Newman left the provision of a better building to his successors.

The foundation stone of the new Oratory church, designed by E. Doran Webb, was laid by the Archbishop of Birmingham in 1903, the new nave was opened in 1906 and the completed church in 1909. In spite of what to my eye is its over-heavy barrel vault, it is a lovely building, especially for anyone with a Mediterranean love of fine marble, with its 12 pillars of Breccian marble, from the Ligurian mountains, said to be the tallest such columns in England. The apse is lined with red African onyx and bands of Sienna marble, with panels of green Mexican onyx, 'veined and translucent'. The altar rails came from the Roman Church of S. Andrea della Valle, as did the greater part of the Lady Altar, though its columns of rare Siberian onyx were originally intended for Westminster Cathedral. The altar incorporates alabaster with various marbles, some named like fine wines, Sicilian, Porta Santa, jasper, peach-bloom, and Bianc' Nero. Westlake designed the mosaics made up at Murano, depicting the scenes from the life of the Virgin in the apse, and semi-domes above the altars. There is a special attractiveness about the shrine of St Philip Neri, copied from his shrine in the Chiesa Nuova, with its floor and walls of various precious marbles, and its relics of St Philip, which include one of his pairs of spectacles cases. The church is a harmonious unity, in spite of the splendour of its various parts, with its great open nave, with side chapels and dome, a reminder in the midlands of southern climes, as well as a memorial to Newman himself.

The Puritan imagination may shudder at such an orgy of marble, but we need these buildings, whose very costliness reminds us that there is nothing

---

63. Tristram, *Newman and the Church of the Birmingham Oratory*, p. 23.

too fine and glorious for worship. 'Ubi est thesaurus eius, ibi est cor tuum', 'Where is thy treasure, there is thy heart'. We now build vast shrines to consumerism, which show that our hearts are there. But what happens at the altar is, according to Catholic tradition, the noblest, the deepest of dramas, of which no theatre can be worthy. Sacheverell Sitwell called one Baroque church 'the dance-floor of God'.[64] Perhaps they are better described as throne rooms of the King of Kings. The proper performance of divine worship in inspiring surroundings has now become almost distinctive to the character of the Oratory, and its rich and noble settings remind us of the meaning of the Mass, as Newman describes it in *Loss and Gain*.

> It is not a mere form of words,—it is a great action, the greatest action that can be on earth. It is, not the invocation merely, but, if I dare use the word, the evocation of the Eternal. He becomes present on the altar in flesh and blood, before whom angels bow and devils tremble. This is that awful event which is the scope, and is the interpretation, of every part of the solemnity. Words are necessary, but as means, not as ends; they are not mere addresses to the throne of grace, they are instruments of what is far higher, of con-secration, of sacrifice. They hurry on as if impatient to fulfil their mission. Quickly they go, the whole is quick; for they are all parts of one integral action. Quickly they go; for they are awful words of sacrifice, they are a work too great to delay upon; as when it was said in the beginning: 'What thou doest, do quickly.' Quickly they pass; for the Lord Jesus goes with them, as He passed along the lake in the days of His flesh, quickly calling first one and then another. Quickly they pass; because as the lightning which shineth from one part of heaven unto the other, so is the coming of the Son of Man. Quickly they pass; for they are as the words of Moses, when the Lord came down in the cloud...[65]

Here, then, is the end and aim of Catholic worship, to show in ritual that this is the evocation of the Eternal, before whom angels bow and devils tremble, in both consecration and sacrifice, like the lightning on the day of judgment and God's presence in the cloud.

Somehow, then, public devotion has to express and communicate these things. And here Pugin and the Oratorians were at one: the belief that the Mass is nothing less than the descent of the most high God upon the altar to his worshippers. Any question of artistic or architectural form is secondary to that. But Pugin and Newman were both right to argue that the form must

---

64. Quoting an unnamed source on the pilgrimage church at Wies. S. Sitwell, *Monks, Nuns and Monasteries* (London: Weidenfeld & Nicolson, 1965), p. 67.

65. *Loss and Gain: The Story of a Convert* (London: Longmans, Green, & Co., 1891 [1848]), pp. 327-28.

try to be worthy of the action it sets forth. From this it follows, not that the setting for devotion must be in the best of taste, for good taste may be mere self-restraint, but that it matters, as it sanctifies the senses and rises or falls to the mystery of the altar, as it shows or fails to show the Eternal. Much modern liturgy seems to be concerned with anything but the divine mystery, and to be centred on humanity and not on God, in having no higher or nobler aim than to confirm a community in a sense of itself. But liturgy is not primarily about community, but transcendence, enchantment, and only then the community which flows from these, as God brings heaven to earth and lifts earth to heaven. Amid the deformation of the shrines of the Victorian era by the kind of modern liturgy in which the community worships itself, the tradition of Pugin and Newman and the English Oratory now has a unique vocation, to declare the glory of God in worship. Professor McLeod, in his paper in this volume, offers a defence of one dimension of Victorian religion. Here is another. We live in a lean and barren time for the faith. May the Victorian witness sustain us with a hope for better days.

Part III

EDUCATION

THE CULTURAL ASPIRATIONS OF THE WELSH CLERGY

Frances Knight

In April 1853, some six months before the publication of what was to become his enduringly popular dissection of 'Church Parties',[1] W.J. Conybeare turned his satirical pen to 'The Church of England in the Mountains'.[2] It was an investigation of how the Church fared in Wales, and to a lesser extent, in Cumberland. Like the 'Church Parties' article, the piece was couched in the form of a review article, although he referred only minimally to the books that he supposed to be reviewing.[3] In order, one assumes, to draw at least some of the sting from Welsh churchmen, Conybeare, who was the son of the Dean of Llandaff, judiciously pointed out that what he

1.   Conybeare's 'Church Parties' article has recently been given a new lease of life in an excellent edition for the Church of England Record Society. A. Burns (ed.), 'W.J. Conybeare: "Church Parties"', in S. Taylor (ed.) *From Cranmer to Davidson: A Church of England Miscellany* (Church of England Record Society, 7; Woodbridge: Boydell, 1999), pp. 215-385.

2.   W.J. Conybeare, 'The Church of England in the Mountains', *Edinburgh Review* 97 (1853), pp. 342-79.

3.   One of them was the immensely controversial *Reports of the Commissioners on Education in Wales* (London: William Clowes & Sons, 1847), the so-called 'treason of the Blue Books', which was widely attacked both then and since as a calumny on the people of Wales. See I.G. Jones, '1848 and 1868: "*Brad y Llyfrau Gleison*" and Welsh Politics', in I.G. Jones (ed.), *Mid-Victorian Wales: The Observers and the Observed* (Cardiff: University of Wales Press, 1992), pp. 103-65. Also E.T. Davies, *A New History of Wales: Religion and Society in the Nineteenth Century* (Landybie: Christopher Davies, 1981), pp. 13-21; K.O. Morgan, *Modern Wales: Politics, Places and People* (Cardiff: University of Wales Press, 1995), p. 148. Conybeare took the report at face value as an accurate account of Welsh educational standards and morality. The other books under review were *Life of R. Walker, Perpetual Curate of Seathwaite* by the Rev. R. Parkinson (London, 1843); *Wales: The Language, Social Conditions, Moral Character and Religious Opinions of the People, Considered in their Relation to Education* by Sir Thomas Phillips (London, 1849); and *Report of the Society for Providing Additional Clergymen in the Diocese of Llandaff* (London, 1852).

was describing was the Welsh Church of the previous generation, rather than its current circumstances, about which he was slightly more positive. His article evoked the early nineteenth-century world in which the clergy were ordained as literates on the basis of a grammar school only education. He characterized them as the sons of hill farmers, who spoke broken English, caroused in taverns, married domestic servants and if they had to visit a big house, only felt at home in the kitchen. As Conybeare accurately noted, the financial rewards of the Welsh Church were so limited that it could not recruit from the same social classes that were ordained in England. This was the heart of the matter. 'No parent whose means enable him to give his son a liberal education, will educate him for a profession in which his probable income would be (at the best) under 200*l*. a year.'[4] It followed that the Welsh clergy were mainly drawn from backgrounds in farming and trade.

Conybeare was voicing the English middle-class perspective on the presumed consequences of ordaining such men. He compared the veneer of civility under all circumstances maintained by those of gentle breeding with the uncouth behaviour of the peasant clergy, who could fight like cats in a sack.

> If one gentleman has outstripped another in the chase of some object of ambition, the unsuccessful candidate (whatever may be his secret feelings) must meet his rival with outward courtesy. But when two Welsh curates have met, after one has obtained a benefice which the other sought, we have known instances of the vanquished assailing the victor with the most scurrilous vituperation.[5]

Worse still, he believed that ill-educated, lower-class clerics were prone to 'scandalous and degrading vice' (of a type unspecified). Indeed, how could such men aspire to a higher form of life, when they were 'surrounded by friends and relatives whose highest enjoyments are found in the conviviality of the village alehouse. They are cut off, by want of cultivation and opportunity, from the pursuits of literature and art.'[6] Conybeare would have laughed at the notion that these men had 'cultural aspirations', and he appears to have been ignorant of the major contribution that Welsh clerics were making to the bardic tradition, the Welsh literary renaissance and the eisteddfod movement. Fuelled by the controversy sparked by the

---

4. Conybeare, 'Church of England in the Mountains', p. 347.
5. Conybeare, 'Church of England in the Mountains', p. 354.
6. Conybeare, 'Church of England in the Mountains', p. 355.

1847 Education Commission report, his article represents a particular moment in the hostile stereotyping of the Welsh clergy. Conybeare would return to them briefly at the end of his 'Church Parties' article, where he declined even to attempt to categorize the churchmanship of the '1000 peasant clergy in the mountain districts, who must be classed apart'.[7]

Yet while Conybeare saw the Welsh clergy as so far removed from the mainstream of ecclesiastical life as not even to be touched by the raging debates of the day, others regarded the clergy who served the Welsh Church as ineffectual English monoglots, addicted to English forms of social exclusiveness. These views were expressed by pressure groups such as the Association of Welsh Clergy in the West Riding of Yorkshire, who as early as 1835 had petitioned Peel's government about the evil effects of English appointments on the Welsh Church. They also came from Sir Benjamin and Lady Augusta Hall (Lord and Lady Llanover after 1859) who made a particular point of canvassing politicians and senior ecclesiastics whenever an important vacancy arose.[8] The clergy were also accused, even by some of their number, of an obsessive—and, it was implied, English—form of clericalism which restricted the talents of the laity. Critics such as H.T. Edwards, the future Dean of Bangor, cast envious glances at the way in which Nonconformity avoided such pitfalls, with its well-established *blaenoriaid* (leaders), networks of elders and deacons.[9] Another vocal clerical critic was the noted classical scholar and Archdeacon of Cardigan, John Williams. Williams was particularly hostile to St David's College, Lampeter, reviling it as an Anglophone institution with an ingratiating, Anglophile principal (Llewellin Lewellin)—he felt both were doing immense damage to the Church.[10] Williams went so far as to state that the only decent Anglican preachers in Wales were either ex-Dissenting ministers or the very old, educated at local grammar schools in the years before the opening of St David's College. But for the vibrancy of Nonconformity, he claimed, Wales would be a nation of heathen.[11] The criticisms of Edwards and Williams are particularly telling because they

7.   'Church Parties', p. 338 (original edition); p. 357 (Burns edition).

8.   E.T. Davies, *Religion in the Industrial Revolution in South Wales* (Cardiff: University of Wales Press, 1965), p. 116.

9.   Davies, *A New History of Wales*, pp. 41-42.

10.   Part of Williams's hostility may be attributed to the fact that he had failed to secure the principalship of the college, losing out to Llewellin Lewellin.

11.   D.T.W. Price, *A History of St David's University College, Lampeter*. I. *From the Beginnings to 1898* (Cardiff: University of Wales Press, 1977), p. 96.

were directed not at the importation of monoglot Englishmen, but at the notion that the Church was actually corrupting young Welshmen by robbing them of their own culture and making them think and behave in alien English ways. Such arguments had parallels elsewhere in the nationalist debate that was then rising. By the late nineteenth century, the Church, as a supposedly English, elitist institution, had, as P.M.H. Bell put it, 'its fixed place in the demonology of Welsh nationalism'.[12]

Hostile stereotyping can develop its own momentum, so what is the truth about the Welsh clergy? This paper explores their cultural aspirations particularly as they were influenced by their varied educational experiences. An attempt will be made to indicate what, besides greater poverty, made their experience different from that of their English brethren. One of the most bizarre, but also one of the most telling, incidents in modern Welsh ecclesiastical history occurred in 1870. Gladstone nominated Joshua Hughes as Bishop of St Asaph, and he was trumpeted as the first Welsh-speaking Welshman (as opposed to Welsh learner) to occupy a bishopric since the time of Queen Anne. Then it emerged that Gladstone had been misled about Hughes's academic attainments. Hughes had not graduated as a BA in 1842 from Queens' College, Cambridge, as his entry in *Crockford's* indicated; indeed he was exposed as never having been at Cambridge. Hughes's higher education, it emerged, had been received at St David's College, Lampeter. Gladstone was shocked by his mistake, because whatever could be said in favour of Lampeter, it was not seen as providing suitable nurturing for a future bishop. Hughes claimed that he knew nothing of his misleading *Crockford's* entry, but it seems odd that anyone's entry should contain such a significant error for so many years without him noticing. Was it a mistake, or had Hughes sought to reinvent his past? The temptation must have been considerable for someone anxious for advancement. On the one hand stood Cambridge, effortless in its superiority; a place where even Welsh grammar school boys could be transformed into national leaders. On the other side stood Lampeter, periodically dogged with difficulty, a place that only two decades before had been attacked by the local archdeacon as 'a blight and curse upon the spiritual and intellectual energies of the Principality...the slaughter-house of the rising talent of my country'.[13]

The incident perfectly illustrates one of the major fault lines within

---

12. P.M.H. Bell, *Disestablishment in Ireland and Wales* (London: SPCK, 1969), p. 239.

13. Price, *History of St David's University College*, I, p. 81.

Welsh clerical culture; that between those who were Oxbridge educated and those who had been to Lampeter. (There was also a third category of seemingly even less fortunate clerics—those who were non-graduates and were ordained just as literates.) In so far as they were the product of three different educational processes, the nineteenth-century Welsh clergy were perhaps a less cohesive body than their English counterparts. Although the English clergy were by no means monochrome in their educational or social backgrounds, they were the products of different educational processes to a far lesser extent. Alan Haig has shown that in the province of Canterbury in 1865 (excluding the four Welsh dioceses) 78% of ordinands had been educated at Oxbridge and only 3% were literates; the remaining 19% had been educated at a variety of newer institutions. In the province of York, 46% had been to Oxbridge and 4% were literates, with the remaining 49% educated elsewhere. In Wales, however, the picture was very different: 25% were Oxbridge-educated, 20% were ordained as literates and 55% had been educated elsewhere—the majority would have been at Lampeter.[14] In the 1860s, therefore, the newly ordained Welsh clergy came from three distinctively different educational backgrounds. This was not a new trend, and it was one which was to continue for many years.

How did their educational background affect their cultural aspirations? To answer this question I will explore something of what was imparted to the three different groups through their educational experiences, in so far as this can be reconstructed. The first category, that of the literates, changed its meaning during the course of the nineteenth century. Initially, it referred to those who were ordained on the basis of a school-only education; later on it referred to those who were non-graduates, but had had the benefit of some period of residence at a college such as St Bees or Queen's College, Birmingham. In Wales, the term 'literate' was seldom used for those who had studied at Lampeter, some of whom were graduates, and others licentiates. Lampeter was seen as superior to the English theological colleges.

The proportion of literates among the total numbers seeking ordination in Wales was always significant, but it fluctuated strongly during the eighteenth and nineteenth centuries. In the huge diocese of St David's, the proportion of literates seeking ordination in the first half of the eighteenth century had been about two-thirds of the total. The figure shot up between 1750 and 1799, when of those admitted to deacon's orders in the diocese,

14. A. Haig, *The Victorian Clergy* (London: Croom Helm, 1984), p. 118.

680 were literates and only 45 were graduates, with an additional 37 who had spent some time at Oxford or Cambridge but had not taken a degree, usually as a result of having run out of funds.[15] The majority of the literates had been educated at the endowed grammar schools, some of which were extremely good in the late eighteenth and early nineteenth centuries. When Samuel Horsley became Bishop of St David's in 1788, he realized that the most effective way of improving clerical education was to try to bring all the grammar schools up to the standard of the best. He sent a circular letter to schoolmasters, urging them to take particular care with the admission of candidates to their divinity classes.

> Admit none as students of divinity of bad moral character, that have been engaged in any low or menial occupation, that have any natural imperfections in the organs of speech, or labour under any remarkable deformity of person. In all which cases you will refer to me if you are under any doubt yourselves. Another caution I would earnestly recommend is to admit no students in divinity who have not made such a proficiency in school learning as to be able to construe the Greek Testament and the common Latin authors with tolerable proficiency.[16]

Horsley also specified the books on which he would examine the ordination candidates, standard works of High Church divinity, together with some classical authors. The best of the grammar school masters seem to have risen to the challenge, providing an education apparently worthy of an English public school. At Cardigan Grammar School in the 1820s, the curriculum included Hebrew, Greek, Latin, French, English and Welsh, and the boys acted Greek plays.[17] The school was one of several licensed by Bishop Burgess for the training of ordination candidates. Grammar school preparation for the ministry was, as Owain Jones has pointed out, a thoroughly English scheme of education imposed on men whose background was thoroughly Welsh. This weakens the arguments of those like Archdeacon Williams, who were to claim that it was the Welsh grammar schools that had been the authentic repositories of Welsh clerical education.

It happened that Archdeacon Williams's father had been headmaster of Ystradmeurig, one of best known of the endowed grammar schools offer-

15. O.W. Jones, 'The Mountain Clergyman: His Education and Training', in O.W. Jones and David Walker (eds.), *Links with the Past: Swansea and Brecon Historical Essays* (Llandybie: Christopher Davies, 1974), p. 167.

16. Jones, 'Mountain Clergyman', p. 174.

17. D.G. Osborne-Jones, *Edward Richard of Ystradmeurig* (Carmarthen: W. Spurrell & Son, 1934), p. 95.

ing preparation for the Church. The school had been originally founded in 1734 by a remarkable High Church layman, Edward Richard, an auto-didact of huge erudition who devoted all his time and money to educating the boys in this remote Cardiganshire valley. He taught them a six-or-seven-year course in classics, divinity and mathematics, and intended that his boys should enter the Church.[18] In fact, some became the leading lights of Calvinistic Methodism, which caused distress to this schoolmaster who strongly disapproved of evangelicalism. Equipped with a classical educa-tion and fluency in both English and Welsh, the Ystradmeurig boys were able to make their mark on Welsh culture in decisive ways. Early students included Evan Evans, one of the eighteenth century's most renowned Celticists, and a whole host of poets, scholars and preachers.[19] The school's second headmaster, John Williams senior, known locally as *Yr Hen Syr* ('the old sir') ruled the school from 1777 to 1818, and improved the level of academic achievement still further, so that in the years before the open-ing of Lampeter in 1827, Ystradmeurig offered the nearest thing to a university education to be had in Wales. Williams *Yr Hen Syr* was himself a former pupil of Ystradmeurig, and had never been to university, but this appears to have been no disadvantage to him. During his headmastership the school produced another distinguished crop of clergy, physicians, preachers, headmasters, classicists and bards,[20] as well as, one assumes, some extremely well-educated farmers. Bishop Burgess licensed the school for the preparation of clergy, and like his predecessors at St David's he was very complimentary about the performance in the ordination exam of Ystradmeurig men.

Impressed though he was with the local grammar schools, Bishop Bur-gess had other ambitions for the training of clergy in his diocese. The open-ing of the college at Lampeter on St David's Day 1827 proved a decisive blow to the diocesan grammar schools, and particularly to Ystradmeurig, which went into a rapid decline. The school began to recover partially only in the 1860s, when it re-established itself as a feeder school for Jesus College, Oxford, specializing in preparation for classical scholarships.[21] After the opening of St David's College, Lampeter, the bishops of St

18. Osborne-Jones, *Edward Richard*, p. 45.

19. Osborne-Jones, *Edward Richard*, p. 34 lists the most distinguished old boys of Richard's day.

20. Osborne-Jones, *Edward Richard*, pp. 61-62, lists the most distinguished old boys of Williams's time.

21. Osborne-Jones, *Edward Richard*, p. 110.

David's were generally less willing to accept candidates who had come straight from school. Compared with the small schoolroom in a corner of the churchyard in remote Ystradmeurig, the facilities at Lampeter were vastly superior, with its larger staff and accommodation neatly arranged in a spacious Oxbridge-style quadrangle. It was no longer necessary for the students to lodge in public houses, where, as Bishop Jenkinson put it, they might 'witness scenes...and acquire habits utterly incompatible with the profession for which they were destined'.[22] Instead, they could be safely locked into the quadrangle every night, and supervised to a much greater extent. (The gates continued to be locked until 1955, and public houses remained out of bounds until 1959.)[23]

In the impoverished diocese of Llandaff, the ordination of men straight from licensed grammar school continued well into the nineteenth century, although Bishop Ollivant withdrew his licence from Cowbridge Grammar School in 1850, in the hope of encouraging more men to go to Lampeter. David Howell, a future Dean of St David's, was one such literate, ordained at Llandaff in 1855 straight from Abergavenny Grammar School. The circumstances of his education and early life provide a revealing insight not only into the lengths to which some went in order to secure ordination, but also the extent to which such men were steeped in Welsh culture. Howell had been born in the vale of Glamorgan in 1831. He attended only a dame school, and spent his early years working the family farm, marrying at the age of 19 after his 16-year-old girlfriend became pregnant. He also embarked on a private study of the Welsh language, moving from a working knowledge to a literary ability.[24] An evangelical conversion swiftly followed his marriage, and Howell was persuaded by the local curate that he should seek ordination. His father eventually agreed to support him financially, and at the age of 20 David Howell entered the Eagle Academy in Cowbridge, in order to gain an elementary knowledge of classics, studying alongside boys half his age. He then transferred to crammers in Merthyr, in order to prepare for Abergavenny's entrance examination. Howell studied at Abergavenny Grammar School from February 1853 until August 1855, renting a cottage in the town for his wife and by now three children. He

22. J.S. Harford, *A Life of Thomas Burgess D.D.* (London: Longman, 1840), pp. 356-57.

23. D.T.W. Price, *A History of St David's University College, Lampeter. 2. 1898–1971* (Cardiff: University of Wales Press, 1990), p. 196.

24. R.L. Brown, *David Howell: A Pool of Spirituality: A Life of David Howell (Llawdden)* (Denbigh: Gee & Son, 1998), p. 10.

described the experience as 'reading for my life, as it were, poring over my books for as many as twelve or fifteen hours every day, in anticipation of the ordeal I shall have to undergo' (i.e. the ordination examination).[25] But despite his heavy workload, Howell maintained a prodigious literary output, submitting poetry to Welsh magazines (irrespective of their denominational allegiance), writing for local newspapers, and making substantial and regular contributions to the Welsh-language Church periodical *Yr Haul*. He adopted the bardic name *Llawdden* and wrote essays and poetry for *eisteddfodau*. His subjects included the history of Talley Abbey, the coming of Christianity to Britain and an ode on the recent opening of the South Wales railway. The fees and prize money that he received made a useful contribution to his expenses as an ordinand with a growing family.

When David Howell was ordained at the age of 25, he was already a well-known figure on the Welsh literary scene. For Bishop Ollivant, he may have been 'merely' a literate, a farmboy who had transformed himself into a curate in the space of five years, but such a disparaging view would have been based on a misapprehension of Howell's own standing within Welsh-speaking South Wales. As his ministry unfolded, he became a leading Anglican Evangelical and a national figure within the principality, occupying a number of important posts including the archdeaconry of Wrexham and the deanery of St David's. The episcopate, however, eluded him, although he was discussed for every see vacant in Wales between 1870 and 1897. The problem was threefold.[26] First, there was his perceived lack of education. In later life, Howell bitterly regretted that the curate who had encouraged his vocation had not persuaded his parents to send him to one of the ancient universities. Secondly, there was his wife, whose lowly social origins meant that she was not seen as bishop's wife material. Thirdly, there was the pre-nuptial conception of his first son, which at the hands of his arch rival A.G. Edwards, Bishop of St Asaph, became magnified into a secret illegitimate child. When the hostile rumours about Howell were once again circulating during the St Asaph vacancy of 1889, an English missioner, Joseph Cullin, was among several who wrote to Archbishop Benson in support of Howell's candidature.

> The allegation of want of culture arises from want of Un[iversity] degree. Canon Howell has in reality more literary culture than 9/10th of the clergy

---

25. Howell to Thomas Stephens, 6 August 1855. National Library of Wales (NLW), MS 964E f.130. Cited by Brown, *David Howell*, p. 16.
26. Brown, *David Howell*, pp. 199-210.

who oppose his nomination... a Bp. like Canon Howell wd. exert nearly as much influence as the four Welsh bishops have done hitherto.[27]

Howell had other supporters, but he had hit the glass ceiling as far as the advancement of a 'literate' in the Welsh Church was concerned. Education and social status were more important than cultural attainments and fluent Welsh.

As we have seen in the case of Joshua Hughes, Lampeter men, however Welsh-speaking and cultivated they might be, became bishops only by mistake in the nineteenth century. So how fared this distinctively nineteenth-century alternative to grammar schools and Oxbridge, and what cultural values did it impart? In the 1810s, its foundation had been strongly supported by the *Offeiriaid Llengar* ('literary priests'), who as well as being strongly supportive of Welsh language and literature, were proponents of the idea of the old British Church as the most ancient and authentic form of Christianity in the land. They planned to collect old Welsh manuscripts, making the nucleus of a national library within St David's College.[28] In cultural terms, this seemed a promising start, but later on, Lampeter's penchant for taking the English side in ecclesiastical disputes (for example, on the nomination of Englishmen to Welsh bishoprics, and over the proposed unification of the sees of St Asaph and Bangor)[29] did not help to endear the college to the Welsh nation, and gave it its lasting reputation as an essentially English institution in the heart of Welsh Wales. But it was an exaggeration to suggest, as Archdeacon Williams had, that the college was a curse on the nation. Lampeter offered a perfectly acceptable and reasonably good-value education, although in the 1870s at an all-inclusive price of slightly less than £50 a year for three years, it was still out of reach of the poorer ordinands, helped though they were by the existence of 24 valuable scholarships. It is doubtful that the kinds of students that had been remembered by Mrs Rowland Williams in the 1850s, the 'men advanced in years, broken-down farmers, blacksmiths, Wesleyan preachers',[30] had ever been typical, although the origins of many students were agricultural. Indeed, the vast majority admitted between 1865 and 1878, 115 out of 306, were the sons of farmers, and the next largest group, 36 out of 306, were the sons of clergymen. Most were aged between 18 and 24 on arrival, 73 per

27. Lambeth Palace Library (LPL), Benson Papers vol. 55, ff.93-94.

28. Price, *History of St David's University College*, I, pp. 11-12.

29. Price, *History of St David's University College*, I, p. 66.

30. *The Life and Letters of Rowland Williams D.D.* edited by his wife (2 vols; London: Henry S. King, 1874), I, p. 167.

cent came from the huge St David's diocese and 93 per cent from Wales.[31]

To a great extent, therefore, half a century after its foundation the college was still doing what its founder, Bishop Burgess, had intended, educating local men for the ministry of the Welsh Church, and particularly for the St David's diocese. Under the influence of Vice-Principal Rowland Williams, the entry requirements were stiff at this period, and by the time the men arrived, they would already have devoted many hours to the study of English, Latin and Greek. Once in the college, they received a general education in the arts and sciences, in addition to a theological course. Outside the classroom, their cultural and recreational needs were met by a range of clubs and societies, with opportunities widening as the century progressed. There was debating, in English and Welsh, a Scientific and Archaeological Society and a Dramatic and Music Society. There were also cricket and rugby, and later athletics and lawn tennis.[32] Most importantly, since 1853 Lampeter had had its own degree-awarding powers, at first for the Bachelor of Divinity, and then from 1865 for the Bachelor of Arts. In 1868, J.W. Burgon, the chief external examiner, declared that the Lampeter BA was equivalent to that at the universities, the level being the same as the ordinary degree at Oxbridge.[33] By insisting that candidates for the BA take papers in classics, mathematics, science and English, as well as theology, and also by offering a good range of extracurricular activities, Lampeter was less vulnerable to the charge that its graduates suffered from 'narrowness'.

This charge was frequently made against the theological colleges at this period. Critics saw establishments such as St Bees as in effect just crammers for ordination exams, places where reprobates who had been thrown out of Oxbridge, stern Calvinist ex-Dissenting ministers and impoverished churchmen, all had to rub along together, with predictably unpleasant consequences.[34] But 'narrowness' is a vague charge, and it is easy to see it as code for something else, something with a whiff of the 'gentleman heresy': disapproval at the whole notion of ordaining those who would not be at ease with the middle and upper classes. It would be wrong to suppose that Lampeter aimed to produce 'gentlemen', with all the associations that that word had in the mid-Victorian world. Indeed, there was an increasing recognition that 'gentlemen' were not of much value to the Welsh Church. As H.T. Edwards, Dean of Bangor, put it bluntly in 1870, 'the social

31. Price, *History of St David's University College*, I, pp. 126-28.
32. Price, *History of St David's University College*, I, pp. 151-53.
33. Price, *History of St David's University College*, I, p. 113.
34. Haig, *Victorian Clergy*, pp. 130-34, 137.

characteristics of Wales render it not only unnecessary, but, even if it were possible, absolutely undesirable, that the majority of its clergy should come from what are called the higher classes'.[35] What Lampeter aimed to produce was well-educated clergy, with broadened horizons. The Vice-Principal Rowland Williams's desire to maintain this priority by retaining the classical curriculum was at the heart of his struggle with Vowler Short, the Bishop of St Asaph, in the 1850s. Short wished to see the syllabus concentrating on English literature, mathematics and divinity, with the study of classical languages reduced to New Testament Greek. Williams believed that abandoning the classics would damage the Church, and severely weaken the theological aspirations of his students.[36] Among other things, Lampeter was a powerful vehicle for social and cultural mobility in nineteenth-century Wales. Any restrictions on the breadth of its curriculum would have limited that influence.

About a quarter of the nineteenth-century Welsh clergy had been educated at Oxford or Cambridge, with a large proportion passing through Jesus College, Oxford, which had been established specifically as the 'Welsh College' in the immediate post-Reformation period.[37] Jesus had numerous closed awards for boys from the grammar schools of north Wales, and some reserved for the former pupils of Cowbridge Grammar School in Glamorgan. The Jesus men usually returned to the north, to serve the curacies and incumbencies of the dioceses of St Asaph and Bangor which were generally wealthier than those of the southern dioceses of St David's and Llandaff. Although attendance at Oxbridge might be expected almost to guarantee the attainment of gentlemanliness and initiation into the very heart of English culture, this was not always the case. Those who entered college as servitors remained isolated from the mainstream of Oxford life, attempting to get through their residence with the minimum expenditure possible. It was ironic that men who had sometimes been treated as the lowest form of academic life in Oxford, were regarded as the highest form of clerical life when they returned to Wales.

There were also perceived to be dangers in sending young Welshmen away. Sir Thomas Phillips, a noted observer of mid-nineteenth-century Wales, and the author of a stinging rebuttal of the 1847 Education Report,

35. H.T. Edwards, 'The Calling and Education of the Clergy for the Church in Wales', a paper read in August 1870, reprinted in H.T. Edwards, *Wales and the Welsh Church* (London: Rivingtons, 1889), p. 375.

36. *Life and Letters of Rowland Williams*, I, pp. 192-204, 219-20.

37. M. Jebb, *The Colleges of Oxford* (London: Constable, 1992), pp. 90-97.

was strongly critical of sending Welsh boys to England, where they might be exposed to vice, debt, the dangers of 'mixed' education and the temptation to remain there.[38] It was a legitimate fear that Wales's brightest young men, carefully groomed for Oxford scholarships by devoted teachers in local grammar schools, might have their heads turned once they crossed the English border, and a proportion never returned to Wales. It was noted that many who did return to their homeland found it very difficult to settle down to ministry in the Welsh Church. There was also a fear that in the English university towns, boys might forget their Welsh, and in 1819, a society was formed at Jesus College, Oxford, to encourage the study of the language.[39] Later on in the century, Welsh students at Oxford found a focus in the Dafydd ap Gwilym Society.

It is difficult to draw firm conclusions about the extent to which an English education affected Welsh boys who were destined for the Church. Some, such as Isaac Williams the Tractarian, a native of Aberystwyth and a product of Harrow and Trinity College, Oxford, seem to have become anglicized in outlook. It was his brother Matthew, rather than Isaac himself, who built Llangorwen as the first Tractarian church in Wales, and the attempts that were made to lure Isaac back to minister in his native land proved unsuccessful.[40] Others, such as Rowland Williams, a native of Flintshire and a product of Eton and King's, remained thoroughly committed to Wales and yet found the return there very difficult. At Cambridge, Williams had taken the lead at St David's day dinners, and had shockingly claimed that if he lived in Wales, he would rather go to Welsh-language chapel services than English services in church. He compared the religious and intellectual life of the Ely diocese unfavourably with that around his father's Flintshire parish.[41] Yet when the time came for Rowland Williams to exchange his fellowship of King's for a post at Lampeter, he embarked upon it, according to his wife, 'with the same spirit that induced Bishop Heber to go to India'.[42] His predecessor, Harold Browne, wrote him a sympathy letter shortly after his arrival: 'If you have no wife, sister, horse or dog, you must sadly want company.I had wife, sisters, horses and dogs, and had not too much company then.'[43]

38. Phillips, *Wales*, pp. 317-29.
39. Price, *History of St David's Unversity College*, I, p. 4.
40. O.W. Jones, *Isaac Williams and his Circle* (London: SPCK, 1971), pp. 92-112.
41. *Life and Letters of Rowland Williams*, I, pp. 41, 46, 97-98.
42. *Life and Letters of Rowland Williams*, I, p. 170.
43. *Life and Letters of Rowland Williams*, I, p. 170.

Williams had none of these things, but he took Browne's advice and acquired most of them. His energy was also channelled in a horticultural direction, and he developed a particular enthusiasm for growing dahlias. As an immensely able Welsh-speaking Welshman, from a very distinguished clerical family, Rowland Williams should have been ideally placed for elevation to the Welsh episcopate. His taste for liberal theology and his involvement in the *Essays and Reviews* controversy meant that this was never to be.

It has been suggested recently that of the Tractarian clergy in Wales, the majority had been at Jesus College, Oxford.[44] Although it seems that the case for Jesus College being a hotbed of Tractarianism has still to be made, it is interesting that these Jesus men did share significant theological and cultural interests. In particular, they were united in their support for and participation in the National Eisteddfod, and in societies such as the Cambrian Archaeological Association. In theology, these High Churchmen looked to the antiquity of the early British Church, rather than to the early Fathers. It followed that they were sternly anti-Roman, believing in the pure and uncorrupted nature of the Celtic Church before the arrival of Augustine. *Eisteddfodau* provided a natural platform for Tractarian poets, and some clergy who were attracted to Tractarianism may also have been attracted by the rituals, processions and vestments of the *Gorsedd*. Morris Williams, a Jesus College graduate whose bardic name was 'Nicander', won a prize at the Aberffraw Royal Eisteddfod of 1849 with a poem which drew attention to the holy days and seasons of the Church's year. He used the Aberystwyth Eisteddfod of 1865 to present a poem which claimed that St Paul had preached in Welsh.[45] Other Jesus College clerics were instrumental in reviving the National Eisteddfod and the *Gorsedd* in something approximating its modern form. This took place at the Llangollen Eisteddfod of 1858, but within a few years the druidic orders were subject to ridicule from some quarters. Morris Williams himself described it all as ridiculous and improbable, 'the half-sister to Mormonism and the half-sister to unbelief'.[46]

Unsurprisingly, Conybeare's insinuation that the Welsh clergy had no aspirations beyond carousing in taverns and eating in kitchens turns out to

---

44. D.P. Freeman, 'The Influence of the Oxford Movement on Welsh Anglicanism and Welsh Nonconformity in the 1840s and 1850s' (PhD thesis, University of Wales Swansea, 1999). Freeman lists those he identifies as Tractarians from Jesus College, Oxford, on pp. 426-28.

45. Freeman, 'Influence of the Oxford Movement', p. 303.

46. Freeman, 'Influence of the Oxford Movement', p. 304.

be without foundation, and it may be doubted if Conybeare really believed it himself. The Welsh clergy, whether they were educated at grammar school, at Lampeter or at Jesus, experienced the intellectual and cultural freedom that their education brought. Wherever they were educated, all encountered a large emphasis on the classical languages, and most were taught to improve their spoken English and their written Welsh, in addition to mathematics and a little science and literature. In 1849, Sir Thomas Phillips drew out the intended consequences of the 'liberal' education offered at Lampeter.

> By accustoming them [the students] to habits of self-respect and communi-cating to them tastes for liberal studies, they will also be preserved from those habits of intemperance, on the one hand, and that spirit of despondency or indolent apathy on the other, which are not uncommonly produced or perpetuated in the solitary parishes so often the dwelling place of a Welsh clergyman.[47]

What the future clergyman learned at college was not simply academic training. It was intended to help him get through life. Obviously, not all were educated to the same level, and not all benefited from the same oppor-tunities—but though the semi-literate curate may have existed, he was certainly not universal. Many of these men, however, came from simple farming or trading backgrounds, drawn from far lower in the social hier-archy than their English brethren. For Englishmen like Conybeare, their ordination was a cause of embarrassment, and the notion of giving them a liberal education, something of a puzzle. For the Welsh clergy themselves, their educational attainments gave them a confident entry into a world of letters in a society that was growing increasingly literate. Every sizeable Welsh town had its printer/publisher, its booksellers and binders. In 1887, a Welsh-language publication advising young married labouring couples on their household finances, took it for granted that they would spend about 13 per cent of the total costs of setting up home on books and subscrip-tions to periodicals.[48] Many clergy (and of course Nonconformist ministers) took a lead in literary productions, writing sermons, poetry, pamphlets and hymns as the need required. The eisteddfod movement, both at local and at national level, provided them with a very important focus. It attracted clergy of different churchmanship and different educational background, and it provided a distinctively Welsh form of cultural achievement.

---

47. Phillips, *Wales*, p. 326.
48. Jones (ed.), *Observers and the Observed*, p. 17.

HONORARY DOCTORATES AND THE NONCONFORMIST
MINISTRY IN NINETEENTH-CENTURY ENGLAND

Timothy Larsen

It was not generally the custom in nineteenth-century England for those with scholarly or professional ambitions to enrol in a doctoral programme at a university. On the other hand, it was a fairly common practice for clergymen of distinction to be awarded doctorates. Anthony Trollope, in the concluding chapter of *Barchester Towers*, suddenly refers to his male hero as *Dr* Arabin, defending his use of the new title on the grounds that 'we suppose he must have become a doctor when he became a dean'.[1] Whether or not one considers a major ecclesiastical promotion a legitimate prompt for such an award, as Arabin had been a fellow of a distinguished Oxford college, he hardly can be considered scandalously ill-suited for the honour. Indeed, British universities have always maintained the right to confer further diplomas on their graduates, with the Cantab and Oxford MA perhaps being the most famous example of this practice. In the case of doctorates, there does not seem to have been a clear consensus as to whether or not one should call these degrees 'honorary', but there is no doubt that a Victorian recipient could make full use of such an award without fear of reproach.

For this study, an effort has been made to establish the nature and source of the doctorates held by as many nineteenth-century English Nonconformist ministers as possible, focusing primarily on the Baptists, the Congregationalists and, to a lesser extent, the Wesleyans and the Methodist New Connexion. Also, in chronological terms, the focus is primarily on the first half of the century. This research has revealed that a small minority of Nonconformist ministerial doctors did receive their awards in this most unobjectionable of ways. The Baptist F.W. Gotch earned his BA and MA degrees at Trinity College, Dublin. Having made this point, his memorialist

---

1. A. Trollope, *Barchester Towers* (Oxford World's Classics; Oxford: Oxford University Press, 1953 [1857]), p. 270.

adds, 'He subsequently succeeded to the higher degree of LLD. His literary distinctions were not therefore honorary, but were honourably won.'[2] The Congregationalists John Clunie, John Hoppus, George Redford and C.A. Simpson all earned MAs from Glasgow University and were later awarded LLDs by their alma mater. Likewise the Baptist Nathanael Haycroft earned a Glasgow MA, and later received a Glasgow DD. The Congregationalists George Legge and James Spence both earned MAs at King's College, Aberdeen; the former subsequently received an Aberdeen LLD and the later an Aberdeen DD. This is the full list of such figures identifiable from the research for this paper, although a few other figures have been discovered whose doctorates have not been traced to a specific institution, although they did possess an earned MA. That is to say, to examine the negative exposure this reveals, the vast majority of the doctorates of Nonconformist and Methodist ministers were honorary ones in the purest sense of the term, namely, diplomas awarded by universities where the recipients had never enrolled as students or submitted themselves for examination.

As the words 'Dublin', 'Glasgow' and 'Aberdeen' serve to remind, English Nonconformist ministers in the first third of the nineteenth century were in the peculiar situation of having been barred from earning degrees in their own country. The situation did improve as the century progressed: the University of London, which had no religious tests, was granted the right to award degrees in 1837, and as the 1840s unfolded a range of Dissenting colleges developed links which enabled their students to participate in London examinations and thereby earn English degrees. This made a noticeable change in the kind of degrees held by the Nonconformist ministry. For example, English Baptists did not produce a list of their ministers between the years 1831 and 1851, and the contrast between the two lists on either side of this gap is revealing.[3] The 1831 list had a total of 841 names, and there was not one 'BA' cited throughout it, although there were 5 doctors (including one MD), and 14 master's degrees (some of which were undoubtedly honorary). The 1851 list had 1,196 names, 10 of which were doctors (including two MDs), and 28 master's degrees were recorded (including those possessed by the Anglican seceders Baptist Noel and J.C. Philpot). So far the two lists show a fairly similar pattern; the real change comes in the 13 BAs cited in the 1851 list: the presence of London University was being felt. Nonconformists won the right to earn Oxford BAs in 1854, and Cambridge ones in 1856 but, all

2. *Baptist Handbook, 1891*, pp. 140-42.
3. *Baptist Magazine* 23 (1831), pp. 590-97; 43 (1851), pp. 794-803.

these changes notwithstanding, it took a considerable amount of time to turn the Dissenting ministry into a degree-possessing body. Even several decades into the twentieth century, the majority of Nonconformist ministers had no degrees of any kind. The net result of these historical realities was the intriguing anomaly that most of the Dissenting ministers using the title 'doctor' had never earned a degree or studied at a university.

This, of course, does not imply that many of them were not intelligent men who had been well-trained in their denominational institutions and who had subsequently written worthy works of scholarship and distinguished themselves in their profession. For such men—or men who flattered themselves that they were such—an honorary doctorate could be a valuable prize. It was a tangible victory over the snub inflicted on them by a society that had excluded them from the university careers they might have had, and it could play a crucial part in fulfilling aspirations they might harbour to be recognized as learned and distinguished by the wider society. When Gladstone wrote in 1897 to the Congregational minister, J. Guinness Rogers, who had been awarded an honorary DD from Edinburgh two years earlier, he addressed him as 'Dear Dr. Guinness Rogers'.[4] However much one might be convinced of one's own worth, to have it formalized in a title used even by one of the most eminent members of the cultural elite must have been very gratifying. Moreover, in Dissenting circles, the doctorate had to fill the void of the numerous ranks which rising Anglican clergymen might acquire as forms of address. If one says 'Dean Stanley' or 'Bishop Wilberforce' (one could mention a handful of such titles), distinction enough is indicated, leaving no reason to inquire whether or not these figures ever happened to have been awarded a DD. Victorian Dissenting ministers, of course, had no incentive to expend their energy in the hopes of being awarded a knighthood. The chairmanship of the Congregational and Baptist Unions and the Methodist Conferences changed annually, and no minister would have thought of signing his name as 'President' on the strength of it. In short, if a Dissenting minister was more eminent or worthy than his ministerial brothers (or thought to be so by himself or others), the only way this could be expressed in his very name was through a doctorate. The honorary doctorate was a rare and therefore valuable vehicle through which the cultural aspirations of Nonconformist ministers could be expressed.

4. See a facsimile of the letter in *J. Guinness Rogers: An Autobiography* (London: James Clarke & Co., 1903), facing p. 232. (Rogers, however, had earned a BA from Trinity College, Dublin.)

Nevertheless, as not all honorary doctorates were equal, and there was a kind of continually shifting scale of their relative value in English opinion, descending from the unreproachable down to the transparently worthless, often a lot of calculations had to be made regarding whether one's own award was more apt to generate prestige or mockery. Although much work has been done on the education of Victorian ministers, scholars have largely ignored the question of honorary degrees. For example, although Kenneth Brown mentions briefly the issue of buying dubious degrees, he nevertheless lumps honorary degrees together with earned ones in his calculations.[5] While such an approach was probably the only practicable one for the kind of sweeping survey he was undertaking (given the fact that one would have to trace every degree in order to make the distinction), it nevertheless begs the question of the worth of these degrees, a question well worth pursuing, even if it has to be done through a less statistical approach.

Crucial to the process of evaluation was the academic prestige of the awarding institution, and how vigilant that institution was about bestowing its honours upon only those who unquestionably merited them. No Nonconformist minister has been discovered who was awarded an honorary doctorate from an English university in the nineteenth century, although the Wesleyan minister W.F. Moulton received a 'much-coveted' honorary MA from Cambridge in 1877.[6] Although Dissenting ministers from some other denominations received honorary doctorates from continental universities such as the Presbyterian William McKerrow (DD, Heidelberg, 1851) and the Unitarian James Martineau (STD, Leiden, 1875), this was not the case for Baptists, Congregationalists and Methodists. The exception that proves the rule was the Independent Samuel Davidson. He did receive an honorary ThD (DD) from Halle in 1848, but he also went on to drift out of Congregationalism and into Unitarianism.[7] Virtually all the honorary doctorates received by English Nonconformist ministers came from either Scottish or North American institutions.

Scottish honorary degrees were not completely above suspicion. The immortal character, Dr Pangloss, in George Colman the Younger's comedy,

---

5.   K.D. Brown, *A Social History of the Nonconformist Ministry in England and Wales, 1800–1930* (Oxford: Clarendon Press, 1988), p. 83, Table 3.1.

6.   G.J. Stevenson, *Methodist Worthies* (6 vols; London: Thomas C. Jack, 1885), IV, p. 544.

7.   A.J. Davidson, *Autobiography and Diary of Samuel Davidson, D.D., LL.D.* (Edinburgh: T. & T. Clark, 1899).

The Heir at Law (1797), was so entitled to be addressed because he had purchased his degree for 'one pound fifteen shillings and three-pence three-farthings' from 'the Caledonian University of Aberdeen'.[8] The journalist James Ewing Ritchie was not impressed by Nonconformist ministerial doctors, grumbling that some 'of the old Scotch diplomas got into strange hands'.[9] Nevertheless, in general terms, a Scottish honorary degree was a genuine prize, rarely derided by anyone.

The same cannot be said for all degrees emanating from North America. Ritchie, having refused to respect Scottish degrees automatically, went on to say 'and the American ones have fared still worse'. The Congregational minister Newman Hall received a DD from Amherst College, Massachusetts, in 1865, but he did not use the title 'outside the United States of America' until he had also received an honorary doctorate from Edinburgh on the grounds that 'degrees other than those of British universities had been somewhat discredited'.[10] George John Stevenson, in a biographical sketch of the Methodist New Connexion minister, James Stacey, reveals that he received a STD (DD) from Ohio Wesleyan University in 1864. According to Stevenson, Stacey was an intellectually gifted man and, if he had been afforded the opportunity, he could have earned a degree, 'even in an English University'.[11]

There is also that intriguingly vague phrase which often recurs in the accounts of Dissenting ministers who were referred to as doctors, 'an American university'.[12] It is interesting to wonder at the reason for this circumlocution. No one ever writes that a minister received his diploma from 'a Scottish university'. On the one hand, the phrase gives the impression that all American universities are the same: that the simple word 'American' tells you well enough the value of the degree. On the other hand, it might have been a way of disguising the fact that the awarding institution could be easily recognized as less prestigious than the more

8. G. Colman, the Younger, *The Heir at Law; A Comedy, in Five Acts* (London: Longman, Hurst, Rees, Orme & Brown, n.d. [originally 1797]), pp. 11-12.

9. J.E. Ritchie, *The London Pulpit* (London: Simpkin, Marshall & Co., 1854), pp. 100-101.

10. C.N. Hall, *Newman Hall: An Autobiography* (London: Cassell, 1898), p. 176.

11. Stevenson, *Methodist Worthies*, IV, pp. 632-33.

12. Even some modern scholars use this phrase, although they might be forced to do so by not being able to find more information than that offered in primary sources which use it: M.R. Watts, *The Dissenters*, II (Oxford: Clarendon Press, 1995), p. 267; E. Kaye, *The History of the King's Weigh House Church* (London: George Allen & Unwin, 1968), p. 82.

celebrated ones. Finally, in some cases, it may be simply that the information was so unfamiliar that it was forgotten by colleagues and friends even though the memory of the honour, in general terms, lived on. Nevertheless, it is revealing that an award could be significant enough to change a person's name for the rest of his life so that he was invariably being referred to as 'Dr So-And-So' in denominational publications and elsewhere, and yet long, sympathetic memoirs or even full biographies nevertheless could neglect to elucidate the basis on which this change was made.

There is, of course, no doubt at all that there were some second-rate American institutions that were unduly indiscriminate with their favours. Nevertheless, discovering the precise level of respectability of any given institution at any given time is a daunting task. Two little lists offered as guides have been discovered. First, an Anglican clergyman, Henry Belcher, published in 1872 a delightful exposé of bogus American institutions which offered degrees for sale. He mentions various truly disreputable institutions, including 'the Clintonian University of Arkansas', but as to the more legitimate end of the spectrum, he lists Harvard, Yale and the University of Pennsylvania as beyond all reproach, while Columbia, Bowdoin, Tusculum and Alabama he censors for having been too 'lavish with their smiles'.[13] Secondly, the journalist Arthur Porritt (writing in 1922, but reflecting on the late Victorian period as well) also decried the market in worthless American degrees, grumbling that any 'backwoods college which secured a State charter as a university—and the charters were easily procured—had the legal right to confer honorary degrees'. Porritt, however, was willing to offer a list only for the respectable side of the equation, citing Yale, Harvard, Princeton and Oberlin as 'beyond all cavil'.[14]

Several ministers received their degrees from institutions that no longer exist, at least under the same name: for example, the Congregationalist Robert Ferguson received his degrees from 'Jefferson College, Pennsylvania', and his co-religionist John Waddington received his DD from 'the university of Williamstown, U.S.A.'. The Baptist William Landels received his degree from 'the Columbian University at Washington' which is also untraceable, if it is not a bad corruption of Columbia University,

13. H. Belcher, *Degrees and 'Degrees,' or Traffic in Theological, Medical and Other 'Diplomas' Exposed* (London: Robert Hardwicke, 1872), pp. 31, 56.
14. A. Porritt, *The Best I Remember* (New York: George H. Doran, [1923]), pp. 184-86.

New York, New York.[15] Nevertheless, it does not follow that just because an institution subsequently became defunct, it never was respectable. On the other hand, the case of the Congregationalist Joseph Parker might illustrate the slipperiness of the terrain. His right to the title 'Doctor' rested on an honorary DD he received from the University of Chicago in 1862. His biographer, William Adamson, writing in 1902, endeavoured to bolster the worth of this award by noting that this institution is 'now one of the largest and wealthiest universities in the world'.[16] The 'now', however, obfuscates a great deal, for Parker received his award from a Baptist seminary that went defunct shortly thereafter. It is true that when John D. Rockerfeller wished to create a modern university in that city a figleaf of continuity was devised between the two institutions, apparently in order to capture the name of the former for the latter, but the *Encyclopaedia Britannica* (which incidentally has its headquarters in Chicago) states unequivocally that the University of Chicago was founded in 1891, almost three decades after Parker received his award.[17]

It is possible, of course, to make a list of all the information available regarding which institutions Dissenting ministers received their awards from, but one could not generalize from it regarding the overall level of prestige because the data is skewed hopelessly: distinguished institutions are apt to be mentioned explicitly, while one suspects that the numerous narratives that avoid mentioning the awarding institution are heavily weighted toward the humbler end of the spectrum. Dubious honours from second-rate institutions meant that the title of 'Doctor' did not afford automatic respect. Ritchie, having heard the Congregational minister John Leifchild preach, brushed aside his DD with contempt.

> We know not where the Doctor got his diploma from, but few Dissenting ministers have diplomas of any worth. Dr. Leifchild is not a scholar, and his degree must be merely honorary… They seem to have been bestowed without the least regard to propriety, and have become anything but titles of honour. They have, however, effected this one good—they have taught the public to put less confidence in titles—to believe rather in men than in honorary degrees.[18]

15. T.D. Landels, *Williams Landels, D.D.: A Memoir* (London: Cassell, 1900), pp. 195, 318.

16. W. Adamson, *The Life of the Rev. Joseph Parker, D.D.* (Glasgow: Inglis Ker, 1902), p. 70.

17. *Encylopaedia Britannica* (32 vols; Chicago: Encyclopaedia Britannica, 15th edn, 1998), III, p. 195.

18. Ritchie, *London Pulpit*, pp. 100-102.

And Ritchie might have had a good journalist's nose. Leifchild was awarded his DD in 1841 from 'the University of the City of New York'. Such a precise title makes it unlikely that New York University, New York, New York (founded in 1831) was in mind, but the 'City University of New York' claims that it was not founded until 1847. Moreover, it does not inspire confidence to read the letter informing him of the award in which his correspondent sheepishly notes that the university does not have a physical diploma to give him, but that if anyone should question the legitimacy of his doctorate they could write to him personally for confirmation.[19] In America, all degrees were not created equal.

There was also a debate, this one an internal one within Dissent, regarding which doctorate was on offer. Essentially, there were only two options, the DD and the LLD, and some Nonconformists had qualms about the DD. Indeed, it seems to have been a point of conscience that was most likely to be adopted by very eminent ministers. The great Baptist minister, Robert Hall, can serve as the first chronologically of a line of such figures stretching across the nineteenth century. His opinion is recorded in a letter that might have been written around the years 1816–17:

> it does appear to me to militate directly against our Saviour's prohibition. The term rabbi, by the consent of Dr. Campbell, and the best writers, coincides, as nearly as possible, with the modern term doctor. It was a religious degree of honour, conferred by their theological schools, to denote a pre-eminence of spiritual wisdom; and if it has not this import, (or rather if the D.D. has not,) I am at a loss [to know] what it means. Nor can I conceive in what manner our Lord, supposing it has been his acknowledged intention to have forbidden it, could have done it more effectually consistent with the genius of the language in which he spoke.[20]

The venerable Congregational minister, John Angell James, who was born 20 years after Hall, made the same argument, adding:

> I am quite aware that it is argued that these diplomas are to be regarded as mere academic and literary honours and distinctions, conferred as the rewards of merit. This may be said of mere secular degrees, such as B.A., M.A., LL.B., or LL.D.—these are all simply literary; but it is not the same with D.D. This is in its true meaning a religious distinction, never conferred but upon a minister of religion, and intended to raise him in public estimation above his fellows.[21]

19. J.R. Leifchild, *John Leifchild, D.D.* (London: Jackson, Walford & Hodder, 1863), pp. 243-44.

20. G. Pritchard, *Memoir of the Rev. William Newman, D.D.* (London: Thomas Ward, 1837), pp. 283-87.

Moreover, although his distinguished successor, R.W. Dale, might have departed from some of James's other convictions, he followed his predecessor on this one. On the strength of the same argument, Dale made use of his LLD from Glasgow, but not his DD from Yale, causing people on both sides of the Atlantic to misconstrue his motivation as snobbishness about American degrees.[22] These are the only comments on this issue which have been found, but other ministers (for whatever reason) followed the pattern of declining to use a DD that had been conferred upon them without their approval, and one source appears to claim (rightly or wrongly) that another eminent Congregational minister, Thomas Binney, also maintained this scruple.[23] It is also curious that the most celebrated nineteenth-century English Nonconformist minister of them all is never referred to as 'Dr Spurgeon'.

Another aspect of the issue of honorary degrees that needs exploration is the motivations of the awarding institutions. The most sordid of these was financial. Many contemporary sources are well aware of this possibility, and some even view it as widespread but, of course, they invariably highlight the issue in order to make a contrast with the sterling nobility of the subject of their memoir. As might be expected, no evidence has been found in order to bring definite charges against any particular nineteenth-century minister, although the *Christian World* proved a case in court in 1903.[24] Nevertheless, there is a *prima facie* case against one particular class of ministers: the very few who claimed to possess a PhD. Memoirs have been found for two such figures, the Baptist Joshua Taylor Gray and the Congregationalist Samuel Bell, and they both conceal the awarding institution (indeed, make no mention of the degree at all other than to cite it after the subject's name), and they both reveal that their subject left the ministry for a season and made his living by establishing a private school.[25] Belcher, his indignation against purchased degrees notwithstanding, not only acknowledged that they were endemic to this particular class of men, but even was willing to offer some sympathy in their case.

21. R.W. Dale, *The Life and Letters of John Angell James* (London: James Nisbet, 1861), pp. 424-26.

22. A.W.W. Dale, *The Life of R.W. Dale of Birmingham* (London: Hodder & Stoughton, 1898), pp. 514-15.

23. J.M. McKerrow, *Memoir of William McKerrow, D.D.* (London: Hodder & Stoughton, 1881), p. 201.

24. Brown, *Social History*, p. 85 n. 6; Porritt, *Best I Remember*, pp. 184-86.

25. *Baptist Manual for 1855*, pp. 49-50; *Congregational Year Book for 1862*, p. 222.

> The use of learned titles is no doubt very attractive to the poorer classes of person who have need of education for their children—and beyond all question it pays… While, then, there seems to be some excuse for a needy schoolmaster, it is hard to find any apology for clergymen or practitioners in their dealings with a merchant of academical shams.[26]

Indeed, beside the few upgrades given to graduates of Irish or Scottish universities (which one may choose to count or not), earned doctorates were virtually never found during the research for this project, although the MDs presumably were legitimate. One rare exception was the Baptist minister, Robert K. Brewer, who studied with distinction for five years at the Royal Academy, and subsequently received the Academy's MusDoc.[27]

One step up on the scale of dubious promptings was volunteering oneself. This practice cannot be pinned down to specific instances either, although the custom of disclaiming that it had happened in a particular case was so common as to make one suspect that the phenomenon itself must also have been widespread. In a typical example, the memoir of the Congregationalist George Legge assures us that his Aberdeen LLD was 'an honour which was entirely unsought by him'.[28] The University of Pennsylvania went so far in 1871 as to print a letter in the British press explaining that its procedures for awarding honorary doctorates were very rigorous, in a determined effort to curb a British nuisance: 'Frequent applications are made to the authorities of this University by gentlemen who desire to obtain honorary degrees.'[29]

A respectable prompt, by Victorian standards although perhaps not by today's, was cronyism. Indeed, a significant percentage of honorary doctorates were awarded because a personal acquaintance or friend happened to have influence in this matter, and it is a common practice in doctoring narratives to mention this. The memoir of the Baptist minister Samuel Wills (who ministered in the United States for a time) states that his friends included: 'the heads of some colleges. Some of these latter, appreciating his literary performances, obtained for him the honorary degree of D.D.'[30] A letter sent in 1830 to the English Congregationalist, Thomas Raffles, from his friend, the American minister, Dr Sprague, is typical of the ingratiating tone of many.

---

26. Belcher, *Degrees*, pp. 8-9.
27. *Baptist Handbook, 1876*, pp. 336-38.
28. *Congregational Year Book, 1862*, pp. 247-49.
29. Belcher, *Degrees*, p. 29.
30. *Baptist Handbook, 1874*, pp. 296-98.

> It gives me much pleasure to inform you that the degree of Doctor of Divinity was conferred upon you at the annual commencement of Union College (of which Dr. Nott is president), this week. I know you will not refuse it, as it comes from one of the most respectable colleges in the country, and if I may be allowed to plead personal friendship as an argument for your acceptance, it has been procured by my own efforts.[31]

Raffles's biographer-son, in a deft piece of writing, manages to intimate that his father had such good manners that he condescended to accept it.

A more curious motivation was political correctness. Rightly or wrongly, a hint in this direction is certainly given in some sources. The *Dictionary of National Biography*, for example, has its mention of the Baptist John Rippon's award immediately follow the comment that he 'gave his warm sympathy to the Americans during the war of independence'.[32] Likewise, a modern biographer of the Wesleyan, William Arthur, has his honorary degree from Dickinson College, Pennsylvania, immediately follow comments regarding his public support for the North in the American Civil War, and an article he wrote extolling President Lincoln.[33] This connection was made embarrassingly explicit when Amherst College, Massachusetts, awarded Newman Hall an honorary DD in 1865. W.A. Stearns, the college's president, wrote him a letter that was heavily preoccupied with his support for the North, noting with hopeless candour:

> And now in these days of returning peace and prosperity, the damning blot of slavery for ever erased, and the National Government re-established to the extent of the Federal Constitution over all our states and territories, we take no little pleasure in expressing our grateful recognition, in such ways as we can, of those strong friends of the Republic who have stood nobly by us in those dark days of anxiety and anguish.[34]

It seems clear that the choice of the particular degree, Doctor of Divinity, was made purely because Hall happened to be a minister, and it is not surprising that the recipient did not feel able to make use of it. Nor was this kind of behaviour confined to American institutions. The Presbyterian William McKerrow received his DD from the University of Heidelberg through the intercession of Richard Cobden, and the letter that Cobden wrote to him in 1851 securing credit for this act is imbued with politics,

---

31. T.S. Raffles, *Memoirs of the Life and Ministry of the Rev. Thomas Raffles, D.D., LL.D.* (London: Jackson, Walford & Hodder, 1864), pp. 288-89.

32. *DNB*.

33. N.W. Taggart, *William Arthur: First Among Methodists* (London: Epworth Press, 1993), p. 22.

34. Hall, *Newman Hall*, p. 177.

leaving the impression that McKerrow was being rewarded for services to free trade and radical causes.[35] Most tangential of all, Thomas Raffles received an Aberdeen LLD in 1820 upon the recommendation of the Duke of Somerset whose letter to him confides that he was prompted by his admiration for the fine work that Raffles's cousin and namesake was doing as Lieutenant Governor of Java.[36]

Along with cronyism, another particularly common motivation was a desire to be hospitable. The surest way to obtain an honorary doctorate while still being able to boast that it had not been bought, was simply to go on a tour in North America, ideally as an official delegate of a denomination or worthy voluntary society. For example, the memoir of the Congregationalist Henry Gill states:

> In 1864 he accepted an invitation from the Committee of the Bible Society, to visit its auxiliaries in North America and Canada… While in Canada he received the degree of 'D.D.' from the 'Senatus of Kingston University,' and also an intimation from the 'Victoria University,' that it had conferred upon him the same honour.[37]

Andrew Reed and J. Matheson went to America in 1834 as a deputation of the Congregational Union of England and Wales, and both came back with DDs from Yale. F.A. Cox went to America in 1838 as a representative of the Baptist Union and returned with a DD from the publicity-challenged University of Waterville, Maine. The Wesleyan T.B. Stephenson 'took an active part in the proceedings of the Methodist Ecumenical Conference of 1881, and, the same year, had the honorary degree of LL.D. conferred upon him by an American University'.[38] One could compile a considerable list of ministers who received their doctorates in the same year as or the one immediately following a visit to America. For example, the Congregationalist Henry Allon crossed the Atlantic in 1870 and received a DD from Yale in 1871.[39] In an account of the life of the Baptist, James Hoby, we are offered the vague, if not incomprehensible, information: 'His visit to America evolved a wisdom, courage, and sympathy which were recognised by the diploma which his name adorned.'[40] Indeed, this practice was

35. McKerrow, *William McKerrow*, p. 201.

36. Raffles, *Thomas Raffles*, pp. 196-97.

37. *Congregational Year Book, 1871*, pp. 311-12.

38. Stephenson, *Methodist Worthies*, IV, p. 529.

39. W.H. Harwood, *Henry Allon, D.D.: Pastor and Teacher* (London: Cassell, 1894), pp. 53, 91.

40. *Baptist Handbook, 1872*, p. 226.

so common that the biographer of the Baptist minister, William Landels, boasted that his subject's DD from the unidentifiable Columbian University, Washington, awarded in 1867, was 'no small honour, in view of the fact that he had never visited America'.[41]

Another factor was denominational solidarity. The Baptists did very well in these stakes. A Baptist college was founded in Rhode Island in 1764, adopting the name Brown University in 1804. Thus one of the older and more prestigious American universities was in Baptist hands. Bristol Baptist College raised funds and donated resources to help its sister college in America get on its feet and it 'in return conferred honorary degrees on many Bristol men'.[42] The Wesleyans, on the other hand, were far less fortunate. The result was that fewer Wesleyan divines possessed honorary doctorates, and those who did almost invariably received them from less distinguished institutions. Even their brightest star in the first half of the nineteenth century, Dr Jabez Bunting, had a right to his title only on the strength of a DD awarded in 1835 by Wesleyan University, Middletown, Connecticut, an institution that had obtained its charter only four years earlier.[43] Beside Middletown, there were only two real American sources of honorary degrees for Methodists. Dickinson College, Carlisle, Pennsylvania, has never been one of the better known American institutions, but it did receive its charter in the eighteenth century. In 1833, its trustees abandoned its Presbyterian roots and aligned it with the Methodist Episcopal Church, and English Wesleyan ministers with cultural aspirations benefited from this change. Ohio Wesleyan University received its charter in 1842. The *Dictionary of National Biography* entry on the Wesleyan leader, W.H. Rule, states that he 'received the degree of D.D. from Dickenson College (methodist episcopal church), Ohio, in July 1854'.[44] This garbled bit of information is suggestive: Wesleyans were apparently apt to assume that an honorary degree must have come from either Dickinson or Ohio, and sometimes muddled the two together. All of this is not to deny the fact that the awarding of many honorary doctorates was occasioned primarily, if not solely, by a recognition of the scholarly and professional achievements of the recipients. Nevertheless, the evidence regarding the influence of personal scheming, cronyism and political and

41. Landels, *William Landels*, p. 195.

42. N.S. Moon, *Education for Ministry: Bristol Baptist College, 1679–1979* (Bristol: Bristol Baptist College, 1979), p. 9.

43. *DNB*.

44. *DNB*.

denominational correctness, all points toward the inescapable conclusion that who did and who did not receive an honorary degree was not a reliable indicator of the relative merits of English ministers.

One simple way to avoid the accusation that an award was not credible or not merited was to decline it or, if presented with a *fait accompli*, to refuse to make use of it. J.A. James made good on his scruples by declining or ignoring no fewer than three honorary DDs. If one wishes to be a particularly suspicious critic, it could be argued that a sense of one's own cultural importance could also be fostered effectively by boasting that one had disdained the favours of Princeton and Glasgow. Moreover, James also moved beyond his biblical argument to make further remarks which were a masterpiece of mingling humility with pride and inverted snobbery.

> And, moreover, apart from this conscientious scruple, I never thought myself warranted on the ground of any superior learning or attainment to be thus called Rabbi. True it is I have written books on religion, not a few, but they are all of a practical nature, and contain no profound theology, nor any new elucidation of holy Scripture. Perhaps I might lay claim to as much as this, and therefore as good a claim to the distinction as very many on whom it is conferred, and who now consent to wear it. This, however, is saying very little.[45]

The Baptist minister, J.P. Chown, declined a DD from Rochester College, New York, and the Wesleyan William Arthur declined a DD from Dickinson College: whether or not their objection was to the DD in particular, however, is not recorded.[46] Thomas Binney was a rare, if not singular, case of a Nonconformist minister who declined to make use of an honorary LLD. Although Aberdeen awarded him this degree in 1852 (and in 1861 he was awarded a DD from an unidentified American university), John Stoughton is right to report that neither 'of these, however, were for some time assumed by him'.[47] Certainly throughout the 1860s he appeared in the *Congregational Year Book* as simply 'Binney, Thomas', while other men had 'LL.D.' or 'D.D.' after their names, and when he published a volume of his sermons in 1869, occasioned by his having completed 40 years of ministry at the King's Weigh House Chapel, the author was iden-

45. Dale, *James*, pp. 424-26.

46. D. Milner, 'J. P. Chown, 1821–1886', *Baptist Quarterly* 25 (1973), pp. 15-40; Taggart, *William Arthur*, pp. 149, 169 n. 37.

47. J. Stoughton, *A Memorial to the late Rev. Thomas Binney, LL.D.* (London: Hodder & Stoughton, 1874), p. 42.

tified on the title page as plain 'T. Binney'.[48] Other humble souls might have concealed their unsolicited degrees with complete success and, one hopes, have stored up eternal rewards for themselves.

Everything that has been elucidated thus far in this paper—notably, question marks over what motivated the award and the possibility that the honourable course might be to reject it—encouraged the writing of apologetic doctoring narratives which, in the memoirs of Dissenting ministers, are just as stereotyped as the conversion narratives they also contained. Of the Methodist New Connexion minister, William Cooke, it is said: 'About the year 1864, two colleges in America spontaneously conferred upon him, unasked and unexpected, the honorary degree of Doctor of Divinity.'[49] The watertight comprehensiveness of a legal document is suggested by the perceived need to use all three words: 'spontaneously', 'unasked' and 'unexpected'. Likewise, of John Leifchild: 'In the year 1841 Mr. became Dr. Leifchild, not from any motion of his own. He neither expected nor desired the distinction; but it came spontaneously.'[50] William Newman's biographer noted:

> Among those upon whom honorary titles have been conferred, perhaps comparatively few could say, as Dr. Gill is reported to have said, when he received his diploma: 'I neither thought it, sought it, nor bought it.' On the contrary, it is more than probable that *most* who have attained to such distinction have previously thought it; that *many* have sought it, and that *some* have not even scrupled to procure it by purchase. No one acquainted with Dr. Newman will, for a moment, suspect that the degree he obtained was either the result of personal request or pecuniary consideration...[51]

Concerning the case of the honorary doctorate of the Congregationalist John Campbell, we are told, in a level of cant befitting the man, that he 'cared little for such distinctions in themselves', but he accepted his DD as an ornament to the Church of Christ in general.[52] The Baptist Jabez Burns defended his acceptance of his doctorates on the paradoxical grounds that he did not feel competent to judge his own intellectual worth.[53] Of the

48. T. Binney, *Sermons Preached in the King's Weigh-house Chapel, London, 1829–1869* (London: Macmillan, 1869).

49. Stevenson, *Methodist Worthies*, IV, p. 614.

50. Leifchild, *John Leifchild*, pp. 243-44.

51. Pritchard, *William Newman*, pp. 283-87.

52. R. Ferguson and A.M. Brown, *The Life and Labours of John Campbell, D.D.* (London: Richard Bentley, 1867), p. 158.

53. J. Burns, *A Retrospect of Forty-Five Years' Christian Ministry* (London: Houlston, 1875), pp. 37-38.

Baptist Benjamin Evan's honorary DD we are told, in a splendid phrase, that 'he reluctantly accepted'.[54] Such apologetic language is so ubiquitous in the doctoring narratives of Dissenting ministers that one positively warms to William Landels, whom, we are told bluntly: 'felt no hesitation in accepting and using the degree, and was known henceforth as "Dr Landels" '.[55] Or even to the Congregational minister, R.W. Hamilton, who, after the usually disclaimer that 'not a man in the world less expected it than I did', disarmingly reveals that he consulted his friends in order to discover whether or not 'I may wear it without self-exaggeration, or as I express it, without making myself perfectly ridiculous'.[56]

Nevertheless, it be would be unfair to give the impression that the only issue at stake was the cultural aspirations of the individual ministers concerned, and that therefore these calculations were purely personal ones in which fairly won position battled with presumption and valid claims with vainglory inside the breast of a solitary servant of Christ. For the doctoring of their ministers unquestionably gratified the cultural aspirations of the congregations they served, and arguably of their entire denomination, or even Dissent generally. Binney might demurely put his name down as 'T. Binney' on his books, but to all who took vicarious pride in his fame he was 'the great Dr Binney' nonetheless.[57] Of the Congregationalist Robert Halley's award it is claimed:

> he mentioned it to his friend and colleague, Dr. Henderson, who whispered it in the classroom; and, whether he would or not, from that time he was 'the Doctor' at Highbury—a soubriquet added to it after years at Manchester, where he was generally spoken of amongst his people as 'the good Doctor,' or 'our good Doctor.'[58]

Likewise Andrew Reed reports of his and Matheson's return from America: 'Our literary honours, which we had not thought of adopting, had already created a change of style in England; and, on arriving at Liverpool, we were received as Doctors, learned in Divinity.'[59] While such

---

54. *Baptist Handbook, 1888*, pp. 94-95. (Evans was a Welshman, but the comment encapsulates well the tone of some English doctoring narratives.)

55. Landels, *William Landels*, p. 195.

56. W.H. Stowell, *Memoir of the Life of Richard Winter Hamilton, LL.D., D.D.* (London: Jackson & Walford, 1850), pp. 365-66.

57. Kaye, *King's Weigh House*, p. 62.

58. R. Halley, *A Short Biography of the Rev. Robert Halley, D.D.* (London: Hodder & Stoughton, 1879), p. xxxix.

59. Andrew Reed, *Memoirs of the Life and Philanthropic Labours of Andrew Reed* (London: Strahan, 1863), p. 189.

narratives might be a bit disingenuous, there is no doubt about the pride being expressed when some leading members of McKerrow's congregation organized a meeting in order to congratulate him formally on his award.[60] An even clearer example is that of the Baptist William Brock who, having been awarded an honorary DD from Harvard in 1860, steadfastly declined to make use of it until, six years after the event, his exasperated, aspiring congregation was reduced to passing a resolution urging him to do so. Thereafter, the members of his congregation referred to him with pride as 'the Doctor'.[61]

From the 1840s onwards, of course, esteem was also focused upon those who had earned degrees in England. In this new phase, a father-and-son pattern emerged in which a ministerial father with an honorary doctorate joyfully shared the glowing approbation of his denomination with a ministerial son possessing an English BA. One thinks, for example, of Robert and R.A. Vaughan, or of Andrew Reed and his namesake son. Moreover, some of the most prominent Nonconformist leaders of the late Victorian period combined the two. One can hardly begrudge the Baptist John Clifford his claim to the title 'Doctor' (even if it was based for several decades on an honorary DD conferred in 1883 by the youthful Bates College in Maine), once one realizes how industriously (if not greedily) he had pursued the English degrees that were open to him, earning from London University a BA in Classics (1861), a BSc in Geology (1864) and a LLB (1866), as well as an MA (1864).[62] These were signs of a coming day when the peculiar pathologies created by the Nonconformist grievances would be largely resolved, and when their passing would mark the end of many of the contortions surrounding honorary doctorates. 1920 may serve as the year in which the final nail was put in the coffin of the old order: not only was the Congregational minister W.B. Selbie an Oxford graduate, and not only was he the principal of a Dissenting Oxford college, but in that year he also became the first Nonconformist since the Commonwealth to be awarded an Oxford DD.[63]

On the other hand, if a comparative postscript may be permitted,

---

60. McKerrow, *William McKerrow*, p. 202.

61. C.M. Birrell, *The Life of William Brock, D.D.* (London: James Nisbet, 2nd edn, 1878), pp. 240, 317.

62. J.H.Y. Briggs, 'John Clifford', in T. Larsen (ed.), *Biographical Dictionary of Evangelicals* (Leicester: IVP, forthcoming).

63. See E. Kaye, 'Cultural Aspiration and the Dissenting Colleges: The First Students at Mansfield College, Oxford', in this volume, p. 173.

although English Baptist, Congregationalist and Methodist ministers became integrated into the university-attending, degree-earning, professional classes, the same pathologies explored in this study do re-emerge elsewhere in modern Christianity. Notably, the modernist–fundamentalist split in America (in which the modernists gained control of the historic universities and seminaries), has caused many of the patterns outlined here to be re-enacted. In certain conservative Christian circles in the English-speaking world, university bachelor's degrees are still rather rare in the ministry, and honorary doctorates from humble, if not dubious, institutions are rather too common. Even closer to the pattern of nineteenth-century English Dissent is the case of the Ulsterman Ian Paisley, who studied in humble, confessional colleges and never earned a degree, but who is standardly referred to in the media as 'Dr Paisley' on the strength of an honorary DD from Bob Jones University, South Carolina, a fundamentalist stronghold, better known for its stand against interracial relationships than as a centre of scholarship. So the pattern is repeated of marginalized religious groups compensating for their lack of cultural capital by brandishing honorary academic titles.

In conclusion, the unique circumstances of nineteenth-century Dissent, in particular the fact that Nonconformists were not allowed to earn degrees in England for the first third of the century, caused the Dissenting community to latch on to honorary degrees as a focus for their cultural aspirations. Many ministers viewed an honorary doctorate as a way to have their intellectual and professional abilities formally recognized, and to distinguish themselves from their peers, and as the only way in which they could gain a title with more cachet than Reverend. Likewise, Dissenting laymen and women viewed the gaining of honorary doctorates by their ministers as a way of offsetting the mark of cultural inferiority that English society placed upon them, and of portraying their leaders, and therefore their communities, as learned and distinguished. Nevertheless, for this manoeuvre to be effective, one had to navigate the dangerous waters where one might get caught attempting to use a title that was procured ignobly or that was awarded by an institution which lacked credibility. If successful, the resulting new status could be very gratifying indeed but, on the other hand, as R.W. Hamilton wisely noted, if it misfired one could end up appearing 'perfectly ridiculous'.

CULTURAL ASPIRATION AND THE DISSENTING COLLEGES:
THE FIRST STUDENTS AT MANSFIELD COLLEGE, OXFORD

Elaine Kaye

In his famous essay on 'Some Lapsed Dissenters: A Study of Ecclesiastical Pathology', first given as a lecture to the Cambridge University Congregational Society in 1931, Bernard Manning commented that 'the Church brings down the heavenly manna to places where there is culture and to places where there is no culture'.[1] This was a warning to those who in Manning's view did not fully appreciate 'the conflict of culture and Dissent'. This paper will examine the experience of five men who were to share in something of that conflict and tension through the decision to move an English Nonconformist theological college to Oxford.[2]

On 18 October 1886 a small group of men gathered together at 90 High Street, Oxford, with the main purpose of interviewing five young men who had applied to study for the Congregational ministry at the new institution which was about to be opened after transfer from Birmingham. Spring Hill College, founded in 1838, was now to be transformed into Mansfield College, named after its original founders. The chairman of the group, which constituted the college's Board of Education, was R.W. Dale, minister of Carr's Lane Church, Birmingham, and the newly appointed principal, Andrew Martin Fairbairn, was in attendance. At their previous meeting the month before, at Steelhouse Lane Chapel Vestry in Birmingham, the board had examined the credentials of the five young men, found them acceptable and summoned them to interview. All were now offered places, and all accepted. They were joined by one Spring Hill student, Frank Purcell Joseland,[3] who had one more year of his course to complete.

1. *Congregational Quarterly* 29 (1951), pp. 159-69 (169).
2. The issues are discussed in detail in M.D. Johnson, *The Dissolution of Dissent 1850–1918* (London: Garland Press, 1987) and Dale A. Johnson, *The Changing Shape of English Nonconformity 1825–1925* (Oxford: Oxford University Press, 1999).
3. Joseland (1863–1945) served with the London Missionary Society in China from 1888 until 1913, when he retired to Australia.

After the five had been told of their acceptance, Dr Fairbairn addressed them, 'saying that while others came to colleges that were full of old traditions, we had got to make the traditions of Mansfield'.[4] The party then removed to the Randolph Hotel for lunch, before returning to 90 High Street at four o'clock to join others in hearing Dr Fairbairn give the inaugural address on 'The Study of Theology and the Theological Student', a lecture which the *Oxford Magazine* reported as one of 'great breadth and power'. Five days later, those who were not already members of the university were matriculated through the Society for Non-Collegiate Students. The rooms which were rented for their lectures and for worship during the next three years had historic associations. One had formerly housed the Oxford Union, a room in which Gladstone had honed his oratorical skills; the other was once occupied by Charles I during the siege of Oxford in the 1640s.

Four of them had these rooms as their college base throughout their entire Oxford course, though they must have watched the college's new building rise on the far side of Holywell. Both Fairbairn and Dale had insisted that the college should not be residential in order to avoid the dangers of the 'seminary mentality' and the students therefore found lodgings in north Oxford. The exception was Dugald Macfadyen, who began his undergraduate course at Merton College in 1886 but simultaneously shared in Mansfield's collegiate life from the beginning. The names of the other students were Charles Silvester Horne, J.A. Robinson, William Boothby Selbie and Thomas Arthur Wolfendale.

Those contemplating admission to an English Congregational theological college in 1886 had a choice of nine colleges—Rotherham, Airedale[5] and Lancashire Independent College in the north, Hackney, New and Cheshunt in the south, Western in Plymouth, the Congregational Institute in Nottingham, and now Mansfield in Oxford. Seven of these colleges offered a general literary course as well as a theological one, a wide curriculum taught by a small number of tutors. The establishment of London University had opened arts degrees to students of these colleges, and the development of local university colleges was now providing new possibilities to students in London, Nottingham and Manchester. But none could yet match the possibilities of Oxford or Cambridge, despite their many deficiencies.

---

4. Charles Silvester Horne, quoted in W.B. Selbie, *The Life of Charles Silvester Horne M.A. M.P.* (London: Hodder & Stoughton, 1920), p. 32.

5. Rotherham and Airedale were about to be amalgamated after several years of negotiation as the Yorkshire United Independent College.

Of the college principals, Fairbairn was the most distinguished theologian, though John Brown Paton of Nottingham and Henry Reynolds[6] of Cheshunt were in different ways also significant figures. The most-needed reform was a clear division between the literary and theological courses, a reform which Fairbairn had recently introduced at Airedale by sending the students to Edinburgh for three years.

Mansfield, a postgraduate college, was able to provide some new opportunities. There were the resources of a university theology faculty, however imperfect, and the opportunities to meet and debate with students from other colleges and studying other disciplines in the Oxford Union and in other societies. The Oxford of 1886 was at last enjoying a more liberal atmosphere. Nonconformists and other non-Anglicans were now free to study there and take all degrees except divinity degrees; women from the new halls were beginning to appear at lectures; college fellows were now allowed to marry and fewer of them were clergymen. Since the death of Pusey in 1882 the Tractarian influence had diminished and liberal Anglican theologians enjoyed a greater freedom.

Matthew Arnold had attacked Nonconformists for their lack of culture in an essay in *Culture and Anarchy*, published in 1869. Was it now possible for them to enjoy the atmosphere of 'sweetness and light' which Arnold found in Oxford without compromising their principles? Opinion was divided and the effort was bound to produce a certain tension. The subject was aired at Congregational Union assemblies from 1870 onwards. The problem was well expressed by Edwin Hatch, Oxford's Reader in Ecclesiastical History, in an article on 'Nonconformity at Oxford' in the *Methodist Times* (11 June 1885). He welcomed the possibility of a Nonconformist college in Oxford, for it would 'show the possibility of a vigorous Christianity which believes in Christ and yet is not sacerdotal', and would bring 'the inspiration of freedom and of progress'. On the other hand he maintained that its previous lack of close contact with the world of society and of letters had deprived it of much that was understood as 'culture'. According to this interpretation, the Nonconformists and the university would have something positive to give to each other.

At least four of the men we are considering were the sons of ministers.[7] Charles Silvester Horne was the son of the Revd Charles Horne (c. 1833–

---

6. Henry Reynolds gave the communion address at the opening of Mansfield's new buildings.

7. It is likely that J.A. Robinson's father was also a minister, but firm evidence is lacking.

1903) who had been a student at Spring Hill in the 1850s in the days of R.W. Dale and John Brown Paton. He had spent some years in pastoral ministry before abandoning that for journalism and political activity in Newport, Shropshire. His eldest son, Leonard,[8] went to St John's, Cambridge, a college much favoured by Nonconformists. Charles Silvester, who was younger, went to Glasgow University when he was 16, after his school, Newport Grammar School, had taught him as much as it could. In Glasgow he was able to develop his debating skills and acquired firm Liberal views. A sermon by John Allison Macfadyen at Elgin Place Church in 1886 deeply impressed him and encouraged him in his desire to enter the Congregational ministry. It was natural for him to think of his father's old college, Spring Hill, but since this was the year 1886, his application to Spring Hill inevitably became an application to Mansfield.

Of J.A. Robinson little is known. He was born in Portugal in the 1860s at a time when foreign Protestants were just beginning to have some freedom to exercise positive influence in the country. He had enrolled in Airedale College when Fairbairn was principal. According to the requirements recently introduced by Fairbairn, he had spent three years in Edinburgh following the arts course, and now presumably had been encouraged by Fairbairn to follow him to Oxford. Like so many of his contemporaries he was fired by the missionary ideal, but in his case not to the East, but to Catholic Europe. He planned to return to Portugal, the land of his birth, to lead an independent mission, 'in the belief that the people will more readily respond to a preaching of the Gospel that is done by no minister of a foreign church'.[9]

Thomas Arthur Wolfendale[10] was the son of the Revd James Wolfendale (1833–89), who had spent four years preparing for ministry at the Rotherham Independent College before beginning his sole pastorate at Tutbury in Staffordshire. He published a number of biblical commentaries and works for Sunday schools. Thomas Arthur was his eldest son; his two younger sons both trained as doctors in Edinburgh and both went out as missionaries with the London Missionary Society.[11] Thomas Wolfendale

8. Leonard Thomas Horne (1860–1934), a civil servant. See *Who Was Who, 1929–40*.

9. Mansfield College *Annual Report 1887–8*.

10. For Wolfendale (1864–1938), see *Congregational Year Book, 1939*, p. 718, and *Mansfield College Magazine* 113 (938), pp. 530-31.

11. Richard Wolfendale (1866–1921) was in China, and George Ashton Wolfendale (1868–?) went out to Central Africa, but had to return after two years because of ill health.

had attended Caterham School and then Burton-on-Trent Grammar School before going up to St John's College, Cambridge, where he evidently distinguished himself in rowing as much as, or more than, in academic work. His fellow students in Oxford later agreed that though he was not marked by outstanding intellectual gifts, he had been instrumental in creating a rowing tradition at Mansfield, then, perhaps as now, considered necessary if the college were to hold its own in the university community.[12]

William Boothby Selbie[13] was the son of the Revd Robert William Selbie (1825–93),[14] who had prepared for ministry at the Lancashire Independent College under Robert Vaughan. His pastorates were in Chesterfield and Salford. The younger Selbie attended Manchester Grammar School, and from there won a scholarship to Brasenose College, Oxford, to read 'Greats' in 1882. He could not, therefore, be charged with that lack of Hellenism that was part of Matthew Arnold's charge against Nonconformity. Selbie experienced occasional prejudice among his contemporaries on account of his Nonconformity, but was encouraged when he found himself among a small group of Nonconformist undergraduates being gathered together by R.F. Horton, Fellow of New College, in the Oxford University Nonconformists' Union. This led him to reflect later that while the Oxford atmosphere 'may not be very healthy for a weak-kneed and anaemic type of Nonconformist…to Free Churchmen who have convictions and have the courage of them it is quite innocuous'.[15] In his second year Selbie was elected secretary of the Nonconformists' Union, and was a frequent contributor to discussion and an occasional speaker.[16] At the end of his course he was placed in the first class in the 'Greats' examinations.

One of the other leading members of the Nonconformists' Union was William Allison Macfadyen,[17] a scholar of Brasenose one year below Selbie; he too had arrived in Oxford via Manchester Grammar School. He was the eldest of the five surviving sons of the Revd John Allison Mac-

---

12. *Mansfield College Magazine* 113 (1938), p. 531.

13. For Selbie (1862–1944), see *Mansfield College Magazine* 125 (1944), pp. 100-10. Selbie did not want his biography to be written, and destroyed his papers.

14. Robert Boothby Selbie was also the son of a minister, William Selbie (1797–1877), born in Aberdeen, who studied in Edinburgh and held pastorates in England.

15. W.B. Selbie, 'Fifty Years at Oxford', *Congregational Quarterly* 14 (1936), pp. 282-90 (289).

16. See the minute book of the Oxford University Nonconformists' Union (Mansfield College Archive).

17. Macfadyen (1865–1924) later taught in colleges in South Africa. See *Who Was Who, 1916–28*.

fadyen—there were also two daughters—and his wife Elizabeth (née Anderson). The second surviving son, Dugald, also attended Manchester Grammar School, and won a history scholarship to Merton, but because he wished to follow his father into the Congregational ministry, had applied for acceptance by Mansfield, and was one of the little group who were interviewed on 18 October 1886.

The father, John Allison Macfadyen,[18] was born in Greenock. After five years at the University of Glasgow he entered the Lancashire Independent College on the advice of Alexander Raleigh, who had been minister of his home church for a time. He had a brief ministry in St Helen's before being called to the new Congregational church in Chorlton Road, Manchester. Here he remained for 26 years, until his comparatively early death in 1888. During those years the membership grew from 70 to 837. Though his parents had been Congregationalists, there was a strong element of Scottish Presbyterianism within him which found an echo in early English Puritanism. His biographer called him 'Puritan in mental build and habit'. He called himself a 'High Churchman' and was an early advocate of the union of Presbyterians and Independents. When he was elected chairman of the Congregational Union for the year 1882–83 he chose as his subject for the May address, 'The Ideal of the Christian Church'.

His life illustrates both the advantages and the drawbacks of close parental interest in education, as well as the problems of 'cultural aspiration'. He brought with him to England Scottish ideals of education, and was a firm supporter of the foundation of Mansfield. He took a very close interest in the education of his children, and took time to talk with them about history, politics, theology and—sometimes—poetry, with a strong emphasis on Puritan characters and ideas. When his sons were at Manchester Grammar School, he would ask to see their examination papers and then go over them, giving his opinion of how they had done and how he would have answered each question. Their essays had to be read to him and then discussed.[19] It was a great disappointment to him, not in the least disguised from his children, that both William and Dugald were awarded second class degrees; Dugald's subsequent first in theology was too late to eradicate the disappointment.

The academic careers of his younger sons were still at an early stage when their father died. Perhaps this was as well, since neither of the two

18. For John Allison Macfadyen (1837–1889), see A. Mackennal, *The Life of John Allison Macfadyen* (London: Hodder & Stoughton, 1891).

19. Mackennal, *Macfadyen*, pp. 256, 266.

who went up to Oxford gained the firsts their father had always hoped for them. Alfred Newth Macfadyen[20] won an exhibition to Wadham College. Eric,[21] the youngest, gained a scholarship to Wadham. Both Alfred and Eric applied to Mansfield at the beginning of their undergraduate courses, and were accepted, but both later withdrew.[22] Alfred followed his eldest brother to South Africa. Eric, who was president of the Oxford Union in his last year, went out to Malaya as a civil servant. His career culminated in a brief spell in the House of Commons, a knighthood and membership of the local hunt.

The Macfadyen daughters, Marjorie and Johanna, and their adopted sister, Ellie Longwill,[23] were all educated at Milton Mount College, Gravesend (opened in 1873 for the education of the daughters of Congregational ministers), and therefore presumably reasonably free from their father's supervision.[24]

Dugald Macfadyen attended meetings and services at Mansfield about three times a week during his undergraduate course, but also seems to have taken a full part in Merton College life, frequently speaking at the debating society. The atmosphere of Merton was likely to have been congenial; Warden Brodrick[25] had been a firm supporter of the coming of Mansfield and had helped to facilitate the sale of Merton's land for the new college. The history tutor was A.H. Johnson,[26] who did much to establish the comparatively new History School in Oxford, and whose wife Bertha was a pioneer in the establishment of the Society of Home Students for women.

Two of the students being considered, therefore—Selbie and Macfadyen —came from that urban, prosperous, confident Manchester Nonconformity

20. Alfred Newth Macfadyen (1869–?). Alfred Newth, after whom he was named, was one of John Allison Macfadyen's tutors at the Lancashire Independent College.

21. Eric Macfadyen (1879–1966) was a civil servant and pioneer rubber planter in Malaya. For a short time he was MP for Devizes. He was eventually knighted for his work for the Imperial School of Tropical Agriculture, Trinidad. See V.S. Macfadyen, *Eric Macfadyen, 1879–1966* (Barnet: Stellar Press, 1968).

22. See Mansfield College Board of Education Minutes (Mansfield College Archive), entries for 20 January 1890 and 15 June 1897.

23. Ellie Longwill was the orphaned daughter of Macfadyen's schoolfriend, David Longwill.

24. It was unusual for a family to send their daughters to boarding school and their sons to a day school.

25. George Charles Brodrick (1831–1903). See *DNB*.

26. Arthur Henry Johnson (1845–1927). See *Who Was Who, 1916–28*.

which was about to take a significant role in promoting and financing the new Mansfield College in Oxford.

How was a Mansfield ministerial course to differ from that in the other Congregational theological colleges? Those responsible for the decision which led to the move from Birmingham to Oxford had to consider whether education within what had for two hundred years been an Anglican institution would destroy or at least weaken the Puritan tradition that had kept Nonconformists separate from the Church of England since the late seventeenth century. For Fairbairn, the opening of Mansfield in Oxford was a *return* to the inheritance from which they had been excluded after 1662. But since that date, the education of Nonconformists, especially that of ministers, had taken place largely in separate institutions, which contributed to that distinct culture and ethos that formed such an important element in Victorian life. In returning to Oxford they would have to adopt something of that Anglican culture which had flourished in Oxford over the previous two centuries unhampered by Dissenting influence. Selbie's comment on his friend Horne that 'his Free Churchmanship was of a very robust type, almost too much so for some of his contemporaries on whom the influence of Oxford was strong', suggests that their reaction varied.[27] That mutual enrichment to which Hatch had referred would not be easy to achieve. However, one Anglican commentator offered the view in 1900 that 'Mansfield College at Oxford, under Dr Fairbairn's headship, is becoming more and more the nucleus and fountain-head of theological culture to which the Church of England is hardly less indebted than the Nonconformist churches', and suggested that leading Nonconformists were now 'fully in line with the highest English culture'.[28]

The two resident tutors in the first years were Fairbairn and Dr John Massie.[29] Fairbairn was already a theologian of some stature, and through participation in the new Oxford Society of Historical Theology and through personal friendships made a positive contribution to Oxford theology. Massie, a Cambridge graduate who taught New Testament and patristics,

27. Selbie, *Horne*, p. 36.

28. R.E. Bartlett, 'The Relations of the Church of England with Modern Nonfonformity', in A.G.B. Atkinson, Christian Conference Essays (London: A. & C. Black, 1900), pp. 223-50 (238, 236).

29. Massie (1842–1925), the son of the Revd Robert Massie, had read classics at St John's College, Cambridge, and taught New Testament and patristics. He was never ordained. From 1906 until 1910 he was Liberal MP for North Wiltshire. See *Who Was Who, 1916–28.*

was both a meticulous scholar, and an active participant in public life. In 1903 he left Mansfield in order to spend more time in politics, and was elected a Member of Parliament in 1906. In addition the students were able to benefit from the teaching of Anglican theologians and biblical scholars, an opportunity not yet available to their contemporaries in other Congregational theological colleges. The first generation of students attended lectures by Edwin Hatch[30] on church history, William Sanday[31] on the New Testament and Thomas Cheyne[32] on the Old Testament. It was Edwin Hatch who most warmly welcomed Mansfield and who made the deepest impression. In his book, *Pulpit, Platform and Parliament* (London, 1913), Horne wrote of the inspiration he had received from Hatch's book on *The Organization of the Early Christian Churches*, and in particular of the sentence from which he said he had never been able to escape: 'The unaccomplished mission of Christianity is to reconstruct society on the basis of brotherhood.' This vision of 'Christian brotherhood' inspired all Horne's future work, and it was to form the basis of his first address as chairman of the Congregational Union in May 1910. Selbie too acknowledged the influence of Hatch on his own thinking when he published a book of sermons preached in Cambridge under the title *Aspects of Christ* (London, 1909), and later referred to Hatch's lectures as having been for him and for his contemporaries 'an almost epoch-making experience'.

Oxford offered other opportunities as well as lectures, seminars and rowing. The Oxford Union offered valuable opportunities for public speaking and debate. Horne, Selbie and Macfadyen all took part in Union debates. The political interests which Horne had first developed in Glasgow were now given further scope. On 3 February 1887, for example, he was one of the main speakers for the motion (which was lost), 'That in the opinion of this House the existence of the House of Lords in its present form, is useless and harmful'. Two years later he spoke alongside Gilbert Murray for the motion, 'That in the opinion of this House it is desirable to close Public Houses altogether on Sunday'.

30.   Hatch (1835–89) was Reader in Ecclesiastical History, author of *The Organization of the Early Christian Churches* (Oxford: Rivingtons, 1881), originally given as the Bampton Lectures. See *DNB*.

31.   Sanday (1843–1920), Dean Ireland's Professor of Exegesis of Holy Scripture and Fellow of Exeter College. Later he was Lady Margaret Professor of Divinity. See *DNB*.

32.   Thomas Kelly Cheyne (1841–1915) was Oriel Professor of the Interpretation of Scripture. See *DNB*.

Oxford in the 1880s was developing its social conscience, and 'was just beginning to take seriously the idea that gilded youth had duties as well as privileges'.[33] The greatest influence in fostering this view was undoubtedly T.H. Green,[34] the philosophy tutor at Balliol and Professor of Moral Philosophy until his death in 1882. His ideas lived on through the charismatic Arnold Toynbee (1852–83) and Toynbee Hall in London, and the less charismatic but conscientious W.H. Fremantle, chaplain of Balliol. Fremantle was a frequent attender at the Nonconformists' Union. The first Mansfield students were involved in the discussions and debates that led to the foundation of Mansfield House Settlement, and their influence is clear in the later activities of both Horne and Macfadyen.

At the end of their course, four of these men went almost immediately into pastoral ministry in England. The fifth, J.A. Robinson, went out to Portugal to begin what he saw as his life's work. Although he wanted to be independent, he no doubt had some association with the group of Congregationalists who had been active in the country since 1880. But his ambition was cut short just before Easter 1892 when he died of typhoid fever at Portalegre. Fairbairn told the college subscribers: 'He had devoted his life to the Portuguese, and it was his great ambition to aid in the creation of a National Protestant Church in the country of his birth.' Although his life was short, the small Congregational church which still survived there 40 years later bore witness to his work.[35]

Thomas Wolfendale went to minister in Durham, where he became particularly interested in the work of the British and Foreign Bible Society. After 13 years in Durham he spent the rest of his working life as a local secretary for the society, first in Lancashire, later in the north midlands. He died in 1938.

The continuing lives of the other three were more closely intertwined, and they are more fully documented. All three were married in the early 1890s. Selbie, who remained at Mansfield for a year as Hebrew tutor after finishing his course, married Mildred Mary Thompson, daughter of Joseph Thompson,[36] chairman of the Manchester Ship Canal Company, and Lord

33. W.H. Walsh, 'The Zenith of Greats', in M. Brock and M. Curthoys (eds.), *History of the University of Oxford*, VII (Oxford: Oxford University Press, 2000), pp. 311-26 (322).

34. Thomas Hill Green (1836–1882), idealist philosopher.

35. See E. Moreira, *The Significance of Portugal: A Survey of Evangelical Progress* (London: World Dominion Press, 1933).

36. Joseph Thompson (1833–1909) was the third generation of his family to serve

Mayor of Manchester in the year of the canal's opening by Queen Victoria. They met when the Thompsons entertained Selbie as the visiting student preacher at Wilmslow, and married in 1890. In later years Mildred Selbie was a formidable matriarch when she presided over the principal's lodgings at Mansfield. She outlived her husband by 20 years and reached her hundredth birthday. Two years after the Selbies' marriage Horne married Katharine Cozens-Hardy, a member of Kensington Chapel, a sister of William Hepburn Cozens-Hardy, a contemporary and friend of the Mansfield trio in Oxford. Their father, Herbert Cozens-Hardy,[37] was a distinguished lawyer from a Norfolk Congregational family. At the time of his daughter's marriage Cozens-Hardy was MP for North Norfolk; eventually he became the first Baron Cozens-Hardy, Master of the Rolls. A further two years later Dugald Macfadyen married Mary Olivia Goulty, the second daughter of Wallis Rivers Goulty, engineer, and Olivia King Young, of Bowdon, near Manchester. She was the chief schoolfriend of one of his sisters, and they first met in each other's houses when she was a child. They met again in Oxford when he lectured to a summer school which she attended. The following autumn, at the beginning of his last year, she came up to Somerville Hall, Oxford, with the intention of training to be a teacher. But on the day of his ordination they became engaged, and she left Oxford. In doing so, she had the approval of her college tutors, who felt she was 'more cut out for married life than for the life of a student'.[38] However theirs was an intellectual partnership, and she was able to help her husband with much of his literary work in the succeeding years.

In the 1890s all three men were engaged in pastoral ministry. Selbie was minister of Highgate Congregational Church,[39] north London, where his great gifts for preaching were first developed. After 1892 Leonard Horne was a member of his church. Charles Silvester Horne was minister at Kensington Chapel, having been called there more than a year before he finished his course. Although, according to his friend Arthur Porritt, he found the congregation 'rather stuffy', he appreciated 'the definite and resolute

on the council of the Lancashire Independent College. He was one of the earliest students of Owens College, Manchester, and wrote a history of both Owens College (1886) and of Lancashire Independent College (1893).

37. For Cozens-Hardy (1838–1920), see *DNB*.

38. See D. Macfadyen, *A Modern Puritan* (London: privately printed, 1912), p. 14.

39. See J.H. Thompson, *Highgate Dissenters: Their History since 1660* (n.p., 2001), for the ministries of Selbie and Macfadyen in Highgate.

Dissenting attitude' of the membership.[40] After a spell in Germany listening to Harnack, Macfadyen went to St Ives Free Church, Huntingdonshire, a lively but not particularly challenging church whose self-confidence was proclaimed by a spire which deliberately exceeded the height of that of the parish church by several inches.[41]

All three had an interest in history and in common with many of their contemporaries felt a need to articulate and defend the principles of Nonconformity through a study of its earlier exponents. In 1893, the tercentenary of the death of Barrow, Greenwood and Penry, Horne wrote one of the celebratory pamphlets on 'The Separatists at the Universities'. He spoke at several commemoration meetings, exhorting young Congregationalists to seek inspiration in the lives and deaths of these martyrs. Two years later came a history of the London Missionary Society on the occasion of its centenary. Another five years later he published 'What we owe to the Puritans', a plea for Christian democracy: 'The Puritans' mission in the Church is to make the Christian People the supreme authority there.'[42] It was in his capacity as organizing secretary of the Congregational Young People's Union that he wrote to George Currie Martin in 1899 to suggest the foundation of a Congregational Historical Society. Martin, then minister in Reigate, soon discovered considerable support for the idea and summoned a gathering during the autumn meetings of the Congregational Union. This led to the formal establishment of the society at a meeting in the Memorial Hall in London in May 1900, when Horne was one of the chief speakers. Selbie and Macfadyen both joined him as members.

The end of the nineteenth century saw the transformation of Nonconformist churches into Free Churches, with the emphasis moving away from the removal of disabilities to a more positive witness. There were also strong hopes for some form of Free Church unity. As the battle lines between the Church of England and the Free Churches began to form around the issue of education at the turn of the century, Horne wrote his *A Popular History of the Free Churches* (London: James Clarke, 1903), introducing the work in the preface with the comment:

> While the men and women of the Free Churches are bracing themselves to renew the fight for unsectarian education and religious equality it may be well that they refresh their memories of those illustrious [sic] who helped to make England great.

40. C.S. Horne, *A Century of Christian Service: Kensington Congregational Church, 1793–1893* (London: Hodder & Stoughton, 1893), p. 16.
41. See M. Wagner, *Not an Easy Church* (St Ives: The Free Church, 1982).
42. C.S. Horne, *What We Owe to the Puritans* (London: H. Marshall, 1898), p. 12.

His history was not based on original historical research, and indeed he was taken to task by John Brown in an early issue of the Historical Society's *Transactions* for an unscholarly use of documents.[43] But, as Selbie commented, Horne's historical work produced a 'convincing story glowing with conviction and at times even with passion'.[44] It offered an interpretation of Congregational origins and identity which was to inspire two or three succeeding generations of young Congregationalists. At the same time Horne's perspective was not narrow. When he was asked to address the students of Regent's Park College—then in London—on 'The Ministry of the Modern Church' (lectures published under that title in 1907), he entitled his final lecture, 'The modern catholic', and exhorted his hearers always to remember that their Christian inheritance was greater than their own tradition.[45]

In his years as minister in Highgate and Cambridge Selbie laid a strong emphasis on the duties and responsibilities of church membership, and his chairman's address to the Congregational Union in 1914 had the same theme. His expositions of Congregational and Free Church principles were published after he became principal of Mansfield, and after his attendance at the World Missionary Conference in Edinburgh in 1910. In 1911 he edited a series of lectures given in the college on *Evangelical Christianity: Its History and Witness*, and a year later he wrote the volume on *Nonconformity: Its Origin and Progress* in the Home University Library series.

Selbie had left Highgate in 1902 for Emmanuel Church, Cambridge, a church whose role in Cambridge was similar to that of Mansfield College chapel in Oxford. Here he had among his church members A.S. Ramsey, the father of a future Archbishop of Canterbury. When the Countess of Huntingdon's college moved to Cambridge as Cheshunt College, Selbie was invited to lecture to its students. He was succeeded in Highgate by Dugald Macfadyen. This link, and the fact that Leonard Horne was the senior deacon at Highgate, kept the three men in continuing contact. Macfadyen had left St Ives in 1896 for Hanley Tabernacle in Staffordshire; he and his wife had felt that they ought to seek a more challenging sphere of work. At Hanley, both husband and wife had thrown themselves

43. *Transactions of the Congregational Historical Society* 1.2 (1900), pp. 79-83 (79). John Brown was commenting on Horne's paper, 'From a Diary of the Gurney Family', published in an earlier number: 1.1 (1900), pp. 39-43 (39).

44. Selbie, *Horne*, p. 137.

45. C.S. Horne, *The Ministry of the Modern Church* (London: James Clarke, 1907), pp. 257-86.

into their work, both inside and outside the church. Dugald was much involved in educational work in the community—a member of Hanley County Borough Education Committee, and first secretary of the Council for Higher Education in North Staffordshire. Olive worked among factory girls and promoted and led a Pleasant Sunday Afternoon for women. While recognizing that the people were friendly, both of them pined for more intellectual companionship. Dugald later reflected that 'the absence of outside intellectual companionship drove me to literary work to keep my soul alive'.[46]

Among the fruits of that literary work was his chief contribution to the rethinking of denominational structures, *Constructive Congregational Ideals* (London, 1902), subtitled 'A series of addresses and essays illustrating the growth of corporate life and feeling in the Congregational churches during forty years, and the significance of this movement as a true modern development of early Free Church ideals'. The first part was a collection of articles from earlier years by Congregational leaders such as Dale, Fairbairn and Macfadyen senior, while the second part by Macfadyen included a series of specific proposals for realizing more fully the corporate life of Congregational churches and for closer Free Church cooperation. Ten years' experience in rural and urban ministry had persuaded him of the need to rethink the relation of autonomous churches to one another, and to overcome the obstacles, as he saw them, of 'individualism in the pew and egotism in the pulpit'.[47] He viewed with favour the possibility of common ministerial education, such as Mansfield offered, at least among the Free Churches, as a contribution towards future organic union.

The move to Highgate in 1904 brought a wider, more congenial, circle of friends and a release from the stress felt in Hanley. He was able to continue with literary work: a substantial biography of Alexander Mackennal (who had written the biography of his father) appeared in 1905. He contributed to the *Mansfield College Essays* of 1909 an essay on 'Final Christianity: Some results of the historico-critical method in the study of religion', and made other contributions to the *Contemporary Review*, the *Encyclopaedia Britannica*, the *Encyclopaedia of Religion and Ethics* and the *Transactions of the Congregational Historical Society*.

All three men were outstanding preachers. Macfadyen's preaching was the most intellectual; in the opinion of one knowing commentator, Mans-

---

46. Macfadyen, *Modern Puritan*, p. 28.
47. D. Macfadyen, *Constructive Congregational Ideals* (London: H.R. Allenson, 1902), p. 13.

field had 'ruined' his style by overemphasizing the intellectual dimension. Selbie's preaching was considered by many to be too academic for his congregation at Highgate at first, but became more 'balanced' as time went on.[48] In Cambridge he soon gained a reputation as an outstanding preacher. One former undergraduate remembered how 'his words would stab your spirit broad awake'.[49] After he returned to Oxford as principal of Mansfield in 1909 he became the best-known preacher in the city, and drew large congregations from all denominations to the college chapel. He frequently said that his primary task as principal was to produce preachers. His comment on a student sermon that 'it wouldn't save the soul of a tomtit' was well known. He was in great demand as a preacher all over the country in the college vacations. Horne, whose preaching was described as 'electrifying', was often booked as a preacher two or three years ahead.

When Horne left Kensington in 1903, it was to take up the challenge of the ailing Whitefield's Tabernacle in Tottenham Court Road. The London Congregational Union had just agreed to sponsor it as a mission, and Horne found it a challenge he could not resist. His recent reading of Charles Booth's *Life and Labour of London*, combined with the continuing influence of Edwin Hatch, had fired him with the vision of an 'institutional church' which would provide premises open throughout the week offering refreshment, physical and mental, appropriate to the needs of people in the neighbourhood. 'The public houses should be compelled to recognise in the Free Church their greatest rival and counter-attraction.'[50] The governing principle was to be, 'the more human our institutions are, the more Christ will be at home in them'.[51] 'We are here, as Dr Hatch said, not to follow John the Baptist into the wilderness, but Christ into the world.'[52] The experiment was a phenomenal success. The church and Toplady Hall were renovated and the institute behind was rebuilt to the design of Morley Horder. Horne enlisted the voluntary help of men and women members of the congregation, and the institute flourished from the beginning. It was open to all: 'We Congregationalists have behind us the

48. This view was expressed by William Blackshaw, one of Selbie's successors at Highgate, in 'William Boothby Selbie, 1862–1944', *Mansfield College Magazine* 125 (1944), pp. 100-110 (101).

49. A.H. Fowler in 'William Boothby Selbie, 1862–1944', *Mansfield College Magazine* 125 (1944), pp. 100-110 (102).

50. C.S. Horne, *The Institutional Church* (London: James Clarke, 1906), p. 24.

51. Horne, *Institutional Church*, p. 60.

52. Quoted in Selbie, *Horne*, p. 195.

tradition of Milton and Cromwell in favour of the rights of the people as against the privileges of any caste or class.'[53] Whitefield's was to exemplify the principle of 'Christian Brotherhood'. The vagabonds of central London were to be as welcome as the middle-class suburban dwellers.

Such work could not avoid the charge of being 'political'. But, responded Horne:

> If the Church is not interested in Education, Licensing Reform, Housing, the Reconstruction of the Poor Law, a Living Wage, Divorce, the arrest of Gambling, the abolition of slavery, and, above all International Peace, the Church may as well disband her forces, and make an ignominious exit from the society she can no longer inspire and guide.[54]

Even before going to Whitefield's he had become embroiled in the controversy over the 1902 Education Act, and his speech at the autumn meeting of the Congregational Union in Glasgow in that year had led to invitations to speak all over the country. He was one of those who withheld payment of rates after the Education Act of 1902. In 1906 he was urged to stand for parliament; he had already had experience of canvassing through supporting his brother, Fred, as Liberal candidate for Ludlow in 1903. This time he resisted the invitation. But he did not resist a second invitation in 1910 to stand for Ipswich. He was elected, the first man in pastoral charge to sit in the House of Commons since the days of Praise-God Barebones in the seventeenth century. Though he spoke on several occasions, he did not make an outstanding impression: 'The brightest star on the Nonconformist horizon, Horne failed to shine in the parliamentary firmament.'[55]

By 1914 he had almost exhausted his strength. He resigned from Whitefield's and sailed to America to give the Yale Lectures on Preaching.[56] He told Arthur Porritt that he doubted that he would return either to Congregational ministry or to parliament, but had thoughts of giving his whole time to the Brotherhood movement. Three days after delivering the last lecture he died suddenly en route to Toronto. He was only 49, and greatly mourned. His old friend, Selbie, wrote his biography, using his diaries and papers.

Macfadyen and Selbie both survived the war, though each lost a son in

---

53. C.S. Horne, *Pulpit, Platform and Parliament* (London: Hodder & Stoughton, 1913), p. 75.

54. Quoted in Selbie, *Horne*, p. 213.

55. S. Koss, *Nonconformity in Modern British Politics* (London: Batsford, 1975), pp. 107-108.

56. Published as *The Romance of Preaching* (London: James Clarke, 1914).

the conflict. Macfadyen's wife had died suddenly in 1912 after nursing one of their children through a serious illness. It was Horne's brother Leonard who spoke at the unveiling of the memorial window to Olive Macfadyen in Highgate Congregational Church. Only a few months after that, Macfadyen resigned from Highgate and moved to Letchworth, where his younger brother Norman had been living for some years. He was only 47, but never again served in pastoral ministry. Apart from work in France with the YMCA, and several visits to the United States, he spent the last 20 years of his life in Letchworth.

His younger brother Norman[57] had broken the family mould by not going to Oxford, but had qualified as a doctor at St Bartholomew's Hospital, London. He then entered general practice, first in Hitchin, then in Letchworth, Hertfordshire, where the Garden City Association, inspired by Ebenezer Howard, had just purchased an estate. He soon emerged as one of the leaders of the new community, serving as medical officer of health and chairman of the executive of the Garden City and Town Planning Association. Mrs Macfadyen senior had joined him in Letchworth in 1904, and after Dugald's wife died, his children spent holidays there.

When Dugald settled in Letchworth he joined a book club, through which members agreed to lend each other books from their own personal libraries. For this purpose Edith Barnett Bates, the daughter of a Manchester businessman who had moved to Letchworth some years earlier, came to catalogue his books. Within months of meeting the two were married. They were parted for much of the remainder of the war when Dugald went abroad, to France with the YMCA and to the United States, lecturing to troop camps.

Dugald Macfadyen had been interested in the problems of housing since his years in Hanley, and after the war he devoted himself to politics, social questions, writing, lecturing in Britain and the United States and supporting the League of Nations. Though he preached there occasionally, he never actually joined the Free Church which had been founded in Letchworth in 1905, finding the rather vague churchmanship and eclectic membership unattractive. He preferred to attend the local Quaker meeting.[58] One of his close neighbours was Henry Cubbon, whose time at Mansfield

57. Norman Macfadyen (1887–?). See *Who's Who in Local Government* (1931) and *Medical Who's Who* (1914).

58. I am grateful to Clyde Binfield for this and other information about Dugald Macfadyen's later life, particularly that derived from his correspondence with Mrs Elspeth Bristow, daughter of Dugald Macfadyen, in 1984.

had overlapped with his own. Both Cubbon and Macfadyen were admirers of Ebenezer Howard, and both engaged in politics, though for different parties—Cubbon supported the Labour Party, while Macfadyen was a Liberal.

Macfadyen's political interests led him to stand for parliament, unsuccessfully, four times, in Reading and in Hertfordshire, and to the presidency of the North Hertfordshire Liberal Association. He was a founder member and secretary of the Council for the Interchange of British and American Ministers, and continued to visit the United States regularly. He chaired the local branch of the League of Nations Union, and visited Geneva in 1924 to see its workings and make a report.[59] As a founder member of the local Rotary Club he visited several countries in Europe. His last book was *Sir Ebenezer Howard and the Town Planning Movement*, published in 1933. When he died in 1936, it was his old friend Selbie who wrote his obituary in the *Mansfield Magazine*, describing him as having been 'a busy, not to say restless, man'. His youngest brother, Eric, continued the family connection with Letchworth by chairing the Garden City company in the 1940s, as Sir Eric Macfadyen.[60]

Selbie survived them all. He remained at Mansfield as principal until 1932—perhaps longer than he should have done—and continued to live in Oxford until his death in 1944. In the later years he had made a special study of the psychology of religion, and gave the Wilde Lectures on that theme in the early 1920s.[61] In 1920, when Oxford University opened its divinity degrees to non-Anglicans, Selbie was honoured as the first Free Church recipient of the degree of Doctor of Divinity by decree. Four years later he became the first Free Church examiner in the Theology Schools. In the 1920s he took a leading role in the ecumenical conversations following the Lambeth Conference of 1920, but his volume on *Congregationalism* (London: Methuen, 1927) in a series of 'Varieties of Christian Expression' showed that his robust defence of his denomination's churchmanship was still strong.

The little group of men who gathered at 90 High Street in 1886 took part in an experiment which raised some fundamental questions about ministerial education and training. All of them remained faithful to their Free Church heritage, and all contributed to Free Church life and self-

---

59. *The Portal: The Monthly Magazine of the Letchworth Free Church* 1 (October 1924).

60. See Macfadyen, *Eric Macfadyen*.

61. Published as *The Psychology of Religion* (Oxford: Clarendon Press, 1924).

understanding. Two of them, Horne and Selbie, were elected chairmen of the Congregational Union. It was Dugald Macfadyen who seems to have experienced an unresolved tension in his life, but this may have been due as much to his family background as to his Oxford education. Selbie lived most of his adult life in either Cambridge or Oxford and took his place among Oxford theologians while remaining essentially 'a Lancashire lad, fond of his pipe and his cup of tea, who never lost his understanding of the common man'.[62] Though four of them were the sons of ministers, none of their children, and (to the best of my knowledge) none of their descendants became ministers.[63] In most cases neither did they remain Congregationalists. But that is another story.

---

62. Geoffrey Nuttall in 'William Boothby Selbie, 1862–1944', *Mansfield College Magazine* 125 (1944), pp. 100-110 (109).

63. Horne had a great nephew, Hampden Nicholson Horne (1903–93) who was a Congregational minister.

Nonconformists at Cambridge
Before the First World War

David M. Thompson

The abolition of religious tests for college fellowships and membership of the Senate has been described as 'the natural beginning of the religious history of modern Cambridge'. 'The admission of Dissenters', wrote Dr Roach, 'took away much of the distinctiveness and exclusiveness of the older Dissenting communities: it certainly enriched the life of the University.'[1] Nevertheless Nonconformists were not barred from Cambridge before 1871. Although the essential barrier was willingness to subscribe to the Thirty-Nine Articles, rather than the fact of being a Dissenter, it should be remembered that for most of the eighteenth century all Dissenting ministers and teachers were required to subscribe to the Articles with the exception of Articles 20 and 34-36, and (for Baptists) Article 7.[2] Only in 1779 was this requirement lifted by the Dissenters' Relief Act, which substituted a declaration against popery and an affirmation of the Bible as the standard of doctrine. The university's requirements depended on its statutes, and, whereas at Oxford it was necessary to subscribe to the Articles at both matriculation and graduation, at Cambridge it was only necessary at graduation. Thus a Nonconformist could attend Cambridge and leave without taking a degree, as did F.D. Maurice, for example. In those days many students did not proceed to the BA degree.

Subscription to the Articles as a prequisite for the BA was abolished by Act of Parliament in 1856. (This happened two years earlier in Oxford.)[3]

---

1. *Victoria County History: History of the Counties of Cambridgeshire and the Isle of Ely*. III. *The City and University of Cambridge* (ed. J. P. C. Roach; Institute of Historical Research, University of London: Oxford University Press, 1959), p. 304.

2. Article 20 concerned ceremonies, and Articles 34-36 concerned the traditions of the Church, the homilies and bishops: subscription to all but these was required by the Toleration Act of 1689.

3. 19 & 20 Vict. c. 88, §45; P. Searby, *A History of the University of Cambridge*.

Pressure for this had developed since the 1830s, but the lead in bringing about the change was taken by James Heywood, MP for North Lancashire from 1847 to 1857.[4] A Statutory Commission was established to negotiate the changes with the university and colleges that were eventually embodied in legislation. The changes in college statutes were probably even more important because of the removal of restrictions which laid down quotas for members from particular counties.

The University Tests Act of 1871 removed religious tests from all other degrees, apart from those in divinity, and opened college fellowships to all, regardless of religion. Even then, however, J.B. Lightfoot was more concerned by the position of men like Henry Sidgwick, who were feeling obliged to renounce formal adherence to Christianity, than the position of Nonconformists. One response to the removal of tests was the foundation of Keble College at Oxford and Selwyn at Cambridge in order to preserve the ideal of an exclusively Anglican college: Selwyn did not abandon this and become a full college of the university until 1957.[5]

The Theological Tripos (leading, of course to the BA degree and therefore without tests) was first examined in 1874. But the degrees of Bachelor and Doctor of Divinity were opened to non-Anglicans only in 1913 (here Oxford was later in 1920) and Nonconformists were not eligible for appointment as Preachers before the University until 1939. So Nonconformity was still a live issue in late nineteenth-century Cambridge.

Yet the number of Nonconformists at Cambridge grew rapidly in this period, and an increasing number gained college and university posts. It is

III. *1750–1870* (Cambridge: Cambridge University Press, 1997), pp. 492-503, 507-44; M.G. Brock and M.C. Curthoys (eds.), *History of the University of Oxford*. VI. *Nineteenth Century Oxford, Part I* (Oxford: Clarendon Press, 1997), pp. 306-36.

4.   Heywood (Trinity) was among the Senior Optimes in 1833, but did not take his degree until 1857 because of the tests. Searby, *History, 1750–1870*, pp. 518-19; J.A. Venn, *Alumni Cantabrigienses*, II (Cambridge: Cambridge University Press, 1940–54), iii, p. 354. For the Nonconformist campaign leading up to these changes at the universities of Oxford and Cambridge, see T. Larsen, *Friends of Religious Equality: Nonconformist Politics in Mid-Victorian England* (Woodbridge: Boydell, 1999), pp. 59-65.

5.   *Victoria Country History: Cambridgeshire*, III, pp. 257-58; C.N.L. Brooke, *A History of the University of Cambridge*, IV, *1870–1990* (Cambridge: Cambridge University Press, 1993), pp. 99-106; D.M. Thompson, 'Lightfoot as Victorian Churchman', The Lightfoot Centenary Lectures, ed. J.D.G. Dunn, *Durham University Journal* (1992), p. 15; G.R. Treloar, *Lightfoot the Historian* (Tübingen: Mohr Siebeck, 1998), pp. 178-81, which also notes that Lightfoot was an enthusiastic supporter of Selwyn College.

a remarkable fact that in 1899 the Secretary of the Council of the Senate and the Secretary of the General Board of Studies were both Congregationalists. These positions were not so significant in the university as today, but they were not without influence. Neville Keynes is better known as the father of John Maynard Keynes, but he was a formidable figure in his own right, who became Registrary in 1907, since when the Registrary has been the secretary of the Council. Alfred Dale was the son of Dr R.W. Dale of Birmingham; he later became Principal and then first Vice-Chancellor of the University of Liverpool, and was knighted in 1907.[6] Dr Roach identified T.R. Glover, son of the Baptist minister, Dr Richard Glover of Bristol, as the leading Nonconformist in the university, partly because of his later office as Public Orator, but also perhaps because he wrote about Cambridge and has a biography.[7]

However, the records of the Cambridge University Nonconformist Union (CUNU) from 1883 to 1916 contain a complete list of members, just over 1,000 in all.[8] This list illuminates the minutes, and gives a picture of the student Nonconformist presence, which was significantly greater than the number of senior members. Nor did the Union contain all Nonconformists, because Methodists and Presbyterians were not usually members.

This provides an opportunity to test Matthew Arnold's thesis about Hebraism and Hellenism in relation to the culture of Cambridge Nonconformity. Does the experience of Cambridge reflect the 'life of jealousy of the Establishment, disputes, tea-meetings, opening of chapels, sermons', which Arnold regarded as the Nonconformist ideal of a human life?[9] To answer this question two overlapping circles will be examined, the dons as represented by Keynes and Glover, and then the Nonconformist Union.

6.   For Dale and Keynes, see Venn, *Alumni*, II, ii, p. 213, and II, iv, p. 34.

7.   H.G. Wood, *Terrot Reaveley Glover* (Cambridge: Cambridge University Press, 1953); but the closer one immerses oneself in Glover's diaries (in St John's College Archives), the more disappointing the book seems. There are no biographies of Keynes or Dale, nor of J.R. Tanner of St John's; despite his Liverpool connections Dale does not appear in the index to Brooke's *History of the University*, nor is there any reference to Keynes's diaries. Nonconformists receive only fleeting attention in the volumes by Brooke and Searby.

8.   I have begun to enlarge this database with other biographical material from the *Index to Class Lists* and Venn's *Alumni Cantabrigienses*, but it is not yet complete. I am grateful to Margaret, Andrew and Stephen Thompson for assistance in the transcription of data.

9.   M. Arnold, *Culture and Anarchy* (ed. J.D. Wilson, Cambridge: Cambridge University Press, 1950), p. 58.

This highlights the choice for Nonconformity, which in many respects corresponds to Arnold's distinction between 'totality' and 'provincialism'.[10]

The first person who was claimed to be a Nonconformist graduate after 1856 was William Henry Farthing Johnson, who attended a meeting of the Nonconformist Union in 1889.[11] His career aptly illustrates the 'Cambridge problem'. He was admitted as a sizar (i.e., an undergraduate paid by the college to undertake menial duties for others) at Corpus Christi on 14 February 1843, the son of William Johnson, who ran a school in Cambridge at Llandaff House in Regent Street. He matriculated in the Michaelmas Term 1843, and became a Scholar in 1844. But he then went no further, and instead secured a London University BA in 1850. He also took over his father's school. After the 1856 Act was passed, he was readmitted as a sizar at Corpus on 10 October 1856, and took his BA in 1857. He took his MA from Trinity College in 1862, and held a variety of public offices in Cambridge, until his death in 1901.[12]

His four sons all went to Cambridge, two of them having been at the Perse School (the old town grammar school), and all had distinguished careers. None of them were members of the Nonconformist Union. Johnson's two brothers were admitted as pensioners at Christ's; but the elder died before coming into residence, while his younger brother took his BA without scruple in 1853, and was ordained in the Church of England, eventually becoming headmaster of the Royal Institution, Liverpool, 1874–79.[13] This is a cameo of one Nonconformist family which encountered Cambridge in the 1840s.

Johnson was a member and deacon of Saint Andrew's Street Baptist Church; the present pulpit was given in his memory by the old pupils of Llandaff House School.[14] Professor W.S. Aldis, who went up as a sizar to Trinity in 1856 and was the son of a Baptist minister, said that in his time

10. Arnold, *Culture and Anarchy*, p. 16. For the theme in general, see J. Munson, *The Nonconformists* (London: SPCK, 1991), especially pp. 67-128.

11. CUNU Minutes, 1883–94, 28 April 1889; Glover noted him at other meetings, Glover Diaries, St John's College, 16 October 1892, 28 April 1895.

12. Venn, *Alumni*, II, iii, p. 586.

13. Venn, *Alumni*, II, iii, pp. 579, 580 (for H.I. Johnson and J.B. Johnson, brothers) and pp. 576, 579, 582 and 585 (for A.H. Johnson, G.W. Johnson, R.B. Johnson and W.E. Johnson, sons).

14. He became a member on 3 December 1845, was elected a deacon on 3 January 1857, and died on 16 July 1901. St Andrew's Street Church Book, 1832–96, pp. 85, 125; 1896–1963, p. 301, cf. K.A. Parsons (ed.), *St Andrew's Street Baptist Church 250th Anniversary* (Cambridge: By the Church, 1971), p. 43.

there were only four others who attended a Dissenting place of worship, and that up to 1870 the increasing numbers attended St Andrew's Street. However, after the death of his father-in-law, the Revd William Robinson (minister 1852–74), that church was deserted by Nonconformist undergraduates.[15] This may have been due to the five-year vacancy before the arrival of the Revd T.G. Tarn in 1879, and also to the attraction of the Great Meeting after it moved from Downing Place to Trumpington Street in 1874 as Emmanuel Congregational Church.[16] The first undergraduate church member was admitted there in 1851, when the theological tone of the church began to move in a more liberal direction under the Revd G.B. Bubier.[17] The new Emmanuel building was a national, as well as a local, undertaking, but Dr Matthew Robertson (minister 1872–78) resigned after a bitter dispute without taking another pastorate and subsequently became editor of the *Cambridge Independent Press*.[18] It was only in the ministry of the Revd W.S. Houghton after 1879 that undergraduates appeared in considerable numbers.[19]

Neville Keynes came from a Salisbury Congregational family; his great-uncle was a minister at Blandford, but his grandfather was a brushmaker and his father a horticulturalist. He was educated at Amersham Hall near Reading, and like several other Nonconformists he studied simultaneously at Cambridge and London. Although the Natural and Moral Sciences Triposes had been established in 1848, the mathematics tradition remained strong. So Neville came up to Pembroke to read mathematics in 1872, but changed to moral sciences after his first year and topped the Moral Sciences Tripos in 1875. He also won a Gold Medal in Moral Sciences in the London MA in 1876. In that year he was elected a Fellow both of Pembroke and of University College, London.[20]

Neville was a lifelong friend of James Ward, who was briefly minister

15. Wood, *Glover*, p. 66. For Aldis, see Venn, *Alumni*, II, i, p. 26; he was Senior Wrangler in 1861 and First Smith's Prizeman.

16. *Victoria Country History: Cambridgeshire*, III, pp. 136-37. Professor Binfield's anticipated history of Emmanuel should clarify this.

17. B.L. Manning, *This Latter House* (Cambridge: Heffers, 1924), pp. xii-xiii.

18. Manning, *Latter House*, pp. 24-25, 27-28; Robertson matriculated as a non-collegiate student on 19 October 1877, but withdrew a year later; he died in 1890: Fitzwilliam College Record Book.

19. Manning, *Latter House*, pp. 1-5, 16-17; Houghton also matriculated as a non-collegiate student, on 2 October 1884, passing Parts I and II of the Previous Examination: Fitzwilliam College Record Book.

20. G. Keynes, *The Gates of Memory* (Oxford: Clarendon Press, 1981), pp. 13-16.

of the Great Meeting from January 1871 to February 1872 before he re-signed and became an Anglican.[21] He was also a schoolfriend and contem-porary of Henry Bond, son of William Bond, a grocer in Trinity Street and deacon of Emmanuel, whose home in Brookside became a meeting place for young Nonconformists at Cambridge. William was responsible for securing university representation on the Cambridge Borough Council in 1889.[22] Henry took the Law and Historical Triposes in 1876 and 1877, and subsequently became a Fellow and eventually Master of Trinity Hall.[23] (Henry did not become a member of Emmanuel, but he was on the church list with a seat into the 1920s.) Neville met his future wife, Florence Brown, daughter of the Revd John Brown of Bunyan Meeting, Bedford, who came up to Newnham in 1878, at the Bonds' house, though he was also involved in supervising her studies. They became engaged in 1880—Florence did not take a degree—and they married in 1882. Neville never became a member of Emmanuel, though he was a regular attender until the First World War. His mother became a member in 1889 when she moved to Cambridge, remaining so until her death in 1907. Florence became a member of Emmanuel by transfer from Bunyan Meeting in 1883 but resigned in 1948 not long before Neville died; she died in 1958, aged 96.[24]

Slightly younger than Keynes was Alfred Dale, son of R.W. Dale, who came up to Trinity from King Edward's School, Birmingham, in 1876, moving to Trinity Hall a year later where he gained a first in classics in 1879. He became a Fellow of Trinity Hall in 1880, Bursar in 1883, and then Tutor and Lecturer in 1887. Dale transferred his membership to Emmanuel in July 1879 from Carr's Lane, Birmingham, and remained until he transferred to Great George Street, Liverpool, in 1900. His wife, May—they also married in 1882—transferred from Queen Square, Brigh-ton, and remained on the Emmanuel roll until her resignation in 1913.[25]

Keynes and Dale became friends, and dined together regularly. Just

21. Ward matriculated as a non-collegiate student on 5 February 1872, migrating to Trinity a year later; he was subsequently a fellow of Trinity and Professor of Mental Philosophy in the University: Fitzwilliam College Record Book; *DNB*; Venn, *Alumni*, II, vi, p. 354.

22. *Victoria Country History: Cambridgeshire*, III, pp. 27, 286; F.A. Keynes, *Gathering up the Threads* (Cambridge: Heffer, 1950), p. 39.

23. Venn, *Alumni*, II, i, p. 315.

24. N. Brown, *Dissenting Forbears* (Chichester: Phillimore, 1988), pp. 107-108; Emmanuel Church membership records. Florence was the first woman town councillor in Cambridge, and the first woman to be mayor.

25. Venn, *Alumni*, II, ii, p. 213; Emmanuel Church membership records.

before his wedding Keynes noted, 'I have dined with the Dales, staying to tea—and have had a capital time almost making up for the absence of the Bonds'.[26] Mrs Dale came round at 3.00 a.m. when John Maynard Keynes was born on 5 June 1883—and the Dales' daughter, Marjorie, was born at about the same time. From an early stage Keynes was involved in the caucus which nominated liberal candidates for the Council of the Senate of the University.[27] In 1892 he was asked by Dale to stand for the council 'on the Liberal ticket' and agreed. He was the second elected, and almost immediately was elected secretary; by April 1894 Henry Bond was telling him that Maitland thought Keynes was an even better Secretary of the Council than MacAlister.[28]

Donald MacAlister was a highlander who came to St John's from the Royal Liverpool Institute. He was Senior Wrangler and then Linacre Lecturer in Physic.[29] According to Glover, 'he handled University and College business with a quickness that shocked people' and he 'could draft a resolution as readily as he seized the issue'. He had a breadth of vision that many of his colleagues lacked and was less bound by local tradition. 'So in the end he lost his seat on the Council of the Senate to a safe man (a very pleasant one) whose mental processes men could more easily foresee and who abode with us for all his genial life.'[30] Was Glover referring to Keynes? MacAlister was a member of St Columba's Presbyterian Church— and was one of the original signatories of the petition to the Presbytery of London which led to its establishment; he became Principal of Glasgow University in 1907.[31]

Keynes cherished his Nonconformist and liberal background. He was anxious about a sermon in Pembroke chapel when the Master had said that the spiritual, rather than intellectual, welfare of undergraduates was their primary concern, and that if any who were not members of the Church of England were induced by their example to join their communion, 'our

26. Keynes Diaries, Cambridge University Library, Add 7832(1): 13 August 1882.

27. Keynes Diaries, Add 7832(2): 1 November 1882.

28. Keynes Diaries, Add 7842: 22 October 1892, 7 November 1892; Add 7844: 15 April 1894.

29. E. Miller, *Portrait of a College* (Cambridge: Cambridge University Press, 1961), p. 105. This was a university lectureship paid for by St John's.

30. T.R. Glover, *Cambridge Retrospect* (Cambridge: Cambridge University Press, 1943), p. 96.

31. Venn, *Alumni*, II, iv, p. 250; E.F.B. MacAlister, *St Columba's Church, Cambridge* (Cambridge: [St Columba's Church], 1950), pp. 14, 39-40. He should not be confused with Professor Alexander Macalister, whose daughter he married.

delight will know no bounds'. The Master was not pleased when Keynes proposed to give a bottle of champagne at high table in May 1882 in honour of Gladstone just after the Phoenix Park Murders.[32] On 4 March 1894 his diary showed his priorities: 'Mr Gladstone's resignation now formally announced, Lord Rosebery will be his successor. Mr Forsyth has accepted the invitation to Cambridge.'[33] He favoured liberal theology; and after Dr Stoughton preached at Emmanuel in 1881, he wrote: 'For a dissenting minister he is remarkably "clerical" in his appearance and manner. He invoked a blessing on *us* at the conclusion of the service in a style worthy of the Pope himself.'[34]

Yet Keynes was a man in transition, and some of the clues to this come in Florence's description of Harvey Road, where they built their house after getting married: 'In our early days Harvey Road was inhabited almost entirely by members of the University, the extensive residential developments on the outskirts of the town having hardly been contemplated.' There follows a list of neighbours, including Mrs Bateson, widow of the Master of St John's, mother of William Bateson, discoverer of Mendel and his principles of heredity; Dr Besant, a distinguished mathematician; the Revd A.H.F. Boughey, Senior Tutor of Trinity; (Sir) Richard Glazebrook, also a fellow of Trinity, later Director of the National Physical Laboratory; (Sir) Charles Villiers Stanford, Professor of Music, organist of Trinity, composer and conductor, 'who waged war upon the Italian organ-grinders or hurdy-gurdy men beloved and encouraged by the junior inhabitants'; Alexander Macalister, Professor of Anatomy; Dr Ryle, afterwards President of Queens' and Bishop of Winchester; Frank Crawford Burkitt, future Norrisian Professor of Divinity; and for a while the twin sisters Mrs Lewis and Mrs Gibson, while they were building their house, 'Castlebrae'. 'It was a friendly community; we shared a ground with tennis-courts, we subscribed to plant trees in the road; we started a book-club which ran for about twelve years.'[35]

The social effects of living in such a neighbourhood for a long period are incalculable. Even the most determined Nonconformist had to struggle hard to remain one. Although both Keynes and Dale were invited to address the Nonconformist Union on several occasions, neither ever did. Keynes never accepted; Dale accepted three times and cried off at the last

32. Keynes Diaries, Add 7832(1): 6 April 1881; Add 7832(2): 10 May 1882.
33. Keynes Diaries, Add 7844: 4 March 1894.
34. Keynes Diaries, Add 7832(1): 13 March 1881.
35. Keynes, *Gathering up the Threads*, pp. 55-56.

moment, until eventually the secretary noted in the minutes that Dale 'will never undertake extra work in term time'.[36] In view of the number of senior members who did address the society, this sounds rather lame. Keynes did remain concerned over traditional Nonconformist issues, as shown by his anxiety over securing the abolition of religious tests for divinity degrees in 1913.[37] But by then that may have become an issue of liberal, rather than Nonconformist, principle.

Glover was less accommodating. He arrived in Cambridge on 28 September 1888. Two days later he wrote, 'Then to College Chapel in a white surplice. After this masquerade went to Congregational Chapel & heard Rev. W.S. Houghton on Paul at Philippi.' On 8 October he called on Neville Keynes and his wife; the following Sunday he was introduced to Neville Goodman (another early Nonconformist graduate)[38] at St Andrew's Street; a week later he went to the Presbyterian service in the Guildhall, borrowed R.F. Horton's *Inspiration and the Bible* from the Union Library, and had supper with the Keyneses; on 30 October he voted in favour of disestablishment at the Union.[39] St John's was a more liberal college than Pembroke. Glover's tutor, W.E. Heitland, was one of the caucus that nominated liberal candidates for the Council of the Senate.[40] When Glover returned from Canada in 1901, he went to live in Glisson Road, only a stone's throw from Harvey Road; but, after opposing the 1902 Education Bill vigorously, he signed a manifesto in favour of passive resistance, and declined to pay the education rate until 1921.[41] It is easy to see why Dr Roach took Glover, rather than Keynes, as the archetypal Cambridge Nonconformist.

What light does the Nonconformist Union shed on this picture? The idea came from Oxford, where R.F. Horton, fellow of New College, 1879–83, formed the Oxford Nonconformist Union in 1881, with Joseph King of Hampstead who was at Trinity as secretary. The plan had the approval of Jowett, Master of Balliol and Vice-Chancellor; Professor Bryce was

36. CUNU Minutes, 1883–94, 10 May 1885, 29 November 1885, 28 May 1893; 1894–1901: 2 June 1899.

37. Keynes Diaries, Add 7863: 20 April 1913, 22 April 1913, 25 April 1913.

38. Venn, *Alumni*, II, iii, p. 85. He was a fellow commoner of Peterhouse from 1862 and obtained a first in natural sciences in 1865.

39. Glover Diaries, 28 September 1888, 30 September 1888, 8 October 1888, 14 October 1888, 21 October 1888, 30 October 1888.

40. Keynes Diaries, Add 7832(2): 1 November 1882.

41. Wood, *Glover*, p. 67.

president and and T.H. Green was a vice-president. Horton had estimated that there were about 200 Nonconformists in Oxford—but probably only about half a dozen Nonconformist dons. The Union met twice a term in Horton's rooms in New College.[42] As an undergraduate Horton had visited Cambridge with two companions representing the Oxford Christian Union and they 'were amazed with the far richer religious life at the sister University'.[43] It is an interesting remark because there is no evidence in the CUNU records of contact with the Cambridge Inter-Collegiate Christian Union, and the negative attitude of CICCU towards Nonconformists was one factor in the secession of CICCU from the Student Volunteer Movement in 1910.[44] However, the Oxford Nonconformist Union disappeared as such after the foundation of Mansfield College, though its functions were carried on by the Milton Society and later the Livingstone Society.[45]

The Cambridge University Nonconformist Union was founded on Wednesday 25 April 1883 in the Alexandra Hall, home of the Cambridge YMCA. Two of those present at the meeting doubted the wisdom of the move. J.D. Batten of Trinity College thought that the tendency of the Union 'would be to open still wider the breach already existing in the University between Nonconformity and the Church of England'. He considered that the 'great need of the present day was that Churchmen should know more of Nonconformists and that Nonconformists should better understand Churchmen'. Mr Harley of King's College considered that 'Cambridge was the place of all others where religious, as social, differences should be placed in the background and that the tendency of the Union would be to provide that Nonconformists should have only Nonconformist friends'. However, J.R. Tanner of St John's, the historian and the eldest of four brothers from the printing firm in Frome who all joined the Union, took the opposite view. He pointed out that 'besides a need that Nonconformists should know more of Churchmen there existed also a need that

42. R.F. Horton, *An Autobiography* (London: Allen & Unwin, 1817), p. 54; A. Peel and J.A.R. Marriott (eds.), *Robert Forman Horton* (London: Allen & Unwin, 1937), pp. 104-106.

43. Horton, *Autobiography*, p. 36.

44. D.M. Thompson, *Same Difference* (Birmingham: SCM Press, 1990), pp. 3-6; J.C. Pollock, *A Cambridge Movement* (London: John Murray, 1953), p. 162; T. Tatlow, *The Story of the Student Christian Movement* (London: SCM Press, 1933), pp. 382-83.

45. W. Selbie, 'Nonconformity at the Universities: I, Oxford', *Congregational Quarterly*, 1 (1923), pp. 76-79.

Nonconformists should know more of Nonconformists, and that such an end would be attained by the proposed Union'. His opinion was 'that Cambridge was the place of all others where such a Union was required'.[46] So the Union was established.

The first president was Norman Hardcastle, BA, of Downing College. Little is known about him because he died ten years later as a result of a fall from his horse. Although a lawyer, he became a Fellow and Lecturer in modern languages at Downing. He had earlier been secretary of the University Society for the Promotion of Religious Equality, which was founded a few years earlier by Courtney Kenny, Neville Goodman and Rendel Harris.[47] There he was active in trying to bring Nonconformists and Anglicans together, along with men like Canon Fremantle. Hardcastle was probably a Congregationalist, though he was not a member of Emmanuel.[48] The vice-president was William Bennett, BA, of St John's College, who subsequently taught at Rotherham and Hackney Colleges and was Principal of Lancashire Independent College from 1913 to 1920.[49] The first secretary was E.R. Tanner of Clare, one of J.R. Tanner's brothers.

The first General Meeting was held on the evening of 20 May, when Hardcastle listed the non-resident celebrities who had not been free to

46. CUNU Minutes, 1883–94, 25 April 1883. For Batten and Harley, see Venn, *Alumni*, II, i, p. 188 and II, iii, p. 246: Batten was called to the bar, but eventually became an artist; Harley was the son of the vice-master and chaplain of Mill Hill School, and became an actor and playwright.

47. H.N. Dixon, 'Religious Life in Cambridge in the Eighties of the Last Century', *Congregational Quarterly*, 20 (1942), pp. 314-15. Kenny and Harris both attended Emmanuel, though Harris resigned in 1877 (perhaps because of the tension over Dr Robertson?). Kenny was of French Huguenot descent—Kenny being a variant on Du Quesne—Fellow of Downing, 1885, Reader in English Law 1888–1907, Downing Professor of the Laws of England 1907–18, MP for Barnsley, 1885 and 1886–88; Harris was Third Wrangler, 1874, Fellow of Clare, 1875–88, 1892–1904, Professor of New Testament Greek, Johns Hopkins University, 1882–86, and founding Director of Studies at Woodbrooke, Selly Oak, Birmingham: Venn, *Alumni*, II, iv, p. 24; II, iii, p. 254; *DNB*; Emmanuel Membership Records. Kenny offered the records of the Religious Equality Society to CUNU after Hardcastle's death, but the offer was declined: CUNU Minutes, 1883–94, 14 May 1893.

48. *Guardian*, 19 April 1893, 26 April 1893; cf. *Recollections of Dean Fremantle* (London: Cassell, 1921), pp. 85, 92, 94-96, 133, 135-36, 147.

49. Venn, *Alumni*, II, i, p. 233; E. Kaye, *For the Work of Ministry* (Edinburgh: T. & T. Clark, 1999), pp. 101-102. Before going to Rotherham in 1884, Bennett had a fellowship at St John's.

deliver an Inaugural Address: Dr Stopford Brooke, Professor Bryce, Canon Fremantle, Mr Horton, Dr MacLaren, Dr Martineau, Professor Robertson Smith, Professor Stuart, Mr Summers, MP,[50] and the Revd Edward White. So Courtney Kenny, who became a stalwart of the Union, spoke instead. The subject of the address was not stated, though it was decided to print it.[51]

The objects of the Oxford Union were significantly more specific than at Cambridge. They included the removal of the feeling of isolation among Nonconformist undergraduates, the investigation of the principles of English Nonconformity and the presentation of its true meaning and aim to members of the Established Church, the presentation of 'a free and simple doctrine of Christianity' to help those with religious doubts, and the establishment if possible and desired of a Sunday Greek Testament or Bible class to assist the religious life of all, especially of those intending to enter the ministry.[52] By contrast the Cambridge constitution simply stated that, 'The object of the Society is to hold meetings on Sunday evenings and occasionally on other days for social purposes, and for the discussion of subjects of common interest'. Furthermore it was not intended that the Society should be identified with the political or religious controversies between Nonconformists and other religious bodies.[53] So there was no suggestion of a Bible class, and no reference to 'a simple doctrine of Christianity' or to those intending to enter the ministry.

Moreover the Cambridge committee decided at its first meeting that there would be no devotional exercises at the beginning or end of meetings. It also affirmed its distinct identity from particular traditions by saying that it could not arrange for the lectures proposed to be delivered by lecturers chosen by the Baptist and Congregational Unions.[54] This partly reflects a characteristic student independence, but also a recurrent sus-

50. Presumably William Summers, MP for Stalybridge, 1880–85, of Owens College and University College, Oxford: M. Stenton and S. Lees (eds.), *Who's Who of British M.P.s.* II. *1886–1910* (Hassocks, Sussex: Harvester, 1978), p. 344.

51. No copy has been traced, but it was repeated in 1895 under the title, 'The Original Aims of this Society', CUNU Minutes, 1894–1901, 19 May 1895.

52. Selbie, 'Nonconformity at Oxford', p. 76.

53. CUNU Minutes, 1883–94, 18 November 1883; the word 'Nonconformist' was defined as including all who were interested in Nonconformity, an original reference to 'sympathising with' it having been deleted.

54. CUNU Minutes, 1883–94, 29 April 1883, 14 October 1883.

picion of denominational links that might destroy the perceived neutrality of the Union. Membership was open to Anglicans, and several members became Anglican clergymen, sometimes, but not always, because of conversion. Neville Figgis, who was the son of a strongly evangelical minister in the Countess of Huntingdon's Connexion, was a member while an undergraduate at St Catharine's.[55]

The records are a clear reminder that it was an undergraduate society. The membership fluctuated, its finances fluctuated, and this led to regular problems about where to meet. They met in the Alexandra Rooms for a period, then had an argument about the rent and retreated to the schoolroom at Emmanuel. Then someone would say that they needed somewhere better; they moved, costs went up, there was an argument about the rent, and it was back to Emmanuel. Nevertheless for most of the Union's existence it met in the Alexandra Rooms.

The corporate memory also tended to fluctuate. Despite a core of supportive senior members, the Union was run by undergraduates and, while some of the rules were remembered, others were not. For example, it was noted in 1883 that although members could introduce visitors, this did not include ladies—but by the 1890s women were starting to appear. Again, despite the original decision not to open meetings with prayer, by October 1884 this was happening. The matter was raised in January 1885, but the practice continued, and in January 1886 18 voted in favour and only 4 against.[56]

The attendance in the early years was very respectable, averaging 40 to 50. Nor was this greatly affected for most of the time by whether speakers were from outside Cambridge. Apart from a few terms with particularly conscientious secretaries there is usually no account of the content of the papers or the discussion, apart from the title.

Who came? The tables give some indication of the ways in which the membership (including honorary members) of 1,054 can be analysed. Table 1 illustrates the fluctuations: an enthusiastic beginning in 1883–85, which settled down to a quite modest annual intake through to the mid-1890s (though 1888 was unusually low). There was a fall in the later 1890s and then a surge from 1903 to 1910, drifting down gently towards

55. CUNU Roll Book, 25 October 1885; Venn, *Alumni*, II, ii, p. 493; M.G. Tucker, *John Neville Figgis* (London: SPCK, 1950), pp. 2-10.

56. CUNU Minutes, 1883–94: 29 April 1883, 19 October 1884, 20 January 1885, 24 January 1886; 1894–1901, 2 June 1895.

1916. There is a rough correlation with periods of Liberal government, but that may be a coincidence. The Union ceased to meet after the Easter Term 1916, by which time the number of undergraduates in residence had fallen from 3,263 (in the Michaelmas Term 1913) to only 575.[57]

Table 1. *New members of CUNU, by year.*

Note: In several years a precise date is not given for each member. These have been included in the totals for the years in which they appear in the Membership Book.

Year	No.	Year	No.	Year	No.
1883	99	1895	32	1907	84
1884	31	1896	28	1908	66
1885	34	1897	12	1909	40
1886	14	1898	8	1910	47
1887	23	1899	26	1911	32
1888	7	1900	11	1912	30
1889	15	1901	17	1913	28
1890	12	1902	21	1914	28
1891	20	1903	49	1915	28
1892	20	1904	37	1916	13
1893	17	1905	46		
1894	40	1906	39	total	1054

The college breakdown is even more interesting. Table 2 shows the dominant position of St John's, with over 20 per cent of the total membership. In the 1880s it was the second largest college, but Trinity was larger still and produced more than 60 fewer; so size alone cannot explain the proportion. Moreover St John's declined from 354 undergraduates in 1879–80 to 253 in 1909–10, because of the pressure on college finances from the agricultural depression—which may partly account for the decline in CUNU membership in the 1890s. By 1910 it had been overtaken in size by Caius and Pembroke.

The readiness of St John's to admit the sons of professional and business men is probably the main explanation, though it must be remembered that members of the Union did not have to be Nonconformists.[58] Of the other colleges, Sidney Sussex, Downing and Emmanuel had high proportions of members and Magdalene, Pembroke, Corpus Christi and Trinity

57. *Victoria County History: Cambridgeshire*, III, p. 287.
58. Miller, *Portrait*, pp. 92, 96-99; Brooke, *History, 1870–1990*, pp. 593-95.

Table 2. *Members of CUNU by college*

Note: Six non-collegiate students and one other student migrated to other colleges and therefore appear twice; one Westminster and one Cheshunt student are also listed under their university colleges.

College	Number	Percentage
no college listed/illegible	28	2.7%
Caius	75	7.1%
Cambridge House	1	0.1%
Cavendish	4	0.4%
Cheshunt	18	1.7%
Christ's	70	6.6%
Clare	42	4.0%
Corpus Christi	12	1.1%
Downing	45	4.3%
Emmanuel	79	7.5%
Jesus	34	3.2%
King's	47	4.5%
Magdalene	3	0.3%
Manchester, Oxford	1	0.1%
Newnham	16	1.5%
Non-Collegiate	37	3.5%
Pembroke	11	1.0%
Peterhouse	23	2.2%
Queens'	27	2.6%
Sidney Sussex	37	3.5%
St Catharine's	18	1.7%
St John's	234	22.2%
Training College	4	0.4%
Trinity	168	15.9%
Trinity Hall	25	2.4%
Wadham, Oxford	1	0.1%
Westminster	3	0.3%
TOTAL	1063	

Hall had low proportions.[59] It is interesting that Arthur Ramsey, father of Michael and Sunday school superintendent at Emmanuel, should have been

59. This is based on a comparison between the numbers for each college and the size of each college in the period between 1879–80 and 1909–10.

a fellow of Magdalene;[60] and perhaps it is significant that Keynes, Dale and Henry Bond should have been at colleges with low proportions of Nonconformists. In passing, it should be added that the schools from which members came seem to have been the old city grammar schools, rather than Nonconformist schools, with the significant exception of Mill Hill. J.D. McClure was a member of the Union and headmaster of Mill Hill from 1891 to 1922, during which time he made it one of the leading Nonconformist schools in the country.[61]

Table 3. *Tripos Subjects of CUNU Members*

Note: Because of changes of subject these figures add up to more than 1054, so no percentages are included.

No evidence of Tripos	340
Classics	114
Economics	14
History	93
Law	69
Mathematics	193
Mechanical Sciences	23
Modern & Medieval Languages	17
Moral Sciences	24
Natural Sciences	243
Oriental Languages	2
Semitic Languages	2
Theology	35

The analysis of tripos subjects in Table 3 is also revealing. The most significant figure is probably the 340 who do not appear in the tripos lists at all because they took ordinary degrees. This is a total over a 30-year period during which things were changing, so a more refined analysis is needed; but it reflects a lower proportion of ordinary degrees than in the university as a whole at this time. In the mid-nineteenth century about half the undergraduates took ordinary degrees, and this proportion gradually declined: in the 1880s at Caius the proportion was approaching a third, and

60. Venn, *Alumni*, II, v, p. 241; O. Chadwick, *Michael Ramsey: A Life* (Oxford: Clarendon Press, 1990), pp. 4-6. He joined the Union in November 1886, and gave a paper on Shaftesbury in 1888.

61. Venn, *Alumni*, II, iv, p. 256; *DNB*. He addressed the Union five times between 1884 and 1903. See also Munson, *Nonconformists*, pp. 87-89.

by 1909 it was only a third at St John's.[62] A closer examination of the results shows a string of firsts and university prizes and medals. Perhaps not surprisingly the performance of CUNU members was above average. The subject spread is also interesting, though it needs to be related to that in the university as a whole. Natural scientists outnumbered those reading the traditional premier subjects of mathematics and classics, while the even newer triposes of history and law were well represented.[63]

A detailed analysis of subsequent career profiles has not been made: as well as ministers and missionaries, there were a significant number of doctors and lawyers—many secured legal qualifications but did not practise—and other professional men, including university teachers and school-teachers. But the new social environment was precarious. Both Keynes and Glover worried about money; jobs were scarce and Keynes gained security from his administrative position at the Local Examinations Syndicate. He gave Glover some examining to supplement his Fellowship income in 1895; it was a grind, but he took comfort from the fact that if he was starving he could be taken on again.[64] The CUNU records also show a number of early deaths—a reminder of the twentieth-century change in life expectancy.

How does the Union's programme fit Matthew Arnold's description of Nonconformist life? The meetings began with coffee (or tea) and, depending on the state of the finances, cake.[65] There was little trace of jealousy of the Establishment, though this did not preclude robust criticism, and the minutes do not suggest many disputes.

In fact, the theology and the general scope of the papers delivered were not at all narrow. Theologically the Union was critical: it wanted to hear about biblical research (literary and archaeological), it expected to hear about critical views. For example, Glover's paper on 'The Mission of Independency' in 1892 advocated 'a broad and undogmatic church'.[66] He described a paper by the Revd Dugald Macfadyen of St Ives on 'Inspiration' in February 1893 as 'masterly'; the secretary's summary noted the

62. Brooke, *History, 1870–1990*, p. 294; Miller, *Portrait*, p. 100.

63. Munson, *Nonconformists*, p. 85. E.A. Benians, later Master of St John's, was President of CUNU in the Lent Term 1902 and was the first history Scholar at St John's. Miller, *Portrait*, p. 114.

64. Glover Diaries, 25 March 1895, 6 April 1895, 14 February 1896.

65. CUNU Minutes, 1883–94, 7 December 1884, 1 February 1885 ('a brief but animated discussion'), 11 March 1892.

66. Glover Diaries, 24 January 1892.

breadth of the use of the word 'inspired' in the Old Testament, pointed out the correct translation of 2 Tim. 3.16, and concluded:

> By careful reasoning the reader of the paper showed that we could not claim infallibility for the bible; in fact that some parts of it were not compatible with the infinite goodness of God. The Jews were not the only people who had inspired men in their midst. But in them alone was there a continued stream of inspired prophecies. The bible as a collection of these contained the most inspired utterances of the past.[67]

Although they never persuaded Robertson Smith to address them, Rendel Harris spoke four times; and Mrs Lewis spoke on her visits to Thessaly, Sinai and Jerusalem in May 1897. But talks on biblical topics as such were rare. There was a series of talks on evolution, especially in relation to religion. Another popular theme was Church history, particularly the history of Nonconformity; the early Church and the middle ages had their share, though there was little about the sixteenth-century Reformation as such. There were talks on other religions—Islam, Buddhism, Hinduism, Zoroastrianism, Chinese religion—sometimes with reference to missionary themes, but more often as subjects in their own right. Contemporary issues, such as education, were regularly discussed, as were the relations of the working classes to the churches and socialism. Lastly, there were literary figures—Robert Browning (on whom Dr Hill, master of Downing and Vice-Chancellor, spoke on 5 December 1897), Tennyson (the subject of Forsyth's only address), Tolstoi, Ibsen, Shelley, Wordsworth and Robert Louis Stevenson.[68]

There was also a strong and recurrent interest in the settlement movement, the first talk on the subject being on 4 May 1884. As well as Toynbee Hall (on which William Beveridge spoke in February 1904), this included the Congregationalist settlements, Mansfield House and Browning House in Walworth. Support was rallied through a special auxiliary, but there was a regular stream of speakers from London, including Will Reason from Mansfield House. T.R. Glover was involved with similar mission work at Tyndale Church in Bristol, and almost as soon as he arrived in Cambridge in 1888 he was recruited by Mrs Whibley to teach a

67. Glover Diaries, 5 February 1893; CUNU Minutes, 1883–94, 5 February 1893. For Macfadyen, see M. Wagner, *Not an Easy Church* (St Ives: The Free Church, 1982), pp. 47-50. Glover spent weekends there in vacations.

68. Obviously it was not so easy to illustrate a talk about music, but Keynes noted once: 'Another fine sermon from Forsyth. He made very effective use of Beethoven's Ninth Symphony as an illustration.' Add 7845: 7 July 1895.

class at the men's Sunday morning school at the Castle End mission.[69] This meant he did not go to St Andrew's Street Baptist Church for morning service, and he went to Emmanuel in the evening instead.

The Union carefully maintained its independence of the denominational authorities. An early example concerned Mansfield College. In May 1885 J.R. Murray of St John's (who later became a Congregational minister in Manchester)[70] suggested a discussion on the establishment of a Congregational theological college at Oxford. A special meeting was arranged, at which Murray moved two resolutions. The first deeply regretted 'the establishment of any college at either Oxford or Cambridge Universities on so doctrinal and sectarian a basis as that proposed for Mansfield College'; the second, 'while sympathising with any attempt to throw open the advantages of a University career to those who are preparing for the Nonconformist Ministry', strongly deprecated 'the establishment of any sectarian theological faculty at either University'. 'A somewhat lengthy discussion' took place on these resolutions; 11 people spoke, including Hardcastle, J.R. Tanner, the Revd W.A. Guttridge[71] and Dr Smith from Oxford. The resolutions were carried *nem. con.*; 33 members were present.[72]

A year later Dr Dale wrote to ask the Union to discuss the matter again. (Dale was a leading protagonist of the Mansfield scheme, and his son at Trinity Hall would presumably have told him of the earlier discussion.) So in May 1886 Professors Massie and Fairbairn spoke to a meeting of a hundred men and women. The discussion lasted until 11.55 p.m. The committee authorized 'a very bald report' to be sent to the *Cambridge Review*, and agreed to pay for a verbatim report of the meeting. Having obtained it, however, the committee decided not to publish it but to print six copies, which the president was to keep and pass to his successors.[73] It was clearly regarded as important to get Cambridge 'on side' in this matter, which presumably was achieved; but there was no comparable

---

69. Wood, *Glover*, pp. 18-19; the mission is in St Peter's Street, north of Pound Hill and close to the back way into New Court of St John's College.

70. Venn, *Alumni*, II, iv, p. 502.

71. Venn, *Alumni*, II, iii, p. 179. Guttridge was the founding minister of Victoria Road Congregational Church in 1877 after graduating from St John's: A. Smith and D. Lawrence, *Victoria Road United Reformed Church: A History of the First Hundred Years* (Cambridge, n.d.).

72. CUNU Minutes, 1883–94, 7 June 1885.

73. CUNU Minutes, 1883–94, 4 May 1886, 23 May 1886, 24 May 1886, 3 June 1886.

discussion about the arrival of Westminster College a decade later, or of Cheshunt College a decade after that.

After a talk in October 1897 by A.J. Wyatt of Christ's, a member of Emmanuel, on 'Congregationalism in Cambridgeshire Villages', it was agreed to form a voluntary village corps within the Union to assist in village preaching. But the motion to appoint an organizing committee was carried only on the casting vote of the chairman. At the beginning of the Easter Term 1898, a proposal for a new clause in the constitution 'that the Union should not restrict its scope to its Sunday night discussion but should show some sympathy and in some way keep in touch with active Christian work in the University Town and Country' was lost.[74]

The same reluctance to get involved was presumably responsible for the defeat in November 1895 of a motion for the Union to be represented on the Cambridge Nonconformist Council; but in June 1899 the president announced that the Union would send two delegates to the next meeting of the Cambridgeshire Free Church Council. Two were nominated, and thereafter it became normal.[75] A final example was the committee's refusal to leave 6 March 1904 vacant so that the society could take part in the centenary celebrations of the British and Foreign Bible Society; but later H.G. Wood carried a proposal to drop the meeting on 6 March and to hold a dinner to mark the coming of age of the society. Fairbairn was one of the guests at the dinner on 13 May 1904.[76]

Membership of the Union was largely confined to Congregationalists and Baptists: Wesleyans and other Methodists rarely became members. The Presbyterian Association emerged as a separate society from a Bible class run by Professor Macalister, and since its meetings were also on Sunday evenings it was not possible to attend both (though Glover occasionally went there rather than the Union).[77] There was an early proposal for a joint meeting with the Wesley Society, which led to one on 6 June 1886 with over a hundred present for a discussion on the form of church government. In May 1889 when J.H. Moulton addressed the Union, the president said that he hoped that the Union and the Wesley Society could be drawn closer together. Scott Lidgett read a paper at a joint meeting in November 1889, and there was a 'return match' in January 1890, when

74. CUNU Minutes, 1894–1901, 31 October 1897, 6 March 1898, 24 April 1898.
75. CUNU Minutes, 24 November 1895, 4 June 1899, 5 November 1899.
76. CUNU Minutes, 1901–1904, November 1903, 21 February 1904, 13 May 1904.
77. Macalister, *St Columba's Church*, p. 20; Glover Diaries, 12 March 1893, 3 December 1893.

Alex Mackennal was the speaker. In 1891 there was a proposal for a joint meeting involving the Wesley Society and the Presbyterian Association; but the Wesley Society declined so that matter was not taken further. Nothing more happened until 1899, when it was agreed to have a joint meeting once a term from Lent 1900. The first reference to the Robert Hall Society (the student Baptist organization, which was founded at the instigation of Glover in 1902)[78] came in 1903, followed by the Congregational Society, which was founded when Selbie became minister at Emmanuel.[79]

Perhaps the most significant feature of the Union was its predominantly male membership. In Nonconformist churches a majority of members were usually women. The first reference to female visitors is in June 1895. When the Livingstone Society deputation came in November 1895, 25 out of the 30 visitors were women. Thereafter it gradually ceased to be a matter of note. The first woman to speak was Dr Margaret Pearce of the Women's Settlement in Canning Town in May 1896.[80] But women were not allowed to become members until 1915, when it almost seemed necessary to keep the Union afloat. In this respect, therefore, the Union mirrors the wider university attitude to women, in which Cambridge lagged significantly behind Oxford.[81]

What picture of the future for Nonconformists emerges from all this? Not surprisingly there was a range of views. At one extreme there was the pessimism of J.R. Tanner; although one of the founding members of the Union, by 1893 he was telling Glover that he thought it was all up with Nonconformity.[82] Glover disagreed, but the cases of both Glover and H.G. Wood illustrate movement (quite apart from that of someone like Figgis who eventually became a member of the Community of the Resurrection). Both were sons of Baptist ministers, but Glover in his first Cambridge period (1888–96) spent more time at Emmanuel than St Andrew's Street, culminating in his marriage to Alice Few, daughter of an Emmanuel deacon, in 1896. On his return from Canada in 1901 he transferred his membership from Bristol to St Andrew's Street, finding Charles Joseph more attractive than Graham Tarn; but he often went to hear Selbie at Emmanuel in the evening, and he also attended the Society of Friends.

78. Wood, *Glover*, p. 65; Parsons, *St Andrew's Street*, p. 43.
79. CUNU Minutes, 1901–1904, 24 March 1903, 8 May 1904.
80. CUNU Minutes, 1894–1901, 2 June 1895, 24 May 1896. Glover noted 'a lot there. But visitors—and women!' Glover Diaries, 10 November 1895.
81. CUNU Minutes, 1910–1916, 24 October 1915, 31 October 1915.
82. Glover Diaries, 30 October 1893; Wood, *Glover*, p. 30.

During the student summer conference at Conishead Priory in 1905, he went to meeting at Swarthmore Hall.[83] Wood was drawn in the same direction, partly through the influence of Rendel Harris and partly through his Quaker wife, Dora; eventually Wood went to Woodbrooke in 1910. Glover stayed in Cambridge, but his five years in Canada were important. Both were looking for broader horizons. Preachers such as Forsyth and Selbie were significant in providing the breadth they sought.[84]

In 1913 the Nonconformist Union celebrated its thirtieth anniversary with a dinner. An article in the *Daily News* doubted 'whether there is a more valuable society at either university than the Cambridge Nonconformist Union'. It noted the range of subjects discussed, and suggested that there was nothing that was militantly sectarian about it: 'Perhaps its chief contribution to university thought has been in the cultivation of a serious and at the same time open-minded attitude towards religious problems.'[85] Ten years later B.L. Manning (who was secretary in the Michaelmas Term 1914 and president in the Lent Term 1915) described the dinner as the Union's swan song, adding that 'the Union died when the University was at its emptiest; and peace did not revive it because conditions have altogether changed'.[86] He emphasized the new significance of the Student Christian Movement, and, of course, one consequence of the secession of CICCU from the SCM was a much greater involvement of Nonconformist students in the latter's life.

Manning's comment has the advantage of hindsight, but is astute in making the point that it is the non-revival of the Union after the war which needs to be explained, not its demise in the Michaelmas Term 1916 when the pressure on the university was at its height. The war crystallized the political and religious aspects of Nonconformity and the post-war landscape looked very different. To adapt Matthew Arnold's terminology, the choice lay between totality or particularity, between a view that empha-

83. Glover Diaries, 23 July 1905. This was the meeting at which the name was changed from British Colleges Christian Union to Student Christian Movement.

84. Wood, *Glover*, pp. 33-34, 81-93; Glover Diaries, 9 June 1901; R.C. Scott, *Herbert G. Wood* (London: Friends Home Service Committee, 1967), pp. 19-21, 33-46. For Forsyth at Emmanuel, see J.C.G. Binfield, 'Principal When Pastor: P.T. Forsyth, 1876–1901', in W.G. Sheils and D. Wood (eds.), *The Ministry: Clerical and Lay* (Studies in Church History, 26; Oxford: Basil Blackwell, 1989), pp. 397-414 (408-14).

85. *Daily News*, 25 April 1913, p. 6.

86. B.L. Manning, 'Nonconformity at the Universities: II, Cambridge', *Congregational Quarterly*, 1 (1923), pp. 179-87 (184).

sized the place of the Nonconformist tradition in the nation and the Church and one that fostered a sense of a Nonconformist or denominational tradition, which had to be preserved in its particularity. That was the importance of the choice between interdenominational societies like the Union, the SCM or indeed CICCU, and the denominational societies, pioneered by the Wesley Society and subsequently followed elsewhere.

There was a symbolic episode in 1915. On 31 January 1915 at a Union open meeting in the Liberal Club in Downing Street Maude Royden spoke to about 200 on 'Conflict of Loyalties'. Manning was in the chair. In the course of her address Maude Royden said, 'He calls for national loyalty but the hatred of nation for his sake. War is contrary to his mind for though He did not rebuke the militarists of his generation, He taught his disciples a better way.'[87] Ebenezer Cunningham, fellow of St John's, who had been involved in the inauguration of the Fellowship of Reconciliation at the beginning of the month, was there, as was H.C. Carter, minister of Emmanuel.[88] After the Emmanuel deacons' meeting the following evening Carter told Cunningham, 'I am off the fence', and Cunningham wrote that this brought 'a new quality of assurance and faith' into his preaching.[89]

A different impression appears in Keynes's diaries. Before war broke out Keynes thought that Carter's theology was 'getting narrower'. In October 1915 he wrote that he was very annoyed with Carter's sermon, although he liked him so much: 'I should like to give up Emmanuel and occasionally go to church.' The same sentiments recur in 1916 until on Christmas Eve he wrote:

> I went to Emmanuel in the morning. But I really cannot stand Carter any more, and I must I think definitely give up going. Like the American President he appears to see no difference between Germany & ourselves. (But this has proved to be very unjust to the American President.)

There are no further references in Keynes's diaries to services at Emmanuel, and golf at Royston increasingly took their place.[90]

87.   CUNU Minutes, 1910–16, 31 January 1915.

88.   Cunningham (president, Michaelmas Term 1902) had spoken on 'The Church and War' at the end of the previous term; he provided a financial guarantee to enable the Union to hire a larger room. CUNU Minutes, 1910–16, 6 December 1914, 20 January 1915.

89.   'Ebenezer', typescript autobiography of E. Cunningham, pp. 48-49. Carter resigned in 1916 because of criticism by the deacons; but the church meeting called for the withdrawal of his resignation, so the deacons resigned (though more than half were subsequently re-elected).

90.   Keynes Diaries, Add 7864: 18 January 1914; Add 7865: 17 October 1915; Add

Manning thought that the disappearance of the Nonconformist Union was 'the sign of the working of deeper forces'. Class consciousness was declining, and the opening of Oxford and Cambridge had drawn into national life those who otherwise would have been the leaders of a militant Nonconformity. By comparison with 30 years before Nonconformity had lost 'almost the whole of its political significance'. 'The type of Nonconformist who stood *as a Nonconformist* for aggressive radicalism in politics is already a curiosity and will soon be a relic.' Although many Nonconformists were enthusiastic Liberal or Labour supporters, their politics were separable from their religion in a new way (even if they did not see it themselves), and this had removed 'much of the zest of Nonconformity'.[91]

Interestingly, when H.G. Wood was deciding whether to go to Woodbrooke in 1909, Foakes-Jackson, who, like Manning, was a fellow of Jesus, told him that two of his advisers, Rendel Harris and Glover, had 'a peculiar bias against Cambridge': they were 'both militant nonconformists and never quite at ease in an atmosphere of indifferent Whiggism'.[92] Manning could not be accused of 'indifferent Whiggism', and Foakes-Jackson's remark tells us more about him than Harris and Glover. But Manning's response to the changed situation was a new emphasis on churchmanship. The collapse of Anglican exclusiveness meant that Nonconformists no longer lived 'in a religious world of their own':

> The more we are admitted to equal privilege and equal service with Anglicans the more our people must compare Nonconformist Churchmanship with that of others; and as the old political hostility and clash of principle has diminished…it seems to contain nothing but what Anglicanism contains, whilst Anglicanism contains some things that it lacks.

The falsity of such a view could only be demonstrated by emphasizing 'the positive side of Dissenting tradition, Dissenting Churchmanship and Dissenting faith'. There was 'another way than that of bad Tractarian architecture and emasculated liturgy', namely the recovery of the austere tradition of 'those mysteries of grace which the well-bred Dissenter will always miss in Anglicanism'. If this was done, it would be clear 'that Nonconformity is more than Anglicanism and water'. 'In Cambridge at

---

7866: 2 January 1916, 5 June 1916, 24 December 1916. He was elected to the Committee of Royston Golf Club in May 1915: Add 7865: 28 May 1915.

91. Manning, 'Nonconformity at Cambridge', p. 186.

92. Scott, *Wood*, p. 45.

least', concluded Manning, 'Nonconformity cannot live as a protest against injustices removed and errors that are dying.'[93]

Manning's verdict is perceptive. But one final reflection must be added. English university experience, by detaching students from their home context often never to return, is quite peculiar in the kind of disorientation that it produces. The diaries of first-generation academics who did stay in this novel environment increases the sense of detachment. How far is what has been described to be understood in social or sociological terms, or political terms (which lie at the heart of Manning's analysis)? How far does it reflect a religious experience? Or, put another way, what degree of inter-generational continuity is it ever appropriate to expect in a religious context? Here there is a theological point that lies at the heart of the matter. Is religion to be understood in a family context where each generation is successively inducted into the ancestral customs? or is it something which has to be freshly appropriated in each generation? This is a reminder of the significance of the Evangelical Revival in English religion, including English Dissent, which in so many ways marks a major discontinuity. One consequence of these reflections may be to raise once more the question of whether the kind of Dissent which emerged in seventeenth-century England ever could be the same after the eighteenth century, and whether the nineteenth-century experience is the outworking of the consequences of that. This is the context for any discussion of Nonconformist culture.

93. B.L. Manning, 'Nonconformity at Cambridge', p. 187.

METHODIST ATTITUDES TO EDUCATION AND YOUTH: HALIFAX, 1800–2000

John A. Hargreaves

The two centuries from 1800 to 2000 embrace not only the period of the most rapid growth of Methodism in Halifax, but also the period of its most dramatic decline. Halifax, with a circuit membership of 1,350, was already a prominent Methodist centre by 1800 and head of a new Methodist district. Experience of both revival and secession stimulated further spectacular growth in membership and spawned a proliferation of new circuits in the half-century before 1851, when Halifax was the only large town in the West Riding where non-Wesleyans outnumbered Wesleyans. However, by 1914 all the branches of Methodism, except the Primitive Methodists, were experiencing declining growth rates in Halifax and a series of circuit amalgamations after 1932 reduced the number of Halifax circuits from eight to one by 1971. Between 1972 and 2000, membership of the Halifax Circuit declined by 45 per cent from 1,983 to 1,088, but throughout the period Halifax remained the largest of the 22 circuits in the West Yorkshire Methodist District.[1] During the nineteenth-century age of expansion, secession and consolidation, Methodist attitudes to education and youth were shaped by dual considerations of mission and control, within a wider social context of relatively limited educational opportunity. During the twentieth-century era of retrenchment and decline, Methodist attitudes displayed a growing adaptability characterized by the rediscovery of mission in the service of youth, within a wider social context of increasing educational opportunity.

1.   J.A. Hargreaves, 'Methodist Growth and Secession in the Parish of Halifax, 1740–1851', *Transactions of the Halifax Antiquarian Society* [hereafter *THAS*] 7 (1999), pp. 51-73; 'Methodism in Halifax: Consolidation and Decline, 1852–1914', *THAS* 8 (2000), pp. 133-49. I am grateful to Professor David Bebbington, Professor Edward Royle and the Revd John Munsey Turner for their comments on a preliminary draft of this article, and to the Revds Stan Brown and David Jones, Stephen G. Lane (Boys' Brigade Archivist), Dr Peter B. Nockles of the Methodist Archives, and Jenny Leach (Chief Guide), for facilitating access to archive material.

While there has been a profusion of general surveys of Methodist attitudes to education at connexional level, there has been a dearth of local studies focusing specifically on Methodist attitudes to education and youth at circuit level. The purpose of this paper is to assess the extent to which Halifax reflected the connexional ambivalence identified by Dr Archibald Harrison in his history of the Methodist Church published to celebrate Methodist reunion in 1932, where he concluded that 'the attitude of Methodism to education has been wavering and uncertain'.[2]

The Age of Growth and Secession: Mission and Control, 1800–51
The age of Methodist growth and secession in the first half of the nineteenth century was characterized by distinctly ambivalent attitudes to education and youth at both connexional and circuit level in Halifax. Nowhere was connexional ambivalence towards education more apparent at grassroots level than in its response to the early development of Sunday schools. The issue came to a head in Halifax in the aftermath of the machine-breaking disturbances, which had erupted in West Yorkshire in 1812. Luddism, variously viewed by historians as a turbulent episode in industrial relations characterized by 'collective bargaining by riot' or as a heroic phase in the emergence of revolutionary class consciousness characterized by 'quasi-insurrectionary' incitement, came to be regarded by contemporary Halifax Methodists as a failure of parenting which exposed impressionable Methodist youths not only to pressures to join illegal trade associations but also to the influence of dangerous Painite republican and anti-clerical ideology. In the aftermath of the Yorkshire Luddite disturbances of 1812, Jabez Bunting, superintendent minister of the Halifax Wesleyan Circuit, expressed his concern that no fewer than 6 of the 17 Luddites who were hanged at York in January 1813 were 'the sons of Methodists'. He confided in correspondence to a friend that the 'awful' episode confirmed him in his opinion that

> the progress of Methodism in the West Riding of Yorkshire has been… more in the increase of numbers, than in the diffusion of that kind of piety, which shines as brightly and operates as visibly *at home* as in the prayer meeting and the crowded love feast.

Professor W.R. Ward, some 30 years ago, made the crucial inference: 'what was needed was less revival and more denominational drill, and in particu-

    2.   F.C. Pritchard, 'Education', in R. Davies, A.R. George and G. Rupp (eds.), *A History of the Methodist Church in Great Britain*, III (London: Epworth Press, 1983), p. 307.

lar, Bunting's current nostrums, the control of Sunday schools and discipline of children'.[3]

The majority of Sunday schools founded in Halifax before 1800 had been undenominational schools with paid teachers, supported by property owners alarmed at the spread of Painite republicanism. Many of the early denominational Sunday schools, which began to proliferate in the parish from the turn of the century, also attracted similar support. The first Wesleyan Sunday school in Halifax, opened in a cottage near the South Parade Chapel on 15 May 1805, included a shalloon maker and two excise officers among its early superintendents. Initially there were 50 children, but within a fortnight numbers had doubled. In 1813, the year in which Jabez Bunting had voiced his concerns about the education of the young, the Sunday school was moved to the vestry of South Parade Chapel where its activities might be more closely monitored. By 1824 the number of children at South Parade had increased to 300 and there were no fewer than 9 other Wesleyan Sunday schools in the Halifax Circuit, 5 of them meeting in chapel buildings, with a total enrolment of 1,600 scholars.[4]

In the parish of Halifax, Methodism established an unrivalled hegemony in Sunday school provision during the nineteenth century, dwarfing even that of the Anglicans. Of the 49 Sunday schools which had been established in the Upper Calder Valley by 1833, 20 were Methodist, accounting for 44 per cent of the 9,669 enrolments, more than double the Anglican proportion. Moreover, the ratio of Methodist to Anglican enrolments remained virtually unchanged ten years later when Edward Baines's survey of the parish revealed that nearly 46 per cent of the 28,346 enrolments were Methodist and nearly 20 per cent Anglican. By 1843 the total number of Wesleyan scholars had increased to 8,040 and there had also been considerable growth of Sunday schools in the other branches of Methodism. The Methodist New Connexion (MNC) had some 2,921 scholars, the Wesleyan Methodist Association (WMA) 1,099 scholars and there were 946 Primitive Methodist (PM) scholars.[5] The Methodist ascendancy in Sunday school provision in Halifax was confirmed in the Education Census of 1851. In the Halifax Registration District 58 of the 136 Sunday

3.   W.R. Ward, *Religion and Society in England 1790–1850* (London: Batsford, 1972), p. 86; J.A. Hargreaves, 'Methodism and Luddism in Yorkshire, 1812–13', *Northern History* 26 (1990), pp. 160-85.

4.   J.A. Hargreaves, 'Religion and Society in the Parish of Halifax, c. 1740–1914' (PhD thesis, Huddersfield Polytechnic, 1991), pp. 181-92.

5.   E. Baines, *The Social, Educational and Religious State of the Manufacturing Districts, 1843* (New York: Augustus M. Kelley, 1969), Table IV.

schools and 40 per cent of scholars on roll were Methodist, almost double the figures for the Anglicans. Moreover, the Methodists also had the largest number of Sunday schools with the largest number of scholars in the municipal borough of Halifax. Within Methodism the Wesleyan Methodists, with 9 schools and 1,576 scholars, had the most impressive provision, followed by the MNC with 4 schools and 1,061 scholars, the PMs with 3 schools and 434 scholars and the Wesleyan Reformers with one school and 174 scholars.[6]

The genuinely popular appeal of Sunday schools in the first half of the nineteenth century was evidenced by the sheer number of scholars and teachers involved in the movement. It also derived, as Professor Hugh McLeod has observed, from 'the skill with which they mixed religion and education with entertainments and outings'.[7] In Halifax the colourful and spectacular quinquennial Whitsuntide Sings held at the Piece Hall between 1831 and 1890 to commemorate the inauguration of the Sunday school movement remained vivid in the memories of successive generations of children. The 17,000 participants in the third Jubilee Sing in 1841 were revealingly described as 'an invading well-disciplined army—cheerful and well-clad'. The training in diligence and obedience that the Sunday schools provided commended them to employers, many willingly closing their factories and workshops for the Whit Sings. Sunday school teaching was also highly regarded by employers. Successive speakers at the Halifax Wesleyan Sunday schools annual tea party in January 1843 reminded their audience that successful candidates for senior positions with the town's improvement commissioners were 'mainly recommended to the offices they sought…on account of their exemplary characters as Sunday school teachers'.[8]

The primary appeal of the Sunday schools to working-class parents and children, however, lay in the social welfare and rudimentary education in literacy which they succeeded in providing without jeopardizing the family economy. Some Wesleyan Sunday schools, for example Sowerby, founded in 1805, taught reading and writing alongside the Scriptures from the outset. However, the Wesleyan Conference, concerned to safeguard religious teaching from the Jacobin taint of secular education, condemned the prac-

---

6.   Census of Great Britain. Report and Tables on Education. England and Wales 1852–53 [1692] vol. XC.
7.   H. McLeod, *Religion and the Working Class in Nineteenth-Century Britain* (London: Macmillan, 1984), p. 41.
8.   Hargreaves, 'Religion and Society', pp. 187-88.

tice of teaching sabbath writing with such frequency between 1814 and 1837 as to suggest continuing problems in the enforcement of the controversial ban. One tract published in Halifax in 1829 bearing the title 'The impropriety and sinfulness of teaching the poor to write on Sundays' drew a swift response from Joseph Barker (1806–75), the radical MNC minister stationed in Halifax. He argued in a publication entitled 'Mercy triumphant, a vindication of teaching writing on Sundays', that teaching children who lacked other educational opportunities to write on the sabbath was an act of mercy. At Heptonstall, the attempt to enforce the controversial ban drove part of the congregation to join the WMA. In 1842 Mary Pratt, who attended a Wesleyan Sunday school in Brighouse told the Children's Employment Commissioner revealingly that she 'could read a little bit', but could not write. Moreover, the earliest extant records for Mount Tabor Wesleyan Sunday School from 1847 emphasize that writing and arithmetic were not to be taught on Sundays, but that weekday evening classes were provided to develop these skills as a reward for regular attendance at Sunday school. By 1849, however, writing was being openly taught at Greetland as well as reading and religious knowledge.

Tension inevitably intensified when some Sunday schools identified with the Reformers during the 'fly-sheets' controversy, which split the Wesleyan Connexion in the 1840s. The majority of the trustees at Southowram Sunday School, for example, gave their support to the Reformers, while the chapel trustees remained loyal to the Wesleyan Conference. Some of the chapel trustees expelled for reading James Everett's pamphlets attempted to take possession of the school and on 31 January 1851 the teachers resolved by a large majority to boycott the chapel services in the belief that the children would benefit

> from staying in the school in the morning instead of going to the chapel and leaving it to the discretion of the superintendent whether they shall attend chapel in the afternoon or stay at school and hear a sermon from one of the expelled or Reform preachers.

While such gulfs between Wesleyan chapels and their associated Sunday schools emerged at times of crisis, the scale of the continuing investment in both the Sunday school movement and the expansion of chapel building during this period suggests that in the majority of Halifax Methodist chapels strong links were maintained and considerable numbers of former Sunday school scholars ultimately nurtured into chapel membership.[9]

9.   Hargreaves, 'Religion and Society', p. 192; Ward, *Religion and Society*, pp. 96-97, 137, 174.

J.T. Smith in a reappraisal of the Methodist contribution to elementary education in the nineteenth century has concluded that 'Wesleyan provision for day-schools was far less laudable than their Sunday school efforts' and that Wesleyans displayed little enthusiasm for either the schools of the National Society, 'with its Anglican formularies', or the British and Foreign School Society, 'which prohibited Methodist catechisms in its schools'.[10] In Halifax, however, there is evidence of early Methodist involvement with the voluntary societies. Jabez Bunting, who has received recognition for his prominent role in the establishment of a northern school for the sons of itinerant ministers at Woodhouse Grove during his superintendency of the Halifax circuit in 1812, is less well known for his role in the foundation of the Halifax British School in 1813. Both Bunting and his Wesleyan colleague, William Leach, together with MNC minister John Grundell and several other leading Methodist laymen, were prominent in raising funds for the new Halifax British School. The school opened in rented premises in April 1813, after an earlier collaborative initiative, which Bunting had also supported, with the Halifax National School, founded in 1812, had failed. Of the 3,532 children who passed through the school during the period 1813–21 nearly half were Methodist. Of these 30 per cent were Wesleyan and 15 per cent MNC. In 1833 there were 508 scholars, 350 boys and 158 girls, enrolled at the school, vastly more than at any other school in the township of Halifax, and by 1836 some 4,700 children had passed through the school.[11]

Methodist denominational day schools attached to chapels were also opened in the parish of Halifax in the first half of the nineteenth century, though as J.T. Smith has argued, financial constraints undoubtedly imposed 'a major brake' on Methodist commitment to day school provision.[12] Day schools were erected by the Wesleyans at Greetland in 1816 and Stones near Ripponden in 1818. In 1837, the PMs started a day school in their newly opened chapel at Lindwell and in 1846 the Wesleyan day school at Sowerby Bridge was extended, with special provision for half-timers, 'the number of scholars having very considerably increased'. Besides basic literacy and numeracy, the curriculum included geography, history, natural philosophy, book-keeping, the higher branches of mathematics,

---

10. J.T. Smith, *Methodism and Education, 1849–1902* (Oxford: Clarendon Press, 1998), pp. 1, 6.

11. Hargreaves, 'Religion and Society', pp. 194-96.

12. Smith, *Methodism and Education*, pp. 1-2.

music, knitting and fancy needlework 'combined with sound religious instruction, based upon the Bible—the Bible without note or comment'.[13] In 1848 a Wesleyan day school was opened in Orange Street, Halifax, which had 63 scholars, 45 boys and 18 girls, enrolled by 1851. However, the Education Census reveals that a majority of Halifax children in 1851 attended the National and British Schools (1,049 and 499 respectively) and 3 local factory schools (1,239 scholars), one of which had been founded by the MNC worsted spinner Jonathan Akroyd after the Factory Act of 1833.[14] A report of 1850 commending Akroyd's factory school, which was conducted by a trained master and mistress from the Glasgow Normal Seminary, observed that 'religious and moral instruction' was 'a prominent feature in the education given'.[15]

Methodists in Halifax were no less ambivalent than were the Methodist connexional authorities in their attitudes towards government educational initiatives during this period. The prospect of government funding for education embracing Roman Catholic schools in 1839 elicited no fewer than 8 petitions from Halifax and its neighbourhood containing almost 1,000 signatures opposing Lord John Russell's proposals and seeking 'to thwart the attempt to introduce Popery into the land'.[16] The rise of Puseyism in the Church of England; the introduction of Sir James Graham's controversial Education Bill of 1843; the announcement of a government grant to the Roman Catholic seminary at Maynooth in 1845; and the 1847 parliamentary election in which Edward Miall's candidature as a radical voluntaryist in Halifax attracted considerable Methodist support intensified sectarian attitudes to education in the second quarter of the nineteenth century. Indeed, sectarian controversy even permeated the seasonal atmosphere at the annual Christmas celebration meeting of the recently formed Halifax Wesleyan Juvenile Missionary Society, when there was applause for a speaker who proclaimed 'No Peace with Rome', in the highly charged atmosphere of 1843, the year in which the Wesleyan Conference had denounced Graham's 'objectionable and alarming' Factory Bill as 'likely to inflict the greatest injury to the numerous Sunday and weekday schools already supported by the voluntary zeal and liberality of the Wesleyan Body'.[17]

13. Hargreaves, 'Religion and Society', pp. 196-97.

14. Census of Great Britain. Report and Tables on Education. England and Wales 1852–53 [1692] vol. XC, Table P.

15. E. Webster, 'Halifax Schools, 1870–1970', *THAS* (1972), pp. 1-49 (7).

16. *Halifax Guardian*, 25 May, 1 June 1839.

17. J.A. Hargreaves, 'Methodism and Electoral Politics in Halifax, 1832–1848',

The Era of Consolidation: Mission Accomplished, 1852–1901

Sunday schools remained the most popular vehicle for Methodist work among children and young people in Halifax in the second half of the nineteenth century, an era of consolidation for Halifax Methodism, when demographically high birth rates gave Halifax a distinctively youthful age profile and the prevalence of part-time factory work continued to deny many youngsters the benefits of a full-time education. Indeed, Dr Simon Green has estimated that by 1877 possibly half the population under 21 and three-quarters of those aged 5–20 were enrolled in Halifax Sunday schools.[18] Of these a high proportion would have been Methodist and during this period Halifax Methodism probably exercised a greater influence over a wider constituency of children and young people than at any other period in its history. Indeed, Methodist Sunday school scholars and teachers accounted for over half of the 28,621 participants in the ninth Sunday School Jubilee Piece Hall Sing in 1876.[19] Moreover, the records for subsequent Piece Hall Sings suggest that Sunday school recruitment in Halifax remained buoyant at least until 1890. Collectively, the Methodists accounted for 17,460 Sunday school scholars and teachers at the 1890 Sing, again comprising more than half of the total.[20] The recollections of contemporaries confirm the impression of a continuing vitality in Sunday school affiliation in late Victorian Halifax. Alderman Harold Waddington recalled that Sunday schools in the 1870s and 1880s were 'in most instances crowded'.[21] Henry W. Harwood, a local journalist, maintained that 'down to the 1890s, and even for some years after, the Sunday schools were full'.[22] James Parker, Halifax's first Labour MP, reckoned that 'the Sunday

Northern History 35 (1999), pp. 139-60; *Halifax Guardian*, 30 December 1843; Wilkinson, *Methodism and Education*, pp. 10-11.

18. S.J.D. Green, *Religion in the Age of Decline: Organisation and Experience in Industrial Yorkshire, 1870–1920* (Cambridge: Cambridge University Press, 1996), pp. 54, 58-59.

19. Plan of Halifax Sunday School Jubilee, 6 June 1876, author's copy and calculations.

20. Halifax Second Commemoration of the Sunday School Centenary, 27 May 1890, author's copy and calculations; J.A. Hargreaves, *Halifax* (Edinburgh: Edinburgh University Press/Lancaster: Carnegie, 1999), pp. 155-56.

21. J.H. Waddington, *Essays and Addresses* (Halifax: C.W. Ibberson, 1939), pp. 33-34.

22. H.W. Harwood, *Centenary Story* (Halifax: Halifax Courier, 1948), p. 34.

schools were filled in the years up to about 1900'.[23] However, denominational statistics reveal that enrolments at MNC Sunday schools in the Halifax circuits peaked in 1884 at 5,032 and that between 1885 and 1907 enrolments declined by nearly 22 per cent to 3,932. Sunday school enrolment in the Halifax United Methodist Free Churches (UMFC) Circuit also declined from 720 in 1893 to 633 in 1899.[24]

The issue of teaching literacy in Sunday schools became less controversial with the extension of the state provision of elementary education in non-denominational schools after 1870, allowing the development of a closer integration between aspirations at connexional and circuit level in the last three decades of the century. The extension and reform of Sunday schools with the aim of 'the gathering of Sunday scholars into the Wesleyan Methodist society' was actively promoted by the Wesleyan Connexion after 1870, when circuits were enjoined 'to promote the opening of new, and the extension and improvement of existing schools'. In Halifax, however, there is evidence of strategic planning at circuit level even before 1870. The initiative for the planting of a new Sunday school in the industrial village of Siddal had come from leaders at South Parade as early as 1857, and a similar initiative from Wesley Chapel, Broad Street, resulted in the building of a new Sunday school at Pellon in 1861. Extension and reform accelerated after 1870 in all the Methodist denominations. King Cross Wesleyan Sunday School was extended in 1870 and a branch school opened in 1874. At Hanover Street MNC Sunday School there was a concerted effort to ensure that scholars 'behave with seriousness' when 'singing the praises of God' and adopt a more reverent attitude during prayers. At the MNC and PM Sunday Schools on Queens Road there was a growing concern for systematic scriptural and catechetical teaching in the 1880s and a willingness to experiment with new teaching methods. The MNC toffee manufacturer John Mackintosh visited different Sunday schools when travelling on business in America 'always carefully observing the methods of work adopted and gleaning information that might be useful to the schools at home'.[25]

23. J. Parker, 'Looking Back a Century', in J.J. Mulroy (ed.), *The Story of the Town that Bred Us* (Halifax: J.J. Mulroy, 1948), pp. 60-63 (61).

24. Hargreaves, 'Methodism in Halifax', pp. 143-44.

25. Hargreaves, 'Methodism in Halifax', pp. 144-45; Green, *Religion in the Age of Decline*, pp. 212, 218-19, 223-28; Siddal Wesleyan Sunday School Minute Book, 1901–33; A.J. Thorpe, *Pellon Wesleyan Chapel and Sunday School* (Halifax: C.H. Milnes, 1904), pp. 1, 3, 12.

The Sunday school and temperance movements also became more closely linked in all branches of Halifax Methodism in the later Victorian era. Initially, however, Wesleyan connexional ambivalence towards temperance, manifested in an official condemnation of teetotalism in 1841, which was never unanimously accepted within the denomination, was also reflected at local level, where the temperance issue provoked secession from the Wesleyan society at Sowerby in 1854. Although the Halifax Band of Hope (BOH) Union had been founded in 1858 'to teach both children and adults the value of abstinence from alcoholic liquors and the evils of intemperance' the Wesleyan Conference did not sanction the foundation of BOH in connection with Sunday schools until 1875, adult temperance societies until 1877 and total abstinence societies until 1892. However, an early BOH was established at Lumbutts UMFC in 1862, and others at the Wesleyan chapels at Pellon in 1869, where early temperance supporters had received 'a fair amount of banter for being temperance advocates', Brighouse in 1870 and Blackshawhead in 1877. By 1901 the BOH at Siddal Wesleyan Chapel was 'in a most flourishing condition' with a total of 260 members.[26]

By 1900, Sunday school and temperance work had been supplemented by other improving activities for young people, mostly in response to local initiatives, but occasionally adopting connexionally endorsed schemes. A young men's class was established at Siddal in 1883 for 'the well-thinking industrial young men of this village', meeting on Monday evenings for regular Bible studies and lectures, with rambles and picnics in the summer.[27] A young men's mutual improvement society was formed at Pellon in 1890 in an attempt to encourage 'young men congregating at street corners' to join Sunday school classes by the provision of a reading room with periodicals, newspapers and 'a few innocent games', which was subsequently closed after the introduction of playing cards, 'secretly at first,

26. W.J. Townsend, H.B. Workman and G. Eayrs (eds.), *A New History of Methodism*, I (London: Hodder & Stoughton, 1909), pp. 465-66; B. Harrison, *Drink and the Victorians* (Keele: Keele University Press, 2nd edn, 1994), pp. 159-60, 168; R. Wilkinson, *Unto the Hills: The Story of Methodism in Lumbutts, 1837–1987* (Lumbutts: Lumbutts Methodist Church, 1987), p. 15; Thorpe, *Pellon*, pp. 22-24, 31; Anon., *A Short History of Blackshawhead Wesleyan Chapel and Sunday School* (Blackshawhead: Blackshawhead Wesleyan Church, 1906); Siddal Wesleyan Sunday School Minute Books, 20 July 1884, 8 April 1901.

27. Siddal Wesleyan Young Men's Class, Minutes, 9 April 1883–24 December 1885.

then openly'.[28] A similar Sunday School Institute, established at Mount Zion in 1895, firmly prohibited 'the playing of cards, dominoes and all games not approved by the stewards' with 'smoking, tobacco chewing and obscene language being liable to the penalty of expulsion'.[29] The Wesley Guild, a young people's movement originating in Leeds, adopted by the Wesleyan Conference in 1896, and designed to bridge the gap between Sunday school and chapel, experienced rapid expansion in its first decade, but subsequently lost ground to other youth organizations. The movement's major rival in Halifax was the Young People's Society of Christian Endeavour, a non-denominational movement inaugurated in America in 1881, which was adopted in Halifax not only by the PM and other branches of Methodism such as the Salterhebble UMFC in 1894, but also by Pellon Wesley in 1895, where it instituted a monthly tract distribution in 1896 and provided a tea and social for the elderly in 1899.[30]

Although at connexional level 'the Methodists had mixed feelings about how to proceed' after Forster's Education Act of 1870, there is evidence of early grassroots Methodist support in Halifax for the new board schools. The Wesleyan grocer Eagland Bray and the MNC leather merchant Samuel T. Midgley were among 11 candidates elected without contest to the first Halifax School Board in 1871, and one of the most prominent campaigners for a board school in Siddal was John Shaw, secretary of the Siddal Co-operative Society and a Wesleyan local preacher. His canvass of 443 households in the village in 1872 revealed strong local support for a non-denominational school, as did a predominantly working-class meeting at the Wesleyan school. The campaign was a successful radical-Nonconformist challenge to the educational monopoly of Anglican Tory manufacturers, the Holdsworths, and resulted in the opening of Siddal Board School in July 1875.[31] Education became free from 1891, much to the relief of 'the artisan population' in Yorkshire, though there had been continuing connexional opposition on the grounds that the remaining fee-paying Wesleyan schools would suffer from the competition. However, the solitary Halifax Wesleyan day school, with 406 pupils

28. Thorpe, *Pellon*, pp. 11, 25.

29. J. Bradley, *Mount Zion Ogden, 1773–1973* (Halifax: Mount Zion Methodist Church, 1973).

30. Thorpe, *Pellon*, pp. 27-28.

31. Webster, 'Halifax Schools', pp. 11, 14, 18; Smith, *Methodism and Education*, p. 67.

on the roll in 1871, finally closed its doors in 1907, 5 years after the Halifax County Borough Council became responsible for education under the terms of the Education Act of 1902, which exposed further divisions at connexional level over the issue of rate aid. In the Calder Valley, however, the most prominent passive resistance campaigners after 1902 were Baptists, though 3 Methodist ministers were among 46 members of the Todmorden Citizen's League summoned for failure to pay their education rate in January 1904.[32]

Retrenchment and the Growth of Uniformed

Organizations, 1902-1950

While there was continuing evidence of vitality in some Halifax Sunday schools during the first decade of the new century—such as King Cross, which was bursting at the seams until the opening of a new purpose-built Sunday school in 1905—there was also growing evidence of numerical decline in the years before the outbreak of the First World War, and the first half of the twentieth century was to be characterized by retrenchment at connexional, district and circuit levels. The number of scholars enrolled at Siddal Wesleyan Sunday School had peaked at 343 in 1898, and by 1914 membership had declined to 245. Moreover, in 1905 it was reported that attendances at the BOH had recently shown 'a marked decrease' owing to 'such a large number of our members' attending evening school classes. The First World War accelerated Sunday school decline. At King Cross Wesleyan Sunday School, 206 teachers and senior scholars served in the forces and no fewer than 30 were killed, but determined efforts were made to return to normality after the war. Record results were obtained in the annual Scripture examinations for 1918–22 and by 1938 success in the recruitment of younger children produced plans for new primary accommodation. At Mount Tabor Wesleyan Church, the primary department was reorganized and provision made for teacher training, suggesting a similar growth in the work with younger children during the 1920s, when there was a slight recovery in circuit membership.[33]

    32.   West Yorkshire Archive Service, Calderdale District Archives, Orange Street Day School records, 1855–1907, MISC: 481/33, 498/11; MR 253-59; Smith, *Methodism and Education*, pp. 90, 195, 224-26; Hargreaves, 'Religion and Society', pp. 331-32.

    33.   E.V. Chapman, *King Cross Methodist Church and School, 1808–1958* (Halifax: King Cross Methodist Church, 1958), p. 12; D. Sutcliffe and G. Sutcliffe, *Mount Tabor Methodist Church 1820–1970* (Halifax: Mount Tabor Methodist Church, 1970), p. 3.

However, the Halifax and Bradford District Methodist Synod received frequent reports in the inter-war years of declining Sunday school membership and adopted a number of strategies, some linked with connexional initiatives, to try to halt the decline. It 'heartily' approved 'a canvas on behalf of Sunday schools' in May 1926 and designated a district children's day in September 1927 with eisteddfods and art and craft exhibitions, but neither strategy succeeded in halting the decline. In 1930, the District Sunday School Council concluded that 'the general remedy for the continual decline in numbers is a quickening of the spiritual life of the whole church, and a sense of the Church's corporate responsibility for the young'. It also recommended 'greater specialization', 'a wider adoption of modern methods' and a greater utilization of 'the excellent services of connexional lecturers'. The continuing decline in 1935 was considered in part a consequence of the 'falling birth rate', new housing developments and 'new social habits'. However, the inescapable conclusion that 'the decreases are persistent and that the number of scholars in our care is becoming steadily less' generated a resolve for a 'greater efficiency, vocational and spiritual, of teachers and officers'. A decline in membership of Christian Endeavour, the Wesley Guild and distinctively Methodist temperance organizations was also reported and synod was urged 'to work the temperance pledge' into all 'Sunday school and young Methodist meetings'. In 1938 a further decrease of 912 in the total number of children was reported, which was about the average of the decreases registered annually for the past quarter of a century, when the number of Methodist Sunday school scholars in the Halifax and Bradford District had been reduced to just over half what it was in 1913. It was reported that 'this alarming state of affairs has caused much heart searching' and that the district was supporting a connexional campaign to address the problem, involving courses for Sunday school workers, house visitations, weekly prayer meetings for workers among young people, and public meetings in each circuit.[34]

Uniformed organizations appeared to offer a remedy for Sunday school decline in the first half of the twentieth century and churches seem to have made their own decisions in determining which organization to embrace without connexional interference. The Boys' Brigade, founded in Glasgow in 1883, had its greatest strength in the Nonconformist denominations, particularly Methodism, where there were over 3,000 officers and boys by 1893. Although Methodist Boys' Brigade companies had been established

---

34. Methodist Church Archives, John Rylands University Library of Manchester [hereafter MCA], Halifax and Bradford District Synod Minutes, 1926–38.

in Leeds as early as 1892 and at Hebden Bridge in 1899, the first Methodist Boys' Brigade company in Halifax was formed at Rhodes Street Wesleyan Chapel in January 1901. By 1901, there were already 41,096 members of the Boys' Brigade in the UK, including 155 members in Halifax, all members of Congregational companies. In 1908, however, Methodist Boys' Brigade membership in Halifax exceeded Congregational membership for the first time and Methodist companies remained numerically dominant within the Halifax battalion for the rest of the century, with the Wesleyans and the United Methodists vying for the lead in the period up to Methodist reunion. While Boys' Brigade numbers fluctuated in Halifax in the early twentieth century, they were generally rising in the period up to the jubilee year of 1932–33, when they peaked at 699, and major recruitment drives in 1944–45 boosted numbers in the closing years of the Second World War. Regular activities included band practice, camping, cricket, drill, football, gymnastics, swimming and Bible classes. Attendances at Bible classes in Halifax were generally high, ranging from 69 to 80 per cent from 1924 to 1938 and strong links were maintained with Sunday schools. At Boothtown in 1945, for example, the senior boys' department of the Sunday school combined with the Boys' Brigade Bible class, and the Whit Sunday school treat at Salem was held at the Boys' Brigade camp at Soyland in 1949.[35]

Although the Boy Scouts had a membership of 1,300 in Halifax in 1928–29, nearly double that of the Boys' Brigade, the organization was less strongly represented among local Methodist churches. The first church-based Scout troop in Halifax was formed at St Hilda's, and Scouting appears to have been generally stronger in Anglican than in Nonconformist churches in Halifax, where there was only one solitary Anglican Boys' Brigade company and where the Church Lads' Brigade was relatively small, with only 250 members in 1928–29. There had also been strong Nonconformist opposition to the South African War (1899–1902) and some consequent mistrust of militarism and the leadership of Baden-Powell, though this appears to have been dissipated by the First World War when large local Boy Scout, Boys' Brigade and Church Lads' Brigade contingents heard Major-General F.H. Kelly declare that 'militarism that was for a just cause and for the maintenance of the honour of the

35.   J. Springhall, B. Fraser and M. Hoare, *Sure and Stedfast: A History of the Boys' Brigade* (London: Boys' Brigade, 1983), pp. 70, 126, 258; Annual Membership Returns, 1900, Boys' Brigade Archives, Hemel Hempstead; Annual Reports of Halifax Battalion; Boothtown UMC Boys' Brigade Company Register; *20th Halifax (Salem) BB Company, Jubilee 1919–69* (Halifax: Salem BB Company, 1969).

country was the finest thing in the world' at a Halifax open air rally in 1916. Scout troops had been formed in 1913 at Queens Road UMC and King Cross Wesleyan Church in 1914, where there had been a short-lived Boys' Brigade company in 1911. Although by 1935 there were 9 Methodist Scout troops compared with 18 Anglican, the Methodists in Halifax had the largest number of Scout troops among Nonconformist congregations.[36]

The Girls' Brigade, with 207 members including officers in Halifax in 1928–29 was a quarter of the size of the Boys' Brigade, but often existed in chapels with Boys' Brigade companies. A Girls' Brigade company, for example, was formed at Siddal Wesleyan Chapel in 1929, with about 30 girls and 6 officers. One founder member later recalled the girls receiving training from the Boys' Brigade captain in 'dumb bells, bar bells, swinging, gymnastics and marching'. However, they formed a relatively small minority alongside the Girl Guides, who were the largest of all the youth organizations in Halifax in 1928–29 with 1,859 members, including officers. The first Guide company to be formed in Halifax was at Queens Road UMC, by Miss D.H. Seed, a Sunday school teacher responding to pressure from her Sunday school class in September 1913, and a second company was formed at Rhodes Street Wesleyan Church in November 1915. Between 1915 and 1950 no fewer than 18 Methodist Guide companies were registered, with many acquiring Brownie packs catering for younger girls after 1920. The majority insisted upon church attendance as a condition of membership, but eight of the companies were registered as open units. In addition to these uniformed organizations there was strong support in Halifax for the Girls' League founded by the Wesleyans in 1908 which united with similar organizations in the other branches of Methodism in 1932 and which was influential in prompting many to offer for missionary service.[37]

The Second World War brought further disruption to work among children and young people as youth leaders and senior scholars joined the

36. Anon, *Institutions and Charitable Agencies of Halifax* (Halifax: Halifax Council of Social Welfare/Rotary Club of Halifax, 1929); *Halifax Courier*, 16 September 1916; E. Wilson, 'The First Twenty Years of Guiding in Halifax, 1913–33' (Halifax: unpublished typescript, 1976); Chapman, *King Cross*, p. 9; Halifax Boy Scout and Girl Guide Handbook (Halifax: Halifax Boy Scout and Girl Guide Associations, 1935).

37. J. Harber, *Siddal* (Halifax: WEA, 1989), p. 47; *Institutions and Charitable Agencies of Halifax*; Wilson, 'Guiding in Halifax'; West Yorkshire West Guide Association, Unit Registrations, Halifax; R. Moore, *Illingworth Moor Methodist Church, 1950–2000* (Halifax: Illingworth Moor Methodist Church, 2000), p. 13.

forces or worked irregular hours in munitions factories. Many Sunday schools were requisitioned for military use. At King Cross, the Sunday school was largely confined to small side-rooms, while at Southowram the entire Sunday school premises were occupied by the military from July 1940 to 1943.[38] Returning to Elland in 1945, Jack Button commented that during the Second World War 'the Sunday School I had known and loved had dissolved into a shadow of its former self'.[39] After the war new teachers had to be recruited and major work was required to restore the premises for Sunday school use at both King Cross and Southowram. However, the opportunity was taken at King Cross to reorganize and regrade the school, teachers were encouraged to attend training courses and more modern teaching methods were introduced, including the use of filmstrips and other visual aids.[40]

H.W. Harwood observed that 'as time went on, there grew a more tolerant attitude' and 'plays, dances and pantomimes became regular features of Sunday school activity'. At Mount Tabor and Illingworth Moor, tennis clubs became the most popular of the organizations for young people during the inter-war years. Both were the precursors of church youth clubs in the later 1940s.[41] These developments attuned well with government and connexional initiatives. In 1939 Government Circular 1486 'The Service of Youth' urged young people to join youth clubs, and Methodists at both connexional and local levels seized the opportunity for the development of informal youth education. In 1943 a new Methodist Youth Department brought together the Sunday School and Methodist Guild Departments to promote new work with the 12–20 age group and the Methodist Association of Youth Clubs (MAYC) established in 1945 became the springboard for a major post-war thrust in informal youth work, celebrating 'the presence of Christ in youth culture'.[42]

38. Chapman, *King Cross,* p. 12; Anon., *Southowram Methodist Sunday School, 1825–1975* (Halifax: Southowram Methodist Sunday School, 1975), p. 5.

39. J. Button, *God Moves in a Mysterious Way* (London: Avon Books, 1997), pp. 29, 32.

40. Chapman, *King Cross*, p. 13.

41. Harwood, *Centenary Story*, pp. 34-35; Sutcliffe and Sutcliffe, *Mount Tabor*, pp. 5-6; Moore, *Illingworth Moor*, pp. 10, 12.

42. J.A. Vickers, *Dictionary of Methodism in Britain and Ireland* (London: Epworth Press, 2000), p. 407.

Rediscovering Mission: In the Service of Youth, 1951–2000

In the second half of the twentieth century Methodist attitudes towards education and youth were characterized at both connexional and circuit level by a growing adaptability and pragmatism in a desperate attempt to rediscover mission in the service of youth and meet the challenge of cultural postmodernity. The number of children and young people on Methodist premises each week halved between 1900 and 1950, prompting the observation in a connexional publication of 1951 that 'the first task of the Sunday school' was to retain the child 'in the worshipping and teaching atmosphere and tradition of the Christian Church'. However, by 1995, there had been a further 'catastrophic' decline in the number of children and young people to 300,000, eliciting the conclusion that most children now associated with Methodist churches were 'there because of parental involvement'.[43] During the 1950s and 1960s Conference minutes record a fluctuating but generally declining junior membership in all six Halifax circuits and a generally declining number of baptisms, which continued after the creation of a single Halifax circuit in 1970. Moreover, the average attendance of children and young people at worship and Sunday school recorded in the annual October census in the Halifax Circuit declined dramatically from 702 in 1980 to 171 in 1999, although community rolls and the recorded number of young people in association with the churches painted a more optimistic if less reliable picture throughout this period.[44]

Notwithstanding the innovations introduced after 1945 the number of scholars on roll at King Cross Methodist Sunday School never fully recovered after the Second World War and by 1958 had fallen from 330 to 244, with an average attendance of 156, of whom the largest proportions were in the primary and junior departments and the smallest in the intermediate and young people's departments. At Siddal Methodist Sunday School, the number of scholars declined from 241 in 1952 to 86 in 1962. During the 1960s changing attitudes towards the use of Sunday, increased mobility and smaller families affected Sunday school numbers. Sunday school sessions moved from Sunday afternoon to Sunday morning at Illingworth and

43. J.M. Turner, *Modern Methodism in England 1932–1998* (London: Epworth Press, 1998), pp. 70-71.

44. MCA, Minutes of Conference, 1950–2000; Halifax Circuit Membership Returns 1972–2000.

elsewhere, embracing concepts of 'Junior Church' and 'Family Church', with monthly family and parade services, which attempted to integrate both the Sunday school and the uniformed organizations into Church life. In the 1970s a Junior Choir made regular contributions to the morning worship and also presented occasional longer works in the modern idiom, for example 'Jonah-man Jazz' and 'Daniel Jazz'.[45]

In 1953 the Boys' Brigade still claimed that it had been 'most successful in retaining thousands of boys in Sunday school and winning them for the Church' and strengthened by the progressive Hayes Report of 1963 and the development of new junior sections, it remained the strongest youth organization for boys in Halifax Methodism down to the end of the twentieth century, with no fewer than 14 Methodist companies in the County Borough of Halifax in 1972 and 5 in the Halifax Circuit in 2000.[46] In 1972 there were five Methodist Girls' Brigade companies in Halifax and four by 2000. However, the Girl Guides remained the strongest uniformed organization for girls in Halifax Methodism throughout the twentieth century, though the numbers enrolled in Ranger, Guide and Brownie units in the Halifax divisions declined by 41 per cent from 1,178 in 1980 to 694 in 2000, but this was partially offset by a growth in the number of Rainbows (the youngest girls) from 15 in 1988 to 225 in 2000.[47] The Boy Scouts remained the largest uniformed organization at King Cross Methodist Church, with twice as many members as the Girl Guides, but this was exceptional.[48] Other Methodist Scout troops struggled and some were abandoned on account of a shortage of experienced leaders: for example a Scout troop formed at Illingworth during the Second World War gave way to a new Boys' Brigade company in 1968.[49]

But Methodist youth work was poised for further expansion in the second half of the twentieth century at both connexional and circuit level. Connexionally there were some 1,500 fully affiliated or associated MAYC clubs by 1950, when it was claimed that 'the club movement seems to have established itself in the minds of a growing section of the Methodist

45. Chapman, *King Cross*, p. 13; Siddal Methodist Church, Sunday School Minutes, 1952–62; Moore, *Illingworth Moor*, pp. 7, 14.

46. MCA, Minutes of Conference, 1953, p. 38.

47. Halifax Youth Service Handbook, 1972; West Yorkshire West Guide Association, Census figures, Halifax Divisions.

48. Chapman, *King Cross*, p. 13; J. Waring, *King Cross Boy Scouts Fortieth Anniversary Celebrations, 1914–54* (Halifax: King Cross Boy Scouts, 1954), pp. 14-15.

49. Moore, *Illingworth Moor*, pp.15-16.

Church as an effective way of attracting into its fellowship young people not normally susceptible to church appeals'.[50] Between 1950 and 1972 there were no fewer than seven Methodist youth clubs in Halifax listed in the Halifax youth service handbooks, more than for any other denomination except the Anglicans. Jack Button, appointed leader of the MAYC-affiliated Hipperholme Youth Club in 1955, saw club numbers rise to 40, 'everybody meeting together on Saturday and Sunday evenings and sitting together at evening service', and the development of a mid-week programme of recreational activities for Sunday school children. From 1961 Methodist youth club leaders met regularly to organize annual dances and coordinate Halifax participation at the MAYC London weekends. There was also strong Methodist support for the annual Easter Long March, started in 1966, a sponsored marathon walk organized by the Halifax Council of Churches and later Churches Together in Calderdale which had raised over £200,000 for Christian Aid by 1998. Support for MAYC fluctuated in the 1970s and 1980s, and when Jack Button resigned as youth leader at Hipperhome in 1991 he lamented that the mid-week groups had dwindled as Sunday school numbers had declined from 120 to a mere 20 scholars and by 1997 that there was regrettably 'no MAYC activity in the Halifax area whatsoever'.[51]

Following the publication of the Albemarle Report in 1960 and the failure of an ambitious £25,000 scheme for town-centre youth and community work based on the imposing Victorian Gothic St John's Methodist Church, Ian Lewis, a former missionary to Kenya, who had commenced his ministry in Halifax in 1959, submitted a bold proposal in 1962 to replace St John's and three other struggling churches on the southern perimeter of the town with a new purpose-built Methodist church and youth centre, the latter funded jointly by the Church and the Ministry of Education, with grants for maintenance and staffing from the local authority. Support for the project from the trustees of the participating churches was virtually unanimous and in its first decade the church with accommodation for 350 proved not nearly large enough for family worship. Moreover, besides a Junior Church of 200 and uniformed organizations with 100–120 members, the new youth club, open 5 nights per week for the wider community, attracted a paid-up membership of over 300. Many members of the

50. L.P. Barnett, *The Church Youth Club* (London: Epworth Press, 1951), pp. 81-82.

51. Halifax Youth Service Handbooks (Halifax: Halifax Youth Service), 1950, 1960, 1972; Button, *God Moves*, pp. 39-79, 100.

church became involved in supporting the youth club in a variety of practical ways, thereby freeing the professional youth leaders to organize a wide range of activities. 'Gone are the days', declared Ian Lewis, the church's first minister, 'when a table-tennis and dartboard in some Methodist cellar or dingy room can operate as a Youth Club.' He believed that the Church must adapt 'if it is to meet the challenge of the age, and grow with the young into new loyalties and a new commitment'. He continued:

> For some the club is as much of Church as they will ever know. For others, it has become the gateway to a larger life of faith. For all who come the club teaches that the Church cares about them, and perhaps something of our common heritage in the Gospel is imparted.[52]

Attendances at the new youth centre were generally considerably lower in the 1980s and 1990s, averaging in the mid 30s, with a slightly higher membership rate, but the club remained committed to the vision of its founders in 2000, despite recurring uncertainties regarding the level of local authority funding and a series of violent disturbances, including one in which two leaders were assaulted before eight police officers succeeded in restoring order. In his report in May 1999, the youth leader commented on the continuing challenges deriving from the work with socially deprived teenagers and also the immense rewards as some of them matured and developed into 'very sociable beings'.[53] Other partnership schemes at Boothtown and King Cross proved less enduring. John Munsey Turner, minister at King Cross from 1981 to 1989, recounted how Miss Enid Bamforth, the leader of a large church youth club in the 1970s, had to intervene to prevent two teenagers injuring each other with knives and how the club had ultimately been overwhelmed by the more aggressive, 'unclubbable' youngsters in the 1980s. However, he also recalled how some of the club members of the 1970s, none of whom had entered the worshipping life of the church, returning for weddings and baptisms in later life had testified to the positive influence of the club on their lives.[54]

Methodist attitudes to state education varied enormously in the second half of the twentieth century. Some Methodist ministers continued to send their children to Woodhouse Grove, the Methodist fee-paying independent

---

52. I.W. Lewis, *The Family Church: An Account of an Amalgamation Scheme in Central Halifax* (London: Methodist Church Home Mission Department, 1968), pp. 19, 22.

53. Senior Youth Leader's Report, St Andrew's Methodist Youth Club, May 1998, May 1999.

54. Turner, *Modern Methodism*, p. 76.

school, while other children of the manse were educated at local church and state comprehensive schools with other Methodist children. Almost half of the local preachers in the Halifax Methodist Circuit in 2000 were teachers or former teachers. Others had experience of involvement in education as governors in both the private and public sectors. Another local preacher serving as chair of the national society of heads of independent schools, was head of a fee-paying secondary school engaged in pioneering partnerships with both neighbouring state and independent schools. One minister was Free Church representative on the local Standing Advisory Council for Religious Education and chair of governors at a local primary school. Another Halifax Methodist minister, serving as chair of governors at the Ridings School in 1996, remained at the helm during the most publicized incident of the breakdown of discipline at a state secondary school in the late twentieth century, seeking 'to add a Christian voice of reconciliation and moderation in a very tense situation'. At the height of the crisis, the Revd Stan Brown was working full-time with the school with the support of his circuit colleagues and received around a hundred messages of support from 'the church at every level', and the loan of the national press secretary of the Methodist Church when the school was at the centre of unprecedented media attention. In a letter to the *Methodist Recorder*, he concluded: 'I would like everyone to know that the Methodist Church as an institution is not afraid to show its commitment to education and is prepared to back its members when they are hard pressed.'[55]

Conclusion

Methodist attitudes towards education and youth at connexional level may have been wavering and uncertain, but there is evidence of a growing Methodist preoccupation with education and youth in Halifax during the period from 1800 to 2000. Children and young people came to be regarded increasingly as a vital element within Methodism, both in the times of rapid growth such as the early nineteenth century, when nervous connexional leaders often appeared motivated by the necessity of maintaining control of Methodist youth in an age of political disaffection and rampant atheism, and in periods of decline when provision for youth was viewed as a crucial strategy in ensuring the future survival of the Church and its mission. The tensions arising from the dual impulses of mission and control often

55. Letter to the *Methodist Recorder*, 27 October 1996.

created an impression of ambivalence at both connexional and circuit level, particularly in the nineteenth century over such issues as teaching literacy on the sabbath and the promotion of temperance. Lacking the financial resources to establish a network of denominational day schools, Halifax Methodists pragmatically supported local factory schools, especially those operated by Methodist manufacturers, the inter-denominational British Schools and later the non-denominational board and local educational authority schools, with their emphasis on neutral scriptural teaching. With a historically limited and diminishing institutional influence on secular education, they hoped to influence the spiritual development of children and young people primarily through the voluntary Sunday school movement, supplemented by uniformed and other more informal youth organizations in the twentieth century. These voluntary associations were viewed predominantly as a means of nurturing children and young people into a faith relationship by the late Victorian era, an age which has been characterized as 'floating on a flood of faith', when Methodist penetration of youth culture in Halifax achieved its greatest degree of success.[56] However, despite every valiant effort to stem the ebbing tide, by the 1930s—which saw a sharp reduction in the number of children attending Methodist Sunday schools and which were acknowledged by contemporaries as 'bleak years in practically every field of Methodist youth activity'—an era of retrenchment was evident at both connexional and circuit level.[57] Moreover, in an age of increasingly commercialized leisure provision and cultural postmodernity in the late twentieth century, which has been characterized as witnessing 'the haemorrhage of British Christianity', Halifax Methodists struggled to maintain a continuing influence on even their own children and young people, as indeed they had in the era of Jabez Bunting.[58]

---

56. K.T. Hoppen, *The Mid-Victorian Generation, 1846–1886* (Oxford: Oxford University Press, 1998), p. 427.

57. Barnett, *Church Youth Club*, p. 61.

58. C.G. Brown, *The Death of Christian Britain* (London: Routledge, 2001), p. 2.

Part IV

POLITICS

THE DISSENTING POLITICAL UPSURGE OF 1833–34

David Bebbington

At no point during the nineteenth century did the cry of 'the Church in danger' seem more justified than in the years 1833–34. With Parliamentary reform just passed and the Reformers in a huge majority, the national agenda was poised to move on from political to ecclesiastical changes. The Church of England was loudly condemned as hopelessly corrupt, a means of keeping the younger sons of the social elite in a job; it suffered notoriously from pluralism and non-residence; and its Irish branch was even more ripe for drastic overhaul. Radicals wanted its Augean stables cleansed. The first Tractarian stirrings at Oxford, however, looked in alarm on proposals for erastian tampering with the divine society; and Thomas Arnold put forward the solution of relaxing subscription so as to welcome Dissenters back into a truly national institution. In this maelstrom Dissent itself underwent a transformation. From being a marginal force in national life, respectful towards the authorities and grateful for the measure of toleration it enjoyed, Dissent turned into a movement sustaining a demand for fundamental change in English society, the separation of Church and state. The disestablishment movement was born. The alteration has been noticed, but, oddly, it has not been analysed in print. Sir Owen Chadwick records the emergence of newly assertive Dissenting claims; Ian Machin and Michael Watts note the expression of a more militant mood; and Jacob Ellens has pointed to developments in 1833–34 as the root of the anti-church rates campaign. Only Tudur Jones, however, has examined the process in any detail, and his account is confined to Wales.[1] It is possible to

---

1.   O. Chadwick, *The Victorian Church* (2 vols.; London: A. & C. Black, 1966–70), I, pp. 60-62, 79-95; G.I.T. Machin, *Politics and the Churches in Great Britain, 1832 to 1868* (Oxford: Clarendon Press, 1977), pp. 39-47; M.R. Watts, *The Dissenters* (2 vols.; Oxford: Clarendon Press, 1978–95), II, pp. 453-64; J.P. Ellens, *Religious Routes to Gladstonian Liberalism: The Church Rate Conflict in England and Wales, 1832–1868* (University Park: Pennsylvania University Press, 1994), pp. 32-40; R.T. Jones, 'The

dig much deeper into what happened on the basis of *The Patriot* newspaper, newly set up in 1832 to articulate the views of evangelical Nonconformists on public affairs, the minutes of the bodies charged with promoting Dissenting interests and, most instructively, the correspondence of Joshua Wilson, the Congregational layman at the heart of the proceedings. An attempt is made here to show how these sources reveal a fundamental contrast between different styles of cultural aspiration.

The received approach among Dissenters to questions affecting their own concerns in the period immediately before 1833–34 was cautious, deferential and modest in its aims. The era of eighteenth-century politics when Dissent formed a sustained seedbed of radicalism, as portrayed by James Bradley, was long past.[2] The French Revolution had put a stop to previous efforts to liberalize the constitution in favour of religious minorities and orthodox Dissent had turned aside from seeking redress in favour of vigorous expansionist evangelism. Only in the 1820s, with the easing of social tensions, had it again become thinkable to call for the most strongly desired concession, the repeal of the Test and Corporation Acts that theoretically excluded those outside the Church of England from office in local government. The disappearance of this discriminatory legislation from the statute book in 1828 did not, however, represent a major change in the political culture of Dissent. A letter sent just after repeal to Lord Holland, the leading aristocratic sponsor of the measure, by William Smith, the chief Dissenting politician, breathes a spirit of scrupulous restraint.

> As for the Conduct prudent to be pursued by the Diss[entin]g Body at the present time, I have publicly advised the most conciliatory Course— declarations of Satisfaction on all proper Occasions, with what has been done, & a constant readiness to meet Members of the Establishm[en]t with open hearts & friendly dispositions; not fastidiously dwelling on the comparative Trifles of Difference that yet remain—treating the remaining prejudices of ye Clergy with moderation, as what must speedily yield to more familiar intercourse... The only <u>Grievance</u> really <u>grievous</u> now

Origins of the Nonconformist Disestablishment Campaign, 1830–1840', *Journal of the Historical Society of the Church in Wales* 20 (1970), pp. 43-71. There are, however, some unpublished accounts in dissertations, notably H.R. Martin, 'The Politics of the Congregationalists, 1830–1856' (PhD dissertation, University of Durham, 1971).

2.   J.E. Bradley, *Religion, Revolution and English Radicalism: Nonconformity in Eighteenth-Century Politics and Society* (Cambridge: Cambridge University Press, 1990).

remaining is too closely interwoven with the establishment itself to be as yet seriously attacked—viz. The compelling us to pay rates for Building, endowing &c &c the New Churches...[3]

Prudence and conciliation demanded that continuing disabilities should be seen as trifles; if a grievance was bound up with the establishment, there was no question of tampering with it; the abolition of tithes, he added, was a nonsense. There must be respectful appreciation of whatever crumbs of assistance might fall from the table of the advanced Whigs such as Holland.

That attitude contrasts totally with what started to become current in the crisis of 1833–34. Again the views that were beginning to arise can be illustrated by a letter, this time one written in January 1833 by George Hadfield, a militant Independent solicitor from Manchester, to Joshua Wilson. A deputation of Dissenting ministers had recently waited on the premier to submit a humble request, in the traditional manner, for sympathetic consideration.

> In the name of patience what have they been about in their interview with Lord Grey?... Lord Grey's family it is known is filled with Church property, & many of the other Ministers are of the staunchest friends of the System... It is obvious that there will be no great Church Reform, but such as will be wrung from them... I trust, however, that in a case so obviously unjust as the appropriat[io]n of 6 or 7 millions annually to the support of a religion professed by so small a sect as the Church of England is, when compared with the people of England Scotland & Ireland something will be done effectually.
>
> If the Dissenters were true to their own Interests & principles, & united in their demand for Justice I am sure that great bane to the progress of vital religion wo[ul]d be put down... That a Church establishment is needed I deny, & a secular, political & jobbery Church is wicked.
>
> That there ought to be a perfect separation of Church & State—That the public property in the Church, the tithes especially, may be legally & righteously resumed by the State, & applied to useful, instead of injurious, purposes, I wo[ul]d demonstrate.[4]

This apoplectic tirade, directed as much against the Whigs as against the Church of England, is an extreme example of the militant spirit that was

---

3.   William Smith to Lord Holland, n.d. [1828], Holland House Papers, British Library.

4.   George Hadfield to Joshua Wilson, 15 January 1832 [sc. 1833], Letters of George Hadfield to Joshua Wilson etc., 1822–1872, Congregational Library, London, H.a.10 [hereafter GH to JW].

being hatched at this time. There are a smouldering impatience with previous delicacy of method, a ready willingness to wrest the tithe income from the clergy and a fierce eagerness to go the whole hog of putting an end to the bond between Church and state. Times were changing.

The underlying explanation for the transformation is to be found in two broad developments of the period, one internal to Dissent and the other circumstantial. Within the Dissenting community the balance of power was shifting. Traditionally the Presbyterians had taken the lead in Dissenting politics. William Smith was himself one of their number. The Evangelical Revival, however, had led to a vast growth of the orthodox denominations, but there was no equivalent expansion among the Presbyterians, now largely Socinian in their theology and often calling themselves Unitarians. The Independents and Baptists increased roughly tenfold between the reigns of George I and Victoria whereas the Presbyterians halved their numbers.[5] At the same time, although there was no decline in the general prosperity of the well-to-do Unitarians, the evangelical Nonconformists, and the Independents in particular, also came to have a business elite of significant proportions in most provincial towns as well as in the capital. These men and their ministers, themselves self-conscious professionals, were the people who corresponded with Joshua Wilson. Aware of representing the big religious battalions and highly conscious of their own standing in society, such men were less likely than their predecessors to accept the leadership of Unitarians whose theology they disdained. George Hadfield, at the heart of the Manchester business elite though himself in law rather than textiles, had launched in 1826 a sustained campaign to seize the assets of Lady Hewley's charity from the Unitarians for the benefit of the orthodox, drawing together a network of likeminded colleagues in northern towns. Nationally a Congregational Union was established in 1831 to weld the disparate Independents into a single entity and show the public that the strength of Dissent lay among the orthodox. Crucially, too, William Smith retired in 1832 as chairman of the Dissenting Deputies, the body that had existed for a century to defend the interests of the community at large, complaining of the growing tendency 'to stigmatize each other on account of their differences'.[6] He was replaced by the Baptist Henry Waymouth, a man of far less political experience and relatively little rapport with the Whig grandees. The scene

5. Watts, *Dissenters*, II, p. 27.

6. B.L. Manning, *The Protestant Dissenting Deputies* (Cambridge: Cambridge University Press, 1952), p. 68.

was set for the emergence of a far more assertive political style reflecting the populist activism of the evangelicals.

The other major development was in political circumstances. The removal of the longstanding grievance of the Test and Corporation Acts meant that, from 1828 onwards, Dissenters were free to consider what benefits they wanted next. But repeal was only the first act in the drama of the constitutional revolution. In the following year Roman Catholics were given the right to enter Parliament. Dissenters predominantly supported the change, but saw no reason why papists should be favoured when they themselves still suffered under disabilities. The struggle for Parliamentary reform ensued, with Dissenters in many cities clamouring for changes that would bring them a greater share of power. As a result of reform Dissenters may have composed about a fifth of the electorate. The first taste for many of the exercise of the vote came at the 1832 election, when, with Anglican Evangelicals, they were at the head of the anti-slavery forces. The 1833 session saw, to their great satisfaction, the abolition of slavery in British dominions. These stirring events taught a lesson. 'It was by the diffusion of information through the press', wrote 'A Consistent Dissenter' to *The Patriot* in March 1832,

> the excitement of feeling by public discussion, and the influence of petitions to Parliament, that Reform in that body has been accomplished. By the same means slavery is brought, we hope, to the verge of extinction; and it must be by such measures…that religion will be emancipated from her long and degrading bondage…[7]

Hadfield was to the fore in the cause of Parliamentary reform and claimed that by a pamphlet he had issued he swung his local constituency against slavery.[8] The agitation of the previous couple of turbulent years sowed the seed in the minds of many that what had been won for the disenfranchised of England and for the slaves of the Caribbean could also be achieved for downtrodden evangelical Nonconformists.

Joshua Wilson was the first to rise to the challenge of mobilizing Dissent for its own emancipation. Wilson was in his late thirties, a Dissenting Deputy and a non-practising lawyer who spent much of his extensive leisure time on the compulsive hobby of Nonconformist history. He avidly collected books for the Congregational Library, opened in 1831 as a centre for the meetings of the Congregational Union, of which he was the prime

---

7.   *Patriot*, 6 March 1832, p. 76.
8.   GH to JW, 26 January 1833.

mover. His father Thomas had made a fortune in ribbon manufacture, retiring early to devote himself to good works, particularly the rescue of provincial meeting houses from the clutches of the unorthodox. It was Wilson money that paid the expenses of the various centralizing ventures of Congregationalism in these years. The Wilsons launched *The Patriot* early in 1832, appointing Josiah Conder, a former bookseller who was editor of the *Eclectic Review*, to take charge of it. Conder was inevitably close to the Wilsons and, though he was normally trusted to exercise his own judgment, he acted as their mouthpiece. The newspaper, Joshua wrote, would 'not be conducted on ultra liberal or extreme principles' but would never hesitate 'to maintain those great principles of religious truth & Christian liberty on which only British Protestant Nonconformity is defensible'.[9] It gave Joshua the press outlet he needed for prosecuting his first campaign. Its target was an alteration in the law of marriage. Since the enactment of Hardwicke's Marriage Act in 1753, mainstream Dissenters (unlike Quakers and Jews) were forced to celebrate their weddings according to the rites of the Church of England. Unitarians complained that they had to hear their marriages pronounced valid in the name of the Trinity, but Wilson's objection was different. The state was interfering with the civil contract of marriage, turning it into a religious ceremony with a semi-popish slant. As a symptom of 'an imperfect Toleration', it would be swept away if only orthodox Dissenters adopted 'a decided tone'.[10] Accordingly Wilson issued a treatise setting out the full case for reform in 1831, a popular pamphlet listing 14 reasons for the change in the following year and a circular to Independents in preparation for the first general election to the reformed Parliament. His aim, he wrote in July 1832, was 'to rouse the Dissenters'.[11]

The campaign, however, was to be run more on traditional lines than on any novel principle of agitation. Thomas Wilson was 'a zealous Whig' and although in 1846 Joshua described his father's political principles as being 'rather of the democratical than of the aristocratical class',[12] in 1832 both

9.   Memorandum of 1832, Letters and Other Papers relating to the Establishing of *The Patriot* Newspaper, 1831–34, Congregational Library, H.a.4.

10.   J. Wilson, *An Appeal to Dissenters on their Submitting to the Obligation Imposed by law for the Religious Celebration of Marriage According to the Form Prescribed in the Book of Common Prayer* (London: Holdsworth & Ball, 1831), pp. 94, 43.

11.   JW to J.A. James, 14 July 1832, Letters relating to the Dissenters' Marriage Bills, 1832–1836, Congregational Library, II.c.29.

12.   J. Wilson, *A Memoir of the Life and Character of Thomas Wilson, Esq., Treasurer of Highbury College* (London: John Snow, 1846), p. 96.

father and son followed the recognized channels that entailed circumspection and deference. Joshua took the marriage question to the Dissenting Deputies, who requested a formal interview with Lord Grey, asking Lord Holland and Lord John Russell to put in a good word for them with the premier. Grey listened courteously but fobbed off the delegation with the recommendation that they should consult the bishops.[13] The Deputies decided nevertheless to go ahead with a Parliamentary bill, finding that nearly all the congregations replying to a canvas would be willing to send in supporting petitions in due course. At this point affairs became more complicated. Some of the replies to the circular seem to have suggested that other grievances (no doubt including church rates) were more pressing than the rather theoretical marriage difficulty that Wilson, with his antiquarian interest in the application of historic Dissenting principles, had chosen to take up. The rising temperature of feeling in the provinces was already playing a part in developments. There was scope for wider action than Wilson had contemplated.

The Deputies responded to the provincial feeling. After discussions with the General Body, the ministerial equivalent of the lay Deputies, it was agreed to set up a United Committee consisting of all the organizations representing Dissent. The Wesleyans and Quakers, preferring to steer clear of inter-denominational ventures that might compromise their independence, declined to participate, but the Deputies' committee and representatives of the General Body were joined by delegates from the Scottish Dissenters in England and, crucially, the Protestant Society for the Protection of Religious Liberty. This body, active in the defence of country congregations since Lord Sidmouth had tried to suppress itinerant evangelism in 1811, was led by the rather touchy John Wilks, MP for Boston. Joshua Wilson had complained to him in 1831 that the Protestant Society was neglecting the marriage question,[14] but Wilks felt that the long efforts of his organization were being slighted by the new campaign mounted by Wilson. The Protestant Society sent its three delegates, including Wilks, to the United Committee under protest that they had been assigned too few places. They took a very different line from the other members of the committee. Before marriage could be dealt with, they argued, there must

13. Robert Winter to Earl Grey, to Lord Holland and to Lord John Russell, 14 November 1832; Winter to Edgar Taylor, 30 November 1832, Dissenting Deputies' Out-Letter Book, 1826–34, Guildhall Library, London, MS 3085.

14. JW to [John Wilks], 27 October 1831 (draft), Congregational Library, MSS II.c.29.

be civil registration, an innovation that the Protestant Society had been seeking for decades; and the exemption of chapels from poor rates, which Wilks was steering through the Commons that session, must not be compromised by any other proposals.[15] When a deputation from the United Committee waited on Lord Grey in May 1833, it was Wilks's measure that struck the Prime Minister as likely to meet with cabinet approval and it duly passed into law. The marriage question that Wilson had wanted to press forward had been shunted into the sidings. For the rest his lordship thanked the committee for its forbearance in not pressing for relief at present and blandly assured the deputation that 'he thought that the sanction of His Majesty's Government might be expected to any reasonable measures proposed by Protestant Dissenters so far as was practicable'.[16] The committee should have realized what that meant. The government had proved less accommodating than Dissenters had hoped.

In the autumn of 1833 the question of strategy for the coming Parliamentary session was discussed over dinner at the home of Thomas Wilson by a group of London Independent ministers. As ministers often do, they felt that the issue before them should be put on a more reasoned theological basis. 'The general opinion was that a spirited & eloquent tho at the same time plain and popular Declaration should be immediately prepared exhibiting the great principles on which Nonconformity is founded.'[17] The drawing up of a declaration was more problematic than they expected. Andrew Reed, minister of Wycliffe Chapel, at first declined the task of drafting one, but then went ahead and issued his own pamphlet anonymously, *The Case of the Dissenters*, which gained a widespread circulation and was often taken to possess an official standing which it lacked.[18] It fell to the United Committee to compose a formal statement on behalf of Dissenters at large. Joseph Fletcher, Independent minister at Stepney, took the lead in drafting it in a sub-committee. When the draft was submitted to the main committee, it ran into trouble. The Unitarians, as the traditional leaders of the Dissenting interest, were still attached to the older ways of

15. Minutes of the Protestant Society for the Protection of Religious Liberty, 18 March 1833, Dr Williams's Library, London, 38.194.

16. Minutes of the United Committee appointed to consider the Grievances under which Dissenters now Labour with a View to their Redress, 14 June 1833, Guildhall Library, MS 3086/1.

17. JW to GH, 18 October 1833 (draft).

18. A. Reed and C. Reed, *Memoirs of the Life and Philanthropic Labours of Andrew Reed, D.D.* (London: Strahan & Co., 1863), pp. 193-95.

expressing their concerns and were growing alarmed at the increasing populist stridency of evangelical Nonconformists in the country. Any truculence on the part of Dissenters would, they feared, prove utterly counterproductive. Robert Aspland and Thomas Rees for the Unitarians moved that the statement should be revised so as to avoid anything that could be interpreted as 'a Declaration of War against the Church of England'. There was lengthy debate before an amendment that they should accept the substance of the draft was carried by fifteen votes to nine. A week later the Unitarians returned to the fray with another proposal, seconded by William Smith himself, that petitions in support of the statement should be confined to grievances, or, if general principles were mentioned, they should be phrased as recommended. This time the effort was swept aside by seventeen votes to three.[19] Smith continued to counsel 'abstinence from all violence and even clamour' in the pages of *The Patriot*,[20] but the decisive battle had been lost. Aspland soon ceased to bother attending the United Committee altogether.[21] The *Brief Statement of the Case of Protestant Dissenters* appeared inflammatory to the more cautious spirits wedded to the methods of the past.

Joshua Wilson, however, together with the London Independents around him, was himself trying to restrain more extreme elements. The pattern of the *Brief Statement* was an attempt to hold the line against vocal demands for disestablishment, which, as we shall see, were beginning to be heard outside the capital. The statement began with a resounding announcement of principle. 'The exertion of political power, for the suppression of Error, or the establishment of Truth, is presumptuous and unjust.' The Dissenters bore witness to their conscientious objection to the alliance of any ecclesiastical body with the civil power. The decision on how that issue was to be resolved, however, was left 'to the progress of Events and the determination of an enlightened Legislature, under the providence of the Most High'.[22] There was deliberately no demand for immediate separation of Church and state because, as Wilson pointed out in *The Patriot*, such a proposal would be impossible. Instead Dissenters should concentrate on practical grievances, but, as in the statement, expound their principles as well. 'We shall not', he went on, '...desert, without good reason, our

19. United Committee Minutes, 10, 16, 23, 30 December 1833.
20. *Patriot*, 8 January 1834, p. 14.
21. R.B. Aspland, *Memoir of the Life, Works and Correspondence of the Rev. Robert Aspland of Hackney* (London: Edward T. Whitfield, 1850), p. 535.
22. United Committee Minutes, after 4 January 1834.

natural leaders and ancient allies, the Whigs.'[23] He was contemplating a separate organization, perhaps to be named the Wycliffe Union, to call for the severance of religion from secular authority, hoping that 'many pious & enlightened Churchmen' would join.[24] It would then not appear to be a sectional demand from Dissent but the will of the Christian community. The alliance of Evangelical Churchmen and Nonconformists in the anti-slavery campaign could be preserved and there would be no risk of the cause falling into the hands of the secular radicals whom Wilson disliked and feared. So the metropolitan strategy over which Wilson presided entailed concentration on pressing grievances, the avowal of a theoretical belief in the separation of Church and state and continued cooperation with the Whigs. It set its face, however, against urgent demands for disestablishment.

In the provinces opinion was far from uniform. Feeling can be gauged from the reports in *The Patriot* of public meetings held up and down the country during the winter of 1833–34 to pass resolutions and approve petitions to Parliament in the name of the local Dissenting community. With Church reform in the air, it was natural for Nonconformists to express their views. Only in Wales, where the Calvinistic Methodists took a firm stand against the whole movement, were meetings rare. John Elias, their outstanding leader, declared that his body had no connection with the three denominations and believed in submission to authority.[25] Many Dissenters, especially in the south of England, did speak out, but confined themselves to asking for relief from disabilities. This was true at Devonport, Bristol and Reading and among Cornish Congregationalists. At Bath, with its heavy respectability, the meeting specifically refrained from obtruding its views on Church and state. At Chatham one of the speakers explained that he did not want the destruction of the Church of England but hoped that it would become pure in the gospel.[26] The commonest attitude was that recommended by the United Committee and embodied in its *Brief Statement*: to protest against the union of Church and state in the abstract and then concentrate on specific grievances. This firm but moderate stance was adopted (to take a few instances) at Staines, Leicester and Liverpool. One of the resolutions of Dissenters at Exeter echoed the

23. *Patriot*, 1 January 1834, p. 3.
24. JW to GH, n.d. (after 21 October 1833).
25. Jones, 'Origins', pp. 48-50, 56-58.
26. *Patriot*, 25 December 1833, p. 429; 12 March 1834, p. 82; 19 March 1834, p. 89; 9 April 1834, p. 117; 26 February 1834, p. 66; 5 February 1834, p. 46.

London view: although the connection of Church and state was a griev-ance, they were willing 'to defer urging its dissolution until more infor-mation on the subject shall have been diffused, and the sentiments of our fellow-countrymen more fully formed and developed'.[27] Whether Anglican dignitaries were much reassured by this postponement rather than renun-ciation of designs on the established Church we can doubt. Nevertheless the predominant attitude in the provinces coincided closely with the view that Wilson hoped, perhaps rather naively, would not alienate the Whig sponsors of Dissent.

Scattered among the expressions of opinion, however, there were some rather more extreme views. At Coventry the first resolution was that the establishment was unscriptural. The meeting could not be satisfied until the legislature had ended it. Although John Sibree, the distinguished Inde-pendent minister at Coventry, claimed that his meeting had not declared in favour of immediate separation, it came closer to doing so than London would have approved. Chard actually announced that it wanted the speedy separation of Church and state and Berwick Baptists contended that noth-ing short of severance was satisfactory.[28] At Leeds as early as November 1833, long before guidance from London was issued, there was a cabal of the leading orthodox Dissenting ministers together with Edward Baines, the son of the influential proprietor of the *Leeds Mercury*, and three other laymen. The host, John Clapham, was a colleague of George Hadfield in the Lady Hewley suit and something of Hadfield's earnest Manchester temper rubbed off on the meeting over the Pennines. The resulting public meeting duly resolved that the alliance of Church and state was 'altogether inconsistent with the law of Christ and the doctrine of Scripture; and in its practice and workings directly and seriously injurious to the spirit of religion'. Hence, although cautiously declaring that Church property should not be touched, the resolution concluded that the alliance should be severed.[29] There was clearly a body of feeling in the provinces that would not rest content with a mixture of merely theoretical disestablishment-arianism and calls for action over nothing but minor disabilities.

Even Methodism was stirred into revolt against the Church of England. It was to be expected that the New Connexion, with its heritage of the

27. *Patriot*, 22 January 1834, p. 25; 29 January 1834, pp. 34, 33.
28. *Patriot*, 5 February 1834, pp. 42, 44; 19 March 1834, p. 90; 26 March 1834, p. 98.
29. John Clapham to GH, 25 November 1833, forwarded to JW. *Patriot*, 11 Decem-ber 1833, p. 419.

rights of man and lay assertiveness, might supply recruits for the Dissenting campaign, and that was true, for example, in the radical centres of Sheffield, Huddersfield and Macclesfield, where the Primitives were also drawn in.[30] The degree to which the Wesleyans were also affected is more surprising. They were roused to attend a meeting in the very unradical town of Petersfield in Hampshire where the establishment principle was condemned. In Durham City the equivalent gathering was actually held in the Wesleyan chapel with a majority of the class leaders on the platform. At Yarmouth, where the meeting confined itself to disabilities, it was also held in a Methodist chapel, but here Thomas Moxon, one of the ministers, denounced even the mild motion 'as tending to subvert our excellent and venerable Church'.[31] Elsewhere, however, ministers identified with the agitation—at Chichester, Macclesfield (again) and even reportedly some in Manchester.[32] At Birmingham there was a meeting of Weleyans only, held in a Baptist chapel because connexional premises were refused them, where a local preacher successfully proposed a motion for separation. A similar gathering, as Hadfield excitedly noticed, was held at Todmorden and another was expected in Leicester. Hadfield obtained his information from the *Christian Advocate*, the first Methodist newspaper, founded in 1830 by John Stephens, son of the Wesleyan conservative stalwart of the same name, to oppose the regime of Jabez Bunting in the Conference.[33] The newspaper unequivocally took the Dissenting side during the winter of 1833–34. The support of the younger John Stephens's brother, Joseph Rayner Stephens, for disestablishment during this episode has often been noticed, but it has usually been supposed to be an isolated incident that Bunting rapidly suppressed by expelling the offender. It is plain, however, that the threat to connexional discipline was far wider, so that Bunting's action was designed as a warning to others. The Dissenting campaign was normally led by Independents and their Baptist coadjutors, but it enjoyed widespread sympathy and scattered support in Methodism.

A strange quixotic figure did his best to make the Dissenting cauldron, seething in so many places, boil over. Robert Mackenzie Beverley sprang from the landed gentry of the East Riding, but claimed to have been disinherited by a good-for-nothing father who gambled away the family

---

30. *Patriot*, 19 February 1834, p. 63; 22 January 1834, p. 30; 5 March 1834, p. 80.

31. *Patriot*, 19 February 1834, p. 58; 22 January 1834, pp. 25, 30; 12 February 1834, p. 54.

32. *Patriot*, 26 February 1834, p. 70; 5 March 1834, p. 80; 19 March 1834, p. 95.

33. *Patriot*, 16 April 1834, p. 130. GH to JW, 8 April 1834.

fortune. He showed signs of a manic depressive personality and carried a huge chip on his shoulder against the Established Church, but at the same time was pursuing a spiritual quest that later took him among the Quakers, then to the Brethren and finally beyond organized religion altogether. In the early 1830s he was circulating among the Independents, often securing preaching appointments. He caused a storm of alarm and disgust as early as February 1831 by issuing a pamphlet addressed to the Archbishop of York that ventilated some recent university scandals, condemned the state religion as 'a mere theatrical ceremony', anticipated the imminent confiscation of all ecclesiastical property and called loudly for severance of Church and state.[34] In his correspondence he denounced the Established Church as 'the Dragon' and spoke apocalyptically of the 'mighty revolution' and 'terrible ordeal' ahead.[35] He was present at the planning dinner held by Thomas Wilson in October 1833, but found the caution of Joshua and his circle irksome to his firebrand temperament. Some of the Dissenters, he told Joshua in February 1834, 'are pluming themselves on being what they call "respectable"' and so were disowning him.[36] In public he called for the United Committee to be superseded by a new body to seek separation of Church and state, an idea that sowed the seed of Joshua Wilson's scheme for a Wyclife Union.[37] In private he urged Wilson to drop Conder as editor of *The Patriot* in favour of a man of more advanced views, perhaps hoping for the post himself.[38] After he had preached in Brighton a meeting was held to call for a 'total discontinuance between Church and State'; he claimed with excited exaggeration that he had found Hull Dissenters to be '*Destructives*'; and he did his best to rouse Joseph Sturge of Birmingham to drag the Quakers into the campaign.[39] This stormy petrel of a man was ever pressing for a fiercer attack on the established Church that he detested.

34. R.M. Beverley, *A Letter to his Grace the Archbishop of York on the Present Corrupt State of the Church of England* (Beverley: W.B. Johnson, 5th edn, 1831), quoted at p. 20.

35. R.M. Beverley [hereafter RMB] to JW [11 February 1834], 4 January 1834, 25 January 1834, Letters of Robert Mackenzie Beverley, 1833–1840, Congregational Library, MSS II.c.2.2.

36. RMB to JW, 20 February 1834.

37. *Patriot*, 27 November 1833, p. 402.

38. RMB to JW, 12 December 1833.

39. RMB to JW, 20 November 1833, 9 January 1834, [23 December 1833]. A. Tyrrell, *Joseph Sturge and the Moral Reform Party in Early Victorian Britain* (Bromley: Christopher Helm, 1987), p. 68.

The most extreme Dissenters were to be found in Nottingham. Since 1808 the *Nottingham Review*, edited by the Methodist New Connexion printer Charles Sutton, had backed a variety of radical causes including Luddism and, after the paper was taken over by Charles's son Richard in 1829, manhood suffrage and annual Parliaments. Disestablishment had been one of its issues since 1828. Charles, who stood as a Parliamentary candidate at the 1832 election, was surrounded by a circle of dedicated and prosperous men who were already looking for an opportunity to campaign against the state Church: Benjamin Boothby, a Dissenting iron merchant who owned premises occupying virtually the whole of one side of a long street; Samuel Fox, a Quaker shopkeeper; George Gill, a Unitarian who frequently worshipped with the Quakers; and William Howitt, a Quaker chemist who in 1833 published *A Popular History of Priestcraft* that sold particularly well in America.[40] Howitt's 1834 edition added an explicit censure of every state establishment as 'a gross insult and standing LIBEL upon Christianity'.[41] It was Howitt who composed what George Hadfield called 'the most able and decisive Memorial that has yet been presented to the Premier of England on the subject of our Claims and grievances'.[42] This document, which was adopted at a meeting on 8 January, significantly in a New Connexion chapel, called for the entire and immediate divorce of the Church of England from the state. It owed nothing to the more tepid views of London's Dissenting organizations. Joseph Gilbert, the leading Independent minister of the town, registered Nottingham's strong dissent from the metropolitan recommendation to confine petitions to the redress of grievances. They were urged to be mute about their principles because they would be derided. 'If this answer can content Dissenters', he wrote, 'they are not the men their fathers were.'[43] The same spirit was evinced when Howitt, with a Nottingham colleague, presented the memorial to Lord Grey in person. Howitt explained that they had not copied other Dissenters but had asked for separation. Grey replied that he wished they had confined themselves to grievances. Did they, asked the incredulous Prime Minister, want to do away with all establishments of

40. R.A. Church, *Economic and Social Change in a Midland Town: Victorian Nottingham, 1815–1900* (London: Frank Cass & Co., 1966). M.I. Thomis, *Politics and Society in Nottingham, 1785–1835* (Oxford: Basil Blackwell, 1969).

41. W. Howitt, *A Popular History of Priestcraft in All Ages and Nations* (London: Effingham Wilson, 3rd edn, 1834), p. 316.

42. GH to JW, 13 January 1834.

43. *Patriot*, 15 January 1834, p. 23, 22 January 1834, p. 27.

religion? 'Precisely!', announced Howitt.[44] Two months later, in March 1834, the incorruptibles of Nottingham issued an 'Appeal to the Dissenters of England' urging that it was time to put down the establishment.[45] They formed the vanguard of militant Dissent.

Manchester thought today what Nottingham thought yesterday. A motion at the chief gathering in the Lancashire town to voice Nonconformist demands in March 1834 gave credit to 'the correct principles and manly resolutions of the Nottingham Dissenters'.[46] Manchester, however, possessed in George Hadfield a devotee of Dissenting claims second to none. Brought up in Sheffield, which he eventually served in Parliament from 1852 to 1874, he had moved as a young man to Lancashire, where he had thrown himself into the affairs of Independency with a will. 'No influences or inducements of any kind', wrote a former pastor,

> could make him swerve by a hair's breadth from what he believed to be the path of duty. Sometimes, no doubt, this stern, unbending integrity gave to his decisions and proceedings an appearance of self-will and ruggedness of temper... He wondered how any persons could halt or hesitate in the prosecution of aims that appeared to him to be so evidently just and good.[47]

In his autobiography Hadfield revealingly admitted that he had 'often been tempted into excessive hilarity, and lamented it'.[48] While still embroiled in the Hewley case, he was a willing helper at an early stage in Joshua Wilson's marriage campaign.[49] By January 1833, however, Hadfield was becoming impatient with the metropolis. The opportunity of a reformed Parliament, in which Manchester was represented for the first time, might be lost. The fruit of Wilson's 'gradual work', he warned his London corespondent before checking his own flippancy, might begin to show only 'in the days of our great-grand-children'.[50] He was already calling on his new MP, Poulett Thomson, to procure 'a perfect plan of Church

44. *Patriot*, 29 January 1834, p. 39.

45. *Patriot*, 26 March 1834, p. 98.

46. *Patriot*, 12 March 1834, p. 105.

47. J. Griffin, *Memories of the Past: Records of Ministerial Life* (London: Hamilton, Adams & Co., 1883), p. 271.

48. 'The Personal Narrative of Me George Hadfield M.P.' (1860), p. 55, Manchester Public Libraries Archives Department.

49. J.A. Coombs to JW, 12 March 1831; Thomas Raffles to JW, 11 April 1834, II.c.29.

50. GH to JW, 15 January 1832 [sc.1833].

Reform', that is disestablishment.[51] In March he was associated with a petition to Parliament from Lancashire Independents demanding redress of all their grievances and not just marriage reform.[52] And Hadfield's zeal for the ending of religious establishments was constantly being enflamed by William McKerrow, the minister in Manchester of the Scottish United Secession Church, a denomination that had already taken up militant agitation for religious equality north of the border.[53] By the autumn Hadfield had decided that it was time for decisive action nationally. With Beverley, he agreed that the best point of attack would be on the deeply unpopular bishops, whose opposition to the Reform Bill had not been forgiven.[54] Accordingly when he wrote a call to arms to *The Patriot* in November, the exclusion of bishops from the Lords stood second on his list of demands, immediately behind the discontinuation of the Church–state connection. [55] The letter reached a sympathetic audience in many places in the north. Even in Brighton it was agreed to print and distribute 5,000 copies of it.[56] 'You may now', he told Joshua Wilson, '...safely assure your friends in town, that their country friends will do the Work without them.'[57] Hadfield was one of the key figures in the national mobilization of Dissent.

Nevertheless Manchester did not immediately take radical steps in the great upsurge of the winter. Its most influential congregation, the Cross Street Unitarians, meekly resolved in favour only of the redress of grievances; and a petition from Hadfield's own Independents avoided the question of disestablishment, no doubt in deference to the dread by their leading minister, R.S. McAll, of any charge of political or sectarian spirit.[58] On 13 February, however, there was a preliminary meeting where it was agreed that all establishments were wrong and the attenders declared their intention to exert themselves for their termination. The gathering clearly

51. GH to JW, 26 January 1833.

52. GH to JW, 16 March 1833.

53. GH to JW, 21 January 1833; GH to RMB, 7 November 1833, H.a.10. Cf. W.R. Ward, *Religion and Society in England, 1790–1850* (London: Batsford, 1972), pp. 129-32.

54. GH to RMB, 21 October 1833.

55. *Patriot*, 13 November 1833, p. 387.

56. United Committee Minutes, 16 December 1833.

57. John Clapham to GH, 25 November 1833, endorsed to JW.

58. *Patriot*, 12 February 1834, p. 54; 26 February 1834, p. 66. *Discourses on Special Occasions by the Late Rev. Robert S. McAll, LL.D., with a Discourse on his Life and Character by the Rev. Ralph Wardlaw, D.D.* (London: Jackson & Walford, 1840), p. cxliii.

represented a wider Lancashire constituency, for its chairman was Joseph Harbottle, the young and energetic Baptist minister at Accrington.[59] Harbottle was again in the chair, perhaps a device for masking the reluctance to participate of Independent ministers swayed by McAll, when a monster meeting was held in Manchester on two successive evenings, 5 and 6 March. Hadfield proposed a resolution that the presence of bishops in the Lords was unjust and McKerrow moved for the separation of Church and state.[60] Manchester was now roused. The strongest feeling, however, as so often on popular issues in the early nineteenth century, was evinced not in the cotton metropolis but in the more radical townships nearby. The most famous case is Ashton-under-Lyne, where a Church Separation Society was formed two days before the huge meeting in Manchester. The underlying cause of resentment there was the refusal of the Earl of Stamford, the lord of the manor, to allow the erection of an Independent chapel on his land. The Dissenting cottonmasters, together with their operatives in the growing town, saw his intransigence as a classic gesture of aristocratic hauteur.[61] The resulting outrage led to mushrooming of a desire for what Joseph Rayner Stephens, the Methodist minister stationed at Ashton-under-Lyne, proposed at the formation of the society, 'the immediate and total separation of the Church from the State'.[62] To the ire of the Wesleyan authorities Stephens stirred up the same absolutist spirit in adjacent towns.[63] Meetings chaired by leading millowners—Henry Kelsall, Charles Hindley, John Cheetham—were held at Rochdale, Oldham and Stalybridge to adopt similar uncompromising resolutions. Bolton and Hyde took the same bold course.[64] 'I think', wrote a gloating George Hadfield to Joshua Wilson on 15 April, 'there will in a short time not be a single town in this neighbourhood that has not sent up a petition for separation.'[65] The core of the manufacturing districts was thoroughly kindled.

The government was dismayed by the novel stridency of the Dissenting campaign. Exactly a week after the Nottingham resolutions, a deputation

59. *Patriot*, 19 February 1834, p. 57.

60. *Patriot*, 12 March 1834, p. 82.

61. *Patriot*, 11 December 1833, p. 416.

62. *Patriot*, 12 March 1834, p. 81.

63. M.S. Edwards, *Purge this Realm: A Life of Joseph Rayner Stephens* (London: Epworth Press, 1994), chs. 1, 2.

64. *Patriot*, 26 March 1834, p. 107; 2 April 1834, p. 115; 16 April 1834, p. 130; 12 March 1834, p. 81.

65. GH to JW, 15 April 1834.

waited on the Prime Minister to commend the United Committee's cautious programme dealing with grievances only. Lord Grey was in no mood to listen. He insisted that the union of Church and state was necessary; if Dissenters adopted violent measures to separate them, he warned, 'it would be the surest way to make their Friends their Foes'.[66] Two of the Unitarians heard from Lord Holland that it was only his intervention that prevented the cabinet from throwing out any plan for helping Dissent at all.[67] But the government knew that Dissenting votes were too valuable to be squandered. Marriage reform proposals were introduced, but caused dissatisfaction because the Church of England was still to exercise a supervisory role over all weddings. This was enormously frustrating for the London moderates around Wilson. The marriage question was the one they had selected for remedy partly because it should cause the government little embarrassment; they had done their utmost to restrain wilder spirits in the provinces; and now the measure offered them was 'nearly nugatory'. Negotiations with Lord John Russell as Home Secretary brought no improvement.[68] On 2 April the resentment burst out in public. Josiah Conder, Wilson's spokesman, abandoned his previous attempt to rein in the agitation through the editorial columns of *The Patriot*. Since the government had not done more, the time had come for a demonstration of the extent of Dissenting feeling. 'No Minister can serve two masters. He must choose between the Church, as the patrimony of the oligarchy, and the people.'[69] Later in the month, the government tried to placate Dissenting wrath by another measure, the abolition of church rates. Again, however, the cabinet miscalculated. The plan of transferring the charge for the upkeep of parish churches to the land tax was objectionable because it continued to treat Anglican buildings as a national responsibility and because it would no longer be possible for opponents to vote down the rates locally. The further insensitivity to the wishes of Nonconformists seemed intolerable. The United Committee decided to organize a display of national Dissenting opinion.[70]

The method chosen was a delegate meeting in London. The idea had been floated in the previous autumn by Brighton Dissenters, but it had been rejected as too dangerous. It was a favourite project of Beverley's

66. United Committee Minutes, 22 January 1834.
67. Aspland, *Aspland*, p. 534.
68. United Committee Minutes, 5 March 1834, 10 April 1834, 7 April 1834.
69. *Patriot*, 2 April 1834, p. 112.
70. United Committee Minutes, 25 April 1834.

because it would allow mass emotions to have free vent; for the same reason it was alarming to the metropolitan elite.[71] To call together deputies from all over the land savoured too much of revolutionary ambitions. In March 1834, however, the Birmingham Dissenters endorsed the plan. The Dissenting interest at Birmingham was sorely fragmented. Cannon Street Baptists wanted a more militant approach; Carr's Lane Independents under the widely respected John Angell James favoured concentrating on disabilities; but Ebenezer Independents under Timothy East were more aggrieved at the government attitude to marriage reform, drawing up a set of resolutions that James refused to sign. A meeting of representatives from Baptist and Independent congregations under East decided that the best way forward was to request a delegate meeting in London to ascertain the general feeling of Dissenters.[72] It was the Birmingham proposal that Conder endorsed in his editorial on 2 April as a way of showing the government that Dissent meant business. At that point, however, there was another proposal for a public meeting, this time from a gathering representing advanced opinion. Calling themselves the Friends of Civil and Religious Liberty, this group, which included Beverley, was willing to admit secular radicals such as Joseph Hume and called unequivocally for the United Committee to sponsor a meeting for the separation of Church and state. After prudently consulting its member organizations, the committee decided not to proceed with the meeting by twelve votes to only one. It was totally unwilling to contemplate advocating disestablishment in alliance with non-religious forces. But then the government's inimical church rates proposals created an emergency.[73] Unless the government was shown the strength of national opinion, Dissenters would continue to be flouted. The task was therefore to set up a gathering for provincial representatives that would demonstrate profound indignation without lapsing into impossible claims for the ending of the establishment or coquetting with the irreligious. The men from Nottingham and Manchester would have to be repressed.

That was the background to the delegate meeting at the London Tavern on 8 May 1834, the climax of the whole agitation. The nervous apprehensions of the Londoners on the United Committee were palpable. Nobody

71. RMB to JW, n.d. [17 October 1833?]. United Committee Minutes, 6 November 1833.

72. *Patriot*, 19 February 1834, p. 57; 26 February 1834, p. 66; 5 March 1834, p. 73; 19 March 1834, p. 89.

73. United Committee Minutes, 7–25 April 1834.

was to be admitted without a ticket signed by the committee's secretary, Richard Winter.[74] Edward Baines from Leeds, a firm supporter of the Whigs, was secured as chairman. Before the start of the meeting Winter buttonholed Angell James, asking him, as 'a MODERATE MAN from the country', to propose the resolutions prepared by the committee.[75] In order to ensure that the question of Church and state could be entirely excluded, a meeting was advertised for the following day to set up a distinct organization to concentrate on that issue alone. The extremists, however, were not to be thwarted. As soon as the proceedings opened, Joseph Harbottle sprang to his feet to bring forward the views of Lancashire, but Baines asked him to wait until a resolution was before the meeting. Immediately after the first innocuous motion had been seconded, Harbottle proposed an amendment, explaining that he had instructions to insist on the recognition of the principle of separation of Church and state. Joseph Gilbert from Nottingham hastened to his assistance, announcing that he too was mandated to take no part unless separation was accepted. The pressure was irresistible. Henry Waymouth, as chairman of the United Committee, graciously conceded that Harbottle's proposal could stand first. James incorporated it in his own resolution, though adding that it was merely an abstract declaration of principle. If it were to be embodied in a petition, he would oppose it himself. Others were even more cautious. Richard Foster, a Baptist banker from Cambridge, wanted to add an explanatory clause to the resolution in order, as he said, to allay the fears of the aristocracy. A delegate named Bunter from Taunton declared that Dissenters from his district did not want separation pressed to the front, and they were as entitled to respect as Manchester. But William Howitt from Nottingham repeated that he could participate only on condition that separation was recognized as the basis. John Wilks for the Protestant Society warned against disunion, and the resolution was carried as amended.[76] It was a triumph of compromise. The extremists had their principle endorsed; the moderates avoided any commitment to action. At least in public there was a show of unanimity.

The sequel was something of an anticlimax. On the following day a fresh organization, the Voluntary Church Society, was duly established to take up the cause of ending the establishment of religion. The model was

74. United Committee Minutes, 5 May 1834.

75. R.W. Dale, *The Life and Letters of John Angell James* (London: James Nisbet, 1861), p. 586.

76. *Patriot*, 10 May 1834, pp. 162-3; 14 May 1834, p. 167.

the set of societies with the same title that had proliferated in Scotland over the previous two years. In conciliatory mood Harbottle explained that the men from Manchester had not come to overturn the work of the United Committee. In truth the venture was primarily a pre-emptive strike by the Wilson circle associated with the committee against any cooperation with secular radicals. Thomas Wilson presided; the basis was expressly designed to welcome any evangelicals; and Conder expressed the vain hope that the Wesleyans would join in.[77] The new body was to hold a series of lectures in 1835–36 but achieved little else. The group it was designed to upstage, the Friends of Civil and Religious Liberty, went ahead with its gathering a few days later under the chairmanship of Joseph Hume, with Daniel O'Connell and other MPs in attendance. Agreeing to petition Parliament for the separation of Church and state, the gathering also drew in radical Dissenters such as William Howitt.[78] Again nothing subsequently came of it. Meanwhile the Whig government realized that its church rates measure had been counterproductive and quietly withdrew it. Furthermore a bill to open the ancient universities to Dissenters failed in the Lords, and so no grievances whatsoever were remedied by the end of the Parliamentary session. But the result was not a redoubling of Dissenting passion. On the contrary, political uncertainties following the resignation of Lord Grey in July showed that further reform was far from inevitable. When, in November, the king dismissed Lord Melbourne's administration from office in order to install the Tories in power, Dissent rallied to its traditional Whig allegiance. The upsurge of the winter of 1833–34 was neither sustained nor repeated.

Yet the episode represented the start of a major shift in the outlook of Dissenters. Whereas in the past they had been content with toleration, they now began to scent the possibility of full religious equality. Previously the leaders of Dissent such as William Smith had been grateful to receive occasional concessions through the Whigs; during a single winter of discontent the old Unitarian leadership of Dissent was swept aside, the Whigs were dismissed as self-interested holders of church patronage and the evangelical Nonconformists publicly voiced their whole ambitions for the first time. George Hadfield saw no reason why they should be 'left out of the social compact, and degraded'. Nor was such an attitude confined to the most mercurial spirits. The Independents and Baptists of Hull denounced the state maintaining 'invidious and offensive distinctions

77. *Patriot*, 10 May 1834, pp. 163-64.
78. Martin, 'Politics of the Congregationalists', pp. 121-22.

between its subjects'.[79] There was a rising preoccupation with ending all discrimination against Dissenters and a Cromwellian conviction that they must be up and doing in their own good cause. Political practicality was not their prime concern; the public sphere was more an arena for bearing witness. Joseph Gilbert expressed this attitude in a letter to *The Patriot* of January 1834 in defence of the Nottingham call for disestablishment.

> It is said, we cannot now succeed. Be it so: we shall still have done our duty; and we may consistently repeat the claim for justice. By asking too much, it is again predicted, that we shall but obtain the less. Still, be it so: not only shall we have freed our consciences, but have retained the honour and the power also, not to be despised, of being sufferers in a righteous cause.[80]

This stance bore the mark of evangelical religion in its moralism, its declamatory style and its refusal to compromise. By no means all evangelical Nonconformists, however, adopted such a policy at this time. Like many in the country, the respectable London group around Joshua Wilson, the initiator of the whole process of mobilization, was much more circumspect. Joseph Fletcher, the Stepney minister who drafted the statement of the Dissenting case for the United Committee, deplored the 'violent and precipitate reasoners', was sure that their petitions for the severance of Church and state were a mistake and feared that Manchester and Nottingham had retarded the progress of their cause.[81] Wilson, Fletcher and *The Patriot* represented a middle position between the traditional Unitarian deference and the new provincial militancy. Their policy continued to act as a brake on Dissenting politics until Edward Miall began publishing *The Nonconformist* in 1841 and set up the Anti-State Church Association three years later.[82] During the events of 1833–34, it emerges, there were three different answers to the question of how to advance the aspirations of Dissent by political means. There were the deferential pragmatism of the traditional Dissenting elite, the controlled campaigning of the London committee men and the populist absolutism of some of their country co-religionists. The episode is remarkable for the rapid eclipse of the first stance and the sudden appearance of the other two in uneasy symbiosis. A new evangelical Nonconformist political culture had emerged.

79. *Patriot*, 13 November 1833, p. 387; 1 January 1834, p. 7.

80. *Patriot*, 22 January 1834, p. 27.

81. J. Fletcher, *Memoirs of the Life and Correspondence of the Late Rev. Joseph Fletcher, D.D.* (London: John Snow, 1846), p. 432.

82. For later developments, see T. Larsen, *Friends of Religious Equality: Nonconformist Politics in Mid-Victorian England* (Woodbridge: Boydell, 1999).

EDUCATIONAL ASPIRATIONS VERSUS SOCIAL HIERARCHIES:
THE 1906 EDUCATION BILL

John Wigley

The 1902 Tory Education Act and the 1906 Liberal bill are at the heart of a historical paradox. The 1902 act is usually regarded as a constructive measure, the 1906 bill as a partisan proposal, yet when the 1902 act was replaced by Butler's 1944 act his religious settlement was very similar to that envisaged in 1906. This paper argues that the 1902 act was in fact largely partisan, that the 1906 bill was eminently reasonable, and that the key to understanding them lies neither in education nor entirely in religion, but in the discriminatory and hierarchical nature of English life since 1660.[1]

The 1902 act abolished the 1870 Liberal act's school boards and transferred their elementary schools to county, county borough, municipal borough and urban district councils. These local education authorities (LEAs) were to appoint an education committee, to which non-elected members could be coopted, to supervise their 'council' elementary schools. Denominational schools ('voluntary' schools) were to have six managers, including two nominated by the LEA. The managers were to appoint and dismiss teachers, subject to the education committee, except in the case of matters of religion, where they had complete discretion. Denominational schools were to be given rate aid, which board schools had received since 1870.[2]

1.   R.C.K. Ensor, *England, 1870–1914* (Oxford: Oxford University Press, 1936), pp. 355-58; J. Grigg, *Lloyd George: The People's Champion, 1902–1911* (London: Methuen, 1991), pp. 25, 151; E. Halévy, *Imperialism and the Rise of Labour* (London: Ernest Benn, 1961), pp. 204-210; K. Young, *Arthur James Balfour* (London: George Bell & Son, 1963), pp. 179, 203. S.H. Zebel, *Balfour: A Political Biography* (Cambridge: Cambridge University Press, 1973), pp. 80, 119.

2.   Halévy, *Imperialism*, pp. 202-204; J.S. Maclure, *Educational Documents: England and Wales 1816–1963* (London: Methuen, 1965), pp. 149-53.

Nonconformists accused the Tories of establishing publicly funded schools that were not publicly controlled, would not employ Nonconformist teachers and would be used to proselytize Nonconformist children in 'single school districts', identifying the state with Anglicanism and Roman Catholicism, and obliging its citizens to finance religious teachings which offended their consciences: 'Rome on the rates'. Liberal opposition kept the measure before the House of Commons for a record 57 days, but it was actually strengthened when the government amended it, making the councils' proposed discretionary power to take over the school boards into an obligation to do so.[3]

The 1906 bill's details were complex. On and after 1 January 1908 only elementary schools provided by LEAs were to receive either grant or rate aid. Daily religious instruction in such 'provided' schools was to be simple Bible teaching. Clause III allowed schools transferred from denominations to LEAs in rural areas of under 5,000 people to claim 'ordinary facilities' for denominational instruction on two mornings a week, although it could not be given by the ordinary teacher. Clause IV allowed transferred schools in urban areas of over 5,000 people to claim 'extended facilities' for ordinary teachers to give denominational instruction every morning if four-fifths of the parents requested it; alternative schools were available for parents who did not want it. Clause VI provided for rights of conscience, stating that parents were obliged to send their children to school for only exclusively secular instruction. The bill empowered LEAs to take over all denominational elementary schools, but if they did so they were to pay rent for them and meet the cost of alterations and repairs.[4]

The bill therefore had several purposes. It was intended to end the dual system of council and denominational schools, create a unified structure of elementary schools and secure full public control. Clause III was intended to solve the employment and proselytism problems in villages, while allowing some flexibility for Anglican and the few Wesleyan schools. Clause IV hoped to meet Roman Catholic and Jewish demands that their town and city schools should retain a distinctive religious atmosphere. These intentions proved incompatible.

The government hoped to satisfy the Nonconformist conscience with

3. J. Clifford, *The Fight Against the Education Bill: What is at Stake* (London: National Reform Union, 1902); G.W. Byrt, *Dr John Clifford: A Fighting Free Churchman* (London: Kingsgate Press, 1947), pp. 104-108.

4. R. Pattison, 'The Birrell Education Bill of 1906', *Journal of Educational History* 5 (1973), pp. 34-40.

sub-section (2) of clause III and sub-section (1) (G) of clause IV, which stated that the expense of providing neither ordinary nor extended facilities was to be paid by the LEA; and by sub-section (2) of clause VII, which declared that teachers 'shall not be required' to give any religious instruction, subscribe to any religious creed or attend or abstain from attending any Sunday school or place of religious worship.

It is usually argued that the 1902 act united and roused the Nonconformist Churches, that they then united and roused the Liberal party, and so that they contributed to its overwhelming victory in the 1906 general election; but that the 1906 bill showed the fragility and weakness of the Nonconformist–Liberal alliance. The truth is more complex. The Nonconformists were not initially united in their opposition to the 1902 act. The chairman of the Wesleyan Education Committee, Dr Waller, supported rate aid for Wesleyan schools. The leader of the old-guard Wesleyans, J.H. Rigg, was reluctant to accept that the act upset the 1870 settlement. His progressive rival, Hugh Price Hughes, urged moderation on the National Free Church Council. The council's president, J. Scott Lidgett, sought English Presbyterian support when trying to distance it from the National Passive Resistance Committee.[5]

Nor were the Liberal leaders united in support of the Nonconformists. Haldane welcomed the 1902 act as a step towards national efficiency. Lloyd George privately welcomed it except for the provision for rate aid to denominational schools, and during his own public agitation in Wales negotiated with the Anglican Bishop of St Asaph. Campbell-Bannerman, the Liberal leader, was suspicious of pressure groups which wished to go beyond what he saw as authentic Liberalism, made an implicit distinction between Nonconformists and Liberals, had a poor opinion of most Nonconformists leaders, and asked Bryce to persuade the most militant to moderate their criticism of Tory education policy lest they alienate the

5.   D.W. Bebbington, *The Nonconformist Conscience: Chapel and Politics, 1870–1914* (London: George Allen & Unwin, 1982); G.L. Bernstein, *Liberalism and Politics in Edwardian England* (London: Allen & Unwin, 1986), pp. 50-52, 55-56, 62-63; S. Koss, *Nonconformity in Modern British Politics* (London: Batsford, 1975); G.I.T. Machin, *Politics and the Churches in Great Britain, 1869 to 1921* (Oxford: Clarendon Press, 1987); J. Telford, *The Life of James Harrison Rigg* (London: Robert Culley, 1909), p. 324; D. Hughes, *The Life of Hugh Price Hughes* (London: Hodder & Stoughton, 1904), p. 496; J.S. Lidgett, *Reminiscences* (London: Epworth Press, 1928), p. 46.

Free-Fooders, with whom he was seeking an agreement.[6]

Campbell-Bannerman had served in Gladstone's government in 1870 and remembered how it had been weakened by the education issue. Forster's bill had proposed to allow school boards to use rates to support board and denominational schools, but had been petitioned against by two-thirds of the Nonconformist ministers in England and Wales, and denounced by Nonconformist MPs prompted by Chamberlain's National Education League. Gladstone therefore accepted the Cowper-Temple clause, that in schools 'hereafter established by means of local rates, no religious catechism or religious formulary which is distinctive of any particular denomination shall be taught'. The great majority of denominational schools, most of which were Anglican National Society schools, refused to accept this condition and so received no rate aid, although their exchequer grants were doubled at Gladstone's suggestion. Cowper-Temple teaching, interpreted as simple Bible teaching, became the norm in board schools. All schools that received public money had to accept a conscience clause, allowing parents to make a written request to withdraw their children from religious teaching, which the National Society had hitherto refused.[7]

After the bill was passed Nonconformists objected to clause XXV which allowed school boards to pay the fees of poor children who attended denominational schools. Clause XXV was of little practical importance: in 1872 only 42 school boards used it, and when it was repealed in 1876 only £18,000 had been spent. It was a matter of principle: the principle that the state should be, if not quite secular, then at least non-sectarian, and not extend the practice of establishment by subsidizing the teaching of any particular doctrine. It was this key principle that separated the Nonconformists from the Liberal leaders: Gladstone's biographer, Morley, called the clause XXV issue 'the smallest ditch in which two political armies ever engaged in civil war'.[8]

6. K.O. Morgan (ed.), *Lloyd George: Family Letters, 1885–1936* (Cardiff: University of Wales Press, 1973), pp. 131-32; J.A. Spender, *The Life of the Rt Hon Sir Henry Campbell-Bannerman* (2 vols.; London: Hodder & Stoughton, 1923), II, pp. 76, 137.

7. Maclure, *Educational Documents*, pp. 98-105; Koss, *Nonconformity*, p. 25; J. Murphy, *Church, State and Schools in Britain, 1800–1870* (London: Routledge, 1971); A. Sykes, *The Rise and Fall of British Liberalism, 1776–1988* (London: Longman, 1978); T.W. Reid, *Life of the Rt. Hon. W.E. Forster* (2 vols.; London: Chapman Hall, 1888), II, pp. 439-98.

8. J.L. Garvin, *The Life of Joseph Chamberlain* (6 vols.; London: Macmillan, 1935), I, p. 172; P. Adelman, *Victorian Radicalism: The Middle Class Experience, 1830–1914* (London: Longman, 1984), pp. 80-81; D.A. Hamer, *The Politics of Electoral Pressure*

Tory governments were responsible for most late nineteenth-century education policy. They were partisan, against Nonconformists and board schools, for Anglicans and their denominational schools. Lord Sandon hoped that his 1876 act would help them, lest 'School boards...in the smaller country towns and villages...become the favourite platform of the Dissenting preacher and local agitator'. However, the 1880 Liberal act, which made elementary education compulsory, caused problems for the denominational schools. Their endowments and grants did not match the board schools' rate-finance, so they often charged higher fees and lost pupils to the board schools. The Cross Commission (1888) was appointed after complaints by Cardinal Manning, supported by the Church of England, about the parlous position of the denominational schools, and its majority report proposed to give all of them rate aid while exempting some from paying property rates. Lord Salisbury was suspicious of educating the working classes, but made Lord Cranborne (his eldest son) the Lord President of the Council and ensured that he produced the 1891 act, which made elementary education free, hoping that it would increase attendance at denominational schools and so increase their income from exchequer capitation grants.[9]

By the middle of the 1890s education policy was influenced by expert opinion and the denominational lobby. The Devonshire Report (1875) had argued that older children in elementary schools should have more science teaching, provided in part by better coordination between the Education Department and the Science and Art Department. The Samuelson Report (1882–84) had recommended the introduction of practical subjects into elementary schools. Thus the Technical Instruction Act of 1889 had authorized county and county borough councils (established in 1888) to use rates to provide technical and manual instruction and from 1890 they received whisky money grants. In 1895 the Bryce Report recommended the extension and reorganization of secondary education by creating a fully fledged central government department which would work with the county and county borough councils. During the 1890s some urban

(Brighton: Harvester, 1977), pp. 126-35; Bebbington, *Nonconformist Conscience*, p. 129; M. Cruickshank, *Church and State in English Education, 1870 to the Present Day* (London: Macmillan, 1963), p. 42; J. Morley, *The Life of William Ewart Gladstone* (3 vols.; London: Macmillan, 1903), II, p. 309.

9.   G. Sutherland, *Policy Making in Elementary Education, 1870–1895* (Oxford: Oxford University Press, 1973), p. 131; A. Roberts, *Salisbury, Victorian Titan* (London: Phoenix, 1999), pp. 556-58.

school boards began to give quasi-secondary education in their higher grade schools.[10]

In 1893 the English Church Union disparaged simple Bible teaching and in 1894 Anglicans won a majority on the London School Board. There they tested the limits of the Cowper-Temple teaching, arguing that since the Apostles' Creed was not 'distinctive of any particular denomination' it might be taught in board schools if teachers were willing to do so. Cardinal Vaughan lobbied for Catholic schools: in 1884 he had founded the Voluntary Schools Association to revise the 1870 settlement, in 1885 had advised Catholics to make the issue an electoral question, and had secured Manning's membership of the Cross Commission. In 1895 Vaughan pressed Salisbury to grant aid to all denominational schools, making a stronger case than Archbishop Temple's in 1896.[11]

When in 1896 Sir John Gorst, Salisbury's vice-president of council, introduced an education bill it showed many of these influences. It proposed to turn county and county borough councils into LEAs; to give them power to provide secondary education; to entrust them with the distribution of grants to all elementary schools; and to help denominational schools to raise their exchequer grants and exempt them from paying rates. Most contentious was the clause that would have allowed parents who objected to the religious instruction provided in board and denominational schools, to request that their children receive separate instruction on the school premises: it was opposed by Nonconformists because it would allow denominational teaching in the board schools, and by Anglicans since it would allow simple Bible teaching in the denominational schools. Salisbury had not expected Gorst to draft such a wide-ranging measure and after the bill was opposed by Tory and Liberal MPs, and its passage hindered by technical detail and procedural wrangling, the cabinet decided to withdraw it.[12]

Henceforth Gorst confined himself to more specific measures. An act of 1897 raised the exchequer grant to denominational schools and exempted them from rates, as had been proposed in 1896. An act of 1899 united the Education Department and the Science and Art Department within a new Board of Education. Then in May 1899 Gorst conspired with Lord Robert Cecil (Lord Salisbury's youngest son) to procure the Cockerton Judgment

10. Maclure, *Educational Documents*, pp. 106, 121, 140.

11. A. McCormack, *Cardinal Vaughan* (London: Burns & Oates, 1966), pp. 169-73, 257-59.

12. Roberts, *Salisbury*, pp. 817-19.

which declared it illegal for school boards to provide more than elementary education. Both wanted to weaken the school boards and strengthen the denominational schools, Gorst to concentrate responsibility for secondary education with the county and county borough councils.[13]

Control of Tory education policy passed to A.J. Balfour, Salisbury's nephew and Leader of the House of Commons. Balfour had in fact guided the 1891 measure through the House, announced the cabinet's decision to withdraw Gorst's 1896 bill, and pushed through the 1897 measure almost single-handedly. Like his uncle, he was determined to help the denominational schools. During the autumn of 1901 he began to work with Morant, perhaps the least experienced but most dogmatic civil servant in the newly-constituted Board of Education, to draft an education bill. He built on Gorst's earlier work by making county and county borough councils responsible for elementary and secondary education, and municipal and urban district councils for only elementary education. The Chancellor of the Exchequer, Sir Michael Hicks Beach, refused Treasury funds for the bill, and although Salisbury feared that rate aid to voluntary schools would reduce charitable donations, and Chamberlain warned that it would create grave political difficulties for Liberal Unionists such as himself, Balfour and Morant had their way. Rate aid for voluntary schools was the most prominent of the 1902 bill's provisions.[14]

The most determined and militant opponents of the 1902 bill were Baptists and Congregationalists. There was an element of anti-Catholicism in some Baptist attitudes; the Revd F.B. Meyer wrote of 'priestly aggression' and the *Baptist Magazine* reviled the 'yoke of Rome'. Indeed, some of the emotion associated with opposition to the 1902 bill and act was caused by concern about Anglo-Catholicism and Ritualism. Nonconformists were horrified that quasi-Catholic doctrine might be foisted on their children in single school districts. Evangelical Anglicans feared that Anglo-Catholic clergymen might similarly influence their own children. Thus the single major change that Balfour allowed to the 1902 bill was the Kenyon-Slaney amendment, which shifted control of religious instruction in denominational schools from the clergyman to the managers.[15]

13. E. Eaglesham, 'Planning the Education Bill of 1902', *British Journal of Educational Studies* 9 (1972), pp. 3-15 (3-5).

14. B.M. Allen, *Sir Robert Morant: A Great Public Servant* (London: Macmillan, 1934), p. 153; B.E.C. Dugdale, *Arthur James Balfour: Years 1848–1905* (London: Hutchinson, 1939), pp. 182-85, 241-45; J. Amery, *The Life of Joseph Chamberlain* (6 vols.; London: Macmillan, 1937), IV, pp. 177-205.

15. F.B. Meyer, *The Religious Basis of the Free Church Position* (London: Edward

However, the best-known Baptist leader, and the best-known opponent of the bill, Dr John Clifford, regarded himself as fighting 'the intolerant and grasping holders of privilege'—namely the Anglican clergy—who were trying to 'fix more securely than ever the tyrannies of the State Church over the land'. The 1902 meeting of the Congregational Union published a statement placing the struggle in the context of Nonconformist history and self-identity. Free Churchmen should object to legislation that

> instructs their children to deny the faith of their fathers and despise the religion of their home...revives the Test Act by making civil appointments dependent upon churchmanship... Free-churchmen as citizens can never... accept the doctrine that because the State makes a law it is the duty of every citizen to obey it...they will shrink from no consequences in their opposition to it. They are the sons and successors of men who maintained for two centuries a stubborn warfare against the legislation of 1662, never resting until they had gained a complete victory...[16]

Nonconformists dwelt on the 1662 Act of Uniformity, the 1661 Corporation Act and the 1673 Test Act which—respectively—required schoolmasters and municipal and government office holders to subscribe to the Church of England. They did not win the repeal of the Corporation and Test Acts until 1828, their ministers were unable to conduct marriages until 1836, their sons were unable to enter Oxford until 1854 or graduate from Cambridge until 1856, their property was liable for church rate until 1868, and they faced discrimination even after death until the 1880 Burials Act (which soon proved in need of amendment).[17]

The Congregational Union had overestimated the extent of Nonconformist victory, as it must have known. The principal overt legal and religious sign of discrimination against Nonconformists remained intact: the Church of England 'as by law established' claimed to define the nation's identity and was an integral part of the state. Not for nothing were the largest meetings held to oppose the 1902 bill organized by the

---

Hughes & Co., 1903), p. 68; *Baptist Magazine*, October 1902, p. 425; Dugdale, *Balfour*, pp. 246-47.

16. J. Marchant, *Dr John Clifford, C.H.: Life, Letters and Reminiscences* (London: Cassell, 1924), pp. 122, 128; Congregational Union, *Seventy-first Annual Report*, 1903, p. 3.

17. W. Claridge, *What has the Church Done for Education?* (Manchester: Northern Counties Education League, 1907), *passim*. For the removal of Nonconformist grievances in the mid-Victorian period, see T. Larsen, *Friends of Religious Equality: Nonconformist Politics in Mid-Victorian England* (Woodbridge: Boydell, 1999).

Liberation Society (founded to disestablish the Church of England) for, as in 1870, it objected to extending the practice of establishment by giving rate aid to denominational schools.[18]

Difficult as it had been and was to change the law, discrimination based on attitude, custom and social status was harder to eliminate. Writing of 1870, Morley noted:

> At bottom the battle of the schools was not educational, it was social. It was not religious but ecclesiastical…quarrels about education and catechism and conscience masked the standing jealousy between church and chapel—the unwholesome fruit of the historic mishaps of the sixteenth and seventeenth centuries that separated the nation into two camps, and invested one of them with all the pomp and privilege of social ascendancy.[19]

In 1902 the Nonconformists were better organized than in 1870. The National Free Church Council dated from 1892. In 1896 Gorst's bill caused J. Hirst Hollowell, a Congregational minister in Rochdale, to form the Northern Counties Education League; and in 1898 he joined with R.W. Perks, the Liberal and Wesleyan MP for Louth, well known for his anti-Ritualism, to found the Nonconformist Parliamentary Council. In 1902 Hirst Hollowell established the Passive Resistance League, which provided a power base for himself and Dr Clifford, and organized the non-payment of local rates. (Their campaign dwelt on rates and ignored direct taxation because rates recalled the emotive church rate struggle, and because rates were more politically significant: only about one million people paid income tax, but almost seven million male rate payers were parliamentary electors.)[20]

Apart perhaps from the Kenyon-Slaney amendment, they had no effect on the 1902 bill. When Balfour succeeded his uncle Lord Salisbury as Prime Minister in June 1902 he sacked Gorst (and Gorst's nominal superior at the Board of Education, the Duke of Devonshire) and appointed Sir William Anson (MP for Oxford University) and Lord Londonderry. Neither knew much about the education issue. They really did not need to. As in 1897 Balfour pushed through the measure almost single-handedly,

18. For the argument that Protestantism rather than Anglicanism per se was a source of national identity, see L. Colley, *Britons: Forging the Nation 1707–1837* (New Haven: Yale University Press, 1992), pp. 18-54.

19. Morley, *Gladstone*, II, pp. 306-307.

20. W. Evans and W. Claridge, *James Hirst Hollowell and the Need for Civic Control in Education* (Manchester: Northern Counties Education League, 1911); D. Crane, *The Life Story of Sir Robert W. Perks* (London: Robert Culley, 1909).

changing the standing orders of the House and using all his considerable verbal and tactical dexterity. H.G. Wells used *The New Machiavelli* (1911) to caricature him as Evesham:

> fighting with a diabolical skill to preserve what are in effect religious tests, tests he must have known would outrage and humiliate and injure the conscience of a quarter—and that perhaps the best quarter—of the youngsters who come to the work of elementary education.[21]

Nonconformists knew that their only hope of redress lay in a future Liberal government. The 1891 Newcastle Programme had committed the party to the public control of publicly funded education, and in 1903 Campbell-Bannerman had promised a new education bill. As several historians have described, the Nonconformists worked might and main for the Liberal Party before and during the January 1906 general election. The Tories were badly beaten: their numbers fell from 369 to 157 (132 Conservatives and 25 Liberal Unionists), Balfour was defeated at East Manchester, and Lord Hugh Cecil (another of Lord Salisbury's sons; the main parliamentary advocate of Anglican denominational schools) lost at Greenwich. The Liberals won a great victory: with 377 MPs they had a majority of 220 over the Tories and 84 over all other groups combined (157 Tories, 83 Irish, 29 Labour Representation Committee, 24 Lib-Labs). Estimates vary, but perhaps some 200 of the Liberal MPs were Nonconformists.[22]

They had high hopes of the new government. Campbell-Bannerman (the Prime Minister) was a Presbyterian, and Asquith (the Chancellor of the Exchequer) had Congregational origins. Birrell (President of the Board of Education) was the son of a Baptist minister. Lough, his Parliamentary Secretary, was a Wesleyan. On 3 January 1906 (before the election campaign was over) Lord Crewe convened a Cabinet Committee which Campbell-Bannerman had asked him to chair in order to draft an education bill. Birrell was necessarily a member. So was Lloyd George. He had made his name in Wales with the Llanfrothen burial case (1888), had opposed the 1896 bill and the 1897 act, was a co-founder of the Parliamentary Nonconformist Council, had inspired and led parliamentary opposition to the 1902 Bill, supported the Passive Resistance League and

21. H.G. Wells, *The New Machiavelli* (Harmondsworth: Penguin Books, 1970 [1911]), p. 275.

22. Bebbington, *Nonconformist Conscience*; Koss, *Nonconformity*; Bernstein, *Liberalism and Politics*; Grigg, *Lloyd George*, p. 97; R. Jenkins, *Asquith* (London: Collins, 1964), p. 163.

was a member of the Liberation Society and the National Council of Free Churches. Fowler was the first Wesleyan to enter a British cabinet (1892, President of the Local Government Board) and Perks's legal partner. However, the trio was balanced by Lord Crewe himself (an Anglican), Buxton (an Evangelical Anglican) and Haldane (an amateur philosopher and convinced agnostic).[23]

The committee was the subject of conflicting rumour. Sir Almeric Fitzroy (the Clerk to the Privy Council) heard that the cabinet was bothered by the Roman Catholic bishops, that Lord Crewe had said that it was troubled by Nonconformist militants, and that Haldane feared they might defeat the government. Others thought the cabinet divided between the claims of Lloyd George and Lord Ripon, a champion of the Catholics (Lord Privy Seal). Others again regarded the bill as Lloyd George's drafting forced on Birrell by a cabinet majority. Sir George Kekewich, perhaps the most experienced civil servant in the Board of Education and a critic of the Church of England's influence on educational development, condemned it as a confused compromise.[24]

In fact, marked religious feeling was almost entirely absent from the cabinet and its committee. Campbell-Bannerman was an easy-going pawky Scotsman. Asquith had moved via Balliol, Lincoln's Inn, Parliament and the Tennant family into plutocratic metropolitan society. Birrell had refused to attend chapel at Trinity Hall, Cambridge, but a lucrative career at the bar, and an amiable life as an essayist, had left him an agnostic. Lloyd George claimed to be a Baptist, but was in reality an agnostic who used Nonconformists and Nonconformist issues to advance his political career. Birrell had lost his seat in 1900, had missed the debates on the 1902 bill, and was not re-elected until 1906. He had no real interest in education. He did not believe that the majority of the British people were interested in it. His aims were to defend simple Bible teaching and Catholic and Jewish schools in large towns. Beyond that he was open to suggestion. The committee quickly agreed to secure a national system of elementary education, in which there would be one type of school, with no exceptions.

---

23. Pattison, 'Birrell Education Bill', p. 35; Public Record Office (hereafter PRO), Education 24/116.

24. A. Fitzroy, *Memoirs* (2 vols.; London: Hutchinson, 1925), I, pp. 282, 287, 291; Spender, *Campbell-Bannerman*, II, p. 274; P. Rowland, *The Last Liberal Governments: The Promised Land, 1905–1910* (London: Barrie & Rockcliffe, 1968), p. 77 n.; G.W. Kekewich, *The Education Department and After* (London: Constable, 1920), p. 206.

Birrell considered allowing facilities for denominational teaching in former denominational schools and council schools, but after further consideration proposed clause III to try to allay Anglican fears, and Haldane proposed clause IV to try to conciliate the Roman Catholics (there were only 12 Jewish schools).[25]

Birrell introduced his bill on 9 April with a lucid, powerful speech. He began with the outcome of the election.

> ...unless electoral promises and pledges are fustian and fudge, unless they are mere 'sound and fury' signifying nothing, no other [course] than this was possible. It does not fall short of our pledge, it does not go beyond our pledge, it is our pledge.

He described himself as 'a Nonconformist born and bred, as a man nurtured in Nonconformist history and Nonconformist traditions, as one who might almost be described as having been born in the very library of a Nonconformist minister'. He illustrated Nonconformist grievances: while he was preparing the bill a deputation of Primitive Methodists told him that they had 200,000 communicants and chapels in 4,000 villages, but that in only 850 villages was there any school but an Anglican one. He explained the justice of ending de facto religious tests for teachers, made a case for a national system and the public control of public money, and stressed the bill's concessions to denominational schools. He commended it to the House.[26]

The Liberal frontbenchers reiterated his arguments. Nonconformists and Liberals supported the bill. MacNamara (Camberwell) spoke as a Congregationalist and as the president of the National Union of Teachers, Yoxall (Nottingham) as a Wesleyan and general secretary of the NUT. Alfred Thomas (Merthyr, Lloyd George's ally, later Lord Rhondda) pledged the support of Welsh MPs. Compton Rickett (Osgoldcross) and George White (Norfolk, in 1902 president of the Baptist Union and one of the first advocates of passive resistance) spoke on behalf of rural Congregationalists and Baptists respectively. Adkins spoke for the Nonconformists of industrial South-East Lancashire.[27]

However, the radical Liberal C.F.G. Masterman criticized the bill be-

25. A. Birrell, *Things Past Redress* (London: Faber, 1937), pp. 63, 183-89; Pattison, 'Birrell Education Bill', p. 36; PRO, CAB 37/82/9.

26. *Hansard*, Fourth Series, 155, col. 1017 (9 April 1906).

27. *Hansard*, Fourth Series, 155, cols. 1057 (MacNamara), 1077 (Thomas), 1085 (Compton Rickett), 1103 (White) (9 April 1906); 156, col. 1503 (Yoxall and Adkins) (10 May 1906).

cause it did not propose a fully unified secular system, did not direct extra funds to slum schools and did not touch secondary education. MacDonald, the future Labour Prime Minister, and Snowden, the future Labour Chancellor, made much the same case. The Irish leaders, Redmond and Dillon, criticized it at the second reading, Dillon telling the House 'simple Bible teaching in the schools is to us Catholics worse than no religion'.[28]

To some extent MPs were responding to pressure from outside the House. Archbishop Davidson, who had been consulted by Balfour in 1902, and who had been shown a draft of the 1906 bill by Morant (who was secretary to Lord Crewe's committee) rallied bishops, clergy and Convocation against it, raising petitions said to bear over 750,000 signatures. Anglicans argued that the bill would virtually confiscate their schools, largely substitute simple Bible teaching for denominational instruction, and believed that the ordinary teacher should give the latter.[29]

Lord Ripon failed to win Roman Catholic support for the bill, so the Catholic Education Council and *The Tablet* denounced it, claiming that under clause IV Catholics would lose control of their schools, and demanding that the state provide public money to support them on their own terms—namely a guarantee that 'extended facilities' for denominational teaching would be allowed without the conditions stipulated by the clause. The government knew that Irish Catholics in England had voted Tory in 1885, 1895 and 1900, and that Irish MPs had voted for Gorst's bill in 1896 and Balfour's in 1902; and in 1905 Herbert Gladstone (the Liberal Chief Whip) had estimated that the Irish vote was significant in 96 seats in England and Wales, but had concluded that Liberal victory at the polls depended on Tory Free-Traders and the education issue; so with an overall majority in the Commons the government envisaged making only limited concessions.[30]

Initial Nonconformist response to the bill was favourable. However, when Scott Lidgett held a meeting of the executive of the National Free Church Council, Dr Clifford and Hirst Hollowell criticized the bill. They objected to clause III, more so to clause IV, because the clauses that allowed denominational teaching in schools receiving rate aid—in Clifford's words, 'created a statutory foothold for sectarian privilege in the

28. *Hansard*, Fourth Series, 155, col. 1051 (Masterman) (9 April 1906); 156, col. 1188 and following (MacDonald and Snowden) (10 May 1906).

29. G.K.A. Bell, *Randall Davidson: Archbishop of Canterbury* (2 vols.; Oxford: Oxford University Press, 1935), I, pp. 516-20.

30. Rowland, *Last Liberal Governments*, pp. 345-46.

state school system' and so betrayed the key principle that the state should not extend the practice of establishment by subsidizing the teaching of a particular doctrine. Henceforth, Clifford campaigned against clause IV and Hirst Hollowell against the whole bill, arguing that clause IV in particular sacrificed the interests of the government's Nonconformist voters to those of its Roman Catholic enemies.[31]

Lloyd George had attended the executive meeting (he was a member) but believed that the 'mass of reasonable Liberals' would accept concessions to Anglicans and Catholics, and Herbert Gladstone considered that his Nonconformist constituents would support compromise. Thus on 25 June Birrell explained that in response to continuing Catholic demands he would amend his bill to create 'contracted out' schools: if the LEA refused to grant 'facilities' under clause IV, schools could contract out and rely on exchequer grants alone under a new clause V. The Irish MPs were unsure how to react: Redmond and Dillon had voted against the bill at the second reading on 10 May (when it passed by 410 to 204), and Redmond voted against and Dillon abstained at the third on 30 July (when it passed by 379 to 177).[32]

Hirst Hollowell's ally, the assertive Wesleyan, R.W. Perks, knew exactly how to react. He had spoken and voted for the bill at the second reading, but at the third denounced clause IV as the point 'against which every Free Church in the country had directed its censure' and predicted 'that what little opposition he had given in the House was nothing to the opposition which would be given to it by prominent Nonconformist communities from one end of the country to another'.[33]

Despite introducing clause V, the government had used its majority to overcome persistent Tory opposition and ensure that the bill passed the Commons substantially intact. However, in the Lords almost 500 Tory peers, including a Catholic lobby led by the Duke of Norfolk, and supported by 25 of the 26-strong Anglican episcopal bench, easily outnumbered some 80-odd Liberals, barely a handful of whom were Nonconformists. Lord Lansdowne, the Tory leader in the Lords, worked to a plan, arranged by Balfour, not to raise constitutional issues, or to defeat the bill, but to amend it in detail, mask issues of principle as matters of detail, and

31. Lidgett, *Reminiscences*, pp. 57-60; *idem*, *My Guided Life* (London: Methuen, 1936), pp. 191-92; Evans and Claridge, *Hirst Hollowell*, p. 121.

32. Rowland, *Last Liberal Governments*, p. 350.

33. *Hansard*, Fourth Series, 162, col. 524 (30 July 1906).

accuse the government of refusing a fair and just settlement.[34]

Thus the bill passed its first reading in the Lords (30 July) without debate and its second (1 August) without division, but emerged from committee and passed its third reading by 105 to 20 (6 December) as a measure to compel LEAs to give full financial support to denominational schools and allow denominational instruction into council schools, reversing its original purpose. The Congregational Union, the National Free Church Council, the Nonconformist Parliamentary Council and the General Council of the National Liberal Federation, urged the government to reject the amendments *en bloc*. Davidson, who showed no sympathy for the Nonconformist case, used his influence with King Edward VII to persuade Campbell-Bannerman to negotiate. Davidson wanted clause III amended to allow ordinary teachers to give denominational instruction, but Birrell had already rejected such an amendment, because willingness to give denominational instruction would remain a condition of employment, and so perpetuate de facto religious tests, and Acland, the former education minister, upon whom Campbell-Bannerman relied for expert advice, believed that the government should not give way over this issue. On 10 December Birrell proposed to reject the Lords' amendments *en bloc*, but offered to consider concessions on clauses III and IV and in the subsequent debate it was clear that many Liberal MPs hoped for a compromise. Cardinal Vaughan told Lord Ripon that he hoped the bill would pass, so when on 12 December the Commons voted by 416 to 107 to reject the Lords' amendments, Redmond and Dillon supported the government.[35]

When the bill returned to the Lords, Lord Crewe (as Leader of the House) presented Birrell's proposals for clauses III and IV. Under clause III the government would allow assistant teachers to volunteer to give denominational instruction in all except single-school district schools. Under clause IV it would be prepared to accept three-quarters instead of four-fifths as the proportion of parents required for 'extended facilities'. On 18 December three leaders from each party met in Balfour's room in the Commons, ostensibly to find a solution. Although he knew that the government would not grant it, he stood out for Davidson's original demand, to Lansdowne's probable surprise and Davidson's certain regret, for they had both contemplated a compromise. Next day Lord Crewe made

34. R. Jenkins, *Mr Balfour's Poodle* (London: Heinemann, 1954), pp. 24, 37-41.
35. Spender, *Campbell-Bannerman*, II, pp. 300, 310; P. Magnus, *King Edward the Seventh* (Harmondsworth: Penguin Books, 1970), pp. 435-39; Cruickshank, *Church and State*, pp. 98-100; *Hansard*, Fourth Series, 166, col. 1580 (10 December 1906).

the government's final offer to the Lords. Lord Lansdowne rejected his proposal for clause III volunteers, since they would need the LEAs' agreement. The Duke of Norfolk rejected his further proposals for clause IV, one of which was a promise that teachers would have to be acceptable to the parents' committee in a school, a point which Lord Crewe admitted implied the continuance of religious tests. The Lords therefore refused to reconsider their amendments and sent the bill back to the Commons.[36]

The Duke of Norfolk opposed the bill because he did not know that Cardinal Vaughan now favoured it. Lord Lansdowne opposed it because Balfour had calculated that Campbell-Bannerman would not dissolve Parliament and call a general election on the issue. The government knew that its concessions had tested its supporters' loyalty to the limit (Perks told the Commons and Clifford told *The Times* that they welcomed the bill's defeat) and suspected that the electorate at large had lost interest in the issue. Therefore on 20 December Campbell-Bannerman moved to discharge the bill, an occasion noted for his peroration: 'I say with conviction that a way must be found, a way will be found, by which the will of the people, expressed through their elected representatives, will be made to prevail.'[37]

The 1906 bill would have created a national system of elementary schools, drawing in rural Anglican schools and ensuring the cooperation of urban Catholic schools. Anglican and Catholic claims that the bill proposed to confiscate their schools were incorrect: the LEAs were not obliged to seek or to accept denominational schools, and clause II stipulated that they must do so only 'by agreement with the owners'. On the other hand, the financial incentives for denominational schools to become LEA ones were very strong indeed. Every one of them that did not would lose rate aid and exchequer grants. Those that did would provide denominational instruction at their own expense, but the LEA would pay rent for the school, it would provide for maintenance and repairs (£1,000,000 was set aside for the purpose) and the denomination could use it out of school hours.[38]

36. Magnus, *Edward the Seventh*, p. 439; Fitzroy, *Memoirs*, p. 308; Cruickshank, *Church and State*, pp. 101-102; *Hansard*, Fourth Series, 167, cols. 1382-1418 (19 December 1906).

37. *Hansard*, Fourth Series, 166, col. 1617 (10 December 1906); *The Times*, 20 December 1906; E. Halévy, *The Rule of Democracy* (London: Ernest Benn, 1961), p. 69; *Hansard*, Fourth Series, 167, col. 1379 (20 December 1906).

38. 'Bill to make further provision with respect to Education in England and Wales' (Bill no. 160), *House of Commons: Parliamentary Papers*, 1906, I, pp. 895-923.

Anglicans opposed the bill because it made denominational instruction an optional extra and simple Bible teaching the norm, so opening appointments to non-Anglican teachers and pupil-teachers; thus changing the nature and function of the school from a privately run institution that served a public purpose, to a public institution that served a public purpose, not religious instruction but education. Catholics opposed it because they wanted to keep total control of their schools, which with very few exceptions served a self-contained Catholic community rather than the general public. Thus the government was prepared to make fewer concessions to rural Anglican schools than to urban Catholic ones.

Nonconformists would have gained much from the bill. It would have created a publicly controlled system of elementary schools, would have made simple Bible teaching (often regarded by themselves and their opponents as Nonconformist teaching) the norm in rural schools, would have ended de facto religious tests for appointments, and would have introduced a much stronger conscience clause than had existed since 1870, replacing the right to request to withdraw from religious teaching with the right not to attend it at all, thus perhaps giving parents the confidence to act according to their beliefs.

Why, then, did Dr Clifford and Hirst Hollowell object to the bill? Their opinions had been formed in 1870. They had fought the rate aid lobby during the mid 1890s and shared the contemporary Nonconformist opposition to Roman Catholicism. According to one of Dr Clifford's earliest biographers, 'he has insisted upon the prejudicial effects of clericalism and Romanism upon the State. He dreads few things more than these.' Clifford believed that 'the function of government was exclusively secular'. He declared, 'I am as strongly opposed to the establishment by Parliament of what is called "undenominational" teaching as I am to Romanism... I oppose anybody's attempt to compel me to pay for the propagation of Romanist or any other doctrine.' He and Hirst Hollowell shared the Congregational Union's view of English history: he delighted in being 'a son of Hampden and Cromwell' and Hirst Hollowell was proud of being born in 'Cromwell country'. Intellectually they fought against the principle and practice of religious establishment; emotionally they fought for parity of social status and political equality.[39]

---

39. C.T. Bateman, *John Clifford: Free Church Leader and Preacher* (London: National Council of the Evangelical Free Churches, 1904), pp. 242, 260, 283-84; Marchant, *Clifford*, p. 120; Evans and Claridge, *Hirst Hollowell*, p. 2.

Before the 1870 act had compelled the National Society to accept the conscience clause, Nonconformist children had shared the trials and tribulations of an underclass with future Liberal leaders. Lloyd George had resisted reciting the Apostles' Creed at his Anglican village school in Wales. Birrell had feared to ask to be withdrawn from denominational instruction at his Anglican school in Liverpool. Dr Clifford's Baptist parents had been charged double fees because they had refused to send him from the Anglican village school in Sawley, Derbyshire, to the Church Sunday school. Hirst Hollowell's father, who had preached for the Wesleyan Reformers, had moved his family from his native village to Northampton after the vicar refused to allow his son to attend the Anglican school without going to its Sunday school as well.[40]

However, the two groups had grown apart. Lloyd George and Birrell, unusually able men, had used careers in law and Parliament to achieve social mobility and join the metropolitan elite, thinking in pragmatic national terms. Clifford and Hirst Hollowell had found mobility in the Nonconformist ministry, but had not risen so far, remaining in touch with their roots and attaining but a precarious position in the social hierarchy. Their failure to cooperate confused the 1906 bill's progress, but it was defeated because the establishment (in the modern sense) united against it, Davidson with his campaign and Balfour with his tactics. There is a stark contrast between the two groups. On the one hand were Lloyd George, the shoemaker's nephew; Birrell, the minister's son; Clifford, the factory hand's boy; and Hirst Hollowell, the local preacher's hope. On the other were Davidson (Harrow, Trinity College, Oxford, one of Queen Victoria's favourite clergymen, Archbishop of Canterbury) and Balfour (Eton, Trinity College, Cambridge, Lord Salisbury's nephew and political heir).

The 1906 bill's defeat certainly showed the fragility and weakness of the Liberal–Nonconformist alliance, but also had a detrimental effect on education in England and Wales. In its final form the bill contained provisions for vacation classes, health and physical education, and scholarships and bursaries, and its discharge was regretted by MacNamara and Keir Hardie, the Labour leader, who both recognized that it would have benefited working-class children in elementary schools. It would also have removed the twopence limit on rate aid for secondary schools, which is

---

40. P. Rowland, *Lloyd George* (London: Barrie and Jenkins, 1975), pp. 14-15; *Hansard*, Fourth Series, 155, col. 1017 (9 April 1906); Byrt, *Clifford*, pp. 11-18; Evans and Claridge, *Hirst Hollowell*, pp. 5-6.

usually regarded as the 1902 act's most constructive provision.[41]

Thus the 1902 act remained in force. The Board of Education's 1904 regulations had contained few signs of the innovations proposed by the Devonshire, Samuelson and Bryce Reports. The Secondary School Regulations (written by Morant, a Winchester classicist and Oxford theologian) ensured that the new secondary schools followed closely the conventional pattern of the existing public and grammar schools. The Primary School Regulations (possibly drafted by Morant) imposed a circumscribed purpose and curriculum on the elementary schools.[42]

The 1902 act left over 14,000 denominational elementary schools (with some 3,000,000 pupils) and about 5,700 council elementary schools (2,600,000 pupils) in an administrative limbo. The Board of Education took few educational initiatives, and many of the over-300 LEAs were incapable of, or too poor to, take any of their own. The 1902 act was less generous to the denominational elementary schools than the 1906 bill had proposed: they received no rent from the LEAs, which paid for only fair wear and tear. Anglicans and Roman Catholics could barely afford to maintain their elementary schools, let alone to improve them, and so resisted educational innovations that would have entailed extra expense. The Churches built hardly any new schools after 1918, and between then and 1939 gave up their existing schools at an average of 70 a year.[43]

When Butler became President of the Board of Education in 1941 he found that more than half of the elementary schools in England and Wales (accounting for one-third of the pupils) were denominational schools, and that most of their buildings dated from before 1902: of 10,553 schools, 9,683 were over 40 years old, and 'Far too many were appallingly out of date'. Fortunately he was able to work with Arthur Greenwood, Labour minister without portfolio (whom he described as a 'disciple of Dr Clifford'), and William Temple, Archbishop of Canterbury, to solve 'the religious problem' which 'proved to be by far the biggest obstacle' to producing a

41. N.J. Richards, 'British Nonconformity and the Liberal Party 1868–1906', *Journal of Religious History* 9 (1977), pp. 390-402 (390-91); N.J. Richards, 'The Education Bill of 1906 and the Decline of Political Nonconformity', *Journal of Ecclesiastical History* 23 (1972), pp. 49-63; *Hansard*, Fourth Series, 167, cols. 1750, 1752 (10 December 1906).

42. Maclure, *Educational Documents*, pp. 154, 156.

43. Maclure, *Educational Documents*, p. 149; Cruickshank, *Church and State*, p. 103.

new framework for schools, the 1944 act. Its provision of 'voluntary controlled' and 'voluntary aided' schools paralleled the 1906 bill's clause III and clause IV schools. As Butler wrote, 'Birrell's Bill of 1906 was not unlike my final settlement'.[44]

Educational progress could resume.

44. R.A. Butler, *The Education Act of 1944 and After* (London: Longmans, 1965), pp. 4-5; Butler, *The Art of the Possible* (London: Hamish Hamilton, 1971), pp. 98-99.

ABRAHAM LINCOLN, RELIGION AND SELF-IMPROVEMENT

Richard Carwardine

Whig Self-Improvement and the Problem of American Slavery

Abraham Lincoln, the first Republican president, grew to political maturity as a Whig. No mere party flag of convenience, his Whiggery was an expression of his deepest values. The Whigs were improvers, devoted to advancing the nation's economic development. During the 1830s and 1840s their so-called 'American System' provided a modernizing programme of government protection for domestic manufacturing, federal support for improvements to commercial roads and waterways, and a national bank to provide a secure supply of reliable credit. Whig improvers offered the young republic a corresponding moral vision. The flowering of Protestant evangelicalism during the Second Great Awakening, a process that reached its peak in the 1830s, helped fashion the party's ethos. Whigs were a diverse group, by no means composed exclusively of pious Christians; nor did the party monopolize evangelical support. But it was very much the home of New England (or Yankee) Protestants, especially Congregationalists and New School Presbyterians; it held a particular appeal for British-Americans. Whig evangelicals' admiration for self-discipline, self-control, sobriety, thrift and moral self-improvement shaped the party's values, sweetly complementing its programme of economic improvement, and giving it the nerve that would help it meet the mid-century challenges of mass immigration, social flux and territorial expansion. Critics of Whiggery, then and now, have seen the Whigs' concern with personal responsibility and social order as an expression of a moral absolutism, an anxious paternalism and a desire for cultural strait-jacketing. More positively, these same concerns led Whig reformers into schemes of public education designed to produce a literate, ambitious and informed citizenry, trained to cultivate their higher faculties.[1]

1. D.W. Howe, *The Political Culture of the American Whigs* (Chicago: University of Chicago Press, 1979), pp. 1-42.

Lincoln's early history is a chronicle of the ambitious self-improver. By the time he reached his majority in 1830 he had had enough of the hard life of the western farmer. He shortly took his leave of the family home, hired himself out as a Mississippi flatboatman and then settled in the aspiring commercial hamlet of New Salem, Illinois, where he progressed through a sequence of occupations: clerk, mill manager, (unsuccessful) store owner, postmaster, surveyor and self-taught lawyer. When he rode out of the village for good in 1837, to join a law practice in the state capital, Springfield, he enjoyed a reputation for diligence, ingenuity and conscientious self-improvement. By then he was already in his second term as a state congressman, fast establishing himself as one of the leading Whigs in central Illinois.[2]

Lincoln shared the Whigs' enthusiasm for economic development and the commercial opportunities of the emerging national market. He became an earnest exponent of the American System, by which the young state of Illinois, with its rich soil and natural resources, might achieve unprecedented prosperity. Here, he believed, poor subsistence farmers and mechanics, through industry, enterprise and self-discipline, could realistically aspire to better themselves as he had done. Lincoln's personal experience and meritocratic convictions combined to make him far less anxious about democratic upheaval than many of his fellow Whigs. Though he married into the respectable middle class and, through politics and the law, became the associate of bankers, large landowners, cattle kings and the professional elite, he continued to evince an empathy for those beyond the charmed circle of bourgeois success, including modest farmers and even town drunks. No admirer of social pretension or aristocratic ostentation, he continued to wear plain and ill-fitting clothes, practised frugality and even austerity, told rustic stories and indulged in crude jokes.[3] He was moved less by concern for top-down social control and order than by a wish to broaden opportunities for individual fulfilment through economic transformation.

The logic of Lincoln's economic thought dictated a social and moral

---

2. Outstanding among the many biographies of Lincoln are B.P. Thomas, *Abraham Lincoln: A Biography* (New York: Alfred A. Knopf, 1952); D.H. Donald, *Lincoln* (London: Jonathan Cape, 1995); and A.C. Guelzo, *Abraham Lincoln: Redeemer President* (Grand Rapids: Eerdmans, 1999).

3. D.L. Wilson and R.O. Davis (eds.), *Herndon's Informants: Letters, Interviews, and Statements about Abraham Lincoln* (Chicago: University of Illinois Press, 1998), pp. 31, 108, 159, 161, 251, 438, 646.

order at odds with southern slavery. He made his first political statement of hostility to the 'peculiar institution' in 1837, in a protest to the Illinois state legislature, when he declared the South's labour system to be 'founded on both injustice and bad policy'.[4] But his anti-slavery temper was a lifelong fact, a disposition in part absorbed from his parents and reinforced by his earliest memories of Kentucky. A year before his death Lincoln wrote: 'I am naturally antislavery. If slavery is not wrong, nothing is wrong. I can not remember when I did not so think, and feel.'[5] His argument pulled together several strands of thought, and drew especially on the doctrines of natural rights and human equality set out in the nation's founding texts. All men, he insisted, black and white, should be free to enjoy the fruits of their own work. (Lincoln, however, took a common Whig view that slavery would die only gradually, and that blacks' best economic and cultural opportunities lay in developing their own self-governed colonies, in Africa or Central America.) Free labour offered the prospect of '[a]dvancement—improvement in condition' and kept the social order fluid.[6] By the 1850s a fast developing industrial sector had spawned a burgeoning wage-earning class, but Lincoln—his judgment shaped by the seeming boundlessness of America and by his own personal experience—had no worries that a permanent proletariat might be in the making. He saw no insuperable barriers to the social progress of any free, enterprizing and conscientious working man. Slavery, however, the enemy of this kind of economic meritocracy, discouraged individual enterprise in both planters and slaves. Lincoln regarded the glitter of slave-owning 'as highly seductive to the thoughtless and giddy young men who looked upon work as vulgar and ungentlemanly'.[7] As he told Hill Lamon: 'you Virginians shed barrels of perspiration while standing off at a distance and superintending the work your slaves do for you. It is different with us. Here it is every fellow for himself, or he doesn't get there.'[8]

Slavery also narrowed African Americans' mental horizons and denied them the cultural opportunities that free labourers enjoyed. Its defenders,

---

4.   A. Lincoln (hereafter AL), 'Protest in Illinois Legislature on Slavery', 3 March 1837, in R.P. Basler (ed.), *The Collected Works of Abraham Lincoln* (9 vols; New Brunswick, NJ: Rutgers University Press, 1953–55), I, pp. 74-75 (hereinafter *CWAL*).

5.   AL to Albert G. Hodges, 4 April 1864, *CWAL*, VII, pp. 281-82.

6.   AL, 'Fragment on Free Labor', 17 September 1859[?], *CWAL*, III, p. 462.

7.   Wilson and Davis (eds.), *Herndon's Informants*, p. 183.

8.   W.H. Lamon, *Recollections of Lincoln, 1847–1865* (ed. D.L. Teillard; Lincoln: University of Nebraska Press, 1994; repr. from the 2nd edn of 1911), p. 15.

Lincoln told a gathering of free farmers, 'assumed that labor and education are incompatible'. Slaveholders wanted each of their workers to be 'a blind horse upon a tread-mill'. They saw education in this instance as:

> not only useless, but pernicious, and dangerous. In fact, it is, in some sort, deemed a misfortune that laborers should have heads at all... A Yankee who could invent a strong *handed* man without a head would receive the everlasting gratitude of the 'mud-sill' advocates.
>
> But...Free Labor argues that, as the Author of man makes every individual with one head and one pair of hands, it was probably intended that heads and hands should cooperate as friends...that that particular head, should direct and control that particular pair of hands...that each head is the natural guardian, director, and protector of the hands and mouth inseparably connected with it; and that being so, every head should be cultivated, and improved, by whatever will add to its capacity for performing its charge. In one word Free Labor insists on universal education.[9]

Lincoln's own formal education had been limited to just a few months in total, in a rudimentary 'blab' school where parrot-learning was the rule, but by strength of will and what his cousin John Hanks termed his 'constant and voracious' appetite for books he had systematically overcome what another contemporary called 'his low breeding and surrounding, his small opportunities for education & culture', and acquired the intellectual and technical tools with which to flourish professionally. Lincoln, whose stated political ambition was 'to lift men up & give 'Em a chance', knew that education was integral to personal transformation.[10]

In 1854 Stephen Douglas's Kansas–Nebraska Act, by repealing the Missouri Compromise, an intersectional compact of over 30 years' standing, opened up the western territories to slavery's expansion. The new law stunned anti-slavery northerners and served as a catalyst in the destruction of the Whigs. From a position of historical defensiveness, with every prospect of its ultimate extinction, slavery now appeared likely to swamp the nation. During his years of state-level politics, slavery had remained largely on the periphery of Lincoln's field of vision. Now, however, the Nebraska Act reawakened him to active politics and set him on a course that would culminate in his election to the presidency in 1860, as the candidate of a Republican party grounded on the principle of quarantining slavery. His rhetorical assault on the institution, as it evolved after 1854,

9. AL, 'Address before the Wisconsin State Agricultural Society, Milwaukee, Wisconsin', 30 September 1859, *CWAL*, II, pp. 479-80.

10. Wilson and Davis (eds.), *Herndon's Informants*, pp. 455, 678, 705.

evinced a new and sharp moral edge. Joshua Speed, his closest friend, wrote of his fellow Kentuckian

> Unlike all other men there was an entire harmony between his public and private life. He must believe that he was right and that he had truth and justice with him or he was a weak man. But no man could be stronger if he thought that he was right.

Likewise, Joseph Gillespie, a trusted colleague, considered Lincoln's powerful sense of justice the key to his actions. '[T]he sense of right & wrong was extremely acute in his nature', he recalled. 'He was extremely just and fair minded. He was as gentle as a girl and yet as firm for the right as adamant.' Gillespie located Lincoln's earnest hostility to slavery and the Nebraska Bill—'about the only public question on which he would become excited'—in an affront to his sense of justice.[11]

Lincoln's was just one of a chorus of voices raised against the repeal of the Missouri Compromise. Indeed, by the time he spoke out, a ferocious storm of protest had emanated from a radicalized northern pulpit. Whig evangelicals preached to overflowing congregations, addressed political meetings and filled newspaper columns with diatribes against Douglas's abomination. Congress was flooded with their remonstrations, including a 200-foot scroll filled with the signatures of 3,000 New England clergy. Their protests dripped with moral absolutes, castigating the 'slave power' and its allies less for an impolitic act, than for wickedness, treachery, criminality and ungodliness. The breadth and intensity of northern Protestantism's reaction to the Nebraska Act provide a measure of the degree to which the reformist, optimistic, post-millennialist evangelicalism of the Second Great Awakening had entered the nation's political bloodstream.[12]

Both Lincoln and the anti-slavery evangelicals feared that Douglas's measure signified an ominous first step towards the moral reorientation of the Republic, and the strong ethical cast of Lincoln's Whiggery and emerging Republicanism inevitably raises the question of how it related to the religious mindset of these fellow Whiggish Republicans. Lincoln's succinct formulation, 'if slavery is not wrong, nothing is wrong', probably owed something to a New Haven Congregational minister, Leonard Bacon, whose essays on slavery, published in 1846, used similar phraseology and

---

11. Wilson and Davis (eds.), *Herndon's Informants*, pp. 183-84, 499, 507.
12. R.J. Carwardine, *Evangelicals and Politics in Antebellum America* (New Haven: Yale University Press, 1993), pp. 235-40.

had found their way to Springfield.[13] But the question of the religious sources of his moral concern is more easily put than answered. Lincoln made no public statement of personal faith in the 1850s and many of those close to him had no idea about his private views. Judge David Davis, in whose company Lincoln spent many hours on the Eighth Judicial Circuit, considered him 'the most reticent—Secretive man I Ever Saw—or Expect to See', and thought it absurd that any but rare intimates should claim to have known his mind.[14] Those who, after Lincoln's death, did profess to fathom him were scarcely disinterested parties, and their unseemly tussle for his soul leaves us chary about accepting their conflicting judgments at face value.

When Lincoln's first biographer, Josiah Holland, poured him into the mould of a Christian president, a disbelieving William Herndon found the outcome unrecognizable from the man with whom he had practised law. He set about interviewing those who might be in a position to know, and in a series of lectures denied there were any christological elements in Lincoln's spiritual thought. Few religious traditions have subsequently failed to embrace him. Friends have pointed to his Virginia Quaker forebears, Baptists to his parents' faith, Methodists to a supposed conversion at a camp-meeting, Catholics to a surreptitious joining of their Church, and Presbyterians to a public attendance at theirs. Masons, Unitarians and Universalists have all clasped him to their bosoms. Following the visits of two or three mediums to the wartime White House, the Spiritualists claimed him as one of theirs, though Lincoln himself was facetiously dismissive, remarking that the contradictory voices of the spirits at these seances reminded him of his cabinet meetings.[15]

Naturally, such chauvinism cuts little ice with modern scholars. Mostly, though, their treatments of Lincoln's religion have offered little more than a plausible sketching of the phases of his evolving faith: the Baptist milieu

13. Bacon, whose uncle taught in Springfield, wrote, 'If that form of government, that system of social order is not wrong—if those laws of the southern states, by virtue of which slavery exists there, and is what it is, are not wrong—nothing is wrong'. L. Bacon, *Slavery Discussed in Occasional Essays, from 1833 to 1846* (Miami: Mnemosyne, 1969 [1846]), p. x; T.D. Bacon, *Leonard Bacon: A Statesman in the Church* (New Haven: Yale University Press, 1931), pp. 269-73. For a cautious judgment, see D.E. Fehrenbacher and V. Fehrenbacher (eds.), *Recollected Words of Abraham Lincoln* (Stanford, CA: Stanford University Press, 1996), p. 446.

14. Wilson and Davis (eds.), *Herndon's Informants*, p. 348.

15. W.E. Barton, *The Soul of Abraham Lincoln* (New York: George H. Doran, 1920), pp. 225-43.

of his upbringing, his dalliance with deistic freethinkers as a young man in New Salem, his more conventional churchgoing as a married man in Springfield, and his maturing theological thoughtfulness in the face of the grisly realities of war. With the exception of Allen Guelzo's recent prize-winning intellectual portrait of Lincoln, his biographers have largely failed to fathom his religious thought or to integrate the reflective Lincoln with Lincoln the politician and president. Rather, the dominant biographical themes have been those of Lincoln's pragmatic shrewdness and political management.

In the course of his adult life, Lincoln faced the traumas of courtship and a broken engagement, embarked on an uncertain marriage, suffered the painful loss of two young sons (Eddie in 1850 and Willie in 1862), and then confronted the carnage of a fratricidal war. It would have been strange indeed had a man so given to introspection not added new layers to his understanding of the meaning of life and death. If, as Gillespie judged, he was not given particularly to metaphysical speculation, Lincoln's old New Salem friend, Isaac Cogdal, was surely right when he asserted that 'his mind was full of terrible enquiry—and was skeptical in a good sense'. Speed was sure that over the years Lincoln 'was a growing man in religion', advancing from religious scepticism in the 1830s to serious Christian enquiry in the White House. Though James Matheny suggested that the only change to occur resided in Lincoln's greater discretion, not in his views, which Matheny thought remained sceptical (at least up to 1861), there are good grounds for believing that the mature Lincoln of the 1850s was more receptive to Protestant orthodoxy than he had been 20 years earlier.[16]

The argument presented here is that the essential elements of Lincoln's religious outlook in the pre-war decade contributed to the new tone and substance of his speeches following his return to politics in 1854. For the first time he devoted whole speeches to the question of slavery, including its corrosive effect on individual enterprise and aspiration, and to exposing the moral gulf that he saw separating Republicans from their opponents. In the Peoria address of 1854, the celebrated Bloomington speech in 1856, the joint debates with Douglas at Galesburg, Quincy and Alton in 1858, and the Cooper Union speech of 1860, to list only the most notable examples, Lincoln found a moral edge for which political opportunism provides only the shallowest of explanations.

16. Wilson and Davis (eds.), *Herndon's Informants*, pp. 156, 441, 476, 505, 521, 576-77.

Lincoln's Religious Faith

Lincoln's earliest experience of religion came, naturally enough, through his parents. As 'hard-shell' Baptists, they subscribed to a predestinarian, hyper-Calvinist system of beliefs, including the view that missionary work was an act of presumption against the Almighty, who needed no assistance to achieve his foreordained plan. When Thomas Lincoln moved to Indiana he became a leading man among the 'Separates' there. It was a milieu of unlettered preachers and few books. Young Abraham generally attended meetings at church but, unlike his sister, who was admitted to membership, he made no profession of faith. 'Abe had no particular religion—didnt think of that question at the time, if he ever did', his stepmother, Sarah Bush Johnston, recalled. 'He never talked about it.'[17]

The Kentucky and Indiana years left Lincoln with a mixed legacy of belief. Negatively, he can have found little to celebrate in the particular rigidities and exclusiveness of a strict Baptist creed, nominally Calvinist, but one that Calvin himself would barely have recognized. He had no time for the sectarian brawling that marked the developing West. It was here that were sown the seeds of his aversion to church creeds and his scepticism about 'the possibility, or propriety, of settling the religion of Jesus Christ in the models of man-made creeds and dogmas'. He saw little to admire in the crude emotionalism and religious 'enthusiasm' of frontier revivalism, and was more likely to parody and deride the gymnastics of uneducated hellfire preachers than to respect them. '[W]hen I hear a man preach', he remarked, 'I like to see him act as if he were fighting bees!'[18]

At the same time, Lincoln held on to much of what he had learnt. Not least, Lincoln's commonly noted fatalism, which he never shed, reflects the continuing legacy of his high Calvinist upbringing. Equally influential were the handful of books that he read over and over. These included such standards of the English Nonconformist tradition as Bunyan's *Pilgrim's Progress* and Watts's hymns: works whose simplicity and strength of language effected an unmeasurable but undoubted influence on Lincoln's own prose, at its best spare and taut. Above all, he encountered the King

---

17. Wilson and Davis (eds.), *Herndon's Informants*, pp. 107, 215, 233, 455; A.C. Guelzo, 'Abraham Lincoln and the Doctrine of Necessity', *Journal of the Abraham Lincoln Association* 18 (1997), pp. 57-81 (66-67).

18. W.J. Wolf, *The Almost Chosen People: A Study of the Religion of Abraham Lincoln* (Garden City, NY: Doubleday, 1959), pp. 50-51, 74-75; Fehrenbacher and Fehrenbacher, *Recollected Words of Abraham Lincoln*, p. 457.

James Bible. He acquired a command of the Scriptures which would continue to inform his rhetoric throughout his life. His stepmother, seeking to puncture overblown claims about Lincoln's early piety, noted that 'Abe, read the bible some, though not as much as said: he sought more congenial books'. But the habit of Scripture-reading was established and thereafter not lost. Allied to his tenacious memory, his close acquaintance with the Bible gave him a formidable weapon for use on audiences steeped in the Scriptures. An Illinois minister, seeing Lincoln in the street regaling a gathering of citizens with a sequence of anecdotes, remarked as he passed, 'Where the great ones are there will the people be'. Quickly Lincoln replied, 'Ho! Parson a little more scriptural; "Where the carcass is there will the eagles be gathered together." '[19]

To know the Bible well is not necessarily to consider it inspired. Dennis Hanks, a cousin who lived with the family in the Indiana years, questioned whether Lincoln really believed in it, and there is barely any doubt that during the 1830s, as a young man in New Salem and Springfield, Lincoln openly contested its authority.[20] Like others in his circle, he read Tom Paine's *Age of Reason* and Constantin de Volney's *Ruins*, and found in their critique of Christianity and the Scriptures, and in their pursuit of a rational theology, much to satisfy his logical, inquiring mind. As an aspiring lawyer, he clearly warmed to their testing of the Bible by the rules of evidence, and to their use of reason and ridicule to expose its contradictions. At the same time he evinced a strong partiality for the caustic poetry of Robert Burns, and delighted in his the mocking satire on Calvinist self-righteousness, 'Holy Willie's Prayer'.[21]

Amongst his circle in New Salem, and then in Springfield as the junior partner of John Stuart, Lincoln had a reputation as 'an infidel'. We need not dismiss as unfounded (as have some of his defenders) the claim that Lincoln wrote an essay questioning the Bible as divine revelation but that New Salem friends made him burn it in order to prevent damage to his public career: the story is of a piece with what else we know of his views

19. Wilson and Davis (eds.), *Herndon's Informants*, pp. 37, 40-41, 76, 106-107, 499, 573 (spelling corrected). Lincoln was quoting Lk. 17.37.

20. Wilson and Davis (eds.), *Herndon's Informants*, p. 106.

21. D.L. Wilson, *Honor's Voice: The Transformation of Abraham Lincoln* (New York: Alfred A. Knopf, 1998), pp. 73-80. Burns's poem includes the stanza: 'O Thou that in the Heavens does dwell, / Wha, as it pleases best Thysel, / Sens ane to Heaven an' ten to Hell / A' for Thy glory, / And no for onie guid or ill / They've done before Thee!'

at this time, and was later conceded by several of his circle. James Matheny recalled that his father, a Methodist preacher, though 'loving Lincoln with all his soul[,] hated to vote for him' in the mid-1830s because of the taint of unbelief. Matheny himself, friendly with Lincoln in the Springfield office, told how he had heard Lincoln 'call Christ a bastard', how he 'would talk about Religion—pick up the Bible—read a passage—and then Comment on it—show its falsity—and its follies on the grounds of Reason—would then show its own self made & self uttered Contradictions and would in the End—finally ridicule it'. Stuart, too, thought Lincoln's unorthodoxy 'bordered on atheism'. He 'went further against Christian beliefs—& doctrines & principles than any man I ever heard: he shocked me—... Lincoln always denied that Jesus was the...son of God as understood and maintained by the Christian world'.[22]

Lincoln was in fact no more of an atheist than Paine, who, despite his popular reputation, had not launched an assault on all religion. Even in his New Salem period Lincoln believed in a Creator. Isaac Cogdal, while conceding the existence of Lincoln's essay denying the inspiration of Scripture, insisted that his friend 'believed in God—and all the great substantial groundworks of Religion'. But this was not a quixotic God who would act on impulse or anger. Cogdal, claiming to have often discussed religion with Lincoln between 1834 and 1859, considered him 'a Universalist tap root & all in faith and sentiment', someone who could not subscribe to the orthodox Calvinist belief in hell and endless punishment. Corroborative evidence comes from Mentor Graham, who gave Lincoln some instruction at New Salem and who recalled reading a manuscript that Lincoln gave him in defence of universal salvation. Denying that 'the God of the universe' would ever become 'excited, mad, or angry', Lincoln 'took the passage, "As in Adam all die, even so in Christ shall all be made alive"', to contradict the theory of eternal damnation. It is unlikely that Lincoln was here endorsing the Christian doctrine of atonement, but rather affirming the case for a Creator who operated according to the maxims of justice and rationality in his dealings with humankind.[23]

22. Wilson and Davis (eds.), *Herndon's Informants*, pp. 24, 61-62, 432, 441, 472, 576-77; W.B. Stevens, *A Reporter's Lincoln* (ed. M. Burlingame; Lincoln: University of Nebraska Press, 1998), pp. 11-12; Wilson, *Honor's Voice*, pp. 81-83.

23. Wilson and Davis (eds.), *Herndon's Informants*, p. 441; Wolf, *Almost Chosen People*, pp. 47-48; Barton, *Soul of Abraham Lincoln*, pp. 347-49. Fehrenbacher and Fehrenbacher, *Recollected Words of Abraham Lincoln*, pp. 110-11, doubt Cogdal's reliability.

Lincoln's personal and religious circumstances in Springfield worked to refine and reshape his opinions. For the first time he belonged to a community that numbered educated, college-trained ministers, settled pastors capable of engaging intelligently with unorthodox opinion. Hesitant at first about attending any of the city's fashionable churches, Lincoln, after his marriage to Mary Todd, became an occasional worshipper at the Episcopal church. When their three-year-old son Eddie died in 1850, the family switched their allegiance to the First Presbyterian Church, whose Old School pastor, James Smith, had conducted the funeral ceremony. Mary entered into full membership, and the Lincolns rented a pew (though Lincoln himself would be by no means the most regular of attenders: he had, as one friendly commentator politely put it, 'western and not puritan views' of sabbath observance). Smith was an intellectual Scot familiar with the works of Paine, Volney and other freethinkers. In *The Christian's Defense*, a substantial work of theology, Smith deployed rational argument and the evidence of historical and natural sciences to plead the cause of orthodox Christianity. He gave a copy of his book to Lincoln, whose home he quite regularly visited, and who, Smith maintained, gave the arguments on both sides 'a most patient, impartial and Searching investigation'. It was not Lincoln's only reading on the issues of faith and reason. He gave Robert Chambers's *Vestiges of the Natural History of Creation* (1844), an analysis of Christianity and evolutionary science, a close examination; Herndon and Jesse Fell lent him the writings of liberal theologians.[24]

In consequence, according to Smith, Lincoln avowed 'his belief in the Divine Authority and the Inspiration of the Scriptures'. Ninian Edwards remembered Lincoln, his brother-in-law, declaring that thanks to his dialogues with his pastor, 'I am now convinced of the truth of the Christian religion'. Several of Lincoln's acquaintances maintained that in the late 1850s he had professed his belief in the atonement of Christ for the final salvation of all men. This was the Methodist Jonathan Harnett's recollection of a discussion in Lincoln's office in 1858, when Lincoln had said 'that Christ must reign supreme, high over all, The Saviour of all'. Isaac Cogdal, a Universalist, recalled a similar, perhaps the same, meeting 'in 1859' at which Lincoln declared 'that all that was lost by the

---

24. Wilson and Davis (eds.), *Herndon's Informants*, p. 549; Wolf, *Almost Chosen People*, pp. 57, 80-87; *Herndon's Life of Lincoln: The History and Personal Recollections of Abraham Lincoln as Originally Written by William H. Herndon and Jesse W. Weik with an Introduction and Notes by Paul M. Angle* (Cleveland: World Publishing Company, 1942), p. 354.

transgression of Adam was made good by the atonement: all that was lost by the fall was made good by the sacrifice'. A colleague on the judicial circuit, John H. Wickizer, considered Lincoln 'very liberal in his views', but he added, 'I think he believed in "Jesus Christ, and him crucified" '. It is, then, possible that Lincoln's intellectual development within a Presbyterian institutional framework in Springfield made him much more receptive to the idea of the inspiration of Scripture. It is also possible that he had embraced a more christological theology, now using the terms 'Lord' and 'Saviour' in more than just a humanist sense.[25]

It is possible, but the weight of evidence is against it. In a rare moment of private openness, during his father's last days in 1851, Lincoln asked his stepbrother John Johnston to tell Thomas Lincoln

> to remember to call upon, and confide in, our great, and good, and merciful Maker; who will not turn away from him any in extremity. He notes the fall of a sparrow, and numbers the hairs of our heads; and He will not forget the dying man who puts his trust in Him.

Were his father to die, he added, 'he will soon have a joyous [meeting] with many loved ones gone before; and where [the rest] of us, through the help of God, hope ere long [to join] them'.[26] The statement confirmed Lincoln's faith in an omnipotent and kindly Creator, but significantly there is no Christology. (If there is anything theologically striking about it then it is its clear allusion to an afterlife—a subject on which Lincoln had moved towards orthodoxy since his New Salem days, when he had allegedly declared, 'It isn't a pleasant thing to think that when we die that is the last of us'.)[27]

The balance of testimony in fact points to Lincoln's inclining towards essentially Unitarian, not Trinitarian, beliefs in the 1850s. Jesse Fell, a Bloomington lawyer and liberal Christian who had 'repeated Conversations' with Lincoln on religious subjects over a period of two decades, argued forcefully that during Lincoln's Springfield years, 'whilst he held many opinions in common with the great mass of Christian believers, he did not believe in what are regarded as the orthodox or evangelical views of Christianity'. Accepting that Lincoln might have changed his outlook during his presidency, Fell was sure that throughout the time of their

---

25. Wilson and Davis (eds.), *Herndon's Informants*, pp. 516, 547; Barton, *Soul of Abraham Lincoln*, pp. 324, 348-49; Wolf, *Almost Chosen People*, pp. 103-108.

26. AL to John D. Johnson, 12 January 1851, *CWAL*, II, p. 97.

27. Stevens, *A Reporter's Lincoln*, p. 12.

friendship his views put him 'entirely outside the pale of the Christian Church'.

> On the i[n]nate depravity of Man, the character & office of the great head of the Church, the atonement, the infallibility of the written revelation, the performance of myricles, the nature & design of present & future rewards & punishments…and many other Subjects, he held opinions…utterly at variance with what are usually taught in the Churches.

In the mid-1850s they discussed at length the Unitarianism of William Ellery Channing and Theodore Parker, whose works Lincoln read and admired. Without subscribing to everything they argued, Lincoln warmed to their liberalism and rationality. 'His religious views were eminantly practical', Fell insisted, 'and are Sumed up on these two propositions, "the Fatherhood of God, and the Brotherhood of Man".'[28]

Lincoln's son Robert wrote that he knew nothing 'of Dr Smith's having "converted" my father from "Unitarian" to "Trinitarian" belief': he had never heard Lincoln speak of it. John Stuart went further. He told William Herndon that Smith had 'tried to Convert Lincoln from Infidelity so late as 1858 and Couldn't do it'. Listening for Lincoln's authentic voice in the recollections of his friends and acquaintances of this time, we perhaps hear it most clearly through James W. Keyes, a Springfield tailor. Lincoln, he said, gave as his reason for believing in an omnipotent Creator 'that in view of the Order and harmony of all nature…it would have been More miraculous to have Come about by chance, than to have been created and arranged by some great thinking power'. As for the theory that

> Christ is God, or equal to the Creator[,] he said [it] had better be taken for granted—for by the test of reason all might become infidels on that subject, for evidence of Christs divinity Came to us in somewhat doubtful Shape— but that the Sistom of Christianity was an ingenious one at least—and perhaps was Calculated to do good.[29]

This wary and qualified formulation of belief has an authentic Lincolnian ring to it.

Whether or not Lincoln moved closer intellectually to a conventional Trinitarian Christian stance during these years, all were agreed that he was not, in Mary Todd Lincoln's words, 'a technical Christian'; he had, she said, 'no hope—& no faith in the usual acceptation of those words'. His neighbours knew this too. One of his warmest evangelical supporters in

---

28. Wilson and Davis (eds.), *Herndon's Informants*, pp. 578-80.
29. Wilson and Davis (eds.), *Herndon's Informants*, pp. 360, 464, 524, 576.

Springfield, the New School minister Albert Hale, was saddened that Lincoln was not 'born of God'.[30] Most, though, were adamant that he was '*naturally* religious', whatever his shortcomings over ceremonials and creeds. 'He would ridicule the Puritans, or swear in a moment of vexation; but yet his heart was full of natural and cultivated religion', insisted one of his closest associates, Leonard Swett.

> [Judged] by the higher rule of purity of conduct, of honesty of motive, of unyielding fidelity to the right and acknowledging God as the Supreme Ruler, then he filled all the requirements of true devotion and love of his neighbor as himself.[31]

Even those who doubted his piety found it hard to question the moral integrity and private behaviour of a man known not to drink, smoke or gamble.

On one feature of Lincoln's thought there was no disagreement. Lincoln described himself as a lifelong fatalist, and none demurred. 'What is to be will be', he told congressman Isaac Arnold. 'I have found all my life as Hamlet says: "There's a divinity that shapes our ends, Rough-hew them how we will."' Mary Todd heard that formulation many times, for as she confirmed to Herndon, Lincoln's 'maxim and philosophy was—"What is to be will be and no cares of ours can arrest the decree."' Not that Herndon needed reminding. He recalled many conversations about predestination in which Lincoln had asserted that 'all things were fixed, doomed in one way or the other, from which there was no appeal' and that 'no efforts or prayers of ours can change, alter, modify, or reverse the decree'. Lincoln often told his law partner that he had a foreboding of 'some terrible end', but when Joseph Gillespie and others urged him to take precautions against assassination, he took a fatalistic view. 'I will be cautious', he told an anxious acquaintance shortly before his final departure from Springfield, 'but God's will be done. I am in his hands... and what he does I must bow to—God rules, and we should submit.'[32]

The predestinarian ethos of Lincoln's hyper-Calvinist, Baptist upbring-

30. M. Burlingame (ed.), *An Oral History of Abraham Lincoln: John G. Nicolay's Interviews and Essays* (Carbondale: Southern Illinois University Press, 1996), pp. 95-96; Wilson and Davis (eds.), *Herndon's Informants*, pp. 358, 360, 453.

31. Wilson and Davis (eds.), *Herndon's Informants*, pp. 167-68, 516.

32. I.N. Arnold, *The Life of Abraham Lincoln* (Chicago: McClurg, 1884), p. 81; Wilson and Davis, *Herndon's Informants*, pp. 185, 358, 360, 426; E. Hertz, *The Hidden Lincoln: From the Letters and Papers of William H. Herndon* (New York: Blue Ribbon Books, 1940), p. 167.

ing undoubtedly moulded this view of fate: throughout his life he would allude to the determining power of 'Divine Providence', 'the Divine Being' and 'the providence of God'. This was a God, he told Isaac Cogdal, that 'predestined things—and governed the universe by Law—nothing going by accident'.[33] Lincoln's determinism, though, had more secular roots. According to Herndon, Lincoln believed that all conscious human action was shaped by 'motives'—that is, self-interested, rational and predictable responses to surrounding conditions 'that have somewhat existed for a hundred thousand years or more'.[34] There was thus no freedom of the will: as Lincoln put it in an election handbill of 1846, explaining his belief in the 'Doctrine of Necessity', he had found persuasive the idea 'that the human mind is impelled to action, or held in rest by some power, over which the mind itself has no control'.[35] Defensively, Lincoln stressed that this was an opinion consistent with religious faith, as 'held by several of the Christian denominations', but there were non-religious influences working here, too. This was not so much the secular determinism of Paine, Volney and Chambers, though their writings helped strip out some of Lincoln's Calvinism, but more probably Benthamite utilitarianism, as mediated by American legal reformers. Lincoln's views on motives, interests and the lack of freedom of the moral will powerfully resembled Jeremy Bentham's. Whatever their sources, Lincoln's views were anathema to many mainstream Christians—Methodists and 'Arminianized' Calvinists—who viewed the 'doctrine of necessity' as a godless creed that denied moral responsibility. Lincoln, though, continued mainly to present his deterministic faith in a religious language that invoked an all-controlling God.[36]

'Mounted on the Eternal Invulnerable Bulwark of Truth': *Lincoln and the Moral Wrong of Slavery*

It was this hybrid religious faith, with its rationalist, Universalist, Unitarian, fatalist, but only residually Calvinist elements, that did much to shape Lincoln's approach to slavery as a morally charged political issue. The Declaration of Independence, in which he rooted his arguments during

33. Wilson and Davis (eds.), *Herndon's Informants*, p. 441

34. Hertz, *Hidden Lincoln*, pp. 142, 167-68, 265-66, 407-408.

35. AL, 'Handbill Replying to Charges of Infidelity', 31 July 1846, *CWAL*, I, p. 382.

36. Guelzo, 'Abraham Lincoln and the Doctrine of Necessity', pp. 70-77.

the 1850s, was for Lincoln more than a time-bound expression of political grievance. It was a near-sanctified statement of universal principles, and one that squared with essential elements of his personal faith: belief in a God who had created all men equal and whose relations with mankind were based on the principles of justice. Lincoln found the scriptural basis for the Declaration in the book of Genesis: if mankind were created in the image of God, then 'the justice of the Creator' had to be extended equally 'to all His creatures, to the whole great family of man'. As he told an audience at Lewistown, Illinois, the Founders had declared that 'nothing stamped with the Divine image and likeness was sent into the world to be trodden on, and degraded, and imbruted by its fellows'. In setting down the Declaration's self-evident truths, they had provided a basis for resistance 'in the distant future' to a 'faction' or 'interest' determined to argue that 'none but rich men, or none but white men, were entitled to life, liberty and the pursuit of happiness'. Sustain that document and you ensured that 'truth, and justice, and mercy, and all the human and Christian virtues…[would] not be extinguished from the land'.[37]

Lincoln's use of the Bible in the struggle over slavery was driven by conviction, not expediency. As Herndon recognized, whether or not Lincoln believed in the divine inspiration of Scripture, 'he accepted the practical precepts of that great book as binding alike upon his head and his conscience';[38] late in life he described it as the means of distinguishing right from wrong. Not that Lincoln brandished the Bible as an all-purpose anti-slavery manual, but he was clear enough where its principles led: ' "*Give* to him that is needy" is the Christian rule of charity; but "Take from him that is needy is the rule of slavery".' He was wryly scornful of those southern divines like the Presbyterian Frederick A. Ross, who had constructed a pro-slavery theology that concluded, as he put it, that 'it is better for *some* people to be slaves; and, in such cases, it is the Will of God that they be such'. But how was God's will to be established? Suppose Ross had a slave named Sambo. To the question 'Is it the Will of God that Sambo shall remain a slave, or be set free?' God 'gives no audible answer' and the Bible, his revelation, 'gives none, or, at most, none but such as admits of a squabble, as to its meaning'. But the fact that the question was to be resolved by Dr Ross, who 'sits in the shade, with gloves on his hands, and subsists on the bread that Sambo is earning in the

37. AL, 'Speech at Lewistown, Illinois', 17 August 1858, *CWAL*, II, pp. 544-47; Wolf, *Almost Chosen People*, pp. 90-91, 95-97.

38. *Herndon's Life of Lincoln*, p. 360.

burning sun', gave little confidence that he would 'be actuated by that perfect impartiality, which has ever been considered most favorable to correct decisions'.[39]

God's words to Adam, 'In the sweat of thy face shalt thou eat bread', provided Lincoln with a text for his theology of labour: that is, the burden of work, the individual's duty to engage in it, and the moral right to enjoy the fruits of one's labour.[40] James Gillespie recorded the animation and neo-Puritan earnestness with which Lincoln discussed the need to meet and check the moral decay that slavery effected: ostentatious wealth, enervating leisure and a view of labour as 'vulgar and ungentlemanly'. Slavery 'was a great & crying injustice [and] an enormous national crime': the country, he told Gillespie, 'could not expect to escape punishment for it'. Surfacing here in Lincoln's thought was the Calvinist view of the political nation as a moral being. God punished wicked nations for their sins, just as he punished delinquent individuals.[41]

Punishment would bring reformation and progress: Lincoln, explained Leonard Swett, expected the 'ultimate triumph of right, and the overthrow of wrong'. Here we see again Lincoln's idea of destiny and his view that the universe followed a course fixed by divine laws. 'He believed the results to which certain causes tended, would surely follow; he did not believe that those results could be materially hastened or impeded', wrote Swett. 'His whole political history, especially since the agitation of the Slavery question, has been based upon this theory.'[42] It was a theory that threw up two areas of paradox in his thought and practice towards the peculiar institution.

First, his scorn for the argument that slavery was good for people ('As a *good* thing, slavery is strikingly perculiar [*sic*], in this, that it is the only good thing which no man ever seeks the good of, for *himself*') stopped short of full-blown censure of slaveholders, or malice towards them. Believing that people are the product of their circumstances, that environments trap them into unbreakable habits and prompt actions according to the laws of motive, Lincoln was remarkably free from hate. Southerners did no more and no less than the people of the free states would have done

39. AL, 'Fragment on Pro-slavery Theology, 1 October 1858[?], *CWAL*, III, pp. 204-205.
40. Gen. 3.19; AL, 'Fragment on Free Labor', 17 September 1859[?], *CWAL*, III, p. 462; Wolf, *Almost Chosen People*, pp. 91, 102.
41. Wilson and Davis (eds.), *Herndon's Informants*, pp. 183-84.
42. Wilson and Davis (eds.), *Herndon's Informants*, pp. 162, 167-68, 441.

had their positions been reversed. Moral opprobrium was inappropriate. 'No man was to be eulogized for what he did or censured for what he did not do or did do', Herndon explained. 'I never heard him censure anyone but slightly, nor'—Thomas Jefferson and Henry Clay excepted—'eulogize any.'[43]

Further, if Lincoln really did believe 'that what was to be would be inevitably', and that slavery was a doomed institution, why did he so energetically engage in efforts to prevent its spread? Those who have alluded to the essential 'passivity' of Lincoln's nature have used a misleading term: he may have been fatalistic, but he was also ambitious, enterprising and determined. He was scarcely inert politically. How, then, does one square the circle? First, we should note that even those who made much of this trait in Lincoln were quick to caution against a picture of blind belief in destiny. As Herndon himself explained, 'his fatalism was not of the extreme order like the Mahometan idea of fate'; Lincoln conceded that 'the will to a very limited extent, in some fields of operation, was somewhat free'. Humans had the capacity to 'modify the environments' that shaped them.[44] Secondly, as Joseph Gillespie shrewdly observed, Lincoln yoked a belief in foreordained *instrumentality* with his faith in predestined ends, 'and therefore he was extremely diligent in the use of means'. As Lincoln told a newly married Joshua Speed, 'I believe God made me one of the instruments of bringing your Fanny and you together, which union, I have no doubt He had foreordained'. This was how he stood in regard to the agitation over slavery, which from the first, according to Swett, he expected to succeed and so 'acted upon the result as though it was present from the beginning'. Much later, as president, he not only trusted deeply in God's purpose to save the Union but, in Gillespie's judgment, concluded 'that he himself was an instrument foreordained to aid in the accomplishment of this purpose as well as to emancipate the slaves'.[45]

The fatalist and activist were thus fused in Lincoln, who was in this respect a by no means unique historical figure. As Allen Guelzo has remarked, the doctrine of inevitability has often generated a psychological

43. AL, 'Fragment on Pro-slavery Theology, 1 October 1858[?], *CWAL*, III, p. 205; Hertz, *Hidden Lincoln*, p. 266.

44. Hertz, *Hidden Lincoln*, pp. 265-67. Donald, *Lincoln*, offers the most authoritative, but still unconvincing, case for Lincoln's 'passivity'.

45. Wilson and Davis (eds.), *Herndon's Informants*, pp. 162, 506; AL to Joshua F. Speed, 4 July 1842, *CWAL*, I, p. 289.

imperative to action, for instance among Puritan revolutionaries or the disciples of Marx and Lenin. In Lincoln's case we may have a sense of paradox, but his views were not absurdly self-contradictory. Driven by a clear understanding of the Union's purpose, by a view of slavery as a doomed aberration in an enterprising, egalitarian society, in which individual Americans should be free to aspire to, and achieve, personal self-fulfilment, a politically reinvigorated Lincoln embarked in 1854 on a period of earnest political activity.

Difficult as it is to pin down Lincoln's religious views, they were clearly not those of the mainstream evangelical communities that acted as the whetstone on which northern Whigs and the subsequent Republican coalition sharpened their moral edge. Those New School Calvinists and out-and-out Arminians who embraced the anti-slavery programme of the Republican party enjoyed a degree of moral certainty that could spill over into self-righteousness, prompting intolerance of the sinner as well as the sin. The cosmology of evangelicals supposed a universe where the forces of darkness were in chronic conflict with the battalions of light. The Manicheanism or dualism of evangelical thought did much to shape the Republicans' appeal.

These elements were not central to Lincoln's own thought-world, though he knew the political expressions of the evangelical and radical Protestant mindset well enough, whether through leaders like Owen Lovejoy and Ichabod Codding, or through his acquaintance with humble voters. They would not have been far from his political calculations when trying to lock Douglas into a pro-slavery conspiracy; or biting his tongue in the face of 'nativist' Protestant intolerance towards Catholic foreigners. Some recalled an even more manipulative cunning. James Matheny told Herndon that he thought Lincoln 'played a sharp game…on the Religious world' between 1854 and 1860, by allowing it to be thought that he was a seeker after salvation.[46] His 1846 congressional contest with Peter Cartwright had left Lincoln reflecting on the damage that a reputation for religious unorthodoxy could inflict, and he was determined not to be victimized again.[47]

But we make a mistake if we believe Lincoln's power in these years derived from claiming to be what he was not. He made no pretence of

46. Wilson and Davis (eds.), *Herndon's Informants*, pp. 577, 587.
47. R.J. Carwardine, 'Lincoln, Evangelical Religion and American Political Culture in the Era of the Civil War', *Journal of the Abraham Lincoln Association* 18 (1997), pp. 27-56.

religious conversion. Rather he benefited from the points of intersection between his hybrid, post-Calvinist Protestantism and the more common evangelical faith to which he could not subscribe. His unbending conviction that slavery was wrong, scripturally wayward and a fire-blanket that smothered the sparks of individual enterprise and aspiration, gave his speeches a tone and substance that inspired more orthodox Protestants. In the summer of 1858, in the wake of Lincoln's campaign speeches in Chicago and Springfield, a certain Abraham Smith of Ridge Farm in eastern Illinois picked up his pen and wrote:

> It is said that the campaign is regularly opened between thee & Douglas... I want to say to thee that while some [cautious] republicans –will say thou hast taken too high ground—(too near up to the standard of the Christianity of the day)—I am rejoiced that...thou art fairly mounted on the eternal invulnerable bulwark of truth—the same that the bible teaches...a higher stand than don't care whether 'the sum of all villanies' should deluge the land. But Douglas is a cun[n]ing dog & the devil is on his side—As I view the contest...it is no less...than for the advancement of the kingdom of Heaven or the kingdom of Satan...and the fate of Douglas or Lincoln is comparatively a trifle.[48]

Smith's language was not Lincoln's, but Lincoln's religious and ethical perceptions so shaped his utterances during the 1850s that he tugged at the hearts of men like Smith. Judge David Davis was no doubt right to think that only the rarest of intimates could have truly known Lincoln's mind. But scores of thousands of Americans thought they knew it well enough, and if they largely overestimated its Protestant orthodoxy, they were almost certainly right about its moral core.

48. Abraham Smith to AL, 20 July 1858, Abraham Lincoln Papers, Library of Congress.

Part V

ECCLESIOLOGY

THE DISRUPTION IN LONDON:
ENGLISH PRESBYTERIANS AND THE
SCOTTISH DISRUPTION OF 1843

David Cornick

James Chalmers Burns addressed the Synod of the Presbyterian Church in England in 1850 as a member of the Free Church of Scotland deputation. Then minister of Kirkliston, later Moderator of the General Assembly of the Free Church of Scotland (1879), he had from 1837 to 1843 been minister of London Wall, the oldest congregation of the Presbytery of London. He came from impeccable evangelical stock. His cousin William was the Presbyterian Church of England's first missionary to China, his uncle Robert had been the founder and influential editor of the *Edinburgh Christian Instructor*, and his uncle George one of the founders of the Presbyterian Church in Canada.[1]

He played a significant role in the history of London Presbyterianism during the Ten Years' Conflict, and was Clerk of Presbytery 1842–43. Immediately after the Disruption he and James Hamilton were chosen as secretaries of the London committee of the Free Church of Scotland.[2] Both men attended the first General Assembly of the Free Church of Scotland, and it was while there that Burns received a call to Kirkliston Free Church,

---

1.   Compiled from a MS biographical sheet and a cutting from *Christian Leader* 3 (1884), pp. 94-95, both in the J.C. Burns file in the United Reformed Church History Society (hereafter cited URCHS) Library at Westminster College, Cambridge, and Hew Scott, *Fasti Ecclesiae Scoticanae* (7 vols.; Edinburgh: Paterson, 1915–28), VII, p. 492. For the effect of the Disruption in Canada, including Robert Burns' role as an advocate of the Canadian cause in Scotland, see B.C. Murison, 'The Disruption and the Colonies of Scottish Settlement', in S.J. Brown and M. Fry (eds.), *Scotland in the Age of the Disruption* (Edinburgh: Edinburgh University Press, 1993), pp. 135-47 (137-40).

2.   J.C. Burns, 'London Reminiscences', in T. Brown, *Annals of the Disruption: With Extracts from the Narrative of the Ministers who Left the Scottish Establishment in 1843* (Edinburgh: MacNiven & Wallace, new edn, 1893), pp. 528-43. James Hamilton (1814–67): Roxburgh 1841; Regent Square, London, 1841–67.

which he accepted. Returning to England, to Liverpool, as a member of the Free Church of Scotland deputation to the Synod of 1850, he noted the irony of his position.

> It is something odd that the last Synod I attended met in Liverpool also. It was in 1843. We met in the old place in Rodney Street; but you had no Free Church deputation then. You did send deputies to the Assembly in Edinburgh; but so cautious were you to commit yourselves, that in the event of a disruption these Deputies were to consider their commission terminated; and some thought there would be no disruption at all.[3]

Burns was a zealous Free Churchman, far more zealous than most members of the 1843 Synod who corporately expressed their sympathy with the Church of Scotland in its sad plight and declared 'their continued adherence to the great spiritual principles of independence and non-intrusion, for which that church had been contending, and for which she is likely to suffer', but instructed their deputation to consider its commission terminated if there was a disruption.[4] The Synod seems to have been a desultory affair, and is only sparsely reported in the local press—*The Albion* for 24 April notes that only 30 members were present with just a few spectators.

The Scottish Presbyterian congregations in England were an embarrassing anomaly to the Church of Scotland—of the kirk, but not of the kirk because south of the Tweed. The history of English Presbyterianism in the nineteenth century was of conflicting aspirations, caught between Edinburgh and London, between deep-seated desires to be thoroughly Scottish yet at the same time part of the mission to England. The shape of their aspirations was to be critically shaped by the Disruption and its aftermath. Throughout the late 1830s the English congregations had pestered the great and the good of the Church of Scotland and petitioned the General Assembly tirelessly to obtain legal recognition as part of the Church of Scotland.[5] However, these were years of increasing tension between Edinburgh assembly and Westminster Parliament, and assembly bowed to Moderate opinion. In Lord Moncrieff's words, there could be 'nothing more dangerous to the Church of Scotland than to connect it with jurisdiction in England', for the Church of Scotland had no legal jurisdiction in England and such action would interfere with the delicate ecclesiastical

3. Newspaper cutting in J.C. Burns file, URCHS Library.
4. Abstract of the Minutes of the Synod of the Presbyterian Church in England in connection with the Church of Scotland, April 1843, p. 32.
5. R.B. Knox, 'The Relationship between English and Scottish Presbyterianism, 1836–1876', *Records of the Scottish Church History Society* 21 (1981), pp. 43-66.

balance of the Act of Union.[6] Such caution bred understandable bitterness in the presbyteries and sessions of England. They looked to their 'mother church' for support but found themselves 'treated it may be with courtesy, but certainly with little love'.[7] It also divided the small English Synod into those who saw an English future for the denomination and those who still hankered after closer unity with the Church of Scotland.

The vacillation of the 1843 Synod reflected not so much the serious division within the denomination over non-intrusion as the 'national' identity of the Presbyterian congregations in England. Of the 72 ministers in pastoral charge in the Presbyterian Church in England in 1843, 36 left their churches for vacant parishes in the Church of Scotland during 1843–44, but only 2 went to join the Free Church of Scotland. Although a few left for honourable motives, almost half the denomination's ministers were Scottish time-servers.[8]

Their commissions expired, Alexander Murdoch,[9] minister of Berwick, and James Hamilton, minister of Edward Irving's Regent Square, addressed the assembly as private individuals. So did two of Hamilton's elders, his namesake William and the publisher James Nisbet. The view from Regent Square vestry was of an English Church rendered impotent by the cancer of Puseyism. The Free Church therefore seemed a genuine alternative national Church, south as well as north of the Tweed. William Hamilton looked forward to union negotiations with the 'Free Protesting Church'. His minister spoke encouragingly of the interest of 'many of the pious and evangelical members of the Established Church' in the gathering at Tanfield Hall which had also gained the 'respect and goodwill [of] the better classes of Dissenters in England'.[10] Together they pleaded for ministers to come to London, 'a vast field for preaching the gospel'. It was inevitable though that the Free Church of Scotland would find the concerns of Scotland more pressing than those of London, and that rather than supplying

6. *Edinburgh Christian Instructor*, July 1836, p. 405.

7. A letter from 'A Scotch Presbyterian in England' M[anchester], 1 May 1838 in the *Edinburgh Christian Instructor*, June 1838. The writer was probably Alexander Munro (1796–1869), minister of St Peter's Square Church, Manchester, 1832–69.

8. Murison, 'Disruption and the Colonies', notes a similar crisis in Canada.

9. Alexander Murdoch (1804–85): Low Meeting, Berwick 1836–57; Moderator of the Presbyterian Church in England, 1843.

10. 'Proceedings of the Free Protesting Church of Scotland'. Bound with 9 *Presbyterian Review*, pp. 1843-44, Appendix 'Proceedings of the Assembly of the Free Church of Scotland October 1843', pp. 73-75 and 138 (75).

ministers for the metropolis and other English cities they would call north ministers like J.C. Burns.

The London Presbyterian Church Extension Society, still dreaming of a trans-national church, sent an aggrieved petition to the Free Church General Assembly of October 1843 protesting that by removing those 'who seemed to be pillars', an opportunity 'such as in all probability will never again occur...of placing the Free Church in that commanding position which it ought to occupy in the capital of the empire, will be thrown away'. It was an argument that had a natural appeal for James Begg. He spoke supporting the motion at assembly because it might be possible to enlist disaffected Anglicans in their cause and 'induce them to come out and be separate, to set up a free Church in the South of the Tweed, as we have done in the north'. Pre-empting a debate on the call of Thomas Guthrie from Edinburgh to a tiny Presbyterian Church in England congregation in London at Edward Street, Portman Square, he argued that Free Church ministers should be planted like trees, 'a considerable number' together that 'they may keep each other warm', not individually 'because the winter storms will destroy them'. Nonetheless Assembly felt that their trees were needed to cast pastoral shadows in Scotland, not London, and refused to loose Thomas Guthrie.[11]

During 1843–44 the dream perished as a steady flow of ministers left England for vacant parishes in the Church of Scotland. As a national body the Presbyterian Church in England could no longer sit on the fence trying to avoid conflict. Hence at the 1844 Synod at Berwick they proclaimed their independence. The proceedings were dominated by the clear, incisive Clerk of Synod, Hugh Campbell, who claimed as early as 1838 that to succeed in England the Presbyterian Church in England must be English, not pseudo-Scottish.[12]

Although the Presbyterian Church in England's Declaration of Independence and the Free Church's Claim of Right both begin from the assumption of the 'Crown Rights of the Redeemer', they are completely different documents.[13] The Scots were claiming the right of independence

---

11. *Presbyterian Review*, 1843–44, Appendix 'Proceedings of the Assembly of the Free Church of Scotland October 1843', pp. 73-75 and 138.

12. L. Levi, *Digest of the Actings and Proceedings of the Synod of the Presbyterian Church in England 1836–1876* (London: Synod's Publications' Committee, 1877), p. 9; P. Lorimer, *In Memoriam: A Sketch of the Life and Labours of the Late Rev. Hugh Campbell* (London: privately printed, 1855), pp. 30-31.

13. The text of the Declaration of Independence may be found in Abstract of the

from the state. The Presbyterian Church in England was declaring its independence from the Church of Scotland, an independence which, following Campbell, they believed had always been theirs, and which had been officially recognized by the Church of Scotland since 1839. Its reasoning was theological and historical, 'according to the Word of God, and the constitutional principles of Presbyterianism'. Each separate, properly constituted hierarchical unit (session-presbytery-Synod/General Assembly) was a 'particular church of Christ upon earth' and as such an 'independent province in the Kingdom of Christ upon earth' with all requisite powers to administer its own ecclesiastical economy.

The Presbyterian Church in England in connection with the Church of Scotland was such a church, and thus independent in theological principle. The overture claimed that the English Synod existed independently without any name prior to adopting the title 'The Presbyterian Church in England in connection with the Church of Scotland' in 1839, and that that title 'was assumed only in order to distinguish this Church from another denomination, *viz.*, Socinians or Unitarians' who were also using the name Presbyterian. It did not imply, and had never in practice meant, that the Presbyterian Church in England was in a subordinate relationship to the Church of Scotland, which had declared in 1834 that it possessed no legal jurisdiction in England.[14] It was therefore permissible for the Presbyterian Church in England, on its own authority, to amend the title it had itself chosen to the 'Presbyterian Church in England', omitting the phrase 'in connection with the Church of Scotland'.

In moving the acceptance of the overture Campbell argued that the conditions that had led them to accept nominal connection had changed completely, so it was imperative that the Synod should now claim and exercise the independence it had always maintained.[15] The future lay in London not Edinburgh, as part of English Dissent not as an alternative 'British' establishment, and the morning after independence had been declared, Synod symbolically accepted its English future by taking the first steps to create a theological college and thus obtain an independent ministry.

Minutes of the Synod of the Presbyterian Church in England (Liverpool, 1844), pp. 44-46, and the Claim of Right in R. Buchanan, *The Ten Years' Conflict* (2 vols.; Glasgow: Blackie & Son, 1849), II, pp. 633-47.

14. 'The Church of Scotland as Established by Law, and our Churches and Ministers in England', *English Presbyterian Messenger* 2, new series, 1849, pp. 179-82.

15. *Berwick Advertiser*, 20 April 1844, unpaginated.

London itself suffered a miniature version of the Scottish Disruption on 13 June 1843. The Presbyterian Church in England in London was a mirror that reflected the ecclesiastical politics of Edinburgh. Although it languished in the sad wake of Edward Irving's tempestuous genius, it still deliberately nurtured a dangerous fusion of nationalism and religion. The office bearers of the Scotch Church, London Wall, exhorted their fellow countrymen to 'try and forget that we are in London where there's no neighbourhood, and fancy that we are back again in Scotland where everybody knows everybody', to worship with the psalm tunes of the Covenanters so that 'you will forget for the time that you are foreigners, you will think of yourselves again at home'.[16]

The Scottish churches in London deliberately created and contributed to a Scottish subculture. London Wall offered a Scottish sabbath school and the possibility of a day school. The London Lay Union tried to link young Scots coming to London with a church and find them lodgings with church members, protecting them from metropolitan vice, and in the process preserving their 'Scottishness'. It is hardly surprising, therefore, that London was more sharply divided by the controversy that affected the Scottish Church than any other part of England.

The division within the presbytery first became apparent in March 1840 when, in the wake of the Auchterarder judgment, John Crombie, minister of St Andrew's, Commercial Road, and John Cumming tried to block a petition to Parliament in support of non-intrusion because 'interference with those dissensions which, at present, are unhappily mending [rending?] the Church of Scotland, can be of little avail'[17] and because the dispute ought to be left to 'those constituted authorities in Church & State to whom it belongs'. The Crombie–Cumming motion failed, but Cumming exercised his right to protest against the decision, and at the June meeting of presbytery[18] he and Crombie lodged their reasons of dissent. First, the

16. *Invitation and Address from the Minister, Elders and Deacons of the Scotch Church, London Wall, to the Scottish People, residing in and about the City of London, who are not at Present in Connection with that or any other Christian Congregation* (London: Johnston & Barrett, 1843), pp. 3-4.

17. Minutes of London Presbytery, 10 March 1840. Since this research was undertaken these records have been deposited with the London Metropolitan Archive. John Crombie (1788–1872): St Andrew's, Commercial Road, London, 1818–41; Aberlemno, Forfar 1841–44; Scone, Perth, 1844–72; Moderator, General Assembly of the Church of Scotland, 1865. John Cumming (1807–81): Crown Court, 1832–79; Moderator, General Assembly of the Church of Scotland, 1856.

18. Minutes of London Presbytery, 10 June 1840.

Veto Act meant that the power of the keys had been taken from the hands of the Church and given to a fraction of the church membership (the male heads of families) who were 'neither designated in Scripture as a distinct body, nor recognised as possessing any special power, privilege or immunity whatsoever, distinct from the other members of the body of Christ', and second, the Church stood in a contractual relationship with the state, and the state therefore had a right to enforce the terms of that contract, even if the Church abandoned their mutual union. This conservative stance was intended to preserve the existing balance of power in the Church.

A long and detailed answer was prepared by the committee, signed by James Burns and William Hamilton. They repudiated the identification of non-intrusion with the Veto Act: 'Non-intrusion is a fundamental law of the Church: the Veto is only the Act of General Assembly; it was in aid of the former, not the latter, that the Presbytery resolved to petition.'[19]

A different doctrine of the Church and a higher concept of the laity was axiomatic to this argument—the rights of the male heads of families granted by the Veto Act prevented the presbytery or the patron from assuming 'an infallibility that they do not possess'. Presbytery considered the formation of the pastoral tie to be by mutual consent. Therefore the people should have the right to stop a minister being intruded against their wishes. To allow the presbytery to overrule this would be to undermine the rights of the people

> and implies that the Church Courts are entitled to treat them as slaves or children, who, however kindly they may be listened to, have no authority to do anything that shall certainly and *ipso facto* be valid and effectual in the management of their affairs.[20]

The committee had effectively demolished (but not, perhaps, answered) the contractual argument about the relationship between the Church and the state by a blunt theological assertion of 'the Crown Rights of the Redeemer'. To accept the authority of civil over ecclesiastical law was erastianism. The division was deep and well defined in London Presbytery as early as 1840.

Over the next three years the writings of John Cumming and James Hamilton proved opposing poles to which opinion gravitated. Cumming had worked in London as a tutor during vacations from Aberdeen

---

19. Minutes of London Presbytery, 10 June 1840.
20. Minutes of London Presbytery, 10 June 1840.

University, and had sat at the feet of Irving when he was electrifying London as minister at Regent Square. At the age of 20 he was licensed by Aberdeen Presbytery in 1827,[21] but returned to tutorial work in London. It was while tutoring in Kensington that he received a request to preach to the declining Scottish congregation at Crown Court. After that there was no doubt in the mind of minister or people that he should become minister of Crown Court, and on 27 September 1832 he was ordained and inducted. Thus began one of the most remarkable ministries of nineteenth-century London, uniting deep pastoral care for the dingy courts around the church just off the Strand, with a pulpit ministry that attracted the carriage trade and the nobility. Hamilton, who had been dandled on Edward Irving's knee as a child in his father's manse at Strathblane,[22] visited England and London as a student of 24 in the summer of 1838. A keen and able botanist, he visited the botanic and zoological sights, and went to the Royal Academy's seventieth exhibition where he admired Turner's landscapes and Landseer's dogs. A devoted churchman, he heard some of the best preachers England could offer, Binney at the Weigh House, Newman at St Mary the Virgin, Oxford, and Cumming at Crown Court, where he noted, 'People seemed heartless; and altogether I should fear that Presbyterianism does not thrive in London. I question how far it is worth the struggle for its lifeless existence.'[23] Doubtless his soul was restored the following Sunday when he attended evensong at St Paul's and heard Sydney Smith, 'very good (some might have been suspicious) on pious men endeavouring to make religion attractive' and the singing of the choir which 'brought tears to some eyes'.[24]

However, while Hamilton was observing the London scene, Crown Court was growing, and along with it Cumming's reputation. It was the ecclesiastical politics of the late 1830s and early 1840s that brought Cumming to prominence. The year before Hamilton's visit he advocated the necessity of a National Church Establishment in England and Scotland in a public meeting held at the Freemasons' Hall under the chairmanship of Lord Ashley. Part of his speech was printed in *Fraser's Magazine*.[25]

21. MS biographical sheet by W.B. Shaw in Cumming file, URCHS Library.

22. W. Arnot, *Life of James Hamilton, DD, FLS* (London: James Nisbet, 1870), p. 66.

23. Arnot, *Hamilton*, p. 116.

24. Arnot, *Hamilton*, p. 117.

25. As part of an anonymous article, 'Should clergymen take part in politics?', *Fraser's Magazine for Town and Country* (April 1837), pp. 423-24.

This led to an increase in the congregation at Crown Court. However, it was the year after Hamilton's visit (1839) when his outstanding ability really captured public interest in the Hammersmith Protestant Discussion. An anti-Catholic High Churchman—he edited Knox's liturgy in 1840 and was first in the Church of Scotland to advocate kneeling during prayers and standing during singing[26]—it was inevitable that Cumming would be the champion of the establishment principle during the early 1840s. His stance at the 1837 meeting in the wake of the Chalmers–Wardlaw debate on voluntarism[27] was the basis of his studied protest with Crombie against the presbytery petition of 1840, and this argument was in turn reiterated in his able pamphlet *A Short Statement of the Origin and Nature of the Present Divisions of the Church of Scotland* (London, 1840). Writing in the wake of Auchterarder, Cumming argued that there was a basic similarity between the English and Scottish establishments. Both were churches of whole nations, and both were episcopal, although Scottish episcope was corporate and conciliar. It was this divinely instituted episcope which distinguished the Church of Scotland from Nonconformists. The Church of Scotland was a true Church, maintaining an apostolic succession via the converted priests of the Reformation, and was patronized, defended and endowed by the state as such.

Although the party lines had been drawn up, the presbytery remained united and conducted its business efficiently and equably throughout 1841–42, keeping a watchful eye on the government's attitude and the emergence of the Middle Party of Matthew Leishman and Alexander Simpson. However, the non-intrusionist response at the 1842 General Assembly, rejecting any *via media* and adopting the Claim of Right, redrew the landscape. Then in August the decision of the Lords in the second Auchterarder case struck a further blow.[28] This led to the convocation of ministers who supported non-intrusion, which met at Roxburgh Church, Edinburgh, where James Hamilton had been minister for five months the previous year. In the spring of 1841 a deputation from the Church of Scot-

---

26. Shaw biography, Cumming file, URCHS Library.

27. For the debate, see D.M. Thompson, 'Scottish Influences on English Churches in the Nineteenth Century', *Journal of the United Reformed Church History Society* 2 (1978), pp. 30-46.

28. G.I.T. Machin, *Politics and the Churches in Great Britain, 1832–1868* (Oxford: Clarendon Press, 1977), pp. 129-40; S.J. Brown, 'The Ten Years' Conflict and the Disruption of 1843' in Brown and Fry (eds.), *Scotland in the Age of the Disruption*, pp. 1-27 (18-19).

land, which included Robert Candlish and Alexander Dunlop, had come to London. While they were there the elders of Regent Square arranged a meeting with them to see if they had any ideas about a minister. They recommended Hamilton who had worked as Candlish's missionary for several months in 1839,[29] and Hamilton came to Regent Square. He had worked with William Burns in Dundee at the centre of the 1839 revival and was a good friend of Robert Murray M'Cheyne. When he was presented to Roxburgh Church, Edinburgh, he wrote to his uncle Thomas, an Anglican London merchant, 'it is an interesting consideration to feel one's self a member of the most venerable Presbytery in the Kirk. John Knox's Presbytery—Dr Erskine's, Sir Harry's [Moncrieff], Dr Andrew Thomson's Presbytery.'[30] Given this understanding of Church history in the tradition of Thomas M'Crie the elder, his spiritual background and literary gifts, it was not surprising that Hamilton became the protagonist of the voluntarist cause in London. Righteous voluntarism and exiled Romanticism blended potently in his pen. Some of his writings of 1842–43 draw their inspiration from Psalm 137. His pamphlet, *Remembering Zion* (London, 1842), which exhorted Scots 'in this busy, tumultuous Babylon' to 'sit down for a little and remember our Zion' and with Romantic nostalgia re-created Scottish sabbaths, neighbours, services, music and communion season solemnities, lay behind the pastoral letter issued by London Wall. However, the future of the Church of Scotland depended on a mainly English Parliament and Hamilton, exiled in the metropolis, became the apologist for voluntarism, expounding the mysteries of Scottish ecclesiastical problems to the ignorant but 'just' English. So, after attending the meeting of the convocation at his former church in November 1842, Hamilton published *The Harp on the Willows* (London, 1843) subtitled 'the captivity of the Church of Scotland'.

He rehearsed the voluntarist interpretation of Scottish Church history, and repeated Chalmers' theory of the Church of Scotland as established, yet free from state interference.

> This theory of an Establishment is, that the nation selects a Church whose constitution and worship it approves and on this Church, for the benefit of the nation, bestows the beauty of an endowment. But they do not see how this necessarily implies subjection to the state, or the loss of any spiritual privilege.[31]

29. Arnot, *Hamilton*, p. 122.
30. Arnot, *Hamilton*, p. 169.
31. J. Hamilton, *The Harp on the Willows* (London: James Nisbet, 1843), p. 21.

It was analogous he suggested, to a rich man endowing a Dissenting chapel. Once it was endowed, he could not interfere with it. If nothing else, this illustrates how little Hamilton knew of English Dissent. But the rich man of the state was interfering, forcing the Church of Scotland to fight for the same cause as 'the early Nonconformists and the New England worthies…that God alone is the Lord of the conscience, and that the highest tribunal on earth may not abridge the liberty wherewith Christ hath made his people free'.[32] Parliament, he felt, would be swayed by the presence of English public opinion, so he ended with an appeal to the people of England to petition Parliament.[33]

The appeal fell on deaf ears, for although the serried ranks of Anglo-Scottish commerce filled the pews of Regent Square on Sundays, the guardians of power and nobility preferred the conservatism of Crown Court, where John Cumming was at the height of his power and popularity. His influence was considerable. Some have argued that had he not been minister of Crown Court, the Disruption might not have taken place, because the government would not then have underestimated the strength of the voluntarist cause.[34] However, this is doubtful. Cumming was merely repeating the opinions that Peel's government wanted to hear, thus reinforcing rather than creating their misunderstanding of the gravity of the crisis facing the Church of Scotland. Cumming was confidently predicting, even at this late stage, that only a handful of clergy would leave the Church of Scotland.[35] It must have been shortly before this that Cumming published his pamphlet on the *Present State of the Church of Scotland: A Letter addressed to the Most Noble Marquess of Cholmondeley* (London, 1843) in which he completely misunderstood the strength of feeling in Scotland about voluntarism. Very few, he suggested, would leave the Church of Scotland, if any, and he considered that the Free Church would be 'a less important because less justifiable dissent'[36] than that of 1731. He had

32. Arnot, *The Harp*, p. 20.
33. Arnot, *The Harp*, p. 23.
34. G.C. Cameron, *The Scots Kirk in London* (Oxford: Becket, 1979), p. 251. H. Watt, *Thomas Chalmers and the Disruption* (London: T. Nelson, 1944), p. 294, is more circumspect.
35. Burns, 'London Reminiscences', p. 536, notes, 'One of my own co-presbyters assured me, in the month of March, that not more than six men would come out; another more given to prophetic calculation insisted that there would only be two, and that one of the two was so clever that if there was a loophole open he would certainly go in again.' The prophetic calculator was Cumming, the 'clever one', R.S. Candlish.
36. J. Cumming, *Present State of the Church of Scotland: A Letter addressed to the*

either been in London too long, or was too carried along on the waves of his own polemic, to be politically acute. However, he was perceptive enough to discern the difference in function of the Scots churches in England and the Church of Scotland in Scotland. He acknowledged the split in London Presbyterianism. The ministers of Swallow Street, St Andrew's and Crown Court opposed the convocationalists. James Hamilton, Peter Lorimer and J.C. Burns were all open supporters of Candlish. He frankly acknowledged:

> I for one believe that these three are too honest not to embrace the consequences, as they have espoused the principles. Were they to adhere to the Established Church after the secession of Mr Candlish, at any new pretext, they would injure their influence for good, but as dissenters they are sure to prosper.[37]

In March 1843 Cumming launched his most bitter polemic on non-intrusionists who had made a better job of wrecking the national church than the Jesuits could have done (there was no greater insult in Cumming's well-stocked armoury than this). The non-intrusionists were an unprincipled bunch of opportunists, who had sought support from Anglicans, Methodists and Independents regardless of deep theological differences. 'It is worth the pope's consideration, whether if his holiness were to become a non-intrusionist, he would not become extremely popular in Scotland, and whether Non-intrusion might not be a capital horse for Dr Wiseman to ride successfully on.'[38]

He objected to the manner in which some of his Scottish colleagues in London (i.e., James Hamilton) had allowed Dissenting ministers into their pulpits, which, he cynically observed, was smoothing the path to future unions. Hamilton had published a tract on unity in the preceding September—*The Dew of Hermon*, following it with the non-intrusionist *The Harp on the Willows*. Cumming commented, ' "The Dew of Hermon" rolls in its descent into the acrid and heavy dew of Non-intrusion... Dissenters will more and more conclude that pious men, such as we doubt not Mr Hamilton is, mean Non-intrusion when they advocate unity.'[39] Candlish

Most Noble Marquess of Cholmondeley (London: John F. Shaw, 1843), p. 13.

37. Cumming, *Present State*, p. 15 n. Peter Lorimer (1812–79): River Terrace, Islington, 1837–44; Professor, English Presbyterian College 1844–78; Principal, English Presbyterian College, 1878–79.

38. 'The Crisis in the Church of Scotland', *Fraser's Magazine for Town and Country* (March 1843), pp. 363-76 (365).

39. 'The Crisis', p. 365.

dryly noted, 'Mr Cumming has happily detected the conspiracy and saved the Capital'.[40] Two months later events in Edinburgh showed that Cumming, although correct in his minor prognostication about his London colleagues was, as ever, wrong in his prophecy. Musing from a distance eleven days before the first meeting of London Presbytery after the Disruption, James Hamilton wrote from Edinburgh to William Hamilton in London:

> even without a formal adherence, I should not wonder though the Moderate brethren should secede from us and adhere themselves *the* Presbytery of London, in connection with the Church of Scotland. From sundry rumours, I think Cumming and Brown contemplate a separation; and at a meeting of Presbytery on Tuesday se'nnight I expect some resolution.[41]

London Presbytery met less than a month after the Disruption, on 13 June, to arrange the induction of James Fergusson to the new pastorate of Whitechapel. Peter Lorimer of Islington was appointed to admit Fergusson and give the charge to minister and people respectively. Lorimer asked to be informed by presbytery if he was supposed to induct him 'into connection with the Established Church of Scotland as now constituted'. If so, he could not in conscience so do. The presbytery then split neatly along party lines, the pro-establishment party gathered around Cumming arguing that Lorimer should be replaced, the sympathizers with the Free Church that the presbytery should sever its connection with the establishment. Hamilton and Lorimer moved a motion to this effect which the moderator Samuel Blair of Dudley, refused to put 'on the ground that it was irregular, incompetent and revolutionary & c'. Hamilton countered this by moving that Lorimer should replace Blair as moderator. Blair refused to put this to the meeting, so it was put by the clerk, J.C. Burns. The roll was called and the motion declared carried. Lorimer then put the motion, but was interrupted by Dr Brown who asked Blair to adjourn the meeting. Uproar followed. Blair went through the form of adjournment, pronounced the benediction and left with Dr Brown, John Cumming, Alexander McGlashan and four elders.[42] The majority kept the minutes.[43]

---

40. R.S. Candlish, *Notes on the Rev. John Cumming's Letter to the Marquess of Cholmondeley, on the Present State of the Church of Scotland* (London, 1843), p. 17.

41. James Hamilton to William Hamilton, 2 June 1843, quoted by Arnot, *Hamilton*, p. 228. James Brown (1792–1860): High Meeting, Berwick, 1824–31; Swallow Street, 1831–43; Middle Church, Greenock, 1843–60.

42. Minutes of London Presbytery, 13 June 1843. James Fergusson (1788–1855): Whitechapel, 1843–50. Samuel Blair (1812–77): Dudley, 1841–44; Dalry, 1844–77.

Fergusson was accordingly inducted as minister of Whitechapel in the presence of three eminent ministers of the infant Free Church—Henry Gray, William Cunningham and Thomas Guthrie—a fraternal gesture rather than an indication that they thought of themselves as the London branch of the Free Church. It was in this vein that Hamilton wrote of this meeting:

> most of us were only waiting, in the altered circumstances of that Establishment, till our ecclesiastical superior, the Synod, should erase from its title any recognition of that Church. However…it might simplify matters to alter it at once, which we were quite competent to do, the Presbytery having existed as a Presbytery before it entered into connexion with the Church of Scotland.[44]

London Presbytery had regained its original English, independent status. Until the Berwick Synod in 1844, their allegiance was to the Free Church of Scotland, and at their September meeting they switched their missionary support from the Church of Scotland to the Free Church of Scotland.[45] They regarded themselves as the true heirs of London Presbytery, ignoring the demand from Alexander McGlashan, styling himself 'Clerk of the Scottish Presbytery in London in connection with the Established Church of Scotland' for the papers, books and belongings of the presbytery.[46] Both the establishment minority and the continuing presbytery wrote to those members with whom they were in disagreement to try and obtain harmony at the eleventh hour, but to no avail.[47]

There were nine churches in the presbytery, six in London and three

---

Alexander McGlashan (1806–71): St Andrew's, Commercial Road, 1841–45; Lanark, 1845-71.

43. Cameron, *Scots Kirk in London*, p. 256, n. 14, quotes a contemporary press report which states that when Lorimer was elected he walked up to Blair, 'and addressing the Moderator in broad Scotch said, "Come oot o'that" ', but he gives no source. For an eye-witness account, see Arnot, *Hamilton*, p. 229, quoting a letter from James Hamilton to William Hamilton, 14 June 1843.

44. Cameron, *Scots Kirk in London*, p. 252, suggests they did think of themselves as the London branch of the Free Church. Hamilton's comment, combined with Peter Lorimer's later evaluation of the effects of the Disruption (*English Presbyterian Messenger* 16 [July 1846], pp. 243-44), and the common Presbyterian practice of welcoming visiting ministers to presbytery meetings, render this a questionable assumption. It was probably a simple courtesy.

45. Minutes of London Presbytery, 12 September 1843.

46. Minutes of London Presbytery, 11 July 1843.

47. Minutes of London Presbytery.

outside. Of those outside, Broad Street, Birmingham, remained intact under its minister, the Revd Robert Wallace (1797–1892), who was elected Moderator of Synod in 1844. He had been educated at Edinburgh under Chalmers, and was a fellow-student of William Hanna, Chalmers' son-in-law and biographer, so it was unsurprising that he remained within the Presbyterian Church in England. The following year he resigned because of a crisis of conscience over infant baptism. He joined the Baptists and was for many years the pastor of Tottenham Baptist Church. Samuel Blair, moderator of the ill-fated presbytery meeting at Woolwich on 13 June, was minister of Dudley. He resigned and returned to Scotland, to Wallacetown in Ayr for one year, before moving to Dalry where he remained a parish minister for more than 30 years. His small, weak congregation, which had been founded only two years previously, split, but the majority remained in the Presbyterian Church in England, and the cause survived thanks to considerable financial and practical help from Robert Barbour, a Mancunian merchant who was a generous benefactor of English Presbyterianism.[48]

The remaining congregation outside London was Woolwich, a garrison church. Its minister since 1838 was William Thompson who, like Wallace, had trained under Chalmers at Edinburgh. He was called to a congregation battered by fortune. After the long ministry of John Blythe (1797–1830), Woolwich had called Sandy Scott, Irving's exciting assistant at Regent Square who was deposed from the ministry in 1831.[49] Thompson, a conscientious evangelical, developed the church as a specialist military chaplaincy. Under his direction a new church had been built on land provided by the government, given because the church was the chaplaincy for the Church of Scotland. It was completed in 1842 and Henry Cooke of Belfast preached the opening sermon. Thompson managed to retain the church, but not without difficulty because the status of his church had changed. In the summer of 1845 he wrote to Lord Bloomfield, the commanding officer at Woolwich, asking for temporary accommodation for his Sunday school in 'the large school-room, R.A. barracks'. Bloomfield replied, 'Since the church, of which you are minister, has separated itself

48. *English Presbyterian Messenger* 30 (April 1847), pp. 412-13.
49. For Scott, see J.P. Newell, ' "Unworthy of the Dignity of the Assembly": The Deposition of Alexander John Scott in 1831', *Records of the Scottish Church History Society* 21 (1983), pp. 249-62; and 'A Nestor of Nonconformist Heretics: A.J. Scott (1805–1866)', *Journal of the United Reformed Church History Society* 3 (1983), pp. 16-24.

from the Kirk of Scotland, it is not in my power to afford you the facilities you desire, though at the same time entertaining for you great respect'.[50] The legal position was complicated. The church had been built with voluntary money, but on ground given by the state for the use of the established Church of Scotland. While Thompson remained minister, there was a possibility that the church might be retained in the hands of London Presbytery, and because of this London Presbytery refused to loose Thompson to accept a call to Pilrig Free Church in Edinburgh, in spite of pressure from Candlish. The gamble paid off, and the church remained in the possession of London Presbytery.

As Cumming had predicted, the ministers of St Andrew's, Swallow Street, and Crown Court who had opposed the convocationalists remained within the establishment. Crown Court, swayed by Cumming, lost 'only one elder and probably a few members'[51] and became even more the focus of the carriage trade, while Cumming became a court preacher with a giddy reputation. St Andrew's, Commercial Road, and Swallow Street were less fortunate. Alexander McGlashan and the minority of the St Andrew's congregation remained in connection with the Church of Scotland, retaining their building, but the majority left to join the recently formed preaching station at Tower Hamlets, renaming themselves John Knox Church, Stepney.[52] Dr James Brown of Swallow Street remained in the Church of Scotland, but the majority of the congregation left.[53] Regent Square, Islington and London Wall remained to form the nucleus of the Presbyterian Church in England in the capital. London Wall, which claimed (probably justly) to be the oldest congregation in presbytery, remained intact, but the minister James Burns accepted a call to Kirkliston Free Church later in 1843[54] and the congregation experienced considerable difficulty in replacing him—the charge remained vacant until October 1844 when William Nicholson, Free Church minister at Ferryport-on-Craig, was inducted. Islington's constitution demanded a Church of

50. Bloomfield to Thompson, 22 June 1845, quoted in J.M. Thompson, *Memoir of the Rev. William Martin Thompson of Woolwich* (London: Presbyterian Church of England, 1902), pp. 52-53.

51. Cameron, *Scots Kirk in London*, p. 134.

52. A.G. Esslemont, 'An Index of Presbyterian Churches in England', MS in URCHS Library.

53. Cameron, *Scots Kirk in London*, p. 134.

54. K.M. Black, *The Scots Churches in England* (London: William Blackwood & Sons, 1906), pp. 64-65.

Scotland minister, and Peter Lorimer therefore resigned in December 1843 to try and ease the inevitable legal problems. He informed the presbytery that he wanted to remain in England, and that he would only accept a post in the Free Church if no possibilities of employment presented themselves in England. Legal opinion was sought on the trust deed, but it was found that the building was tied to the established Church of Scotland. The mortgagee foreclosed the mortgage because the trustees had no hope of meeting the outstanding debt now that the majority of members adhered to Free Church principles. A congregational meeting was held, addressed by Lorimer, whose vision of the function of the Presbyterian Church in England was already forming. He begged the opposing faction

> to remain united and those who would have preferred a connection with the Est. Church having expressed a willingness to remain and unite with the brethren of the Free Chh in an effort to maintain and support a Gospel wit[ness] it was unanimously resolved that the Congn should remain together and that an effort should be made to raise funds to purchase the lease of the Chh from the Mortgagee.

Financial support was forthcoming, and the building purchased. They elected to be taken under the care of London Presbytery, and in the following August called Josias Wilson of Belfast.[55]

Regent Square, one of the most important churches in the denomination, remained firmly within the Presbyterian Church in England. Seriously threatened at first, ironically it was saved by debt. The new structure cost £21,000, and £5,000 was outstanding. That may have dissuaded those who might have tried to obtain possession.[56] However, the danger still remained that the Church of Scotland would attempt to secure the building at the first vacancy. The congregation remained in secure possession of the property until early 1860 when the need for extensive repairs raised the issue again. The difficulty was solved by exposing the church to sale by the mortgagee, and its subsequent purchase for the congregation.[57] Thus,

---

55. Minutes of the Congregational Committee of the Trustees from November 1843 to January 1866 (Islington), unpaginated MS. Now transferred from the URCHS Library to the London Metropolitan Archives. William Nicholson (1796–1890): Ferryport-on-Craig, 1828–43, London Wall, 1844–52; charges in Tasmania, 1852–79. Josias Wilson (1800–47): Drogheda, 1822-36; Belfast, 1836–44; Islington, 1844–47.

56. J. Hair, *Regent Square: Eighty Years of a London Congregation* (London: James Nisbet, 1898), pp. 288-89, following Arnot, *Hamilton*, p. 231.

57. Arnot, *Hamilton*, p. 499.

by a judicious retention of debt Regent Square was saved by the Presbyterian Church in England.

With James Burns called to Kirkliston Free Church and Peter Lorimer out of pastoral charge, London Presbytery was severely undermanned. In a speech at the General Assembly of the Presbyterian Church of Ireland on 7 July 1846, James Fergusson, whose induction to Whitechapel had sparked off the miniature Disruption in London, commented that 'about the time of the Glasgow Assembly' the Presbyterian Church in England had but two ministers in London, and as he was one of them and had only recently been ordained to care for a tiny flock meeting in a temporary hall, 'Mr Hamilton was left in London almost alone to "Hang his harp upon the willows" '.[58]

London Presbyterianism owed its reconstruction to the remarkable energy of the minister of Regent Square and the shrewd financial and business expertise he was able to tap from men such as William Hamilton, Alexander Gillespie and James Nesbit. Hamilton had a methodical, scientific, statistical brain. He noted in his journal that in 1844 he had preached 124 times (57 not at Regent Square), paid 492 visits, received 1,112 visitors, written 855 letters, studied for 1,254 hours and read 21 volumes amounting to 9,010 pages. On top of this, he had attended Synod, the commission of Synod, 19 presbytery meetings, 119 miscellaneous meetings and committees, 20 kirk sessions and 78 meetings connected with his congregation. He had travelled to Edinburgh through Berwick, to Bristol, Manchester, Ipswich and Brighton (3 times) beside pleasure trips, published 3 sermons, 1 review, 2 articles, 1 book and 1 lecture besides various official letters and circulars for the church.[59] He pushed himself relentlessly, and it is not surprising that in 1846 his health broke. His doctor ordered him abroad for 20 weeks' rest, but this did not deter him. Pressure of outstanding work was so great that in November 1847 Hamilton, always a conscientious craftsman in the pulpit, had to leave the preparation of his morning sermon to 5 o'clock on the Sunday morning. His wife Annie made him coffee, he wrote in a letter to his mother, 'and lay on the rug and cried. She has as great a horror of London work as you.'[60] That was the human cost of the Disruption in London. But Hamilton survived and, thanks to his work, so did London Presbyterianism.

The Disruption was the most important domestic event in the history of

---

58. *English Presbyterian Messenger* 17 (August 1846), pp. 268-69.
59. Arnot, *Hamilton*, p. 255.
60. Letter to his mother, quoted in Arnot, *Hamilton*, p. 321.

Scotland in the nineteenth century, at once a triumph and a tragedy. Its interpretation remains a matter of study and dispute, but it was undoubtedly both a principled stand in defence of the spiritual independence of Christ's Church, and part of the dislocation of British society in the wake of the break-up of the *ancien régime*.[61] Theological realignment and the redistribution of power and influence are, therefore, inseparable. The work of Allan MacLaren and Ian MacIver was the first to show how the emergence of the Free Church both contributed to and benefited from that profound social change. MacLaren showed how the 'arrival of the new urban-based bourgeoisie' was determinative of Free Church fortunes in Aberdeen, a local instance of the changing social and political structure of the eldership which MacIver charted in his study of the General Assembly from 1820 to 1843.[62] Lairds and Edinburgh lawyers were giving way to an increasing number of middle-class, provincial elders, nominated to support the evangelical cause.

A narrow social base was both the strength and weakness of the Free Church, just as it was for English Nonconformity. Dr Alexander MacLeod, Moderator of the English Synod of the United Presbyterian Church in 1874, marvelled in his moderatorial address at the generosity of the Free Church.

> The 474 Ministers of the Disruption have grown to 947. And the Churches they serve in, and the manses and schools and mission stations besides, have been built and sustained,—and an annual income, which last year rose to £5,511,084, supplied by the Free Will offerings of the people alone.[63]

Yet that social base also reduced the effectiveness of the Free Church from the Disruption onwards. The tone of the Church became increasingly

---

61. Brown, 'Ten Years' Conflict', pp. 23-25. For surveys of the historiography of the Disruption, see A.C. Cheyne, 'The Ten Years' Conflict and the Disruption, an Overview', in his *Studies in Scottish Church History* (Edinburgh: T. & T. Clark, 1999), pp. 107-23; D.J. Withrington, 'The Disruption: A Century and a Half of Historical Interpretation', *Records of the Scottish Church History Society* 20 (1993), pp. 118-53.

62. A.A. MacLaren, *Religion and Social Class: The Disruption Years in Aberdeen* (London: Routledge & Kegan Paul, 1974), p. 211; I.F. McIver, 'The Evangelical Party and the Eldership in General Assemblies 1820–43', *Records of the Scottish Church History Society* 20 (1978), pp. 1-3.

63. *Proceedings of the English Synod of the United Presbyterian Church* (London, 1874), pp. 100-101. Alexander MacLeod (1817–91): Strathaven, 1844–55; John Street, Glasgow, 1855–64; Trinity, Claughton, 1864–91; Moderator, UP English Synod 1874; Moderator, Presbyterian Church of England, 1889.

moralistic and self-righteous. The Church of Scotland, which had a wider social base, consequently became a far more attractive agent of transformation in Victorian Scotland, and grew steadily while the Free Church and United Presbyterian Churches made little progress.[64]

The Disruption was, of course, exported. The British North American (Canadian) Church was riven, and the Colonial Committee of the Church of Scotland forced Disruption on the Australians, despite that Church's initial reaction that unity should be preserved at all costs.[65] Scots in England were part of that diaspora. However, the fortunes of the Presbyterian Church in England presented a different story due to the peculiar legal status of Presbyterian churches in England. Very little of the hardship endured by the ejected ministers in Scotland was echoed in England, although some churches were lost to the denomination through expensive, draining legal battles. In many areas desperate deployment problems were created by the departure of virtually half the denomination's clergy to fill vacant parishes in Scotland. Some were openly ambitious time-servers, others men of strong conviction. Some had served the English churches diligently and were to be sorely missed.

The Disruption produced different results in different parts of England. Opinion on intrusion polarized early in London, where the Scottish community was a little Edinburgh in exile, the aristocracy gravitating to Crown Court while the new entrepreneurs of Regent Square launched fundraising committees for the Free Church. The chapels of Northumberland with their English Dissenting heritage and Protestant Dissenting trust deeds remained mostly in control of their congregations, but in Berwick on the Scottish border there were severe divisions, as there were in Liverpool, the most racially divided city in England. However, it should be emphasized that only 7 of the 72 congregations in England adhered to the Church of Scotland in 1843, and in 3 of those considerable factions broke away to form continuing Presbyterian Church in England congregations. The vast majority of congregations remained within the Presbyterian Church in England, and the Disruption unleashed a vast surge of energy— the growth of the Church after 1844 exceeded all reasonable expectations. The Disruption and the consequent Declaration of Independence made the Presbyterian Church in England what it had always been but never completely acknowledged, an English denomination, as J.C. Burns realized.

64. A.L. Drummond and J. Bulloch, *The Church in Victorian Scotland, 1843–1874* (Edinburgh: St Andrew Press, 1975), pp. 1-33.

65. Murison, 'Disruption in the Colonies', pp. 136-37.

> Though we had always been 'Nonconformists' in fact, we were not regarded as such (except by the Establishment), so that the position between the two great parties of 'Church and Dissent' was alike anomalous and difficult… The Disruption changed all that. We became a denomination.[66]

The Disruption in Scotland saw the rise to ecclesiastical power of the new bourgeoisie, and this class factor lent an added bitterness to the events of 1843. In England, however, the Presbyterian Church in England even when connected with the Church of Scotland had always been voluntarist by necessity. In Scotland the Disruption made one Church into two denominations, but it made the English Presbyterian churches an English Nonconformist denomination.

---

66. Burns, 'London Reminiscences', p. 531.

FROM UNION TO CHURCH:
AUTOBIOGRAPHICAL RECOLLECTIONS ON
CONGREGATIONAL ECCLESIOLOGY IN THE 1960S

Alan P.F. Sell

By comparison with other themes addressed in this volume—politics, Abraham Lincoln, education, Cardinal Newman—I am concerned with a minor footnote in Congregational history. I was, however, asked to introduce a theological theme, and it seemed appropriate to reflect upon the doctrine of the Church as expressed within Clyde Binfield's own tradition.[1] The following autobiographical reflections are those of one among a number who, in the 1960s, had theological reservations concerning certain proposals which were put before the Congregational *Union* of England and Wales but who, following intense discussion, were reassured and proceeded into the Congregational *Church* in England and Wales and thence into the United Reformed Church. Whereas the story of those who did not thus proceed has been told,[2] this paper represents, so far as I am aware, the first account of one in the category of the initially anxious but subsequently reassured.

It is not too much to say that for most of my life I have been haunted by ecclesiology. When I was four years of age I met Jimmy in the ice cream shop. He also was four. A month or two ago a Solemn Mass was held in celebration of the fortieth anniversary of the ordination of Father James (as he has since become). He was born, not so much with a silver spoon in his mouth, as with a silver censer in his hand. He has never deviated from the

---

1.   With this paper I seek to honour Clyde Binfield in general for his valuable contribution to historical studies and, more particularly, for his grasp of Congregational catholicity—both words carrying equal weight. Other contributions to this volume refer to ecclesiology in its original sense, namely, the study of church buildings and decoration. I here use the term, as has become customary, as shorthand for 'the doctrine of the Church'.

2.   See notes 96 and 98 below.

highest of High Anglicanism. When other boys would be arguing over whether Burnley were robbed when Charlton Athletic beat them 1-0 in the 1947 FA Cup Final, Jimmy and I would be arguing the toss about the apostolic succession, the propriety of extempore prayer, the place of bishops and the like. On our many cycle tours of churches within a ten-mile radius of our homes he always had the advantage in that when it was raining we could shelter in his buildings, mine always being firmly locked.

I was baptized in Godalming Congregational Church, but by the time I met Jimmy we had moved to Cranleigh. Apart from a non-Union Baptist church and an Evangelical Free church, there were no Dissenters around. My maternal grandparents, however, were there. They were members of the Methodist Church, and that is how I fell among the Methodists. By one of those turnings of the circle so frequent in church life, Godalming Congregational (now United Reformed) Church is today locally united with the Hugh Price Hughes Memorial Methodist Church in that town— the very building on whose behalf my grandfather, when a young man, had gone from his home in Devonshire on fundraising singing tours in South Wales. I attended the Cranleigh Methodist Sunday School, later joined the youth fellowship, found my way around the organ, and became what was called a Junior Church member. It was not long before I felt an inescapable call to the Christian ministry, something which was utterly incomprehensible to my headmaster.

Of more concern to me than my headmaster was the question, How should I fulfil my calling—and among whom? I was happy with the Methodists, and I clearly remember the ministers who came to our village: Howard Belben, F.G. Healey, Brian Boshier, Frederick Bagshaw, Francis Case, Fred Russell, Herbert Harris and Charles Venn—all of these in nine or ten years, and this was one of my problems. I had the idea that ministers should live longer among those they served: this on grounds both of pastoral care and efficient edification. It seemed to me that the Methodist system of those days, as we received it in our village, militated against that depth and continuity of fellowship between pastor and people which seemed important to me.

My other query concerned the church members. The ministers came to us, we knew not how; indeed, the members did not gather in fellowship as a whole, though class meetings were held.

I resolved to take no hasty action, and instead gave rein to my already burgeoning research instinct. I spent most of my pocket money in Thorp's secondhand bookshop in Guildford. I ransacked the place for books on the polity of the several Nonconforming denominations, and what I could not find there I sought from the public library and from denominational offices. Much later I discovered that the eminent John Stoughton, who served Kensington Congregational Church with distinction from 1843 to 1875, went through the same exercise as a young man.[3] Like Stoughton, I concluded that 'on the whole' the Congregational system 'came nearest to the principles laid down in the New Testament'.[4] In particular, as far as I was concerned, it provided for consistent ministry and Church Meeting. I therefore explained myself to the understanding Methodists and, following a period of cycling to Godalming to church, became a member of Worplesdon Congregational Church when my family removed to that area.

To this day I continue to regard the relation of pastor and people as sacred: the analogy drawn by John Robinson, pastor to the Pilgrims, that that relationship is comparable with the relation of husband and wife in marriage does not seem to me to be at all inappropriate.[5] There are many ramifications of this which I cannot pursue here, but I should like to mention just one. Over 50 years ago Alexander Grieve, a former principal of my college, Lancashire Independent, pleaded among other things that the 'Exposition' be restored 'to its old place in Ordination and Induction services—as instruction for our own folk rather than as apologia for outsiders'.[6] The reason, of course, is that the pastoral relationship is rooted in the gospel to which personal and not merely formal testimony is made. I fear, however, that far from restoring the Exposition, it is not even present as an option in the latest Ordination and Induction orders of the United Reformed Church.

As for Church Meeting, I believe more strongly than ever in its importance as the years go by, and I have sought to commend it to Anglicans

---

3.   *John Stoughton: A Short Record of a Long Life*, by his daughter (Georgina King Lewis) (London: Hodder & Stoughton, 1898), pp. 15-16.

4.   *John Stoughton*, p. 16.

5.   See J. Robinson, *Works* (3 vols.; London: John Snow, 1851), II, pp. 396-97. This conviction has fuelled my critique of the uncritical adoption of the corporate model by churches, whereby the doctrine of vocation becomes a casualty. See, e.g., A.P.F. Sell, *Aspects of Christian Integrity* (Eugene, OR: Wipf & Stock, 1998 [1990]), p. 140; Sell, *Conservation and Exploration in Christian Theology* (Caernarfon: Gwasg Pantycelyn, 1993), pp. 18-19. See further R.T. Jones, *John Robinson's Congregationalism* (London: Congregational Memorial Hall Trust, 1987).

6.   Quoted by C.E. Surman (his son-in-law), *Alexander James Grieve, M.A., D.D. 1874–1952* (Manchester: Lancashire Independent College, 1953), p. 47.

and Presbyterians when I have had opportunity.[7] It is the point at which the congregationalists of England and Wales, whether Congregational or Baptist, completed the Reformation from the point of view of polity. Where Calvin stopped at elders, they, undeniably influenced by the socio-political circumstances in which they found themselves, brought matters down to the priesthood of believers corporately conceived; and I have always warmed to John Robinson's protest against any undue clericalism in the church which would lead to a situation in which 'Simon the saddler, Tomkin the tailor, Billy the bellows-maker must be no churchmen, nor meddle with church matters'.[8] Incidentally, another of Robinson's remarks might be taken as a challenge to the builders of megachurches in our own time: 'a particular church under the new testament, ought to consist of no more members than can meet together in one place'.[9] I readily concede that, like all polities which are operated by saints who are also sinners, Church Meeting is not always all it might be. I can understand something of R.F. Horton's frustration when forced to admit after an unusually long ministry at Hampstead, 'They do not know what a Church Meeting is. In fifty years I have failed to teach them.'[10]

Certainly, if it is at least democratic, it should be much more than democratic. The true church

> [wrote Lovell Cocks] is constituted by believers whom the Holy Spirit has gathered and over whom Christ presides; yet the believers constitute the church not as an aggregate of 'saved' individuals, but as a living fellowship or commonality which seeks in all its acts of worship and witness to acknowledge the sovereign authority of its Lord.[11]

7.   See further, A.P.F. Sell, *Commemorations: Studies in Christian Thought and History* (Calgary: University of Calgary Press; Cardiff: University of Wales Press, 1993; repr. Eugene, OR: Wipf & Stock, 1998), ch. 14.

8.   Robinson, *Works*, II, p. 390.

9.   Robinson, *Works*, III, pp. 12-13.

10.   A. Peel and J.A.R. Marriott, *Robert Forman Horton* (London: Allen & Unwin, 1937), p. 186.

11.   H.F. Lovell Cocks, 'The Gospel and the Church', in John Marsh (ed.), *Congregationalism To-day* (London: Independent Press, 1943), pp. 30-44 (37). For this unduly neglected theologian see Sell, *Commemorations*, ch. 13. Cf. B.L. Manning, *Essays in Orthodox Dissent* (London: Independent Press, 1953 [1939]), p. 99: 'We Congregationalists and Baptists have never been able to conceive of a churchless Christianity, a private sect, a Christian experience that is not also an ecclesiastical experience. We have always associated the grace of our Lord Jesus Christ with the communion of saints.'

Applying this to Church Meeting he elsewhere declared, 'It is our under-standing of the Gospel that makes [it] indispensable. It is not a convenient form of organization, but a way of Gospel obedience.'[12] Hence, of course, the close association of Church Meeting with the church's worship: it is a credal assembly where the lordship of Christ is proclaimed, his will sought, and where those who by grace are one in him seek, by the Spirit, to be one in their decisions and judgments.[13] Moreover, it is not simply the local church gathered. Expecting the answer, 'Yes', Samuel Davidson of Lancashire College asked in 1848, 'Does not every church-meeting present a miniature image of the church universal?'[14] Thus, whereas to the present pope 'to be in communion with the Bishop of Rome is to give visible evidence that one is in communion with all who confess that same faith',[15] to those who stand in, or are heirs of, the Congregational Way, the Church Meeting—or, indeed, any service of worship-yields visible evidence at once more impressive and more catholic (because less sectarian) of rootedness in the faith of the ages. I cannot restrain myself from echoing R.W. Dale's well-known testimony to Church Meeting:

> [T]o be at a Church meeting—apart from any prayer that is offered—any hymn that is sung, any words that are spoken, is for me one of the chief means of grace. To know that I am surrounded by men and women who dwell in God, who have received the Holy Ghost, with whom I am to share the eternal righteousness and eternal rapture of the great life to come, this is blessedness. I breathe a Divine air. I am in the new Jerusalem which has come down out of Heaven from God, and the nations of the saved are walking its streets of gold. I rejoice in the joy of Christ over those whom He has delivered from eternal death and lifted into the light and glory of God. The Kingdom of God is there.[16]

12. H.F. Lovell Cocks, 'The Foundation of a Congregational Church', typescript/MS in the Lovell Cocks papers, Dr Williams's Library, London, p. 7.

13. See W.E. Rix, 'The Inner Workings of a Congregational Church', in Marsh (ed.), *Congregationalism To-day*, pp. 62-70 (64-65); A.P.F. Sell, 'The Worship of English Congregationalism', in L. Vischer (ed.), *Reformed Worship, Yesterday and Today* (Grand Rapids: Eerdmans, forthcoming).

14. S. Davidson, *The Ecclesiastical Polity of the New Testament Unfolded, and its Points of Coincidence or Disagreement with Prevailing Systems Indicated* (London: Jackson & Walford, 1848), p. 409.

15. This remark, delivered in the course of a sermon preached in my hearing in the Ecumenical Centre, Geneva, is taken from the text of the sermon translated from the French by the World Council of Churches, 1984.

16. R.W. Dale, 'The Evangelizing Power of a Spiritual Fellowship', address to the

Having become a Congregationalist by conviction, my call to ministry was tested in the usual ways, and although from the 'deep South', I sought entry to Lancashire Independent College, which would enable me to take advantage of three years of arts prior to theology, and enable me to sit at the feet of Manchester's then distinguished group of theological teachers. It would also give me plenty of preaching experience in places very strange to me. I read the texts set for the entrance examination in Congregational history and polity: Albert Peel's *Brief History* and E.J. Price's *Handbook*, and found on entering the college that I had landed among teachers— Gordon Robinson, George Phillips and Eric Hull—each of whom in his distinctive way represented the best traditions of English Dissent. My ordination took place in 1959, and in that same year the Congregational Union took a decision of considerable importance, which provoked my next series of ecclesiological excitements.

The Next Ten Years

In 1957 Howard Stanley, the general secretary of the Union, began to promote the idea of a review of the entire life of the denomination from the point of view of administrative and other practicalities. Suggestions were welcomed, and at the council meeting of 17–18 November 1958, it was resolved to submit to the next assembly a plan under the heading, 'The Next Ten Years'. The idea was to establish eight commissions which, between them, would examine all aspects of the denomination's life. Howard Stanley was a dynamic leader of forthright opinions bluntly expressed. Although he had a sense of humour (something of which I was unaware until I read his obituary, wherein the fact is clearly stated), he really could look quite terrifying on occasion.[17] His saving graces were his enthusiasm, his deep Christian commitment, and his ability to change his mind—and admit that he had done so. Thus, in 1947, he had led the opposition to the union talks with the Presbyterian Church of England, and the project foundered.[18] For this reason John Huxtable, his successor as

Congregational Union of England and Wales, 1886, in D. Macfadyen (ed.), *Constructive Congregational Ideals* (London: Allenson, 1902), pp. 129-44 (136).

17. *URC Year Book*, 1977, p. 272.

18. The executive committee of the Lancashire Congregational Union, of which Stanley was then secretary (a post he combined with that of provincial moderator for Lancashire, Cumberland and Westmorland), appointed a special committee, whose members included Gordon Robinson, George Phillips, Kathleen Hendry and T.T. James. Their report on the Congregational–Presbyterian union proposals was published

Union secretary, was among those who opposed Stanley's candidature for that post.[19] But Stanley's views changed, and he became the one who did more than any other to set Congregationalism on its way towards the very union he had once opposed. Again, when he first pondered a review of the denomination's life, he had practicalities in mind—not least funding; but at the council meeting at which he introduced 'The Next Ten Years' he declared that events had taken what, for him, was an unexpected turn, and that his proposals were now 'more theological than practical; more concerned with the why than the how; less a call to action than a call to clear and brave thinking'.[20]

This was a most significant change of direction. It gave the promise that while practical concerns and the signs of the times constituted the occasion for the review, the discussions would be grounded in the theology, and especially the ecclesiology, of Congregationalism. To a considerable degree the promise was fulfilled. P.T. Forsyth would have rejoiced. Reflecting upon J.H. Shakespeare's determined efforts in the early years of the twentieth century to pull the Baptist Union into shape, he referred to Shakespeare's quest of 'practical unity' and declared:

> There is but one thing that can overcome the inertia he has to meet, and that is the kind of faith, creed, and passion that makes a Church great in spite of us. For Church union ever to come about we must be more ruled by a faith of power than by a fear of fizzling out...[T]he Church can be unified only by the faith, insight, and passion of the same Gospel as made it.[21]

in 1948. The unanimous special committee submitted its report to the executive committee, two of whose members abstained from voting upon it. Among others who expressed reservations in print was C.J. Cadoux, *The Congregational Way* (Oxford: Basil Blackwell, 1945), pp. 30-35. One wonders whether Independent Press declined to take the tract—an unsanctified suspicion, no doubt. Of those who produced the abortive *Joint Conference Report* (London: Independent Press, 1947), Gordon Robinson only was a member of the Lancashire special committee.

19. J. Huxtable, *As it Seemed to Me* (London: United Reformed Church, 1990), p. 37.

20. Quoted by N. Goodall, 'Congregationalism Looks at Itself: A Momentous Session of the Union Council', *Christian World*, 17 November 1958, p. 7.

21. P.T. Forsyth, *Church, Ministry and Sacraments*, bound with J.V. Bartlet and J.D. Jones, *The Validity of the Congregational Ministry* (London: Congregational Union of England and Wales, n.d.), p. 34. For a comprehensive account of Shakespeare's efforts, see P. Shepherd, *The Making of a Denomination: John Howard Shakespeare and the English Baptists, 1898–1924* (Carlisle: Paternoster Press, 2001). See especially Shepherd's comment (p. 48) on the growing tendency to refer to the 'Baptist Church' (as distinct from 'Union'): 'For Shakespeare, this development had

On 12 May 1959 Howard Stanley introduced and enthusiastically commended the eight-commission scheme to the Union assembly, which body committed itself to the task ahead.[22] While I am most concerned here with Commission I on the relations of local churches to their counties and to the national Union, Church unity and oversight, it is well to list the themes of the other seven commissions in order to show the way in which their work was theologically informed. Commission II was responsible for preparing a *Short Confession of Faith*, and a more substantial *Declaration of Faith*;[23] Commission III concerned church extension, while Commission IV examined the local church's nature, purpose, worship and practice (including the Church Meeting construed as 'part of the worship that we offer to God'),[24] the Christian use of Sunday, the place of the Church in local ecumenical life and the pattern of church organizations. Commission V considered the Church's missionary obligation; Commission VI, recruitment for the ministry, the nature of the ministry and the meaning of ordination; Commission VII the moral influence of local churches and the Union; and Commission VIII the Union itself.

There can be no doubt that while local churches and individuals responded to all of the interim reports which were faithfully distributed to them, it was Commission I on the nature of the Church, the relations between the churches and the Union, and oversight, which hit the headlines. Some smelled the burning rubber of connexionalism, and, unlike Howard Stanley, by no means all had adjusted their principled opposition to union with the Presbyterians—a matter which had been intermittently on the table since the mid-1930s.[25] From their point of view it was almost

more to do with pragmatism than with any question of principle. If Baptists were going to use their ministerial and financial resources efficiently to meet the challenge of twentieth-century urban society, they needed to organise themselves effectively.' See also p. 178.

22. His address was published as *The Next Ten Years* (London: Congregational Union of England and Wales, 1959).

23. Published in 1967, the *Declaration* remains one of the most substantial twentieth-century productions of its kind from any branch of the Reformed family. For essays on the *Declaration* see R. Tomes (ed.), *Christian Confidence* (London: SPCK, 1970).

24. *Third Interim Report of Commission IV* (London: Independent Press, 1961), p. 4.

25. See R. Bocking, 'The United Reformed Church: Background, Formation, and After', in J.C.G. Binfield (ed.), *Reformed and Renewed 1972–1997: Eight Essays Journal of the United Reformed History Society* (Supp. 5.2, 1997), pp. 8-9.

certainly not the most tactful thing to set up the Joint Committee with the Presbyterians in 1963, in the midst of the debate over Commission I, and three years before the Congregational Union became a Church. A representative query from the grassroots is that of Michael Taylor of the Bolton and Farnworth group of Congregational churches. In 1962 he reflected upon the proposal to change from 'Union' to 'Church', and asked, 'are the demands from the World Council of Churches or Presbyterians being anticipated too strongly?'[26] There can be no question that the support which many Congregationalists gave to the findings of Commission I was motivated at least in part by the conviction that union with the Presbyterians would thereby be facilitated, or that some Presbyterians who were suspicious of union with Congregationalists felt that the Congregational transition to 'Church' was nothing more than a cynical ploy designed to mask obdurate independency.

The Historical Background

It would be quite wrong to leave the impression that the matter of the relations between local Congregational churches and the wider fellowship did not surface until the middle of the twentieth century. On the contrary, the question had been discussed intermittently from the days of Congregationalism's Separatist harbingers onwards. Thus while Robert Browne declared that 'The Church planted or gathered, is a companie or number of Christians or beleeuers, which by a willing couenant made with their God, are vnder the government of god and Christ, and kepe his lawes in one holie communion',[27] he also had a place for synods; and his synods were to be gatherings of whole churches, not of representatives only: 'A Synode is a Ioyning or partaking of the authoritie of manie Churches mette togither in peace, for redresse and deciding of matters, which can not wel be otherwise taken vp.'[28] Elsewhere, in connection with church practice

---

26. M. Taylor, 'A Call for Restraint', *Group Life* (Bolton and Farnworth Congregational Group Churches), no. 37, May 1962, pp. 2-3 (3).

27. R. Browne, *A Booke which Sheweth the Life and Manners of All True Christians*, in A. Peel and L.H. Carlson (eds.), *The Writings of Robert Harrison and Robert Browne* (London: Allen & Unwin, 1953), pp. 221-395 (253). For a fuller study of the history of the Congregational polity, see A.P.F. Sell, *Saints: Visible, Orderly and Catholic: The Congregational Idea of the Church* (Geneva: World Alliance of Reformed Churches; Allison Park, PA: Pickwick Press, 1986).

28. Browne, *Booke*, p. 271.

and discipline, he advocated 'seeking to other churches to haue their help, being better reformed, or to bring them to reformation'.[29] Some Separatists, however—Francis Johnson among them—resolutely declined any guidance from other churches, maintaining that the local church was omnicompetent in all matters of faith and practice. This, however, was a minority opinion. Many others, including Richard Mather and Jeremiah Burroughes, contended for synods, while in the most concise statement of all Thomas Hooker declared that consociation was 'not only lawful, but very useful also'.[30] The *Cambridge Platform* of 1648 underlined the point and specified a number of duties, including prayer, financial aid and assistance in times of division, which the churches owed to one another. Ten years later the *Savoy Declaration of Faith and Order* followed suit. Although in ch. 26 of *Savoy* the *Westminster Confession* is modified in such a way as to make it clear that 'the visible Catholique Church of Christ...is not intrusted with the administration of any ordinances, or have any officers to rule or govern in, or over the whole Body', the appended paragraphs on church order, while stating that 'there is not instituted by Christ any Church more extensive or Catholique entrusted with power for the administration of his Ordinances, or the execution of any authority in his name' than particular churches, nevertheless enjoin communion between the churches, and admit consultative and advisory synods or councils whose determinations have moral authority only.[31] To the mind of John Owen, the leading theological light behind the *Declaration*, synods, though not expressly commanded by Christ, are entirely in accordance with the Lord's mind. Indeed, 'the *end* of all particular churches is the edification of the *church catholic* unto the glory of God in Christ'.[32] Synods are to be composed of representatives from local churches (not of whole churches as in Browne's scheme), and their powers are, first, '*declarative*, consisting in an authoritative teaching and declaring of the mind of God in the Scripture; the second is *constitutive*, appointing and

29. R. Browne, *A True and Short Declaration*, A. Peel and L.H. Carlson (eds.), *Harrison and Browne*, pp. 396-429 (423).

30. T. Hooker, *A Survey of the Summe of Church Discipline, Wherein the Way of the Churches of New England is warranted out of the Word* (1648), IV, p. 1.

31. *Savoy Declaration of the Institution of Churches, and the Order appointed in them by Christ*, paras. XV, XXVI-XXVII.

32. J. Owen, *The True Nature of a Gospel Church and its Government* (1689), in *The Works of John Owen* (ed. W.H. Goold; 16 vols.; London: Banner of Truth, 1968 [1850–53]), XVI, pp. 1-208 (196).

ordaining things to be believed; and, thirdly, *executive*, in acts of jurisdiction towards persons or churches'.[33] The findings of synods 'are to be received, owned and observed on the evidence of the minds of the Holy Spirit in them, and on the ministerial authority of the synod itself'.[34]

With greater or lesser regard to the principles thus sketched, the Congregationalists cooperated with one another in manifold ways as time went on. There were associations of ministers in various counties, among them the London Board of Congregational Ministers, founded in 1727. By the end of the eighteenth century there was the London Missionary Society (1795), the Congregational Society for Spreading the Gospel in England,[35] as well as the earliest county unions of Congregational churches, and the Home Missionary Society (1819).

By 1831 there were 34 county unions, and to many the time seemed ripe to inaugurate a national Union. Earlier attempts from 1806 onwards had failed owing to suspicions regarding the possible usurpation of the rights of the local church, and despite the powerful advocacy of a number of prominent ministers, among them John Angell James, whose book of 1822, *Christian Fellowship; or the Church Member's Guide*, was widely circulated. The *Eclectic Review* lent its weight to the cause, as did the *Congregational Magazine*, founded in 1818 and edited by John Blackburn.[36] John Morison, who was to edit the *Evangelical Magazine* for 30 years, published a lecture 'On the best Methods of promoting an effective Union among Congregational Churches, without infringing on their Independence'. While agreeing that the New Testament sanctioned no such thing as a national Church, he argued that

> there existed among all the apostolic churches (though complete in themselves in point of government), an unbroken sympathy of fellowship; such a sympathy as that if '*one member suffered all the members suffered with it; or, if one member was honoured, all the members rejoiced with it.*'[37]

33. Owen, *True Nature of a Gospel Church*, p. 205.

34. Owen, *True Nature of a Gospel Church*, p. 208.

35. For this largely forgotten body, see R.F.G. Calder, 'The Congregational Society for Spreading the Gospel in England, 1797–1809', *Congregational Historical Society Transactions* 19 (1964), pp. 248-52.

36. For Blackburn, see C.E. Surman, 'The Rev. John Blackburn (1792–1855), Pioneer Statistician of English Congregationalism', *Congregational Quarterly* 33 (1955), pp. 352-60.

37. Quoted by A. Peel, *These Hundred Years: A History of the Congregational Union of England and Wales, 1831–1931* (London: Congregational Union of England

In 1831 the *Congregational Magazine* published contributions, many of them anonymous, for and against a national Union. 'Roffensis' warned that 'Hierarchies have sprung from the most inconsiderable beginnings', and declared:

> It is our glory that hitherto we have been no sect. We subscribe to no creed. We submit to no synod or conference. We are not properly a body. We recognize but two definitions of the term church. It designates the separate assembly of believers united together for the observance of religious ordinances; and it designates the whole number of the redeemed.[38]

To the definition of 'church' we shall return shortly. From John Nelson Goulty, a high Calvinist of the old Independent school, there came dire warnings. He saw in the projected Union

> a Trojan horse full of mischief; predicted the rise of spiritual assumption; suspected the approach of a controlling money power; deprecated the perils of centralization; and strove to hark back his brethren from deceitful bye-ways to the well and wisely trodden paths of the old Dissent.[39]

Suspicions and hesitations notwithstanding, the proposal for a Congregational Union of England and Wales was promulgated in May 1831, and the Union was consummated on 11 May 1832. It was made very clear that the Union was to be 'founded on the broadest recognition of their own distinctive principle, namely, the scriptural right of every separate church to maintain perfect independence in the government and administration of its own particular affairs'.[40] It followed that the Union had no legal authority over the churches, and that its objectives were to foster cooperation between them, to promote evangelism, to raise funds for new buildings, to gather accurate statistics, and to work for the removal of the remaining disabilities under which Protestant Dissenters chafed. The moderate Calvinist *Declaration of Faith and Order*,[41] promulgated in 1833, declared it 'the duty of Christian churches to hold communion with each other'.[42]

and Wales, 1931), p. 41. I am indebted to this book for much of the information in the present paragraph.

38. Quoted by Peel, *Hundred Years*, p. 54.

39. So J. Stoughton, *Reminiscences of Congregationalism Fifty Years Ago* (London: Hodder & Stoughton, 1881), pp. 71-72.

40. From the motion of May 1831 in support of the idea of a Union. It was moved by John Angell James and seconded by J. Baldwin Brown. See Peel, *Hundred Years*, pp. 62-63.

41. Prepared by George Redford, one of my predecessors at Angel Street, Worcester.

42. Clause X.

However, the fact that at the autumnal assembly held at Devonport in 1845 the Union's secretary, Algernon Wells, was still finding it necessary to insist that the Union claimed no scriptural authority for its constitution and plans, but was a voluntary, human and legitimate expedient for accomplishing the purposes for which it had been established, suggests that some were finding reasons for their less than enthusiastic embracing of the duty.[43] In a word, at its inception the Union's basis (and, no doubt the only means by which it could have been achieved) was that whereas the local church had Scripture behind it, the Union as such did not. This point was to be reiterated during the 1960s.

As the nineteenth century moved on it became increasingly clear that modern biblical criticism would no longer countenance the idea, on which many Congregationalists had hitherto relied, that there was only one polity sanctioned by the New Testament, namely theirs. Forsyth made no bones about it, referring to the double fallacy, 'first, that the polity in the New Testament is sole and sacrosanct; and, second, that the polity was Independency. History has shown that neither is true. Neither is true for any Church.'[44] For his part, John Stoughton, while believing that extreme Puritan restorationism was 'one of those unguarded positions into which ardent minds are betrayed by a blind consistency', nevertheless upheld 'the principle of the authority and unchangeableness of a revealed Church polity'.[45] As to the nature of the Church—and here we return to a point alluded to earlier—modern New Testament scholarship clearly revealed that in the New Testament 'church' refers to the local congregation and to the whole body of believers only (understand: not to an intermediate

43. It would seem that like Howard Stanley after him Wells was able to change his mind; for Thomas Binney remarked in his funeral oration for his friend that 'When the Congregational Union was first projected, he did not feel quite sure that it was allowable or safe!' Quoted by Stoughton, *Reminiscences*, p. 60. Samuel Davidson took an intermediate position regarding consociations. They were legitimate, he thought, but should not be called too frequently—indeed, only 'in cases of great difficulty'. He faulted the New England Congregationalists in this connection, and, against them, thought it was not the business of councils to license preachers of the gospel, or deliberate on their removal from one pastorate to another, or depose them. See Davidson, *Ecclesiastical Polity of the New Testament*, p. 343.

44. P.T. Forsyth, *Congregationalism and Reunion* (London: Independent Press, 1952), p. 63.

45. J. Stoughton, 'Primitive Ecclesia: Its Authoritative Principles and its Modern Representations', in H.R. Reynolds (ed.), *Ecclesia* (first series; London: Hodder & Stoughton, 1870), p. 1-55 (24).

'denominational' body). In making this point a number of Congregational-ists appealed to the researches of the distinguished Anglican scholar, F.J.A. Hort, which were published as *The Christian Ecclesia* in 1897.[46] Not, indeed, that some Congregationalists were prevented from continuing to regard their polity as most consonant with the New Testament. If, half a century before Hort, William Bengo Collyer, who ministered at Peckham from 1800 to 1853, could say, 'I cannot but consider Congregational churches most consonant with the constitution of primitive churches',[47] others, among them A.J. Grieve, were saying much the same thing same thing half a century after Hort. In an address on 'The Congregational Tradition' delivered at Carr's Lane Church, Birmingham, on 1 June 1948, Grieve warned:

> Do not...be misled by any assertion that all derive from and broke away from Episcopacy. Both it and Presbyterianism are offshoots from us and from the New Testament Church. The Early Church Universal was a Congregational type. Two points are decisive: (i) the exercise of discipline as the act of the whole body of church members—a point on which our fathers in the sixteenth century laid the greatest stress; (ii) the manner in which the ministry of the church was conceived and applied. Each Con-gregational 'bishop' or pastor was elected by the whole people...[48]

A further 50 years on, it is not altogether idle to speculate that the occa-sional Nonconformist historian in receipt of a *Festschrift* may be of a similar mind!

Reverting to the Victorians, we may first note Charles Berry's address delivered to the Union in May 1896. He took as his title, 'Congregational Churchmanship: its Principles, its Privileges, its Obligations'. 'Congrega-tionalists', he declared, 'are churchmen, as opposed to individualists. We are living members of an organism, not loose atoms wandering in eternal isolation.'[49] Pursuing a line that was to be followed from Forsyth to Daniel Jenkins, he continued:

---

46. D. Macfadyen was one who thus referred to Hort. See his *Constructive Congre-gational Ideals*, pp. 293-94. He does not, however, have in mind the ideal of 'Church' as used of a denomination, but rather two things which the New Testament excludes: '(1) any use of the word which makes the Church equivalent to the "clergy"; (2) any use of the word which makes political or geographical boundaries natural boundaries for a spiritual society.'

47. Quoted by Stoughton, *Reminiscences*, p. 69. For Collyer see *DNB*.

48. Quoted by Surman, *Grieve*, p. 48.

49. Quoted by J.S. Drummond, *Charles A. Berry, D.D.: A Memoir* (London:

A Congregational Church is not a club, in which membership depends upon pew rents. Neither is it a theological society, the purpose of whose existence is to discuss speculative questions and to attempt the settlement of a philosophy of religion. It is more even than an association of admirable people, met for the promotion of ethical culture and philanthropic enterprise. Clubs and societies are makeable and manageable by men. Churches are the creation and instrument of the Holy Ghost. Christ in the heart of each, Christ in the midst of all is the spiritual factor which translates a mere human association into a Christian Church.[50]

Secondly, we should note the curiously oscillating position of Joseph Parker. In his address to the Union of 1876, Parker was highly critical of the Congregational Union and, by implication, of its then secretary, Alexander Hannay. The Union, he felt was becoming autocratic, and Congregationalism was under threat. In 1901, without offering any explanation of his change of heart, he gave two addresses, complete with a draft constitution, in which he argued for the constitution of The United Congregational Church. While stoutly affirming that 'We are not contemplating the destruction of Congregationalism, but its perfection. The individual Church is the primary and indestructible unit of Congregationalism', he declared, 'I wish to take part in the creation and full equipment of an institution to be known and developed as the United Congregational Church'.[51] Invited to comment upon Parker's scheme under the title, 'The Congregational Church', R.F. Horton began, 'The title, which is not of my choosing, is one which would never occur to a Congregationalist'.[52] As late as 1898, when Parker wrote the preface to his autobiography, he was still contending against those who wished for a more tightly structured Congregationalism, branding Hannay 'my chief opponent'.[53] In the fifth edition of the autobiography (1903), the passage stands unaltered, Parker's 1901 crusade for The United Congregational Church notwithstanding. Meanwhile Parker had died in 1902, but the dates 1898 and 1901 do

Cassell, 1899), p. 139. The idea of the Church as an organism grew in popularity under the influence of post-Hegelian idealism. The Mercersburg theologians, Nevin, Schaff and others, majored on the theme, but I have no evidence that Berry was influenced by them, his American connections notwithstanding.

50. Drummond, *Berry*, p. 140.

51. J. Parker, *Two Addresses on The United Congregational Church* (London: Congregational Union of England and Wales, 1901), pp. 10, 8.

52. Quoted by Peel and Marriott, *Horton*, p. 143.

53. J. Parker, *A Preacher's Life: An Autobiography and an Album* (London: Hodder & Stoughton, 5th edn, 1903), pp. 258-61.

indicate the relatively brief time which it took him to effect his startling ecclesiological about-face.

A somewhat closer relationship between local churches and the Union was secured by the adoption of the latter's new constitution of 1904, the preamble to which specified the 'powers and duties' of local churches and the 'duties and responsibilities' which concern Congregational churches as a whole. A further step towards the recognition of mutual responsibility was taken when the scheme of provincial moderators became a reality in 1919. As might be expected by now, a number of voices were raised against the project, of which surely the most hysterical was that of the assembly speaker who opined that this was simply a devious plot to push bishops down our throats behind our backs! But even the most sophisticated, W.B. Selbie among them, were at pains to point out that 'The work of Modera-tors is purely consultative and advisory. They have no sort of authority over the churches.'[54] E.J. Price had invoked the same considerations in 1924, but with respect to the Union as such: 'like the county unions, it possesses no legislative authority. It is a voluntary association with no power to override the autonomy of its members.'[55]

During the next 30 years we begin to breathe a different air. Nathaniel Micklem, Lovell Cocks and various members of the Church Order Group began to emphasize the catholicity of Congregationalism (though just to show that they did not have a monopoly on the term A.J. Grieve asserted that 'It is one of the divine paradoxes that separatism and catholicity meet in the Congregational way'[56]). Lovell Cocks went so far as to weigh the celebrated R.W. Dale's *A Manual of Congregational Principles* (1884) and find it wanting.

> Why does he equate Congregationalism with the autonomy of the local church to the point of making it seem that…outward-looking concerns and compassions are optional rather than obligatory?… Dale establishes to his own satisfaction, if not to ours, that the New Testament churches were Independent in their polity; but in the course of his argument the *koinonia* of those churches in Christ drops out of sight.[57]

54. W.B. Selbie, *Congregationalism* (London: Methuen, 1927), pp. 186-87. Cf. R.K. Orchard, 'The Place of Church Councils', in Marsh (ed.), *Congregationalism Today*, pp. 86-87.

55. E.J. Price, *A Handbook of Congregationalism* (London: Independent Press, 1924), pp. 31-32.

56. Quoted by Surman, *Grieve*, p. 47.

57. H.F. Lovell Cocks, 'Where Two or Three', *World Congregationalism* 3 (1961),

Lovell Cocks welcomes the way in which the term 'covenant' was coming back into Congregational usage, but now with respect to the wider family of churches, and not in relation to the local church alone. Indeed, he went to far as to say:

> Atomistic Independency is dead or dying. But the Congregational pattern of two or three gathered in Christ's name is the very hall-mark of true catholicity. We have come to see that what has made us a denomination will not let us stay a denomination, as the tides of the Spirit sweep the divided communions of Christendom towards a deeper understanding of one another.[58]

In somewhat more down-to-earth fashion, Joseph Figures, Howard Stanley's successor as Lancashire moderator, blending theology, history and administrative pragmatism, asked 'what we mean by Congregationalism when we think of it in a corporate or denominational sense?'[59] He pointed to the indispensability of the county unions, regretting that they were grounded in expediency rather than doctrine, and arguing that 'the attitude and relationship of a local church to the Union and its reactions to decisions of the Union should be precisely the same as the attitude and relationship of a church member to his church'.[60]

With this we return to 'The Next Ten Years' and in particular to that aspect of Commission I's work which concerns the relations between the local churches and the national Union.

Commission I and the Ensuing Debate

The 14 members of Commission I met under the chairmanship of John Huxtable, with Charles Haig as vice-chairman and John Buckingham as secretary. Daniel Jenkins and Aubrey Vine were the best-known theologians on the panel, while the two women were the Revd Kathleen Hendry and Mrs. H.S. Stanley. An interim report entitled *Oversight and Covenant* was presented to the council of the Union in November 1960. The document opens thus:

pp. 31-32. The Presbyterian T.W. Manson quotes H. Cunliffe-Jones who, in an address to the Yorkshire Congregational Union (see *Yorkshire Congregational Union Year Book*, 1947–48, p. 15), found Dale wanting at the same point. See Manson, *The Church's Ministry* (London: Hodder & Stoughton, 1948), p. 94.

58. Lovell Cocks, 'Where Two or Three', p. 39.

59. J.A. Figures, 'Corporate Congregationalism', *Congregational Quarterly* 35 (1957), pp. 44-54 (44).

60. Figures, 'Corporate Congregationalism', p. 54.

> Christ is both Lord and Shepherd of His people. Christian oversight
> (episcope) is the attempt to express His rule and care through the offices
> and officers of His Church. This oversight is exercised through the Minister
> and deacons and the Church Meeting, and also through Councils, Synods,
> and Assemblies, and men called to serve them in positions of leadership, for
> example Secretaries and Moderators.[61]

Leaving on one side the fact that neither those who commended the
commission's report nor those who queried or opposed it batted an eyelid
at the assumption that those called to be in positions of leadership would
be men—notwithstanding that women had been ordained since 1917 and
Elsie Chamberlain had occupied the chair of the Union in 1956–57—we
can see at once the point at which guardians of the Congregational Way,
whether evangelical or liberal, would plunge the dagger in. The opening
statement begs the question whether the oversight exercised through the
minister, deacons and Church Meeting is similar in kind to that exercised
by the other bodies and persons specified: indeed, whether the latter is
properly called 'oversight' at all. The entire thrust of the document,
however, is that oversight as described is actually experienced within the
denomination, and that what is needed is the recognition of the fact. This
recognition, it is argued, will best be expressed if the churches of the
Union dip into their heritage for the term 'covenant' but apply it now to
the fellowship as a whole. The covenant of 1946 entered into by the saints
at Banstead is printed as an example of such a document,[62] and the
conviction is expressed that it is 'necessary for Congregational churches to
covenant with one another for the purpose of their distinctive Churchmanship'.[63] Presumably in anticipation of the objection that the move from
Union to Church would further, and unhappily, entrench denominational-
ism in an increasingly ecumenical age, the commissioners explain:

> The churches thus associated have no wish to appear as a Denomination in
> distinction from other Denominations, or to weaken their own sense of
> ecumenicity; but since it is not at present possible to gather all Christians

---

61. *Oversight and Covenant* (London: Congregational Union of England and Wales,
1960), p. 4.

62. This, of course, was a *local* covenant. According to the then minister at
Banstead, the Revd Eric Allen, he and other members of the Banstead church regretted
that their covenant, originally prepared under the guidance of Daniel Jenkins, was 'de-
contextualized' when used as an example by the commissioners. They felt that a
covenant for the denomination as a whole would necessarily be different in kind.

63. *Oversight and Covenant*, p. 5.

into one Church Order it is necessary that Congregational churches should express in some corporate form their belonging together which is so plainly a fact of their experience.[64]

They therefore propose that the churches enter into a national covenant. They state their unanimous view that the name 'Congregational Union of England and Wales' no longer adequately describes the present relationship of the churches, but they note that while 12 of their number are content that the new body be known as the Congregational Church in England and Wales, two commissioners (afterwards revealed as John Buckingham and Daniel Jenkins) felt that this would be too great a departure from tradition. Accordingly the options presented were, 'The Congregational Church in England and Wales', or, 'The Synod of the Congregational Churches in England and Wales'.[65]

A two-page insert accompanied the interim report. In it John Huxtable defines 'synod' and writes briefly on the use of covenants in Congregationalism, though some were soon to pounce upon what they perceived as the *non sequitur* between the traditional local covenants and any kind of national covenant. The New Testament scholar George Caird contributes a note on the term 'Church' in the New Testament. He explains that, fundamentally, there is one Church, the people of God, the new Israel; but there is also the church of the Laodiceans as well as the church in Nympha's house in Laodicea. In a word, he concludes, reasonably enough, that there was fluidity of usage, though some objectors (some of them only very selectively restorationist in habit) were shortly to point out that not even Caird could find 'Church *qua* denomination' in the New Testament. A pamphlet bearing the title *A Bible Study on 'Covenant'* was also circulated on behalf of Commission I. It was anonymous, the author in fact being Gordon Robinson, not himself a member of the commission. It is characteristically lucid and informative, but, strictly true to its title, it does not stray from biblical texts or draw any inferences from them regarding later churchly practice. However, he also contributed an article to *Christian World* of 8 June 1961 entitled, ' "Covenant Relationship": Its History in Congregationalism'. He here sought to remind Congregationalists of the place of covenants in their tradition, while admitting that if they recaptured the historic idea, they would be prepared for 'the next step—which is in-

---

64. *Oversight and Covenant*, p. 6.
65. *Oversight and Covenant*, p. 7.

formed consideration of the *newer* idea of the covenanted relationship of Congregational churches with each other'.[66]

John Huxtable introduced the report to the November council meeting, and underlined the fact that the commission's intention was to begin from the state of affairs actually pertaining: the denomination has 'in fact accepted a notion of oversight which is not confined to the local church; and the Commission has started from this fact'.[67] The point was reiterated at the following May Meetings, and the churches began to consider the report for themselves. A considerable discussion ensued in the religious press, notably in the *Christian World* (until its demise on 7 December 1961) and the *British Weekly*. Thus, for example, in his column, 'Answers to Your Questions', the respected minister, John Murray, explained:

> My own reason for supporting Commission I is that I think that, through it, we are now seeking to give theological and churchly expression to so much that has been happening to us over recent decades. The face of Congregationalism has changed, and many of our fathers would be astounded if they sat in the May meetings today and heard of all that the Union does, and saw the extent to which we have 'grown together', so that we are no longer a loose-knit association of churches, but one fellowship ordering a common life and the many agencies needed in it. One has only to mention the Moderatorial system, the Home Churches Fund, the denominational action to recruit candidates for the ministry, the nation-wide ordering of training for lay preachers and lay pastors, to be reminded of the striking extent to which we have been drawn together, and have set ourselves to do things together.[68]

In writing as he did, Murray had in mind three published letters of Sydney Myers.[69] With regard to the expressed intention of the leadership that the work of Commissions I and V should be regarded as indivisible in order that mission be brought fully into the life of the Church, Myers argued that precisely because Congregationalists were able to do all that they were doing as a Union, they could integrate the missionary work forthwith, whether or not they eventually became a covenanted Church—an out-

---

66. W.G. Robinson. ' "Covenant Relationship": Its History in Congregationalism', *Christian World*, 8 June 1961, p. 7; my italics.

67. Quoted in 'Congregationalism: Union or Church? Council Debates an "Historic" Report', *Christian World*, 17 November 1960, p. 7.

68. *Christian World*, 5 October 1961, p. 8.

69. *Christian World*, 20 July 1961; 17 August 1961; 14 September 1961. Norman Goodall replied to Myers on 3 and 31 August 1961; 21 September 1961.

come, he felt, which was not a foregone conclusion. With reference to the Home Churches Fund, Lovell Cocks found it necessary to endorse Murray's point, if more impishly, eleven years later in connection with the proposed scheme of union with the Presbyterians:

> Listen to this rule of the Congregational Union—you'll find it in the Year Book for 1912 or thereabouts. 'In the interest of the Aided Churches it is required as an absolute condition of grant that no invitation be given to any person to accept the pastorate, or even to supply the pulpit with a view to the pastorate, without the approval of the Executive of the County Union.' You won't find anything in the Scheme of Union half as grimly peremptory as that! What has happened to the absolute autonomy of the two or three gathered in Christ's name? Some churches it seems are more independent than others. Absolute autonomy costs more money than our aided churches can afford. If Independency means financial dependence, then anyone looking for New Testament warrant for that won't find it—though he seek it diligently and with tears.[70]

John Huxtable was indefatigable in commending the findings of Commission I. In September 1961 he acquainted the wider family of Congregationalists with the covenant proposal, and at the same time attempted to allay some of the fears at home. 'We do not envisage', he said, 'that the local Church will be told what to do.' Rather, 'we should recognise that there are, in fact, three spheres at least in which we are made aware of receiving the guidance of the Holy Spirit, the local Church, the County Union and the National Union'. Moreover, these three spheres are equal in importance; no hierarchy is envisaged.[71]

It is interesting to note in passing that the idea underlying Commission I's report was not original to its authors, as the following quotation proves:

> Our chief Constitutional doctrine—the independence of the particular Church—remaining untouched substantially (although certain definitions and practical implications of it, which have not been uncommon, may have to be set aside), we might, quite well, if we will, put our *external relations* under some common law, to which we should all be subject. We might be as *de*pendent mutually, as we are *in*dependent singly.

---

70. H.F. Lovell Cocks, Sermon preached at the Congregational Council Meetings, Argyle Church, Bath, on 14 March 1972, p. 2. Typescript in the Lovell Cocks papers Dr Williams's Library, London.

71. J. Huxtable, 'A Covenant Fellowship of Churches', *World Congregationalism* 3.9 (1961), pp. 10-14 (14).

These words appear in an address entitled 'Questions and Duties of the Time', delivered by Alexander Raleigh to the Congregational Union in 1868.[72]

Returning to the 1960s, a further dimension was added to the debate by twenty-seven self-styled evangelical ministers who disseminated a twelve-point *Statement* almost as sombre as Zechariah's flying scroll. Among their number were Gordon Booth and Edward Guest, later to be prominent in An Evangelical Fellowship of Congregational Churches, and Gilbert Kirby of the Evangelical Alliance. It is at least mildly interesting that the 27 came into the Congregational ministry by the following collegiate/non-collegiate routes:

Brecon/Swansea	7
CUEW Examinations	5
New	4[73]
Paton	4
Mansfield	2
List B	2
Cheshunt	1
Western	1
? layman	1

The fact that Lancashire/Yorkshire United/Northern and Bala-Bangor Colleges are absent from the list should not prompt unsanctified suspicions concerning the 'soundness' or otherwise of their alumni.

In response to what they call a 'serious crisis' facing the Congregational churches the evangelicals first set down the gist of their faith in five affirmations:

a.   There is one God, in three Persons, Father, Son, and Holy Spirit, each being fully God.

b.   Man has fallen and is in a lost condition before God.

c.   Salvation is only through the atoning death of Christ and is received by faith.

72. See *Congregational Year Book*, 1869, p. 70.

73. The four from New College were ordained in the same year, 1950. When contemplating succeeding Sydney Cave as principal of New College in 1953, John Huxtable recalls that he sought Nathaniel Micklem's advice. Micklem cautioned him not to make the mistake he himself had made on coming to Mansfield, namely, that of thinking that the battle against fundamentalism was over. Huxtable comments, 'I found out later not only how wise that judgement was; I also discovered how much Cave had suffered himself from the arrogance of those who would not, or could not, learn.' See Huxtable, *As It Seemed to Me*, pp. 30-31.

d. Conversion is necessary and, in this, the work of the Holy Spirit is indispensible [*sic*].

e. The Scriptures of the Old and New Testaments are divinely inspired and of supreme authority.[74]

The co-signatories claim that these doctrines are consistent with those specified in the Savoy *Declaration* of 1658, the Congregation Union *Declaration* of 1833, and with the trust deeds 'which originally governed the vast majority of our churches and Congregational foundations'. They continue in paragraphs four and five:

> We hold these doctrines to be essential to the truth of the Gospel, yet we know there are ministers and churches in the Congregational Unions which, by statement and practice, deny them.
>
> We therefore declare that to enter into any proposed covenant with such ministers and churches would, we believe, seriously compromise witness to the Gospel.

They tell us that they have studied Commission I's report, and have noted Huxtable's address, and they are in no doubt that where the findings are accepted 'the full autonomy of the local church will be lost', with the result that Congregationalism would not be modified, but abandoned.[75]

Under the headline, 'Evangelical Veto', the *Christian World* reported the circulation of the *Statement*, and uttered its first 'reaction of regret... that these ministers should have contemplated what must be called a new form of separatism within the "separatist churches"'.[76] The following week 'Nemo' observed against the evangelicals' strong plea for uninhibited local autonomy, that 'An independency that will not listen to testimony as to what Christ is saying to the churches has always been a false Congregationalism.'[77] In the same issue John Ticehurst presumed to find the evangelicals' statement of faith an 'emasculated affair which does not, for example, mention the Manhood of our Saviour', and he boggled at their non-Congregational fondness for a credal test on the basis of which they will decide the Christian status of others and agree to covenant only with those who think as they do. He cheekily noted that the signatories are located in various parts of the country and thus are not a Church Meeting, and hence, on their own premisses, cannot be divinely guided; and as for

74. *A Statement*, privately circulated, para. 3.
75. *A Statement*, paras. 7, 8.
76. *Christian World*, 5 October 1961, p. 1.
77. *Christian World*, 12 October 1961, p. 2.

their call to others to urge the rejection of Commission I's proposal in County Union meetings, this, he declared, 'seems to smack of casting out devils by the Prince of Devils'.[78] In a circular letter to his co-signatories Edward Guest wrote, 'We have been accused of being strong in our Statement. Well—we were sounding an alarm, not crooning a lullaby. Enough dreamers around already!'[79]

Meanwhile there were stirrings in the most north-westerly parts of the Yorkshire Dales (as they then were); and here I revert to autobiography. A Congregationalist by conviction, and less than two years into my first pastorate at Sedbergh and Dent, I attended the annual Dales Conference at Hawes on 29–30 May 1961. On the evening of 30 May Norman Beard, secretary of the Yorkshire Union, introduced the Commission I's report and, according to my diary, I made some critical comments, with which Norman Beard agreed. Later in the year, on Saturday 28 October, a special meeting of the Dales churches was held at Hawes, with Norman Beard again present. Two days previously the Dales ministers had held a fraternal at which, to quote my diary again, 'we planned our campaign for Saturday'. It transpired that the general feeling among the Dales churches was that the commission's proposal could not be endorsed until certain matters had been clarified—if then. In view of the Dales discussions and the wider debates in the press, I was by now increasingly concerned on the one hand that there were ecclesiological issues which had yet to be adequately addressed and, on the other hand, that claims were being made

---

78. J. Ticehurst, 'The New Separatists', *Christian World*, 12 October 1961, p. 2. Letters for and against the evangelicals were published, *Christian World*, 19 October 1961; and on 26 October Charles Haig published 'An Open Letter to the Evangelicals' in which he addressed them (knowingly using the 'language of Canaan'?) as 'My dear brothers in Christ'. On 2 November 10 evangelicals signed an article in reply to Haig. It is thus surprising that one of the evangelical signatories, Walter H. Denbow, should begin the second of four privately circulated pamphlets with the remark that 'the publishing facilities of both Independent Press and Christian World are reserved exclusively for the support of the Commission Reports. Both definitely decline to publish criticisms of the Reports, direct or implied, while they are before the Churches.' Unlike the evangelical *Statement*, Denbow's pamphlets major on autonomy rather than more general doctrine. Indeed, having regard to the evangelicals' doctrinal criterion of fellowship, it is faintly ironic that in the second pamphlet (p. 2) he can write in block capitals, 'COVENANT WILL NO MORE BIND OUR CHRISTIAN CONDUCT THAN CREED WILL BIND OUR CHRISTIAN BELIEF'.

79. Quoted by G. Booth, 'Winds of Change in Congregationalism', *The Christian*, 23 February 1962, p. 8.

by the defenders of Congregationalism which seemed to me to be spurious. Accordingly, I wrote a draft article under the title, 'A Dales View of Commission I', and went up to the manse at Ravenstonedale to discuss it with my senior colleagues, George Curry and Arnold Mee.

These two colleagues could not have been more different from each other, or from myself, though I suppose that we could all consistently have labelled ourselves 'evangelical' had that word not been so sadly hijacked, and provided that we could also call ourselves liberal, catholic and Re-formed. George Curry (1901–91), a larger-than-life Greatheart from the north-east, who had been raised among the Methodists and who, after an engineering apprenticeship, had served as a circuit rider in deepest Saskatchewan, finally returning to his native parts via a two-year sojourn on the Isle of Wight, had become a Congregationalist by conviction. By now he was the Dales minister, enjoying his roving ministry over a vast tract of country extending from Newton-in-Bowland to Keld, and from Sedbergh to Richmond. He faithfully tended his extensive patch in all weathers, and it cannot in truth be said that the winding, undulating roads were made less terrifying by the presence of his hurtling Mini upon them. At the time of our little crusade he was chairman of the Yorkshire Union.[80]

Arnold Mee (1901–66) was a lifelong Congregationalist, raised in Leeds under the celebrated ministry at Salem of Bertram Smith and Francis Wrigley. Never robust in health, he eventually went blind, and to those who looked on this was a particularly cruel blow upon one who was a fine scholar, not least of Hebrew. For a period Arnold had served with great success as tutor at Yorkshire United College, but failing eyesight dictated that the rest of his ministry would be in rural pastorates. A man of deep faith, sharp yet kindly wit, and no mean poet, Arnold Mee was a blessing to all who met him.[81]

These were the two who cast their eye over my draft article. To my considerable surprise they approved it without amendment and said that they would happily endorse it should it appear in the *Christian World*. On 31 October 1961 I wrote to the editor to ask if he would accept the piece, pointing out that my co-signatories and I felt that 'out of our bewilderment arise certain questions which have not so far been raised in the columns of your paper'. By the same post I sent a copy of the article to John Huxtable,

---

80. For his obituary see *Congregational Year Book, 1991/1992* (Nottingham: Congregational Federation), pp. 30-31.

81. See further, J.W. Moody [daughter], *Arnold Francis Mee, 1901–1966* (privately printed); *Congregational Year Book*, 1966–67, pp. 460-61.

whom I had never met, assuring him that 'there is no connection between the submission of our effort today, and Luther's action [in nailing up his theses] 444 years ago today!!' Huxtable replied by return. He felt that we had not sufficiently considered the actual state of current Congregationalism, and that we had made too much of the proposed change of name. Indeed, he pointed out that

> we make no recommendations about it at all if you look at the document carefully. We state the fact that some of us think that we might as well call ourselves a church and be done with it, since, in fact, we are functioning as one, and that a small minority thought that the word 'synod' would cover the matter better.[82]

I circulated Huxtable's letter to my colleagues, and could not forbear to point out to them that even if the name 'Church' were not, technically, the subject of a commission recommendation, it could not be denied that the alternatives of 'Church' and 'Synod' had formally been proposed for consideration by the commissioners themselves.

The burden of the Dales article, which on publication was retitled, 'Commission I: From the Camp of the "Bewildered"',[83] was that there was more theological work to be done before final decisions could be made. The first question was that of the relative authority of the several *foci* of churchly life. Secondly, the statement in the commission's report to the effect that national covenanting was a necessity 'for the purpose of [our] distinctive Churchmanship'[84] was queried as to the nature of the 'necessity' involved: 'It cannot be logical necessity', I boldly declared, 'for we are not covenanted at present and yet believe that we have a distinctive Churchmanship. Surely the implication is not that if we do *not* covenant we shall have a distinctive Churchmanship no more?' Thirdly, we sought more guidance on the nature and implications of the covenant sought, noting that dissatisfaction with the term 'Union' had not adequately been explained.

> For the people behind the Report obviously do not subscribe to the erroneous belief that the only factor which provides our present sense of fellowship is the payment of an affiliation fee. If they did believe this, they could hardly employ the 'regularising of what already obtains' argument.

Finally, we sought a stronger theological justification of the use of the terms 'Church' or 'Synod' with reference to the national body. 'What's in

---

82. Huxtable to Sell, 1 November 1961.
83. See *Christian World*, 9 November 1961, p. 8.
84. *Oversight and Covenant*, p. 5.

a name?' we asked in conclusion: 'In this case the answer is "Our doctrine of the Church." And that is why the matter is so important.' Our position thus was that we could not vote for or against the proposal until further illumination had been granted.

The article drew a gracious response from Charles Haig, in which he reiterated the commission's line, sought to reassure us that 'We are interested in forming a Congregational Church, not any other sort' (though he was deficient in the detail), and was even prepared to believe that the term 'covenant' might not be the best to express what the commission had in mind—albeit it was difficult to think of an adequate alternative term.[85]

To my very great surprise I began to receive letters from many quarters, mostly from people whom I had never met. All unwittingly I found myself in the position of a communications channel which involved much correspondence, and this at a time when I was writing two sermons and an evening lecture every week, serving on the local council, and finishing my MA thesis. The first response was from Hugh Kember, one of the 27 evangelicals, who had given the charge at my ordination, and with whom I continue in close friendship. The next was from Principal Maurice Charles of Paton College, with whom George Curry and I were to work closely over the next few months. Through him we came into contact with Reginald Cleaves, a successor of P.T. Forsyth at Clarendon Park, Leicester. The correspondence continued to flow, and on 25 November 1961 the Dales trio decided to support a petition to the Congregational Council urging that in view of the serious division of opinion among Congregationalists over Commission I's proposal, any resolution assuming that churches were ready to make a final decision in May 1962 be postponed. R.W. Cleaves sent the letter to Howard Stanley on 5 January 1962, with copies to C.J. Buckingham, secretary of Commission I, Norman Goodall of Commission V, and the press. There were 21 signatories, and no overlap between this list and the evangelical one. Indeed, Cleaves wrote in his letter to Stanley, 'The signatories are not members of any organised group, nor have they met at any time to deliberate on the matter in question'.

The petition duly appeared in the *British Weekly* of 22 February 1962, under the headline, 'Anxious Congregationalists Advise Delay'. Thereafter we were labelled, and further letters were published for and against the petition, including one from Charles Haig, who felt that the petitioners

85. C.A. Haig, 'Commission I: A Word to the Bewildered', *Christian World*, 23 November 1961, p. 8.

were overestimating the degree of divided opinion among Congregational-ists.[86] To some of the points raised in correspondence the Dales trio replied. Haig had suggested that the way to see how great the division of opinion was was to have a full-scale debate in the assembly, with a view to testing the 'main principle'. We felt that since the materials had been circulated to every church, every church should be permitted to submit the finding of its Church Meeting as data for consideration by the assembly. We countered that the division of opinion between the supporters of the commission's proposals and, for example, the evangelical signatories was great. And we pressed again the fundamental point that many were still unclear as to what the 'main principle' was, and that a theological justifi-cation be given of the leap from our present (welcome) degree of unity to an assertion concerning the nature of the Church which we had not hitherto made—namely, that a denomination is a Church. We were con-cerned lest we should be 'undermining part of our distinctive testimony to the essential oneness of the Church, by making it appear that we think there is more than one Church'.[87]

Once it became known that a motion was to be put at the May Meetings urging that 'a serious attempt be made to implement the main findings of Commission I', and to appoint 'a fully representative committee' with that end in view, a meeting was convened at Paton College on 24 April 1962. George Curry and I went down from the Dales, and there I met not only Maurice Charles and Reginald Cleaves for the first time, but also Gordon Booth, one of the evangelical signatories. The upshot of the meeting was that an amendment to the council's motion was prepared consistent with our wish for further consideration of the theological principles prior to a final vote. Our amendment was 'That a serious attempt be made to con-sider the implementing of the main findings of Commission I'. It was signed by 15 ministers (all that could be mustered in the time available) and duly published in the *British Weekly* on 10 May, as was a letter ex-pressing the opposition of 30 evangelicals. Early in May I received a letter from Gordon Booth in which he pledged the support of what he called the evangelical 'Resistance Movement'.[88] I rushed a note to the editor of the *British Weekly*, which he appended to our letter. In it I said that a group of evangelical ministers was prepared to support the amendment.

86. *British Weekly*, 1 March 1962, p. 8.
87. *British Weekly*, 1 March 1962, p. 8.
88. Booth to Sell, 3 May 1962.

I do not know their precise reasons for this, and it would be unjust to give the impression that our motives necessarily coincide. The fact of this support, however, confirms my opinion that the introduction of the word 'consider' into the original proposition, which is what our amendment suggests, would have a valuable therapeutic effect.

On 7 May Reginald Cleaves agreed to move the amendment. To my very great surprise, others having been approached and being unavailable, I found myself in the position of seconding it. So it came to pass that on 16 May 1962, in a packed Westminster Chapel, Hubert Cunliffe-Jones, the proposer of the official resolution, asked in the name of himself and his seconder, John Huxtable, for permission to substitute the phrase 'work out the implications of' for the word 'implement'. This was not allowed, so the motion as published was moved and seconded: 'That a serious attempt be made to implement the main findings of Commission I'. Then Reginald Cleaves moved our amendment, proposing the introduction of the words, 'consider implementing' in place of 'implement'. His speech emphasized the Congregational heritage and especially the autonomy of the local church. I, having first pointed out that I had never before addressed so large a congregation, adduced four reasons for the introduction of the word 'consider'. First, it would make sense of the resolution; for 'If we really want a fully representative, ungagged, committee, the word "consider" must be in'. Secondly, 'The word "consider" is needed so that more homework will be encouraged'. In particular, more work is needed on the so-called 'third Church' subsisting between the local church and the great Church; a fuller statement of our doctrine of the Church is required—in the year of the tercentenary of the Great Ejectment of all years; and we should learn from recent merger history, especially in America, the folly of undue haste. Thirdly, 'The word "consider" is desirable because it will help to heal. Many of the anxious and many evangelicals can support the amendment.' Finally, 'further consideration will enable us to discover what is our distinctive contribution for the sake of the great Church'. Let us not confuse dying in order to live with committing suicide. I concluded, 'Mr. Chairman, I second the amendment because it makes better sense of the original proposition, it will encourage more homework, it will help to heal, and it is for the good of the whole Church'. Cleaves and I were then asked in the pulpit whether we could accept the phrase, 'work out the implications of' I thought that this was ambiguous: was it assumed that we knew what the implications were, and all we had to do was to put them into effect? Or, did we need to work out what the implications were? I could be happy with the latter. Cleaves addressed the assembly again, arguing that the words 'work out the implications of'. meant the same as 'consider', to which those gathered responded 'Yes' in chorus. Cunliffe-Jones' wording carried the day; at least it was preferable, even in its ambiguity, to the original; and assurances were given that the points raised in the debate would be addressed by the representative committee. As I came down the steps of the enormous pulpit, Norman Goodall was passing at the bottom. He said, 'I hope we shall hear more of you'. Whether he did or not, I have no means of knowing, for that was our first and last meeting.

Geoffrey Beck's report of the debate in the *British Weekly* of 24 May was so compressed as to be misleading, and in response to a request from Cleaves,[89] the official minute was published in the paper on 7 June, over the signatures of John Huxtable, H.A. Hamilton, the Union chairman, and Howard S. Stanley. The minute stated that Cleaves and I withdrew our amendment. However, we did not; we accepted Cunliffe-Jones' wording as an interpretation of it—a point which Cleaves made to Huxtable and Hamilton in a communication of 11 June.

Meanwhile on 18 May I wrote to John Huxtable expressing my pleasure at the way things had gone in the assembly, reiterating my hope that the theological issues would receive due consideration, and reminding him that in his letter responding to the Dales article he had said that 'It would be much easier to discuss this in conversation.' I requested a meeting, and on 28 May we met in his office. We then had lunch together, and our conversation continued in a taxi heading for an up-market gents outfitters, where he was to purchase a black Homburg in anticipation of a junket with the Archbishop of Canterbury. I was thus able to put my two main points directly to him: the first concerning the importance of oversight conceived mutually as between the several *foci* of churchly life; the second concerning the need, on ecumenical grounds, of admitting that the use of the term 'Church' for 'denomination' is biblically and theologically irregular. The main outcome of the meeting from my point of view was his reiteration of the assurance that the theological work would be done, and that he was on the representative committee to ensure that it would be.

The committee duly went to work, and in May 1963 a *Draft Constitution* together with *A Commentary* on it written by Robert Latham was presented to that assembly and remitted to the churches for consideration.[90] It is most unfortunate that in his *résumé* of the events leading to the

89. Cleaves to Sell and Curry, 31 May 1962.
90. John Marsh contributed a balanced article, 'Understanding the Draft Consti-

drafting of the constitution Latham, in an otherwise able exposition, should have quoted the *original* motion that the main findings of Commission I be implemented, as if it were the Assembly's final resolution. I wrote to Cunliffe-Jones about this and in reply he said:

> I am sorry there is a misstatement in Robert Latham's Commentary. But I don't think there is anything sinister in this. This has been done in a great hurry and the resolution may have been copied wrongly by the typist. By all means write to Howard Stanley, call his attention to the misstatement and I think he will cancel it publicly. He likes to have things correctly stated.
>
> On the point of substance, we are not going to implement anything that we do not agree to. I am sorry that this mistake has occurred at a point where there is, understandably enough, considerable feeling.[91]

From Draft Constitution to Congregational Church

How far was I reassured by the *Draft Constitution*? The strategy adopted was that the question of the name of the denomination should not be considered unless and until the principle of a national covenant had been agreed. There was thus no discussion of the definition of 'Church' in the documents. There was, however, a clear statement of the mutuality of *episcope* as between the local and wider *foci* of churchly life.

> Both the local church and this covenanted body are under the same authority—the Lordship of Christ. Both are pledged to discern the mind of Christ for themselves and to listen to the testimony of others as to what the mind of Christ is.[92]

This I greatly welcomed, because it seemed to me to honour that catholic thrust which had ever been inherent in Congregationalism, but which had too frequently been obscured by restrictive understandings of local autonomy. Moreover, only along the lines of mutual *episcope* could due weight be accorded to the remark (sadly, one of relatively few remarks published) of my teacher of doctrine, the much loved George Phillips:

> The active presence of the Holy Spirit is...the principle of Church unity rather than any form of external authority... Hence the imposition of an

tution', to the *British Weekly*, 9 May 1963, p. 3.

91. Cunliffe-Jones to Sell, 4 May 1963.

92. *Draft Constitution* (London: Congregational Union of England and Wales, 1963), p. 8. Cf. the pamphlet, *Some Questions and Answers*, para. 6. This was published to accompany Commission I's Interim Report.

external authority upon the Church of Christ seems to us, as to our fathers, a humiliation, and a usurpation of the sole right of the Divine Spirit.[93]

I took further encouragement from Commission I's report on *The Nature of Christian Unity and its Challenge to our Churches*, which was submitted to the 1963 assembly of the Union:

> Neither man nor party, nor Church Meeting nor Assembly can arrogate the right to be considered the sole authoritative interpreter of the Mind of the Spirit. It is not possible to exclude the possibility of error, even when a Council or Assembly of the Church has spoken. Nor, on the other hand, can a minority or dissident individual make good the claim to be the sole medium of the Spirit's guidance. Majorities may be arrogant, but minorities can be self-willed.[94]

It is difficult to conceive that the transition from Union to Church would have been made at all had the principle of mutual *episcope* not clearly been written into the *Draft Constitution*. As it was, the transition was not accomplished without a parting of the ways.

By now I was feeling increasingly that the labels attached to Congregationalists—'Commission supporters', 'bewildered', 'anxious', 'Evangelical'—were obscuring more than they revealed. I was able to see the point of Nathaniel Micklem's assertion that while the local church has a 'faith-structure' in that the final appeal is to the authority of Christ, 'Our denomination has an expediency-structure, not a faith-structure.'[95] I felt that some of those alongside whom I had pressed for further theological clarification were more concerned with local autonomy as such, than with the idea that the local church is an expression of the Church catholic, with all that that means in terms of wider fellowship not on grounds of expediency or utility, but of right. I was not surprised, therefore, when Reginald Cleaves and George Curry subsequently became leaders of the Congregational Federation.[96] Again, while a number of evangelicals were

---

93. G. Phillips, 'Freedom in Religious Thought', in *The Fourth Freedom* (London: Independent Press, 1943), p. 51. George Phillips was raised among the Strict Baptists.

94. *The Nature of Christian Unity and its Challenge to our Churches*, p. 5.

95. N. Micklem, *Congregationalism and the Church Catholic* (London: Independent Press, 1943), p. 30.

96. See R.W. Cleaves, *Congregationalism, 1960–1976: The Story of the Federation* (Swansea: John Penry Press, 1977). It is to be feared that some statements herein are tendentious. For example, of those who eventually became part of the United Reformed Church it is said that 'For them, Historic Independency no longer mattered and was thrown to the wind' (p. 9). This is a libel, and one suspects that it is not how

willing to support those who appeared to be striving for local autonomy—
in their case because they did not wish to be unequally yoked with those
whose understanding of Scripture differed from their own—they knew and
I knew that their credal criteria appeared to many as a 'new circumcision'
on the basis of which they would judge the Christian status of others. The
sensitivity of my ecclesiastical antennae to evangelical sectarianism did
not, of course, preclude me from agreeing with Robert Mackintosh, who
said:

> The body of Congregationalism might continue to exist for a season, though
> it had ceased to be an expression of evangelical faith and life; but the soul
> which has animated it would be gone. And a body without a soul is a corpse.[97]

In due course a number of the evangelicals constituted An Evangelical
Fellowship of Congregational Churches.[98]

some uniting Presbyterians, trying to get their minds around the idea of Church
Meeting, viewed matters. See also the review of the book by F.R. Tomes in the *Journal
of the United Reformed Church History Society* 2 (1978), pp. 25-26. It should be noted,
however, that in his presidential address to the Congregational Federation, 'Jesus is
Lord', delivered to the 151st Congregational Assembly on 8 May 1982, John C.
Travell sought to place some of the 'autonomy' talk in its theological context: 'May I
confess that it makes me uneasy that our Year Book states that the Foundation
Principle of our Federation is "the scriptural right of every separate Church to maintain
perfect independence in the government and administration of its affairs"... [T]he
reason *why* this Assembly or the Federation shall not assume legislative authority is
because Christ alone is head of his Church. That is our true distinctive principle and
the reason why we believe in the independence of the local church is so that it may be
free more directly to be obedient to its Lord. It is not a matter of rights but of faith'
(p. 1). See also J.C. Travell, 'The Congregational Federation, 1972–1997', in Binfield
(ed.), *Reformed and Renewed*, pp. 29-42.

97. R. Mackintosh, 'The Genius of Congregationalism', in A. Peel (ed.), *Essays
Congregational and Catholic* (London: Congregational Union of England and Wales,
[1931]), p. 125.

98. For a brief account of An Evangelical Fellowship of Congregational Churches
see that body's *Year Book*, 1990–91, p. 21; A. Tovey, 'An Evangelical Fellowship of
Congregational Churches, 1972–1997', in Binfield (ed.), *Reformed and Renewed*, pp.
42-50. The difference in attitude between the founders of the Federation and the evangelicals is captured by Gordon Booth in an article entitled, 'Continuing Congregationalists', published in *Evangelical Times* (June 1972), p. 10, in the wake of the
constitution of the Congregational Federation on 13 May 1972. There are in addition
some independent Congregational churches which, in order to receive their due from
the assets of the Congregational Church in England and Wales, were designated
Unaffiliated by the Charity Commissioners. Their story is told by J. Franks, *Stewards*

While so far reassured, I continued to feel that it was ill advised to discuss the nature of a covenanted body apart from its name, for the one could not really be divorced from the other. I argued along this line at the Dales Conference on 2 November 1963. Speaking for the commission was Martin Shepherd, the Yorkshire moderator and member of the representative committee. In responding to my paper he, according to my diary, 'got a bit overwrought'. In all of this I was hoping for the recognition that to call our national body a Church was a departure from our tradition, and a development of New Testament teaching, which could be countenanced only on the grounds that it was an interim usage given the divided state of the whole Church.[99] I did not wish us to become a sectarian bloc—a consideration which did not seem to weigh so heavily upon some of my 'anxious' and 'evangelical' friends. Embedded in the Sedbergh church's response of 28 February 1964 to the *Draft Constitution*, submitted to Howard Stanley, is the following passage:

> ...if we become *a* churchly body (as though we believed that there are numerous Churches), may we not be surrendering a part of our historic witness *too soon*—i.e. outside the context of a truly representative round-table conference of churchmen? Or, alternatively, has it been found already that nobody will listen to us on this point and that we are destined to be eternally out on a limb unless we amend our views?

It is true that Commission I's original report had declared:

> The churches thus associated have no wish to appear as a Denomination in distinction from other Denominations, or to weaken their own sense of ecumenicity; but since it is not at present possible to gather all Christians into one Church Order it is necessary that Congregational churches should express in some corporate form their belonging together which is so plainly a fact of their experience.[100]

But how this bore on the doctrine of the Church to be espoused was not, in the initial stages of the debate, clear.

As the discussion proceeded, however, encouraging comments from various quarters began to coalesce. I have already mentioned the principle of mutual *episcope* which was built into the constitution, and, consistently with this, the witness to the local church as an expression of the Church

---

of God's Bounty: The History of the Unaffiliated Congregational Churches Charities (Manchester: Unaffiliated Congregational Churches Charities, 1996).

    99. See further, Sell, *Saints*, p. 115.

   100. *Oversight and Covenant*, p. 6.

catholic. This latter point was underlined in the *Declaration of Faith* produced by Commission II and finally adopted in 1967.[101] In addition, members of Commission I began more frankly to endorse the truth that the New Testament knows nothing of a 'third Church' between the local church and the whole Church. Thus, for example, John Huxtable declared that the proposed use of 'Church' of the denomination as a whole 'certainly has no literal warrant in scripture'.[102] He reiterated the point elsewhere, but asked, 'in the present unhappily divided state of the Church, in which Anglicans, Presbyterians and Methodists can speak of Churches, might we not, without too great a damage to language, so describe ourselves?'[103] It is not without interest that, according to its secretary, Martin Cressey, the exegetical point was conceded by the Joint Committee of Presbyterians and Congregationalists who were preparing the *Basis of Union* of the United Reformed Church, and that to call a denomination a Church is to demonstrate 'that the failure and weakness of the Church have in particular been manifested in division which has made it impossible for Christians fully to know, experience and communicate the life of the one, holy, catholic, apostolic Church'.[104] What seems undeniable is that the covenanting together of the Congregational churches in 1966 as the Congregational Church in England and Wales facilitated the eventual constitution of the United Reformed Church in 1972. The theological tasks sufficiently done, I happily accepted both decisions, believing that the insights of Congregational catholicity had been preserved in a Church order that emphasized the *mutuality* of *episcope* as between the local and

101. See *A Declaraton of Faith*, p. 34.

102. J. Huxtable, *Proceedings of the International Congregational Council* 10 (1966), p. 33.

103. Huxtable, *As It Seemed to Me*, p. 38. Among earlier stalwarts in denying the 'third Church' idea was C.J. Cadoux. See his *The Congregational Way*, pp. 18-19; 'Congregationalism the True Catholicism', in Peel (ed.), *Essays Congregational and Catholic*, pp. 53-77 (69-70). John Marsh, on other matters significantly apart from Cadoux, reiterated the point in 'Obedience to the Gospel in terms of Churchmanship and Church Order', in *idem* (ed.), *Congregationalism To-day*, pp. 45-61 (48-49). Erik Routley was among more prominent authors who in the 1960s queried the proposed application of 'Church'. See his *Congregationalists and Unity* (London: Mowbray, 1962), pp. 31-33. He preferred to think of Congregationalism as 'an order within the church catholic', p. 34. For a 'classical' statement on the matter, see Dale, *Manual of Congregational Principles*, p. 212.

104. *Basis of Union*, para. 7, quoted by M. Cressey, 'The Theology of Union', in Binfield (ed.), *Reformed and Renewed*, p. 22.

wider *foci* of churchly life, and that the anomalous, interim, denominational use of the term 'Church' was a stimulus to work to render it redundant.[105] Indeed, in that spirit I spoke in the Union assembly debate on 19 May 1965, when the motion to change the Congregational denomination's name from 'Union' to 'Church' was successful. The consummation came one year later in a Service of Thanksgiving and Dedication held on 22 May 1966 at Whitefield Memorial Church, London.

Epilogue

I little thought, during the ecclesiological excitements of the early 1960s, that 20 years on I would be regularly engaged in international bilateral dialogues on largely ecclesiological issues as Theological Secretary of the World Alliance of Reformed Churches, or that 40 years on I would still be summoned as a consultant to such dialogues. That is another chapter, but it is all part of the story which began when I met Jimmy in the ice cream shop in 1939.

105. R.W. Cleaves was thus mistaken in implying that all those who has earlier been labelled 'anxious Congregationalists' found their way into The Congregational Association. See his 'The Congregational Association', *Congregational Monthly*, June 1969, p. 4. I corrected the error in *Congregational Monthly*, July 1969, p. 14, concluding that in my opinion 'what is of value in Congregationalism is to be found within the C[ongregational] C[hurch in] E[ngland and] W[ales]'.

BIBLIOGRAPHY OF J.C.G. BINFIELD'S PUBLISHED WRITINGS

a. *Books*

Binfield, J.C.G., *The Contexting of a Chapel Architect: James Cubitt, 1836–1912* (Occasional Publications, 2; London: The Chapels Society, 2001).

—*George Williams and the Y.M.C.A.: A Study in Victorian Social Attitudes* (London: Heinemann, 1973).

—*Pastors and People: The Biography of a Baptist Church: Queen's Road* (Coventry: Queen's Road Baptist Church, 1984).

—*So Down to Prayers: Studies in English Nonconformity 1780–1920* (London: J.M. Dent, 1977).

—*This Has Been Tomorrow: The World Alliance of YMCAs since 1955* (Geneva: World's Alliance of Young Men's Christian Associations, 1991).

b. *Books and Volumes Edited*

Binfield, J.C.G. (ed.), *The Cross and the City: Essays in Commemoration of Robert William Dale, 1829–1895* (*Journal of the United Reformed Church History Society* Supp, 6.2; Spring 1999).

—*Reformed and Renewed, 1972–1997: Eight Essays* (*Journal of the United Reformed Church History Society* Supp, 5.2; September 1997).

—*Sainthood Revisioned: Studies in Hagiography and Biography* (Sheffield: Sheffield Academic Press, 1995).

—*Sir Francis Chantrey: Sculptor to an Age* (Sheffield: Sheffield University, City Libraries, City Polytechnic, 1981).

Binfield, J.C.G., and D. Hey (eds.), *Mesters to Masters: A History of the Company of Cutlers in Hallamshire* (Oxford: Oxford University Press, 1997).

Binfield, J.C.G., and J. Stevenson (eds.), *Sport, Culture and Politics* (Sheffield: Sheffield Academic Press, 1993).

Binfield, J.C.G., *et al.* (eds.), *The History of the City of Sheffield, 1843–1993*. I. *Politics* (Sheffield: Sheffield Academic Press, 1993).

—*The History of the City of Sheffield, 1843–1993*. II. *Society* (Sheffield: Sheffield Academic Press, 1993).

—*The History of the City of Sheffield, 1843–1993*. III. *Images* (Sheffield: Sheffield Academic Press, 1993).

c. *Journals Edited*

Binfield, J.C.G., Co-Editor, *Journal of the United Reformed Church History Society*, 1976–85 (Vols 1–3), Sole Editor, 1985– (Vols 3–7) with Supplements.

Binfield, J.C.G., Editor, *Reformed Quarterly*, 1989–95 (Vols 1–3; NS Vols 1–2).

d. *Contributions to Volumes*

Binfield, J.C.G., 'A Chapel and its Architect: James Cubitt and Union Chapel, Islington, 1879–1889 (Presidential Address)', in Diana Wood (ed.), *The Church and the Arts* (Studies in Church History, 28; Oxford: Basil Blackwell, 1992 [Pbk 1995]), pp. 417-48.

—' "A Crucible of Modest though Concentrated Experiment": Religion in Sheffield, c. 1840–1950', in H. McLeod (ed.), *European Religion in the Age of Great Cities* (London: Routledge, 1995), pp. 191-215.

—'A Matter of Appearances: The Boothroyds and Southport Congregationalism', *Transactions of the Lancashire and Cheshire Antiquarian Society* 96 (2000), pp. 133-42.

—'A Working Memorial? The Encasing of Paisley's Baptists', in W.M. Jacob and N. Yates (eds.), *Crown and Mitre: Religion and Society in Northern Europe since the Reformation* (Woodbridge: Boydell Press, 1993), pp. 185-202.

—'Alexander,W.L. (1808–84)', in N.M. de S. Cameron *et al.* (eds), *Dictionary of Scottish Church History and Theology* (Edinburgh: T. & T. Clark, 1993), pp. 9-10.

—' "An Artisan of Christian Unity": Sir Frank Willis, Rome and the YMCA', in R.M. Swanson (ed.), *Unity and Diversity in the Church* (Studies in Church History, 32; Oxford: Basil Blackwell, 1996), pp. 489-505.

—'An Excursion into Architectural Cousinhood: The East Anglian Connexion', in Norma Virgoe and T. Williamson (eds.), *Religious Dissent in East Anglia: Historical Perspectives* (Norwich: Centre of East Anglian Studies, University of East Anglia, 1993), pp. 93-140.

—' "An Optimism of Grace": The Spirituality of Some Wesleyan Kinswomen', in Binfield (ed.), *Sainthood Revisioned*, pp. 67-91.

—'Antinomianism', in J. Cannon (ed.), *The Oxford Companion to British History* (Oxford: Oxford University Press, 1997), p. 38.

—'Architects in Connexion: Four Methodist Generations', in Jane Garnett and C. Matthew (eds.), *Revival and Religion since 1700: Essays for John Walsh* (London: Hambledon Press, 1993), pp. 153-81.

—'Art and Spirituality in Chapel Architecture: F.W. Lawrence (1882–1948) and his Churches', in D.M. Loades (ed.), *The End of Strife: Death, Reconciliation and the Expression of Christian Spirituality* (Papers from the C.I.H.E.C. Colloquium held at Durham 1981; Edinburgh: T. & T. Clark, 1984), pp. 200-226.

—'Bible Christians', in J. Cannon (ed.), *The Oxford Companion to British History* (Oxford: Oxford University Press, 1997), p. 103.

—'Bible Society', in J. Cannon (ed.), *The Oxford Companion to British History* (Oxford: Oxford University Press, 1997), p. 103.

—'Boys' Brigade', in N.M. de S. Cameron *et al.* (eds), *Dictionary of Scottish Church History and Theology* (Edinburgh: T. & T. Clark, 1993), pp. 92-93.

—' "Bridled Emotion"; English Free Churchmen, Culture and Catholic Values, c. 1870–c. 1945', in A.C. Duke and C.A. Tamse (eds.), *Britain and the Netherlands. VII. Church and State since the Reformation* (The Hague: Nijhoff, 1981), pp. 176-206.

—'Broad Church', in J. Cannon (ed.), *The Oxford Companion to British History* (Oxford: Oxford University Press, 1997), p. 111.

—'Business Paternalism and the Congregational Ideal: A Preliminary Reconnoitre', in D. Jeremy (ed.), *Business and Religion in Britain* (Aldershot: Gower, 1987), pp. 118-41.

—'Catholic Apostolic Church', in J. Cannon (ed.), *The Oxford Companion to British History* (Oxford: Oxford University Press, 1997), pp. 176-77.

—'Charles Silvester Horne', in C.S. Nicholls (ed.), *The Dictionary of National Biography: Missing Persons* (Oxford: Oxford University Press, 1993), p. 329.

—'Charles Silvester Horne (1865–1914)', in J.O. Baylen and N.J. Gossman (eds.), *Biographical Dictionary of Modern British Radicals*. III. *1870–1914* (Hemel Hempstead: Harvester/Wheatsheaf, 1988), pp. 453-58.

—'Church of Scotland', in J. Cannon (ed.), *The Oxford Companion to British History* (Oxford: Oxford University Press, 1997), p. 210.

—'Clapham Sect', in J. Cannon (ed.), *The Oxford Companion to British History* (Oxford: Oxford University Press, 1997), p. 215.

—'Collective Sovereignty? Conscience in the Gathered Church, c. 1875–1918', in Diana Wood (ed.), *The Church and Sovereignty, c. 590–1918, Essays in Honour of Michael Wilks* (Studies in Church History, Subsidia 9; Oxford: Basil Blackwell, 1991), pp. 479-506.

—'Congregational Union of Scotland', in N.M. de S. Cameron *et al.* (eds.), *Dictionary of Scottish Church History and Theology* (Edinburgh: T. & T. Clark, 1993), p. 206.

—'Congregationalism', in N.M. de S. Cameron *et al.* (eds), *Dictionary of Scottish Church History and Theology* (Edinburgh: T. & T. Clark, 1993), pp. 206-208.

—'The Cutlers' Company and the Churches', in Binfield and Hey (eds.), *Mesters to Master*, pp. 284-311.

—'Dale and Politics', in Binfield (ed.), *The Cross and the City*, pp. 91-119.

—'The Disruption', in J. Cannon (ed.), *The Oxford Companion to British History* (Oxford: Oxford University Press, 1997), p. 295.

—'The Dynamic of Grandeur, Albion Church Ashton-Under-Lyne', *Transactions of the Lancashire and Cheshire Antiquarian Society* 85 (1988), pp. 173-92.

—'English Free Churchmen and National Style', in S. Mews (ed.), *Religion and National Identity* (Studies in Church History, 18; Oxford: Basil Blackwell, 1982), pp. 519-33.

—'Episcopal Church of Scotland', in J. Cannon (ed.), *The Oxford Companion to British History* (Oxford: Oxford University Press, 1997), pp. 354-55.

—'Episcopalianism', in J. Cannon (ed.), *The Oxford Companion to British History* (Oxford: Oxford University Press, 1997), p. 355.

—'*Et Virtutem et Musas*: Mill Hill School and the Great War', in W.J. Sheils (ed.), *The Church and War* (Studies in Church History, 20; Oxford: Basil Blackwell, 1983), pp. 351-82.

—'Fairbairn, A.M. (1838-1912)', in N.M. de S. Cameron *et al.* (eds.), *Dictionary of Scottish Church History and Theology* (Edinburgh: T. & T. Clark, 1993), p. 313.

—'Free Church of Scotland', in J. Cannon (ed.), *The Oxford Companion to British History* (Oxford: Oxford University Press, 1997).

—'Freedom Through Discipline: The Concept of Little Church', in W.J. Sheils (ed.), *Monks, Hermits and the Ascetic Tradition* (Studies in Church History, 22; Oxford: Basil Blackwell, 1985), pp. 405-450.

—'Garvie, A.E. (1861–1945)', in N.M. de S. Cameron *et al.* (eds), *Dictionary of Scottish Church History and Theology* (Edinburgh: T. & T. Clark, 1993), pp. 351-52.

—'George Whitefield', in J. Cannon (ed.), *The Oxford Companion to British History* (Oxford: Oxford University Press, 1997), p. 982.

—'Hebrews Hellenized: Nonconformity and Culture, 1840–1940', in S. Gilley and W.J. Sheils (eds.), *A History of Religion in Britain: Practice and Belief from Pre-Roman Times to the Present* (Oxford: Basil Blackwell, 1994), pp. 322-45.

—'Henry Joseph Wilson (1833–1914)', in J.O. Baylen and N.J. Gossman (eds.), *Biographical Dictionary of Modern British Radicals. III. 1870–1914* (Hemel Hempstead: Harvester/Wheatsheaf, 1988), pp. 874-78.

—' "I suppose you are not a Baptist or a Roman Catholic?" Nonconformity's True Conformity', in T.C. Smout (ed.), *Victorian Values: A Joint Symposium of the Royal Society of Edinburgh and the British Academy, December 1990* (Oxford: Oxford University Press; also published as *Proceedings of the British Academy* 78 [1992], pp. 79-105).

—'Industry, Professionalism, and Mission. The Placing of an Emancipated Laywoman. Dr. Ruth Massey 1873–1963', in D. Lovegrove (ed.), *The Rise of the Laity in Evangelical Protestantism* (London: Routledge, 2002), pp. 187-201.

—'Jews in Evangelical Dissent: The British Society, the Herschell Connexion and the Pre-Millenarian Thread', in M.J. Wilks (ed.), *Prophecy and Eschatology* (Studies in Church History, Subsidia 10; Oxford: Basil Blackwell, 1994), pp. 225-70.

—'John Remington Mills (1797–1879)', in J.O. Baylen and N.J. Gossman (eds.), *Biographical Dictionary of Modern British Radicals. II. 1830–1870* (Brighton: Harvester, 1984), pp. 352-54.

—'Memory Enstructured: The Case of Memorial Hall', in M. Campbell, Jacqueline M. Labbe and Sally Shuttleworth (eds.), *Memory and Memorials, 1789–1914* (London: Routledge, 2000), pp. 160-74, 223-26.

—'Mormons', in J. Cannon (ed.), *The Oxford Companion to British History* (Oxford: Oxford University Press, 1997), p. 656.

—'Muggletonians', in J. Cannon (ed.), *The Oxford Companion to British History* (Oxford: Oxford University Press, 1997), p. 660.

—'Networking through Sound Establishments: How Gladstone Could Make Dissenting Sense', in D. Bebbington and R. Swift (eds.), *Gladstone Centenary Essays* (Liverpool: Liverpool University Press, 2000), pp. 133-62.

—'The Pastor as Professional: Some Preliminary Steps in a Victorian Investigation', in W. Conze and J. Kocka (eds.), *Bildungsbürgertum im 19 Jahrhundert. I. Bildungssystem und Professionalisierung in internationalen Vergleichen* (Stuttgart: Klett-Cotta, 1985), pp. 279-300.

—'Peculiar People', in J. Cannon (ed.), *The Oxford Companion to British History* (Oxford: Oxford University Press, 1997), pp. 736-37.

—'Pentecostal Churches', in J. Cannon (ed.), *The Oxford Companion to British History* (Oxford: Oxford University Press, 1997), p. 741.

—'Peter Taylor Forsyth: Pastor as Principal', in A. Sell (ed.), *P.T. Forsyth: Theologian for a New Millennium* (London: United Reformed Church, 2000), pp. 7-40

—'Pike's New Century Series: An Edwardian Panorama', Introduction to P. Bell (ed.), *A Dictionary of Edwardian Biography* (Master Index Volume) (Edinburgh: Peter Bell, 1986), pp. i-v.

—'Plymouth Brethren', in J. Cannon (ed.), *The Oxford Companion to British History* (Oxford: Oxford University Press, 1997), p. 757.

—'Principal When Pastor: P.T. Forsyth, 1876–1901', in W.J. Sheils and Diana Wood (eds.), *The Ministry: Clerical and Lay* (Studies in Church History, 26; Oxford: Basil Blackwell, 1989), pp. 397-414.

—'P.T. Forsyth as Congregational Minister', in T. Hart (ed.), *Justice the True and Only Mercy: Essays on the Life and Theology of Peter Taylor Forsyth* (Edinburgh: T. & T. Clark, 1995), pp. 168-96.

—'The Purley Way for Children', in Diana Wood (ed.), *The Church and Childhood* (Studies in Church History, 31; Oxford: Basil Blackwell, 1994), pp. 461-76.

—'Religion in Sheffield', in Binfield *et al.* (eds.), *The History of the City of Sheffield, 1843–1993.* II. *Society*, pp. 364-428.

—'Samuel Morley (1809–1886)', in J.O. Baylen and N.J. Gossman (eds.), *Biographical Dictionary of Modern British Radicals.* II. *1830-1870* (Brighton: Harvester, 1984), pp. 360-66.

—'Seventh Day Adventists', in J. Cannon (ed.), *The Oxford Companion to British History* (Oxford: Oxford University Press, 1997), p. 855.

—'Sir George Williams', in D.J. Jeremy and Christine Shaw (eds.), *Dictionary of Business Biography*, V (London: Butterworth, 1986), pp. 828-33.

—'Sir Makepeace Watermaster and the March of Christian People: An Interaction of Fiction, Fact and Politics', in J.P. Parry and S. Taylor (eds.), *Parliament and the Church, 1529–1960* (Edinburgh: Edinburgh University Press [for Parliamentary History Yearbook Trust], 2000), pp. 164-84.

—'Sir Samuel Morton Peto, 1st Baronet (1809–1889)', in J.O. Baylen and N.J. Gossman (eds.), *Biographical Dictionary of Modern British Radicals.* II. *1830–1870* (Brighton: Harvester, 1984), pp. 407-11.

—'Sir Titus Salt, 1st Baronet (1803–1876)', in J.O. Baylen and N.J. Gossman (eds.), *Biographical Dictionary of Modern British Radicals.* II. *1830-1870* (Brighton: Harvester, 1984), pp. 446-50.

—'Smith, Sir William Alexander (1854–1914)', in N.M. de S. Cameron *et al.* (eds.), *Dictionary of Scottish Church History and Theology* (Edinburgh: T. & T. Clark, 1993), p. 782.

—'Socinians', in J. Cannon (ed.), *The Oxford Companion to British History* (Oxford: Oxford University Press, 1997), p. 875.

—'The Story of Button Hill: An Essay in Leeds Nonconformity', in Alastair Mason (ed.), *Religion in Leeds* (Stroud: Alan Sutton, 1994), pp. 79-107.

—'Towards Baptist Architecture', in K.W. Clements (ed.), *Baptists in the Twentieth Century* (Papers Presented at a Summer School, July 1982; London: Baptist Historical Society, 1983), pp. 114-42.

—'Tractarians', in J. Cannon (ed.), *The Oxford Companion to British History* (Oxford: Oxford University Press, 1997).

—'True to Stereotype? Vivian and Dorothy Pomeroy and the Rebels in Lumb Lane', in S. Mews (ed.), *Modern Religious Rebels: Presented to John Kent* (London: Epworth Press, 1993), pp. 185-205.

—'Unitarians', in J. Cannon (ed.), *The Oxford Companion to British History* (Oxford: Oxford University Press, 1997), p. 945.

—'Victims of Success: Twentieth-Century Free Church Architecture', in Jane Shaw and A. Kreider (eds.), *Culture and the Nonconformist Tradition* (Cardiff: University of Wales Press, 1999), pp. 142-81.

—'"We Claim our Part in the Great Inheritance": The Message of Four Congregational Buildings', in K. Robbins (ed.), *Protestant Evangelicalism: Britain, Ireland, Germany and America, c.1750–1950: Essays in Honour of W.R. Ward* (Studies in Church History, Subsidia 7; Oxford: Basil Blackwell, 1990), pp. 201-223.

—'The White Church, Fairhaven: An Artist Trader's Protestant Byzantium', in *Transactions of the Historic Society of Lancashire and Cheshire* 142 (Liverpool, 1993), pp. 155-77.

—'Worlds of Ambiguity: the YMCA, the YWCA, the WSCF and Mission, Nationalism, Ecumenism and the Explosion of Empire', in A.R. Cross (ed.), *Ecumenism and History: Studies in Honour of John H.Y. Briggs* (Carlisle: Paternoster Press, 2002), pp. 69-88.

Binfield, J.C.G. and J.A. Cannon, 'Lady Huntingdon', in J. Cannon (ed.), *The Oxford Companion to British History* (Oxford: Oxford University Press, 1997), p. 499.

—'Thomas Harrison', in J. Cannon (ed.), *The Oxford Companion to British History* (Oxford: Oxford University Press, 1997), p. 457.

e. *Articles and longer reviews*

Binfield, J.C.G., ' "A Climate for Art's Encouragement": A Provincial Architect and His Contacts: John Mansell Jenkinson (1883-1965)', *Sheffield Art Review 1992* (Sheffield: Sheffield Society for the Encouragement of Art, 1992), pp. 2-11.

—'A Learned and Gifted Protestant Minister: John Seldon Whale, 19 December 1896–17 September 1997', *Journal of the United Reformed Church History Society* 6.2 (May 1998), pp. 97-131.

—'A Methodist Diary', *Proceedings of the Wesley Historical Society* 45.2 (September 1985), pp. 61-63.

—'All Muswell Hill and Little Betty Martin: The Establishing of a Congregational Church, 1890–1925', *Victorian Values, Hornsey Historical Society Bulletin* 31 (1990), pp. 2-20.

—'An Edwardian Letter from Australia and its Bearing', *Journal of the United Reformed Church History Society* 3.8 (May 1986), pp. 348-55.

—'An Obituary Footnote: Sir Edgar Williams CB, CBE, DSO (1912–95) and the Revd. J. Edgar Williams (1877–1938)', *Journal of the United Reformed Church History Society* 5.7 (October 1995), pp. 431-36.

—'Another Note on Nonconformists', *Poetry Nation Review* 5.4 (1978), pp. 3-5.

—'Asquith: The Formation of a Prime Minister', *Journal of the United Reformed Church History Society* 2.7 (April 1981), pp. 204-242.

—'Behind a Bath Stone Facade: Josiah Viney, Thomas Roger Smith and Pond Square, Highgate', *Hornsey Historical Society Bulletin* 27 (1986), pp. 2-9.

—'Bernard Lord Manning, 1892–1941', *Reformed Quarterly* NS 1.3 (Winter 1993–94), pp. 5-11.

—'Bias Is As Bias Does' (Long Review), *Poetry Nation Review* 6.1 (1979), pp. 60-61.

—'The Building of a Town Centre Church: St. James's Congregational Church, Newcastle upon Tyne', *Northern History* 18 (1982), pp. 153-81. (Reprinted as a booklet by the church, 1983).

—'Chapels in Crisis: Men and Issues in Victorian Eastern England', *Transactions: Congregational Historical Society* 20.8 (October 1968), pp. 237-54.

—Chapters I and II of *George Williams in Context* in *ITY Bulletin* 4 (trans. Takero Tejima; Tokyo: Bulletin of the Institute of Tokyo YMCA, July 1998), pp. 10-35.

—'The Coats Family and Paisley Baptists I', *Baptist Quarterly* 36.1 (January 1995), pp. 29-42.

—'The Coats Family and Paisley Baptists II', *Baptist Quarterly* 36.2 (April 1995), pp. 80-95.

—'Coffee Kirk Sundays' [Thomas Coats Memorial Church, Paisley], *Landscape* (October 1988), pp. 26-29.

—'Congregationalism's Baptist Grandmothers and Methodist Great Aunts: The Place of Family in a Felt Religion' *Journal of the United Reformed Church History Society* 2.1 (April 1978), pp. 2-9.

—'Congregationalism's Two Sides of the Baptistery', *Baptist Quarterly* 26.3 (July 1975), pp. 119-33.

—'Hackneyed in Hampstead: The Growth of a College Building', *Journal of the United Reformed Church History Society* 4.1 (October 1987), pp. 50-71.

—'Hindhead Highmindedness: I', *Poetry Nation Review* 12.3 (1985), pp. 42-44.

—'Hindhead Highmindedness: II', *Poetry Nation Review* 12.5 (1986), pp. 26-29.

—'Hindhead Highmindedness: III', *Poetry Nation Review* 12.6 (1986), pp. 21-24.

—'Holy Murder at Cheshunt College: The Formation of an English Architect: P.R. Morley Horder, 1870–1944', The Westminster College Commemoration Lecture, *Journal of the United Reformed Church History Society* 4.2 (May 1988), pp. 103-134.

—'Hymns and an Orthodox Dissenter: In Commemoration of Bernard Lord Manning, 1892–1941', *Journal of United Reformed Church History Society* 5.2 (July 1993), pp. 86-109. (Also circulated as Occasional Paper No. 3, with *The Hymn Society of Great Britain: Bulletin 197*, 13.12 [October 1993].)

—'In Search of Mrs. A: A Transpennine Quest', Essays in Honour of Professor R. Buick Knox, *Journal of the United Reformed Church History Society* 3.6 (June 1985), pp. 234-51.

—'Introduction', *Miscellany* 1 (London: The Chapels Society, 1998), pp. iii-iv.

—'James Cubitt and Emmanuel Church, Cambridge', *Chapel Society Newsletter* (December 1992), pp. 80-84.

—'On the Nonconformist Conscience', *Poetry Nation Review* 8.4 (1981), pp. 26-29.

—'The Pleasures of Imagination: A Conundrum and its Context', *Durham University Journal* 86.2 (NS 55.2) (July 1994), pp. 227-40.

—'Profile: Geoffrey Nuttall. The Formation of an Independent Historian', *Epworth Review* 25.1 (January 1998), pp. 79-106.

—'Review Article: The Unitarian Heritage', *Transactions of the Unitarian Historical Society* 19.1 (April 1987), pp. 43-48.

—'Revised Review—"The Shining Brother"', *Christian Parapsychologist* 9.1 (March 1991), pp. 14-20.

—' "Shining Brother": F.W. Lawrence (1882–1948) and His Churches', *Christian Parapsychologist* 4.5 (March 1982), pp. 151-58.

—'Six Letters of Robert Robinson: A Suggested Context and a Noble Footnote', *Baptist Quarterly* 40.1 (January 2003), pp. 50-60.

—'Some Abiding Virtues of the Victorian Church', *The Fraternal: Journal of the Baptist Ministers' Fellowship* 159 (January 1971), pp. 24-32.

—'Temperance and the Cause of God' (Review Article), *History* 57 (October 1972), pp. 403-410.

—' "There was a Festival in Rome". The Shaping of a Congregational Temper', *Journal of the United Reformed Church History Society* 6.3 (December 1998), pp. 185-203.

—'This Chorale of a Church: A Worship-Eye View', *Union Chapel: Stability and Change* (Islington, 1995), pp. 6-9.

—'Thomas Binney and Congregationalism's "Special Mission"', *Transactions: Congregational Historical Society* 21.1 (June 1971), pp. 1-10.

—'Thomas Coats Memorial Church, Paisley', *Proceedings of the Summer Meeting of the Royal Archaeological Institute in Glasgow in 1986* (London: Royal Archeological Institute), pp. 28-30.

—'The Thread of Disruption: Some Nineteenth-Century Churches in Eastern England', *Transactions: Congregational Historical Society* 20.5 (May 1967), pp. 156-66.

—'Three Personalities and a Theological College', *Transactions of the Hunter Archaeological Society* 14 (1987), pp. 19-31.

—'Transacting our History: The Congregationalists' Dimension', *Journal of the United Reformed Church History Society* 6.6 (May 2000), pp. 384-98. (Centenary Lecture, originally delivered at the Annual Meeting of the Society, Summer 1999).

—'Travelling Preachers and Lay Popes: The Case of R.M. MacBrair', *Proceedings of the Wesley Historical Society* 49 (May 1993), pp. 29-43.

—'United Reformed Church, Broughton Park', *Proceedings of the Summer Meeting of the Royal Archaeological Institute in Salford, July 1987* (London: Royal Archeological Institute), pp. 26-29.

—'The Wills Family of Bristol', *Congregational History Circle Magazine* 2.6 (1990), pp. 3-14.

Binfield, J.C.G., and C.J. Lawson, 'Raw Materials for Ministry I—in Yorkshire', *Reformed Quarterly* NS 2.3 (Winter 1994/5), pp. 16-19.

Binfield, J.C.G., review of *The English Churches in a Secular Society: Lambeth 1870–1930*, by J. Cox, *Journal of the United Reformed Church History Society* 3.1 (May 1983), pp. 30-33.

Binfield, J.C.G., review of *The Nonconformists: In Search of a Lost Culture* by J. Munson, *Journal United Reformed Church History Society* 4.9 (December 1991), pp. 571-75.

Binfield, J.C.G., review of *Victorian Quakers*, by Elizabeth Isichei, *English Historical Review* 86.341 (October 1971), pp. 810-15.

f. *Booklets*

Binfield, J.C.G., *A Congregational Formation: An Edwardian Prime Minister's Victorian Education* (London: The Congregational Memorial Hall Trust, 1996), pp. 1-23. (Delivered as the 10th Congregational Lecture [New Series] in October 1996).

—*A Man in his Setting: The Relevance of George Williams* (National Council of YMCAs, 1975), pp. 1-15 (Lecture originally given at the Russell Hotel, 18 June 1975.)

—*A Public Meeting House in Sheffield: Upper Chapel (Unitarian), 1700-2000: A Sermon and a Lecture* (Sheffield: Upper Chapel, 2001), pp. 1-56.

—*Belmont's Portias: Victorian Nonconformists and Middle-Class Education for Girls* (London: Dr. Williams's Trust, 1981), pp. 1-35. (Originally delivered as the 35th annual lecture to the Friends of Dr Williams's Library, 13 October 1981.)

—'*For Charitable and Public Purposes': A Short History of The Sheffield Town Trust 1297–1997* (Sheffield: Sheffield Town Trust, 1997), pp. 1-12.

—*George Williams in Context: A Portrait of the Founder of the YMCA* (Sheffield: Sheffield Academic Press, 1994), pp. 1-62.

—*...that dear man, George Williams: A Personal Portrait of the Founder of the Y.M.C.A.* (London: National Council of YMCAs, 1970), pp. i-vi, 1-26 (Originally delivered as the 3rd Sir George Williams Memorial Lecture, November 1969.)

—*150 Years on the Winning Side: The First George Williams Lecture* (George Williams College, Occasional Paper No. 2; London: YMCA 1995), pp. 1-49.

Binfield, J.C.G. (ed.), *Towards World YMCA Action on Palestinian Issues* (World Alliance of YMCAs, Geneva: World's Alliance of Young Men's Christian Associations, 1990) (Author of pp. 31-63).

Binfield, J.C.G., and J.E. Newport, *Role and Response: The YMCA and the Modern Ecumenical Movement*, Report of a working party (London: National Council of YMCAs, 1975), pp. 1-52.

g. *Other published material*

Since 1966 Professor Binfield has published reviews in *History, English Historical Review, Journal of Ecclesiastical History, Times Higher Education Supplement, Journal of United Reformed Church History Society, P.N. Review, Reform, Scottish Journal of Theology, New Society, Journal of Labour History, Political Quarterly, Post-Medieval Archaeology, Journal of Welsh Ecclesiastical History, Business History, Wiltshire Archaeological and Natural History Magazine, Journal of the Society of Archivists, Journal of American History, Mortality*

Binfield, J.C.G., 'A Conservative Layworm Turns in His Pew to the Minister of His Dreams', *Reformed Quarterly* 1.5 (Autumn & Winter 1990), pp. 7-10.

—'A Nonconformist Conscience', *The Times* (10 December 1990).

—'Albert Cumberland (9 July 1922–21 February 1996)' (obituary), *The Chapel Society Newsletter* 14 (May 1996), p. 58.

—'Convenient Front, Geriatric Excuse, Declining Sub-Culture', *Free Church Chronicle* 37.4 (Winter 1982), pp. 15-19.

—'Crotchets, Conscience and the Embodiment of Christ', *Free Church Chronicle* 25.1 (Spring 1980), pp. 4-23.

— 'H. Godwin Arnold (1920–1999)' (obituary), *The Chapel Society Newsletter* 21 (December 1999), pp. 2-4.

—'Habakkuk in Pykecrete: A Sermon in Celebration and Anticipation', *Free Church Chronicle* 40.3 (Autumn 1985), pp. 26-30.

—'History is…', *The Fraternal: Journal of the Baptist Ministers Fellowship* 141 (July 1966), pp. 24-29.

—'How Reformed?', *Reformed Quarterly* 1.1 (Autumn 1989), pp. 3-8.

—'The Point of the Spire', *Free Church Chronicle* 39.1 (Spring 1984), pp. 18-22.

—'Professor Kenneth Haley' (obituary), *The Independent* (11 August 1997).

—'Raymond Evans' (obituary), *The Independent* (11 February 1992).

—'Reflections from a Former Chairman of Governors', *Reformed Quarterly* NS 2.2 (Autumn 1994), pp. 5-7.

—'Reflections of a Lay Chaplain', *Free Church Chronicle* 20.2 (March/April 1975), pp. 3-7.

—'William Carr' (obituary), *The Independent* (June 1991).

INDEX OF AUTHORS